OPIUM
AND THE
ROMANTIC IMAGINATION

OPIUM

and the Romantic Imagination

Alethea Hayter

UNIVERSITY OF CALIFORNIA PRESS

Berkeley and Los Angeles

1970

UNIVERSITY OF CALIFORNIA PRESS
BERKELEY AND LOS ANGELES, CALIFORNIA
© 1968 BY ALETHEA HAYTER
INTERNATIONAL STANDARD BOOK NUMBER 0-520-01746-3
LIBRARY OF CONGRESS CATALOG CARD NUMBER 68-29700

SECOND PRINTING
FIRST PAPERBOUND EDITION

PRINTED IN THE UNITED STATES OF AMERICA

CONTENTS

ILLUSTRATIONS

Illustrations

Plates v, vi and vii are reproduced by permission of the Trustees of the British Museum.

FOREWORD

In 1962, when I first planned to write a book on the effect of opium addiction on the creative imagination of nineteenth-century writers, the subject seemed to have only a historic interest in this country. I thought that I was investigating a mental phenomenon of the past like, for instance, the duelling code or the practice of witchcraft. No one who reads the newspapers or watches television could think that today, in 1967. A stream of articles and letters, broadcasts and television programmes has in the last few months forced into our minds the knowledge that the number of drug takers of all kinds, including those who take the opium derivatives heroin and morphine, is large and getting larger. The Brain Committee on Drug Addiction, which in 1961 reported that there was little evidence of any considerable addiction to dangerous drugs in Britain, reported very differently in 1965.[1] In 1958 there were 62 known heroin addicts in Britain; in 1966 there were 670; one responsible forecast has suggested that by 1972 there will be 11,000. And of these known addicts there were none under twenty in 1959, but in 1965 there were 145 under twenty; many were under sixteen; one doctor reported a case of a twelve-year-old boy already addicted to heroin. There have been tense debates in Parliament, in the press, on the B.B.C., about the prescribing of heroin to addicts, about black market prices and supplies, about beat clubs and pop singers involved in drug practices, about the relationship between addiction and crime, about the comparative advantages of the permissive British treatment of addicts and the prohibitive American one, about whether addiction to drugs is a choice or a disease or a symptom.

My chosen subject therefore seemed to have become much more topical than I had intended. When I read about the eighteen-year-old boy in Salford who died in March 1967 as a result of giving himself three 'fixes' of heroin in a day, and by whose bedside a book on drug addiction was found, I thought for a little of abandoning this book altogether. But I am not really afraid that these chapters of unsensational literary analysis will become a junkies' hagiology, nor have I much hope that the experiences of a group of nineteenth-century intellectuals will be of any help to those who today are trying to cure a widespread social evil. This book is concerned with adults of creative genius and wide learning, living in an age of sterner moral sanctions and milder legal ones for the eccentric personality than anything that the drug addict of today meets with. No conclusions can be drawn from the mental processes of such men as Coleridge and De Quincey, exceptional in any age and living in a psychological environment now utterly vanished, which will be valid for the defiant ignorant adolescents who are the great majority of today's drug addicts. I have not tried to relate my account of nineteenth-century literary addicts to the phraseology or the anthropology of present-day addiction. Moreover I have limited myself to writers who took opium, in the form of laudanum. This book is not concerned with those who take cocaine, or cannabis (hashish and marijuana), or any of the hallucinogens—the psychedelic drugs like mescalin and L.S.D.—or amphetamine, or the barbiturates; the action and the dangers of all these drugs are different from those of opium. My object has been to describe one constituent of nineteenth-century literary sensibility, not to make a contribution—for which I have neither the qualifications nor the experience—to twentieth-century social medicine.

Does opium affect the creative processes of writers who use it? I first had occasion to look for studies of this subject when I was reading up the life history of a Victorian poet who at one time took morphine. The most illuminating studies which I found

Foreword

were two books by American scholars, which reached completely opposed conclusions.

The first was a pamphlet of less than eighty pages, published in 1934, *The Milk of Paradise* by M. H. Abrams.[2] The writer had the very original idea of tracing a pattern of imagery—images of lights, sounds, movements, variations in the consciousness of time and space, watching eyes, towering buildings—in the work of four opium-addicted writers, Crabbe, Coleridge, De Quincey and Francis Thompson. He deduced that opium created a dream world of its own 'as different from this as Mars may be', and that memories of that world could be recognized when they reappeared in the works of opium-addicted writers.

This little paper-bound book seems to be now quite unobtainable, but it has had an influence out of all proportion to its size and availability. One comes across its name constantly in the footnotes, source lists and bibliographies of critical works on nineteenth-century literature. As an authority on the effects of opium addiction on the creative imagination of poets, it held the field completely for nearly twenty years.

Then in 1953 Professor Elisabeth Schneider, of the University of Chicago, published her *Coleridge, Opium and 'Kubla Khan'*, whose motive force seems to have been an impatience both with symbolist interpretations of Coleridge's poetry and with the idea that *Kubla Khan* could have been composed entirely in a dream under the influence of opium.[3] To refute this latter theory, Professor Schneider made a study of recent American medical reports on the effects of opium, and deduced from these that the opium habit does not of itself confer either imaginative stimulus or fantastic dreams and visions; all the effects attributed to it are in fact due to the previous mental and emotional make-up of the opium addict. That is a very sketchy summary of a detailed and scholarly investigation which will often be quoted later in this book. The remainder of Professor Schneider's study was devoted to a long argument, supported by much learned detail, to establish that *Kubla Khan* was written as late as October 1799 or in May or June 1800, that it was inspired by the influence of Landor's *Gebir*, Southey's *Thalaba*, Milton, and the contemporary

Foreword

literary fashion for Oriental themes, and also by scenery in the Harz Mountains and in Westmorland seen by Coleridge in 1798 and 1799, and that it has a straightforward logical meaning with no particular concealed symbolism.

Here, then, were two radically different theories, advanced by two learned American scholars, on whether opium addiction can colour the imagination of writers. My curiosity was aroused, and I turned to the sources which both writers cited in support of their theories, and then went on to a good many other medical, biographical and critical books on the topic, widening the inquiry to include other writers known or believed to have had the opium habit. The conclusions which I finally reached, and which are the subject of this book, lie somewhere in between the extremes of the two American scholars, but are rather at a tangent to them. But without the ideas and the information in their two books, my own would never have been written, and here at the start I acknowledge my debt to them.

I am grateful to the following publishers for permission to quote copyright material; the Clarendon Press for *Collected Letters of Samuel Taylor Coleridge*, edited E. L. Griggs; Messrs Routledge and Kegan Paul for *The Notebooks of Samuel Taylor Coleridge*, edited Kathleen Coburn; the Liverpool University Press for *New Poems by George Crabbe*, edited Arthur Pollard. The Trustees of the Wordsworth Library, Dove Cottage, have given me permission to quote a sentence from an unpublished letter of Thomas De Quincey. The Masters and Fellows of Trinity College Cambridge have allowed me to quote from an unpublished Commonplace Book by Monckton Milnes in Trinity College Library.

I am also grateful to the Librarian of the Royal Society of Medicine for giving me access to its Library, whose staff, like the library staff of the British Museum and the London Library, have been very helpful.

The experiment in *Kubla Khan* interpretation described in Chapter IX, pages 220–1, was carried out by Mrs J. R. Fogg-Elliot and her pupils in Form Lower V, 1965, of Manor House School; I am most grateful to them.

Foreword

The research for this book was made possible by a research grant awarded to me by the Trustees of the Leverhulme Research Awards, to whom I here express my grateful thanks.

London. August 1967

PART I
SETTING

I

TRADITION

Watching Othello burn in the sulphur mines of jealousy which he had set alight, Iago said to himself

>'Not poppy nor mandragora
>Nor all the drowsy syrups of the world
>Shall ever medicine thee to that sweet sleep
>That thou owedst yesterday'.

For us these lines now have the aching grief of a great happiness lost, which makes them an incantation above the level of precise meaning. But Iago was an efficient unimaginative man, who would have known just what drowsy syrup (which was a medical term, not an emotive description) to ask for, in the nearest apothecary's shop in Venice or Famagusta, for the commonplace physical ills—insomnia, indigestion, toothache, a hangover. To himself, he was saying no more than 'That has looked after you, my friend; you won't get over that with a mere opium pill at bed-time'. His words have (and of course were intended by Shakespeare to have) a resonance for us beyond what they had for Iago himself, but they are also a plain statement of sixteenth-century medical practice.

In Egypt and Asia Minor, where the opium poppy first grew, doctors have treated their patients with opium since the practice of medicine began. In an Egyptian medical treatise of the sixteenth century B.C., Theban physicians were advised to prescribe opium for crying children just as, three and a half millennia later, Victorian babies were dosed with the opiate Godfrey's Cordial by their nurses to keep them quiet. The doctors of classical Greece knew and used opium; it is mentioned by Theophrastes

Setting

and by Dioscorides, as a drug to bring sleep and kill pain. But of its mental effects, which are the concern of this book, less is heard from ancient Greece. It may have been used by the initiates of the cult of Demeter; there is a legend that in her wanderings in search of her daughter Persephone, the goddess came to Sicyon, once called Mecone, the city of poppies, and in its fertile fields she found and gathered a handful of the white and purple flowers. She slit their unripe seed-cases, and a bitter soon-drying gum oozed out, the ὀπός or juice from which the name of opium comes. Tasting it, she forgot her sorrows; and so she was sometimes portrayed holding a poppy in her hand instead of a sheaf of corn, and the flower adorned her altars and its drug was perhaps used in her rites at Eleusis, to bring forgetfulness of the sorrow of the dying year and to share, by a short winter sleep of the emotions, in the death and re-birth of the plants—the juice of the flower bringing the men who drank it back into its own vegetative nature.

The doctor-priests of Aesculapeius may have administered opium to the patients who came to Epidaurus to seek cures by incubation, sleeping in the sanctuary to procure a divinely-inspired healing dream. Perhaps, too, Helen's nepenthe, the drug that brought oblivion of grief, was opium. Homer says that Helen learned of it in Egypt, one of the homes of opium; the fields of poppies round Egyptian Thebes gave to opium the alternative name of thebaicum. When Telemachus was entertained by Menelaus at Sparta, and miserable memories of the Trojan War and their lost friends made all the company weep, Helen brought them a drink, a drug dissolved in wine, which had the power to banish painful memories, and calm both grief and anger, so that the worst afflictions would hardly move them. It sounds very much like laudanum, which is a solution of opium in alcohol and, as will be seen later in this book, was constantly used in this way as a tranquillizer, to protect the mind from fears and hateful thoughts of the past. Some have thought that Helen's nepenthe was hashish, not opium, but it seems to have produced the calm euphoria of opium rather than the delirious excitement of hashish.

Rome inherited Greek medical knowledge of opium. Galen

prescribed it for most of the ailments of his Roman patients, and launched the famous opium compound 'mithridate' on its sixteen centuries of popularity in the European pharmacopoeia. Virgil mentioned opium as a soporific, both in the *Aeneid* and in the *Georgics*. The Arab physicians knew and used it—Avicenna himself is said to have been an opium addict—and Arab traders spread the opium habit and the cultivation of the opium poppy to Persia, India and China. In Europe its use, perhaps lost after the skills of the Romans faded away with their empire, was brought back by returning Crusaders who had learned of it from the Arabs. And here first rises that great stream of poetic myths and images, which began with the Old Man of the Mountains and the hashish which he is supposed to have given to his followers, and which so linked together the ideas of drug addiction and of hidden raptures that this forbidden garden, joining itself to older and holier myths, became an image lurking below the consciousness of European literature, till Baudelaire brought it out into the light by naming it the Artificial Paradise.[1]

The legend of Aloadine, the Old Man of the Mountains, his young Assassins and the drug he gave them, and their waking to the sound of music in a paradisal garden among green lawns and fountains of milk and honey, to see dancing damsels in silk and gold, was caught up from Marco Polo and Mandeville and Purchas into the poetic imagination of Europe. The paradise gardens of Aloadine, if they ever existed, were reached through the door of hashish, not of opium, but the two legends blended, as can be seen in Southey's reference, in a letter of October 1799, to the Assassins being transported to the gardens of the Old Man of the Mountains 'after an opium dose'.[2] The mythology of opium flowed into Europe in the stories of returning travellers from the East, who told of the endurance feats of the Tartar couriers, and even of their horses, when both man and beast were fortified against fatigue by opium; of the Turkish soldiers who took the drug to nerve their courage before going into battle; of the travellers in Africa and Asia who valued it because, as Purchas puts it, 'they suppose I know not what conjunction and efficacie both of Mars and Venus therein; but being once used, must daily be continued on paine of death', though some escape by taking to wine instead.[3]

This awareness that opium is addictive is rarely found so early as 1613, when *Purchas his Pilgrimage* was published. Opium was by then a normal medical remedy in Western Europe. Earlier it had been used for sorcery; there was a spell to bring a dream of an unattainable loved one, in which morning-glory flowers, tortoiseshell and beaver fat were boiled with opium, buried through a whole winter, and then brought up to be rubbed on the navel and the nape of the neck.[4] Half way from this to true medical practice was the feat of Paracelsus, who in the early sixteenth century had compounded laudanum, tincture of opium, and had given it wide renown; he called opium the 'stone of immortality' and prescribed it for almost every disease. In England before the mid-seventeenth century it seems to have been used chiefly as a narcotic; as such it is mentioned by Chaucer, by Shakespeare, and by Sir Thomas Browne who, as a doctor, found it a very ready image. 'The iniquity of oblivion blindly scattereth her poppy' he says, and again 'there is no antidote against the opium of time'; and of his colloquy with God in his prayers at night, 'I need no other laudanum than this to make me sleep.'[5] Burton in his *Anatomy of Melancholy* speaks of laudanum Paracelsi as an insomnia remedy; 'waking, by reason of their continual cares, fears, sorrows, dry brains is a symptom that much crucifies melancholy men' for whom he proposes poppy as a sleepy simple to be inwardly taken (together with violets, roses, lettuce, mandrake, henbane, nutmegs and willows, among other sweet-sounding remedies); or you may smell at a ball of opium, as the Turks do, he says, or anoint your temples with a mixture of opium and rose-water at bed-time, or, less agreeably, apply horse-leeches behind the ears and then rub in opium.[6]

To all these writers, opium was an occasional remedy, to be taken and stopped at will, like any other. But now in the seventeenth century appears the first known English opium-addict writer, an ignoble founder of the tragic dynasty. This was Thomas Shadwell, the bête noire of Dryden who both annihilated and immortalized him in half a line as the writer who pre-eminently 'never deviates into sense'. This dull and dirty playwright suffered from gout, and took opium continually for it, a weakness of which his enemies were quick to take advantage. In *Mac-Flecknoe* Dryden gives Shadwell a wreath of poppies; in *Absalom and Achitophel* he plainly mentions Shadwell's opium-eating; and Shadwell was no sooner in his grave than a mock epitaph proclaimed

> 'Tom writ, his readers still slept o'er his Book,
> For Tom took Opium, and they Opiates took'.

The preacher of his funeral oration, in a more edifying reference, declared 'His Death seized him suddenly, but could not unprepared, since (to my own certain knowledge) he never took his Dose of Opium, but he solemnly recommended himself to God by Prayer, as if he were then about to resign up his Soul into the Hands of his faithful Creator'. He seems, in fact, to have died of an overdose of the drug.[7]

By the end of the seventeenth century opium addiction—not just the use of opium as a medicine, but the habitual taking of it by addicts who were unwilling or unable to give it up—had become a known practice in England. This is shown by a curious book, *The Mysteries of Opium Reveal'd*, by Dr John Jones, published in 1700, on which it is worth pausing for a time as it is a foretaste of many of the theories and errors about opium which were to fill so many later books.[8] The writer, who described himself on the title page as 'Chancellor of Landaff, a Member of the College of Physicians in London, and formerly Fellow of Jesus College in Oxford', was an odd character, combining much practical experience and shrewd clinical observation as a doctor, and a buoyant expressive turn of phrase, with a very limited power of general deduction, a quite unlimited self-confidence, and occasional outbursts of eccentric speculations on philology, or of near-raving about his idol William III or his own inspired discoveries, which he compares for their general benefit to mankind with Harvey's discovery of the circulation of the blood.

> 'For till God was to my Enquiries kind,
> Millions sought and felt what they ne'er could find'

he complacently concludes. But his prose is a good deal better than his verse; his frequent italics give it a lively tone of voice, as he vigorously compares the happy effect of opium to 'a most delicious and extraordinary *Refreshment* of the spirits upon very good *News*, or any other great cause of *Joy*, as the sight of a dearly-loved Person etc thought to have been lost at *Sea* . . . 'tis as if a Good Genius possessed, or informed a Man; therefore people do commonly call it a *heavenly Condition*, as if no *worldly Pleasure* was to be compar'd with it'. But the effect of this is rather spoiled by his adding immediately afterwards 'It has been compar'd (not without good cause) to a permanent gentle *Degree* of that Pleasure, which Modesty forbids the naming of'. Modesty did not, moreover, prevent him from discussing this parallel in a good deal of detail later on in the book. He goes on to list eight other kinds of agreeable and beneficial effects from taking opium, which include pleasant dreams, freedom from anxiety, indolence or exemption from pain, and a delightful series of states of mind— 'Promptitude, Serenity, Alacrity and Expediteness in Dispatching and Managing of Business . . . Assurance, Ovation of the Spirits, Courage, Contempt of Danger, and Magnanimity . . . Euphory, or easie undergoing of all Labour, Journeys etc . . . Satisfaction, Acquiescence, Contentation, Equanimity etc.'

He was not too besotted with the benefits of opium to recognize some of its dangers. He listed many unpleasant physical and mental symptoms from excessive doses ('A dull, mopish and heavy Disposition . . . Decay of Parts, Weakness of Memory') and also painful sufferings from sudden withdrawal of the drug ('Great, and even intolerable Distresses, Anxieties and Depressions of Spirits, which in few days commonly end in a most miserable *Death*, attended with *strange Agonies*') but he seems never to have seen any danger in moderate addiction, or any difficulty in gradual withdrawal. It is evident from various references that he was an addict himself, and had observed a good many others in the course of his practice; when he indignantly claims that 'millions can affirm' from experience the truth of what he says about opium, we need not take him literally, but when he speaks of 'one near *Banbury*, that takes Two Ounces a *Day*', the detail is plausible. He thought that opium could cure

24

or relieve an extraordinary variety of ailments—gout, dropsy, catarrh, ague, asthma, fevers of all kinds, travel sickness, stone, colic, wounds, fractures, amputations, smallpox, dysentery, cholera, measles, rheumatism, and even plague, as well as psychological troubles like hypochondria and insomnia. He listed the different preparations of opium then in use: Venice Treacle, Mithridate, Sydenham Laudanum, Dr Bate's Pacific Pill, London Laudanum, and so on. He discussed at length the nature of sensation and perception, to prove his point that opium operates by causing a pleasant sensation, which cures pain and its effects by the operation of contraries. The theory of Sensation was, through Hartley, to play a great part in the speculations of Coleridge and other opium-addict writers; and the illustrations that Jones uses in his discussion of the theory—candle-flames and their reflections, bells 'heard along hollow valleys', the reverberating sound of a pin's head falling into a brass cauldron—remind one of many jottings in Coleridge's Notebooks, and passages in *The Confessions of an English Opium Eater*.

The Mysteries of Opium Reveal'd is an insidious misleading book, not the less engaging for being slightly mad. The author claims to have scrupulously told the whole story about opium's contradictory powers 'without any sly or sordid Evasion, or considerable Omission (which has been the perfidious Course of *Authors* in this case)'. We shall hear that claim again; most writers on opium claim that everything previously written about it has been prejudiced or misinformed.

By the eighteenth century the opium addict could be met in most walks of life in England. Clive of India started taking opium because of a painful bowel disease, and continued it ever after, and when he was only forty-nine it killed him; he died in a fit caused by a double dose, which he may have taken in error, or may have deliberately swallowed in an excess of the depression which was both the cause and the consequence of his addiction. Clive's tragedy was at one extreme; at the other may be set the lively Lady Stafford whom Horace Walpole remembered having seen when he was a child, and who used to say when she arrived to see her sister 'Well, child, I have come without my wit today', meaning that she had not taken her opium which, said Walpole, 'she was forced to do if she had any appointment, to be in particular spirits'.[9] Clive took opium for a negative effect—to relieve pain, anxiety, depression; Lady Stafford for a positive one —to enable her to dazzle her friends by her wit. A character very different from either of them, William Wilberforce the Emancipator of the Slaves, took opium every day for the last forty-five years of his life. He first had recourse to it for a serious digestive illness, perhaps at the suggestion of Isaac Milner, Dean of Carlisle, who powerfully influenced him in other ways, and who was widely believed to be an opium addict himself, taking 850 drops of laudanum a day in spite of what De Quincey called his strenuous wrestlings against the habit. Wilberforce's illness was cured by the opium, but he was never afterwards able to leave off taking it, though he was strong-minded enough never to increase his dosage beyond a moderate amount. He got nothing from it; it was neither sedative nor stimulant to his mind; the effects began only when he tried to stop taking it. His son quoted him as often saying 'If I take but a single glass of wine, I can feel its effect, but I never know when I have taken my dose of opium by my feelings'. But his son adds grimly 'Its intermission was too soon perceived by the recurrence of disorder'. His example was pleaded later in extenuation by Coleridge—'Who has dared blacken Mr Wilberforce's good name on this account? Yet he has been for a long series of years under the same necessity'—and by De Quincey.[10]

These chains and networks of addicts, influencing those who came after, justifying themselves by those who went before, now became common among the hierarchies of intellect. The greatest of these family trees of poison sprang from the brilliant aberrant Dr John Brown of Edinburgh, who told his medical students and, through his books, all Europe that the vital process depended on the ability to experience stimulation and maintain excitability, and that laudanum was one of the best means of regaining the right degree of excitability. One of Brown's students—an 'ardent Brunonian' as he called himself—was James Mackintosh, who later became well known as a philosophical writer and as a

Tradition

lawyer. He was generally reported to be an opium addict, and his letters from India, where he was for a time Recorder of Bombay, often mention taking laudanum. His son's filially pious biography of him refers cautiously to the 'self-indulgent habits' which prevented him from ever finishing the major work on philosophy which he projected for so many years. The intention but failure to write a great philosophical work is a regular feature in the biography of addict writers.

Mackintosh was an early and life-long friend of the Baptist divine Robert Hall, famous for his preaching. Hall, too, was an addict, taking as much as 120 grains of solid opium a day. Another follower of Dr John Brown, and later an editor of his works, was the Bristol physician Dr Thomas Beddoes, father of the poet T. L. Beddoes. Among his friends and patients Dr Beddoes numbered Coleridge, De Quincey, Charles Lloyd and Tom Wedgwood, all opium eaters. The story of Coleridge's and De Quincey's addiction will be told in later chapters; De Quincey first took opium, he said, on the advice of an Oxford friend, but it is probable that Coleridge's first real habituation to it was the result of a recommendation in Beddoes' edition of Brown's *Elements of Medicine*. Coleridge and De Quincey were linked by an uneasy arm-hold of obligation and admiration, but they could never refrain from comparing and analysing their own and each other's opium addiction.

Charles Lloyd, who took large quantities of opium as a remedy against the irritability and spasmodic affections of incipient insanity, was at first a disciple and afterwards an enemy of Coleridge, whose opium habit he revealed in *Edmund Oliver*, his roman à clef. In later years when he was living in the Lakes, and the trampling armies of his imaginary persecutors were closing in on him, he confided in De Quincey and took refuge with him. Tom Wedgwood, the charming and inventive hypochondriac who has been called the discoverer of photography, took opium to ward off the moods of terrible depression which beset him, and which may have been caused by some digestive trouble. He was a close friend of Coleridge's, and together they experimented with drugs and their effects, with hashish as well as opium. Two of

27

Setting

Tom Wedgwood's brothers married two sisters, whose third sister was married to James Mackintosh. Mackintosh, moreover, knew Coleridge, and thought Beddoes the best doctor in England. The spider's web of opium cast its viscid reticulation from point to point of this group of thoughtful men.[11]

A habit that was lifelong with such well known and revered figures as Wilberforce and Isaac Milner, Mackintosh and Robert Hall, was obviously not then regarded as a stain. No one who thinks of the early nineteenth-century opium addicts in terms of what their position would be today—forced to pester reluctant doctors daily for a barely sufficient dose, or to pay large sums for illicit supplies, in danger of prosecution and of blackmail—will be able to understand the frame of mind of someone like Coleridge, who had no obstacles between him and the drug but his own conscience and the reproaches of his immediate family and closest friends; no difficulty and little expense in getting supplies, no public opprobrium, no legal danger, a divided opinion among doctors about the merits and dangers of the drug, and many widely-read travel books about the opium eaters of the East to stimulate curiosity and experiment. The earlier tales of Purchas and Mandeville were reinforced by more recent accounts, telling how the Persian opium eaters enjoyed raptures and pleasant visions, and reviving the opium-primed horse and rider, now changed from a Tartar courier into an Indian messenger, and able to travel a hundred miles without food or rest. Most widely read and frequently quoted, constantly recurring in footnotes and prefaces, was the Baron de Tott's *Memoirs of the Turks and the Tartars*, with its vivid picture of the addicts of Constantinople repairing every evening to the Market of the Opium Eaters where, reclining on sofas under the shade of arbours, they took their evening dose and then walked home in stately abstracted happiness, deaf to the hootings and mockery of the passers-by.[12]

Eighteenth-century doctors, hearing such tales as these and knowing how essential opium was as an occasional analgesic in their ordinary medical practice, were puzzled whether it could be safely confided to the general public. A Greenwich apothecary writing in 1763 thought that it was probably wiser not to say too much about the properties of opium, for this might 'take from that necessary fear and caution, which should prevent their experiencing the power of this drug; for there are many properties in it, if universally known, that would habituate the use, and make it more in request with us than the Turks themselves: the result of which knowledge must prove a general misfortune'.[13]

But not all medical opinion was as cautious as that. Some celebrated physicians of the eighteenth century, such as Cullen and John Brown, regarded opium as an almost wholly beneficent drug, which could be recommended and used to cure nearly anything—tetanus and typhus, cancer and cholera, rheumatism and smallpox, malaria and venereal disease, violent hysteria and gout. They might not agree as to how opium operated; it had a sedative action, according to Cullen, but a stimulant one according to John Brown. But sedative or stimulant, or both, it was the doctor's prop and stay, sometimes for himself as well as his patients; we hear of a surgeon who always took a large dose of opium before performing any difficult operation.[14] One might prescribe it in the form of *Tinctura Thebaicum*, or *Elixir Paregoricum*, or as an electuary, *Confectio Opiata*; or as a powder combined with hart's-horn or ipecacuanha, this last compound being the famous Dr Dover's Powder, the nostrum of that Thomas Dover of Warwick who was both doctor and pirate.

The most balanced summary of late eighteenth-century medical opinion on opium is given by Dr Samuel Crumpe in *An Inquiry into the Nature and Properties of Opium*, published in 1793.[15] This is a much more sensible and sober affair than John Jones's extravagant work of a century earlier. Crumpe had experimented on himself, but was not an addict; he was aware of the possibility of addiction, and could to some extent distinguish between opium's early and late effects and the effects of withdrawal from it; and he thought that even as a medicine, and apart from the dangers of addiction, opium was noxious for certain complaints such as pneumonia, and was liable to produce insomnia.

At the start of the nineteenth century, then, most doctors and patients still thought of opium not as a dangerous addictive drug but mainly as a useful analgesic and tranquillizer of which every household should have a supply, for minor ailments and nervous crises of all kinds, much as aspirin is used today. It was used for travel sickness: Jane Austen's mother, suffering from fatigue and the motion of the carriage on a journey back to Steventon from Kent, stopped in Basingstoke to consult an apothecary, and was ordered to take 'twelve drops of laudanum when she went to bed as a composer'. (A semantic shift has made this sentence from Jane Austen's letter read very oddly now; Mrs Austen was to take a soothing draught, not go to bed disguised as a writer of music.)[16]

It was used for hysteria; from Emily Eden's letters we hear of the preposterous Lady Goderich, a frantic hypochondriac, being given 'a quantity of laudanum' as a tranquillizer by her exasperated relations when she was in a rage about taking a house.[17]

It was used for hangovers and alcoholism; George IV's doctors gave him laudanum to calm the irritation produced by his excessive drinking—though they disagreed among themselves about it, Knighton saying that laudanum would drive him mad, while Halford said that spirits would drive him mad if he wasn't calmed by laudanum.[18]

It was used as a pain-killer; the philologist Elizabeth Smith, racked with a tubercular cough, took it as she sat in her tent on a lawn by the Lake of Coniston.[19] It was used to ease the passage of the dying; Southey's gruesome old mother demanded laudanum in her last illness, and when the unnerved Southey dropped it out for her with a shaking hand, 'she saw the colour of the water, and cried, with a stronger voice than I had heard during her illness, "That's nothing, Robert! thirty drops—six and thirty!" '.[20]

Every one, in fact, at that period took laudanum occasionally. All the Romantic poets, except Wordsworth, are on record as having experimented with it. When Byron's marriage was breaking up, he kept by him, as a tranquillizer, a phial of Black Drop, a popular opium compound; Lady Byron found it in his trunk, together with a copy of Sade's *Justine*, when she searched his belongings after they had parted. It was a double find that must have given her righteous horror. But in 1821 Byron noted in his diary 'I don't like laudanum now as I used to do' and he told

Moore that it never exhilarated him, sometimes made him suspicious and quarrelsome, but more often had no effect on him at all.[21]

Moore took laudanum for an attack of cholera in Edinburgh, Lamb took it for a bad cold, Shelley took it for nervous headaches, Southey took it for hay fever, for insomnia, and perhaps because he was afraid he had contracted tuberculosis.[22] There was of course no question of any of these men becoming addicts, they took opium simply as an occasional remedy. A further group of writers, Scott and Keats among them, will be discussed in later chapters as having taken opium—though still only occasionally and not as chained habituates—in quantities sufficient to have detectable effects on their writing.

All of them, whether or not they tried opium as a cure for their adult ailments and anxieties, almost certainly had it given to them when they were children. Godfrey's Cordial, Dalby's Carminative, McMunn's Elixir, Batley's Sedative Solution, Mother Bailey's Quieting Syrup—the sinister names of these patent medicines for children, some of which contained as much as half a grain of opium per ounce, pervade the treatises on drugs and even contemporary novels, where they sometimes provide the catastrophe of the plot. Readers of Charlotte Yonge will remember that Flora Rivers' baby in *The Daisy Chain* is killed by an overdose of Godfrey's Cordial administered for fretfulness by an ignorant nurse, while the Julius Charnocks' more fortunate baby in *The Three Brides*, drugged by her truant nurse to stop her crying, lived to tell the tale. 'It only remains to be proved' said the doctor drily when the panic-stricken Lady Rosamond Charnock brought her child to him 'whether an aristocratic baby can bear popular treatment. I dare say some hundred unlucky infants have been lugged out to the race-course today, and come back squalling their hearts out with fatigue and hunger, and I'll be bound that nine-tenths are lulled with this very sedative, and will be none the worse'.

It is a grim little vignette, and the doctor's callous optimism is not borne out by other doctors of the day. An American physician wrote bitterly that these 'elixirs and syrups . . . as administered whether by deluded mothers or crafty nurses, have *soothed* many and many a luckless infant into that state of *quiet* that knows no after-disturbing'.[23] Working-class mothers who had to go out to work in factories gave these soothing syrups to their babies to keep them quiet during their absence. In one town in Lancashire in 1843 there were sixteen hundred families who were regular purchasers of Godfrey's Cordial, and the infant mortality from it was frightfully high.[24] But middle-class children were not safe either; an American addict reported that he had become addicted in his childhood because paregoric (camphorated tincture of opium) was 'a favourite medicine of my excellent mother, and in all the little ailments of childhood was freely administered', and that she thought so highly of it that when he was sent to a university at the age of sixteen 'she put a large vial of it in my trunk, with the injunction to take of it, if ever sick'.[25] In 1856 De Quincey was still recommending half a dozen drops of laudanum as an excellent remedy for childish pains,[26] and even as late as 1883 a child in Mrs Ewing's story *Mary's Meadow* is made to say casually that the smell of a garden poppy was 'like laudanum when you have the toothache'; it was obviously still to be found in every nursery medicine cupboard.

This universal practice makes it almost impossible to say of any nineteenth-century writer that he had never tasted opium. Nearly all children were given it; some middle-class and many working-class children died suddenly from an overdose of it or more gradually from its cumulative effects; but even when it was administered rarely and moderately, and the child escaped any dramatic effects from it, it may have left some physical and psychological traces.

The perfect ease with which opium could be bought helped to build up its empire. The greatest demand was in the cotton-spinning districts of Lancashire, and there, as De Quincey was told by a local chemist, 'on a Saturday afternoon the counters of the druggists were strewed with pills of one, two or three grains, in preparation for the known demand of the evening'.[27] A medical report declared that 'there was not a village in all that region round but could show at least one shop and its counter loaded with the little laudanum-vials, even to the hundreds, for the accommodation of customers retiring from the workshops on Saturday night'.[28] Laudanum was cheaper than beer or gin, cheap enough for even the lowest-paid worker; so in one Lancashire parish a single chemist could sell 200 lbs of opium in small packets in one year, and still say that this was less than half the demand, while the druggist in the little town of Thorpe told Coleridge that he sold two or three pounds of opium and a gallon of laudanum every market day.[29] Lancashire was the worst area, but many of the big industrial towns, among them Sheffield, Birmingham, Nottingham, had an exorbitant demand for opium, and the whole counties of Yorkshire, Cambridgeshire and Lincolnshire had a reputation for the number of their opium eaters.[30] In the Fens they had special names for the drug—they called it 'opic' or 'elevation'. There is a grating little dialogue about it in Kingsley's *Alton Locke*.

' "Yoo goo into druggist's shop o' market-day, into Cambridge, and you'll see the little boxes, doozens and doozens, a' ready on the counter; and never a ven-man's wife goo by, but what calls in for her pennord o' elevation, to last her out the week. Oh! ho! ho! Well, it keeps women-folk quiet, it do; and it's mortal good agin ago' (ague) 'pains''.

"But what is it?"

"Opium, bor' alive, opium!" '.

Nor was London much behindhand. De Quincey was told by chemists in three different parts of London that they had immense numbers of customers who came to them for regular supplies of opium, and that 'the difficulty of distinguishing these persons, to whom habit had rendered opium necessary, from such as were purchasing it with a view to suicide, occasioned them daily trouble and dispute'.[31] It was a common suicide weapon, for neurotic characters like Mary Shelley's half-sister Fanny Imlay, who killed herself with it, or that pathetic student whom De Quincey describes in *Early Memorials of Grasmere*, who climbed the heights of Blencathra, 'took a dose, such as he had heard would be sufficient, of laudanum', and lay down to die with his face upturned to the stars.

Setting

Dickens showed the ludicrous side of this traffic in poison when he described the predicament of the juryman in the case of Bardell *v.* Pickwick, who was a chemist and had had to leave the errand-boy in charge of his shop, and told the judge piteously 'he is a very nice boy, My Lord, but he is not much acquainted with drugs; and I know that the prevailing impression on his mind is, that Epsom salts means oxalic acid, and syrup of senna, laudanum'.

No addict, no intending suicide, can have experienced the least difficulty in getting all the opium they needed from some such bewildered chemist's assistant, or even from the experienced chemist in person; many druggists must actually have recommended its use for the numerous maladies it was supposed to cure. It is not surprising that Britain imported 22,000 lbs of opium in 1830, and that by 1860 the amount had more than quadrupled. It was imported as solid opium, a brown bitter granular powder, but much of it was sold in tinctures, above all in the form of laudanum which was a reddish-brown liquid varying in colour according to its strength.[32] De Quincey dignified his by calling it ruby-coloured, and kept it in a decanter where it was sometimes taken for port by unwary guests who attempted to help themselves to it.[33]

It is against this background of general custom and opinion about opium that one must see the addiction of Crabbe and Coleridge and De Quincey and the other writers with whom this book is concerned. Their habit was not considered an exotic and secret vice, but the excess of a normal indulgence, as drunkenness was. Even the doctors were not sure how dangerous it was, and the general public took it for granted. It was not till *The Confessions of an English Opium Eater* was published, and at once aroused enormous interest, that opium addiction began to be considered as a separate medical and psychological phenomenon which ought to be studied. Till then, even the medical writers who had devoted books to the study of opium had spent little observation on the different effects of addiction and withdrawal from addiction, on the differing symptoms of the early and the later stages of addiction, on the different types of addict—the man who can stick to a moderate never-increasing dosage and the

Tradition

man who must always be piling his dosage higher and higher, the occasional indulger and the utterly enslaved daily habituate. But now the scientific study of drug addiction was to begin. De Quincey is often blamed, and rightly, for the terrible fascination of his masterpiece in drawing in others to follow his example, but he is not often given credit for the impetus which his book undoubtedly gave to the scientific investigations which have helped and saved other addicts. It is now time to leave the history of opium, with its conjectures and superstitions, its anecdotes and false trails, and to turn to the medical case-histories of the drug and its operation.

II

CASE - HISTORIES

Ever since the publication of *The Confessions of an English Opium Eater* in 1822, most statements on the effects of opium addiction on the imagination and mental processes of addicts have been either derived from the untypical case of De Quincey, or made in reaction against it. De Quincey himself gave a warning about this; he was a philosopher, he said, and therefore his opium visions were philosophical; but the plain practical man who took opium would have either no visions at all, or visions of his plain practical affairs.[1] But the warning was disregarded. Generalizations as to how opium affects the mental operations of all addicts began and continued to be made from the individual cases of De Quincey and Coleridge. Before I discussed them and the other well-known literary addicts mentioned later in this book, it therefore seemed essential to make a short survey of how opium affects the non-literary addict, for comparison. The statements in this chapter are based on reports and case-histories by doctors on the addicts under their care in hospitals, prisons and asylums and under treatment at home, and in a few cases on accounts by the addicts themselves. These drug-takers were men and women of all kinds—lawyers, clergymen, actors, soldiers, housewives, prostitutes, clerks, waiters, workers in textile factories. Some were respected figures in regular professional employment, some were convicted criminals, some were insane. None were well-known writers.[2]

The Americans and the French have produced much of the published work on opium addiction, in both the nineteenth and twentieth centuries, though medical and general studies are now beginning to appear in Britain, as our own experience of addicts grows with the recent growth of the habit here. The recent American surveys, based on carefully controlled experiments made on statistically adequate samples, are far more valuable for the general study of the subject than the nineteenth-century reports, which were often distorted by preconception, superstition and emotion, though the writers were sometimes excellent clinical observers. But in its bearing on the nineteenth-century literary addicts, recent scientific research on opium can be misleading in another way. Most modern American research is based on addicts who take the opium derivatives heroin or morphine by injection; recent French research sometimes also includes the smoking of opium. But the early nineteenth-century literary addicts all took their opium in the form of laudanum, alcoholic tincture of opium; this has a weaker opium content than morphine or heroin, and its action is affected by the addition of the alcohol. Moreover both the pipe of the opium smoker and the hypodermic syringe of the heroin addict have come to have a mystique of their own, a complex of feeling and ritual which affects the addict's reaction to his drug in a way not known to the laudanum drinker. What the modern addict takes is different in itself, and differently administered; and he takes it in a different climate of opinion. All the American addicts on whom recent medical surveys have been based were guilty of what is now in itself a crime; they knew themselves to be legally and socially reprobated; they endured danger and ruinous expense in getting supplies of their drug. In Britain the fact of being a heroin addict is not at present in itself a crime, but even for those who get heroin legally on prescription it is an act of defiance and protest, of separation from normal society, generally dominating the addict's time and thoughts and creating a special way of life. And there are increasing numbers who depend on illicit supplies, and who therefore have the same dangers and high costs as the American addicts.

These are the states of mind and feeling on which opium now operates in those who take it, and since—as all authorities, early and recent, agree—it can only work on what is already in a man's mind, it produces different effects in the minds of the self-conscious and ever-anxious addict of today from its effects in the minds of the early nineteenth-century addicts. They indeed felt guilt and anxiety, but guilt towards God and their families and their own wasted talents, not towards society and the law; anxiety about earning their living, but not about finding the money for the drug, or how they could get supplies. Different guilts and anxieties produce different patterns in the imagination, and not all the mental processes and limitations of a man in a prison infirmary in Kentucky in the 1950s, or a boy in a beat club in Chelsea in the 1960s, can be adduced to explain those of Coleridge, a century and a half earlier, living with his family among admiring friends beside a mountain lake. The argument works in both directions: because learned and brilliantly imaginative writers like Coleridge and De Quincey saw fantastic visions under the influence of opium, it does not follow that ordinary addicts will do so; but equally because uneducated unimaginative delinquents today see no visions under opium, it does not follow that Coleridge or De Quincey were either lying when they said they had such visions, or psychopaths because they had them.

In what follows, therefore, I have not taken only the pronouncements of recent researchers, but have made a consensus of the many points on which nineteenth-century and twentieth-century authorities agree, and where they differ, have given both views. I have not, however, adopted the most recent approved phraseology. The words 'addiction' and 'habit' or 'habituation' are now out of favour with the experts on drugs, who prefer to speak of 'dependence', which includes both physical and psychic dependence on a drug, whether taken periodically or continuously, and whether or not it includes tolerance. I have continued to use the word 'addiction' because it was the one known and used in the nineteenth century for the laudanum-drinkers with whom this book is concerned. In the early nineteenth century they were generally but rather illogically called opium-eaters, though they almost all took the drug in liquid form. There is no single word in English equivalent to the useful French word 'opiomane'; 'opium addict' seems to me the nearest English equivalent which will be generally understood, and I have therefore continued to use it. For the same reason I have used the more familiar phrase 'withdrawal symptoms' in preference to 'abstinence syndrome' which is now preferred by the experts.

One of the most disputed problems is whether there is any type of personality specially liable to become a drug addict. In one classic modern American study of the subject, *The Opium Problem* by C. E. Terry and M. Pellens, the authors shrewdly suggest that doctors are biassed on this point by their own experience—prison doctors think that most addicts are criminal types, lunatic asylum doctors think that most addicts are mental defectives, doctors who run expensive private clinics think that most addicts are eminent intellectuals. The authors of *The Opium Problem* conclude that 'this condition is not restricted to any social, economic, mental or other group . . . there is no type which may be called the habitual user of opium, but that all types are actually or potentially users'.[3] At the other extreme from this view may be set the nineteenth-century doctor who felt able to pronounce that 'a delicate female, having light blue eyes and flaxen hair' was the most likely addict.[4] There is plenty of evidence that opium addiction is not confined to any social class or any type of physique. But certain mental traits may predispose their possessor to become an addict. Leaving aside those who started taking opium simply as a pain-killer, on medical prescription, and the extreme cases of social deprivation or of mental abnormality, there seem to be two main and one lesser group of mental characteristics which may lead to addiction.

The first is a restless mental curiosity about strange and novel mental experiences; the defect of those who wish to enjoy or to observe special states of mind, and to do this by taking a short cut. This predisposition has been noted specially by such French authorities on addiction as Pichon, Chambard and Dupouy, and is found in the more imaginative and sensitive intellectual temperaments. In such minds as these, the example and the descriptions of other addicts can be fatally contagious. The whole literature of opium addiction, French and American, is strewn with quotations from addicts who avowed that they were first led to experiment by reading De Quincey. Roger Dupouy in his book *Les Opiomanes* tells of the French colonial administrators who had already made up their minds, before ever they left France for the Far East, to become opium addicts when they got there, because they had read De Quincey and Baudelaire and were excited by their descriptions of their visions.[5] The fear of arousing curiosity to experiment is a heavy weight on anyone who undertakes to write even the soberest account of the effects of opium.

But this curiosity about a new kind of mental experience is not likely to be found in very many minds. The second predisposition to opium addiction is a much more common mental trait, the longing for peace and freedom from anxiety. Men and women who feel all kinds of suffering keenly, exaggerate its extent and the impossibility of bearing it, and lack the energy and resolution to conquer it; who are unable to face and cope with painful situations, who are conscious of their own inadequacy and who resent the difficulties which have revealed it; who long for relief from tension, from the failures and disappointments of their everyday life, who yearn for something which will annihilate the gap between their idea of themselves and their actual selves—men and women most preyed on by these feelings, which are present to some degree in all of us, are liable to the temptation of opium. It is a mental type severely characterized by a leading American authority, Dr D. P. Ansubel, under the heading of 'The Inadequate Personality'. Such a man, we are told, 'fails to conceive of himself as an independent adult and fails to identify with such normal adult goals as financial independence, stable employment, and the establishment of his own home and family. He is passive, dependent, unreliable, and unwilling to postpone immediate gratification of pleasurable impulses. He demonstrates no desire to persevere in the face of environmental difficulties, or to accept responsibilities which he finds distasteful', so he seeks in drugs 'increased self-confidence and feelings of self-esteem, decreased anxiety'.[6] The list of 'normal adult goals', particularly their order, may not seem to all of us to comprehend the Whole Aim of Man, but the personality portrayed is recognizable, and its likeness will often be met later in this book.

A third mental trait which may predispose its owner to drug addiction is a combination of the first and second ones, and is more rare. It is that element in personality which delights in secret rites and hidden fellowships, in being an initiate. French opium-smokers talk of their drug in terms of sanctuaries and sacrileges, of 'une vie opiacée' in the same sense as 'une vie monastique', a vocation.[7] American morphine addicts of the 1950s had a whole secret language and set of passwords of their own for their symptoms and sensations, and muttered and boasted to each other about Chinese needlework, whips and jingles, the lamp habit, Miss Emma; they were hooked, loaded, in high, they got the kick, they had a monkey on their back.[8] The young English addicts of today have inherited some of these passwords and evolved some more of their own, and get an extra initiate pleasure out of the junkies' jargon of fixes and joy-popping, skin popping and mainlining and the horse (heroin). 'When you're a junkie, you feel apart from society. You can't be hurt; ordinary people are like another race'.[9] Those who cannot make a place and a relationship for themselves in the daylight world of humanity persuade themselves that their isolation is a distinction, a setting-apart of the chosen ones, and they join the secret close communities of the dark.

What do the opium eaters really get out of their drug? The most important point here is to distinguish between the earlier and later stages of addiction, and between the moments when the drug is working and when its effects are wearing off, either because the time for the next dose is near or because the addict is trying, or being made, to give up his drug. Nearly all the positive advantages, if they can be called so much as that, of taking opium belong to the first, and generally short, stage of experiment with the drug. After that, it can confer little but freedom from the torture of not taking it. I have nothing to say here about the moral implications, or about the physical symptoms, often disgusting, which follow on taking opium and on withdrawing from

41

it. My concern is only with its mental effects, so far as these might influence the work of literary creation.

First, then, the honeymoon period, as some writers have grimly called the first embraces of this swarthy bridegroom. The first sensation from taking opium, in nearly all cases, is a relaxation of tension and anxiety, the onset of a special kind of calm enjoyment usually summarized, as far back as Dr John Jones in 1700, under the word euphoria, in its original meaning of well-bearing, the condition of being borne along by a favourable breeze. There have been cases of experimenters with opium who feel nothing at all, or nothing but nausea; but these are probably calm lethargic unimaginative characters. The more usual effect is that cares, doubts, fears, tedium, inhibitions, sink away and are replaced by a serene self-assurance, for which there is no objective justification; the opium-taker's real situation has not changed in the least, only—and transiently—his feelings about his situation. He is now in a state of listless complacent tranquillity. Nothing worries him, nothing moves him; he is at peace with his fellow-men because he does not care about them; their sorrows do not move him, their injuries and slights of which he was so conscious now rebound harmlessly off his invulnerable self-esteem. An American doctor recently summarized what his patients said when he asked what drugs did for them: 'It puts an end to my despair: it makes me feel happy; it restores my self-confidence; and it does all that in a moment, without any effort on my part. The drug is a miracle. I cannot live without it'.[10] A French addict told his doctor that a quarter of an hour after taking opium he felt as though he were plunged in a bath of tepid milk, or in cotton-wool.[11] Addicts have likened their feelings under opium to flying or floating, to an 'exquisite don't-care attitude', a Buddha-like calm, an admission to paradise. Often at first there is a transient stimulus, a feeling of excitement and vivacity, of fire in the veins, but this soon gives place to the calm rêverie in which all thoughts dangerous to the cherished image of self have been annihilated, and the mind floats in its sea of warm milk.

Many drug-takers have claimed that in this early stage of addiction their mental powers and activity have been enhanced. Their intellectual faculties are ready, vivacious, lucid, and their ideas copious and original; opium, said an addict, made him think of things he would not otherwise have thought of. The power of associating ideas is immensely stimulated, in long unfolding links and networks of thought which can be creatively revealing. Projects are formed for huge philosophical works which will be a synthesis of all knowledge and will explain the pattern of existence. The most difficult works, the most elaborate conceptions, can be read and understood with ease. Abstract ideas become images, brilliantly distinct but melting and evolving in swift metamorphoses, or the mind leaps with intrepid audacity and self-reliance across the gaps between idea and idea. Anything could be achieved—if it were worth achieving; but there is no need to make an effort, for the thing is, in effect, done already; intention and performance are no longer distinguished. Every emotional impulse—pious feeling, kindness to others, sexual love—is consummated in thought but may remain unexpressed in action. In fact, much of the supposed intellectual impetus from opium is a subjective delusion in the addict—he *feels* that he is having brilliant thoughts and doing difficult intellectual feats with extraordinary ease, but the results are not often shown by achievements objectively measurable. The unusual associations of ideas, the distinct and self-evolving images, the easy flow of words and the brilliant conversation may be powers genuinely conferred or stimulated by the drug; but the vast philosophical works which will explain everything do not get written—or if they do, explain nothing.

One of the most hotly contended facts about opium, and the one most relevant to the subject of this book, is whether it stimulates artistic creation. Most nineteenth-century writers on opium were convinced that it did. The American addict who was quoted in the last chapter as having been sent off to college by his mother with a bottle of paregoric in his trunk was quite positive on this point. 'If a man has a poetic gift, opium almost irresistibly stirs it into utterance. If his vocation be to write, it matters not how profound, how difficult, how knotty the theme to be handled, opium imparts a before unknown power of dealing with such a theme; and after completing his task a man reads his own composition with utter amazement at its depth, its grasp, its beauty and force of expression, and wonders whence came the thoughts that stand on the page before him'.[12]

Later authorities have almost totally rejected this theory. Nothing, they maintain, is imagined under the influence of opium which could not be imagined equally well by the same mind in a voluntary and conscious rêverie; the addict has not gained in imaginative force, he has simply deteriorated in the critical faculty which would enable him to judge the value of what he has imagined when under the influence of opium. It is, however, certain that, as will be related in Chapter XIII, some addicts have been at any rate completely surprised when reading what they themselves have written under the influence of opium; it was unrecognizably alien even if it was not unrecognizably good.

But this leads to another mental effect of opium, the tricks it plays with the memory. There is much disagreement about these among the experts. The memory is generally asleep during an opium rêverie, so an American physician is quoted in 1862 as saying; memory is the first faculty to be affected, declared a French doctor in 1889.[13] But addicts have maintained that under opium they could recall every note of whole symphonies, every detail of childhood experiences; and medical authorities mainly agree that though the opium addict's memory may be treacherous as to recent events and their sequence, it is phenomenally retentive of long-past ones. The opium-orientated memory selects, adapts, rearranges past experiences to a formula of its own, a magic pattern to exclude anxiety, like the pentagram on a sorcerer's floor within which the demons cannot penetrate.

There is flat contradiction between the experts as to whether opium produces hyperaesthesia or intensification of the sense perceptions. In 1871 a doctor declared that, under opium, the susceptibility of the senses may become so acute that 'not so much as an articulated sound, not the jar from a footstep, shall be endurable';[14] ten years later another doctor, a specialist in the treatment of drug addiction who had made experiments on himself, reported that his tactile sensibility was much increased;[15] and Roger Dupouy, writing in 1912, agreed that most addicts find even slight noises or bright lights painful.[16] But an American medical report of 1941 declared that after morphine injections the hearing was dulled, the tactile sensitivity sometimes diminished, the sense of smell was not affected, nor was visual acuity, though the field of vision was sometimes decreased.[17]

There is not much positive evidence on whether synaesthesia—that exchange of sense perceptions, by which colours are heard and smelt and sounds are seen and tasted, which was so dear to German and French nineteenth-century writers—can be induced by opium. But a good deal has been written on the question whether, at least in the early stages of addiction which I am now describing, the objects perceived by the senses are totally misreported by the brain, so as to cause hallucinations, or whether the mind under opium is a distorting mirror but one still reflecting reality. The contact with the external world is certainly attenuated during opium rêveries; sudden stimuli may still violently shock the addict, objects close at hand may be seen with painful distinctness, but general awareness of the outside world is lessened. A French addict of the 1880s reported that about an hour after taking opium, he began to feel pleasantly torpid; his legs felt leaden, his arms powerless, his eyelids too heavy to raise. He was not asleep, he was still conscious of the outside world, but sounds like the ticking of a clock or the rumbling of carriages seemed very distant and muted.[18] An American doctor of the 1860s made the point that in an opium trance 'the senses convey no false impression to the brain; all that is seen, heard or felt is faithfully delineated, but the imagination clothes each object in its own fanciful garb. It exaggerates, it multiplies, it colours, it gives fantastic shapes; there is a new condition arising out of ordinary perception'.[19] The addict sees a real object, but the normal thought-processes which would enable him to place it—its size, its situation, its use or meaning—may have been disconnected from each other. As Paul Bonnetaire wrote in *L'Opium*, the drug was like a looking-glass; 'miroir, il reflétait, en grossissant, mais il reflétait, et la refraction seule de ses images était anormale'.[20]

Most vital to the consideration of opium and the literary imagination is the question of opium dreams and rêveries. Nearly all authorities, from De Quincey himself onwards, agree that these experiences under opium are conditioned by the addict's heredity, original education, temperament, habits of thought and of mental association, degree of talent and imagination, and innate capacity for dreaming vividly and remembering dreams. The 'silken garment of the imagination' is woven from the strands already there. Only one book on opium known to me, written by a life-long habituate, firmly rejects the theory that De Quincey had opium dreams because he had an aptitude for dreaming anyway, and issues a challenge: 'Let any one, bold enough to undertake so costly an experiment, try the virtues of opium in the capacity of producing dreams, and, my word for it, he will either claim a special aptitude for dreaming himself or, with me, give all the credit to the subtle and mighty power of opium'.[21] But it is incontestable that many addicts have no memory of having dreamed at all, or they dream only vague subfusc scenes or sequences of monotonous slightly-varying images linked to some obsessive triviality. In any case the so-called 'dreams' of opium takers in the early stages of addiction are often not real dreams of sleep, but waking rêveries. The sleep which may overcome the addict from half an hour to some hours after taking his dose is often dreamless, but it is preceded by the rêverie state in which many of the so-called 'dreams' are enjoyed.

Opium, then, cannot give the power of vivid dreaming to those who have not got it already, and to those who have, the dreams and reveries that it brings will be mixed from the paints already on the palettes of their minds—there will be no colours entirely new, beyond the spectrum. But opium can cause the dreamer to select certain elements among the powers and experiences given to him, and to blend, deepen, heighten some and ignore or distort others. The effects of opium make these visions, even when they are experienced in waking rêverie and not in dreams of sleep, not such a fully voluntary activity as the day-dreams of ordinary imagination. The addict can control them to some extent; he may start from, and even pursue, a chosen theme; one of Dupouy's patients, an opium-smoker, said that he could evoke and control at will the mental presentations which passed before him, and some have claimed that they could choose and steer even their dreams in sleep. But something not entirely within their control is at work in the theatre of their minds, presenting to them masques and dramas which they can watch with detached fascination.

Such was the fantastic rêverie of Walter Colton, an American parson who as a young man was inspired by *The Confessions of an English Opium Eater* to try the effects of the drug, and having taken a large dose, 'lapsed into a disturbed slumber, in which it appeared to me that I retained my consciousness entire, while visions passed before me which no language can convey, and no symbols of happiness or terror represent'. In this apocalyptic vision, he was flying high in the heavens, listening to celestial music, when he was flung down onto a thunder cloud, and from thence onto the verge of a cataract over which he plunged into a roaring gulph, and then rose to shoot across the sea, whose waves he seemed to be organizing into the bass harmony of a world anthem. Then again he hovered sky-high over the ocean, looking down on an immense circle of blue waves over which ships were skimming, but at its outer edge there was an abyss, immeasurable and lividly gloomy, full of the wrecks of worn-out worlds. He saw the Pole Star dying, and the planets bending over it and lowering it into a bottomless grave. He was caught up on the dripping shelf of an onrushing iceberg, and carried through stormy seas where huge lightning-struck serpents lay in the troughs of the waves. Paralysed by the icy cold, he fell down through the depths of the sea to a grotto where a mermaid lit a fire to warm his frozen veins back to life, and sang to him; but her song merged into the Last Trump, and the whole earth from the shores to the mountain-tops was black with the risen dead. The sun vanished leaving a huge dark chasm in which the moon span and the planets sank and were quenched, and palpable darkness streaked by lightning filled all space, and all motion—of ships, of waves, of birds, of cataracts—was frozen for evermore.[22]

No doubt Colton heightened and tidied up his memories of this vision when he wrote it down some years after he had it, and introduced some allegory and edification; no doubt he had read Jean-Paul Richter and had seen engravings by John Martin; but allowing for all that, there still remain the traces of a remarkable experience, with elements that are not the obvious ones to have invented.

Few opium-takers have had and recorded such a vision as that, but some of its elements are found separately in many case-histories of addicts. The feeling of buoyancy, of flying and hovering, is often mentioned; 'a pleasurable dreamy sensation of floating away' is a typical description. An American doctor in Constantinople, experimenting with two grains of opium, felt as he went home that he was floating and sliding along the street, and that his blood had been changed into an ethereal fluid which made his body lighter than air. Such dreams are not confined to opium addicts, of course; many normal people fly often in their dreams. But the flying or floating of opium rêveries is linked to a special feeling of being immaterial, ethereal, of having lost or merged one's identity, and to an alteration in the perception of time and space, a 'universal expansion of mind and matter. My faculties appeared enlarged, everything I looked at increased in volume' as one opium-taker described this experience.[23] William Blair, a Scottish addict who ended his days in America, described his first opium vision, during a 'waking sleep' in the theatre after taking an experimental ten grains; the theatre expanded around him into an endless succession of vast halls and high-piled galleries, roofed with blazing stars and thronged with gigantic figures.[24] Hyperaesthesia and associative disorder, according to Dupouy, make the addict 'incapable in his dream of fixing accurately a date, or the age, situation or size, of anything; everything becomes for him immeasurable, imponderable, indefinite; he counts by thousands of years or kilometres'.[25] And so the dreams of the addict are liable to become cosmic in scale, and he presides with detached calm over the deaths of worlds and the unreeling of millennia. He dreams, too, of paradises and utopias, reached by aerial voyages. 'I saw, on a rock in mid-ocean, a magnificent temple bespattered with gold; two superb statues stood on an altar of jade; a priest officiated; the congregation prostrated themselves in prayer' related one of Dupouy's patients.[26]

These rêveries, since they are experienced in a partly conscious state and may be controlled, or at least steered, at will, are naturally pleasant in content for the most part, though the pleasures are limited in range. Erotic rêveries seem rare (though in the nineteenth-century case-histories this may be due to prudery in recording them); there are no dreams of eating or drinking; nothing active or aggressive, and nothing warm or companionable. All is solitary and remote. And even at this early stage, less pleasant elements sometimes intrude into dreams and rêveries—sensations of falling down precipices, of cold, of coiling snakes and grimacing countenances.

But at this stage, when a man is taking opium only occasionally, or has only been taking it for a short time, he can still stop without too much difficulty, and many who have experimented with it have in fact stopped at this stage. But with many others, this early phase of addiction, with its baseless euphoria and self-confidence, begins to fade away into the darkness that is to follow. After a period that may be only a few weeks, or may even extend to years in the case of those who space their doses very widely, the opium-taker begins to find that the drug no longer produces the euphoria for which he started taking it; but now it is too late to stop. The drug can no longer raise him above his normal level of happiness; but unless he goes on taking it, he falls excruciatingly far below his normal level, into a crater of restless misery.

Many addicts, when they find that they have developed tolerance for the drug and can no longer get the positive pleasure and relaxation which they got from it at first, go on increasing their dose in the attempt to recapture euphoria. But there is one class of addicts, not a large one, who when they have discovered the dosage which preserves them from the wretchedness of with-drawal symptoms, will restrict themselves to that amount and continue for many years, perhaps for all the rest of their lives, taking only so much opium and no more. Opium now gives them nothing positive, nothing that they would not have had if they had never taken it at all; it simply saves them from the pains of giving it up. They are like diabetics dependent on their regular in-jections of insulin to keep them in normal health. Addicts of this type can lead conventional responsible lives, and their addiction may not be detected even by their family and friends. Examples of this type of addiction were William Wilberforce and the poet George Crabbe, whose forty-year-long addiction to opium will be considered in Chapter VIII. Such men and women are rarities, because only strong and well-balanced characters can maintain such a régime, never yielding to the temptation to increase their dose, and strong and well-balanced characters do not generally take to opium in the first place.

Since opium is not in itself necessarily life-shortening or physically deleterious, addicts of this kind may live to a great age. There are records of a woman of eighty-one, who had taken three grains of morphine daily for sixty-five years, but was still mentally alert and able to manage her household affairs very efficiently.[27] An Englishman, a retired Army officer living in New York, who took more than forty grains of opium daily for half a century, lived to be 103 and preserved much mental and physical vigour.[28] Such addicts may retain all their original reputation and intel-lectual power. Opium taken in this way leaves you where it found you; if you were a useful member of society before you started taking it, you may remain so; but you will have gained absolutely nothing by the habit, only (at best) not lost by it. These confirmed but moderate addicts are called 'users' in the jargon of the addict world, and it is to this condition that doctors who prescribe for heroin addicts today attempt to bring those for whom there is no hope of complete cure. There are not many of them, though—like the undetected murderers—there may be more than we think.

Case-Histories

Apart from these rare controlled addicts, how does the typical addict react when he finds that his cherished euphoria is lost, that he no longer feels the first moment of thrill and stimulus, the floating on from that into serenity? He may not be aware of the change in its naked fullness; he may now have forgotten that he ever got positive pleasure from the drug, and may even indignantly deny this; he takes it, he says, and always took it, only to avoid pain or unbearable anxiety. But some are more sophisticated than this. 'Rien ne vaut les débuts . . . maintenant je ne connais plus que le bien-être physique' said a man who was smoking 150 pipes of opium a day to Dupouy.[29] In an attempt to get the 'kick' once again, addicts increase their dose, inject it intravenously, or postpone their injection till mild withdrawal symptoms have started. One adolescent addict, who had come back five times to be cured, when he was asked why, said 'I take the treatment to get off the drug in order to have the sensation of beginning again'.[30] Addicts sometimes take ten times the dosage which would be needed to prevent withdrawal symptoms. It is all useless; the most they can now hope for is to escape the pain of craving, not to secure the pristine pleasure.

The mental vivacity and rush of ideas have now generally disappeared, and the mind is gloomily stagnant and apathetic. Relationships with other human beings are out of gear. The addict is indifferent to the sufferings of others, often feels no strong affections even for his own family and friends, cannot so much as guess how other people will feel—he is as much cut off from them as though he came from another planet. He feels that he is an outcast, a pariah, and he cherishes his solitude and isolation, hating to be interrupted and ready to tell any lie if his drug habit is endangered. Left alone, he is unaggressive and even condescendingly complacent to the sins of others, but withdrawn and secretive in his shell of apathy.

But behind this dark façade which shuts him in from the world, he may be cogitating huge plans. Though humanity treats him as an outcast, he feels that he is omnipotent and holds the secrets of the universe; he alone is percipient, sensitive, wise, superior to dull conventional minds. He has penetrated the hidden analogies

Setting

and associations behind all the phenomenal world, and in his mind he builds vast metaphysical constructions, which will astonish and enlighten mankind when they are revealed, and plans great empires of power and achievement. He is confidently sure of his own powers to carry out these plans, because the faculty which criticizes and foresees difficulties has been paralysed. He has no anxieties for the future, he is protected by his complacent superiority. The gigantic scaffolding of his projects is insecurely lashed together, tottering, unable to bear any weight; he has put it together out of incongruous and irreconcilable elements, and is unaware of the dangerous gaps; to him it is a heaven-aspiring temple with foundations of adamant—and sometimes to the rest of us, as we catch glimpses of it, it seems to have a cobweb iridescent beauty.

I have been piling up generalizations, and must pause to say again that none of them can cover all cases of addiction, since opium, as has been said, only works on what is already present in the mind. It cannot make a really loving man indifferent, or a really sociable man morose and secretive, or a really uneducated man able to construct vast philosophical systems. In the advanced stage of addiction which I am now describing, all a man's tendencies may be clouded and distorted, but they will not be changed beyond recognition.

If the authorities differ on whether opium addiction in its first stage stimulates poetic creation, there seems to be general agreement that in its later stage it makes any sustained imaginative creation impossible. It does not prevent a man from writing, or painting, or composing; many addicts have gone on earning their living to the end of their days by practising one of the arts. But the paralysis of the critical faculty makes them no longer able to distinguish their best work from their worst, and the haunting idea of the great universal masterpiece which they are one day to produce causes the work which they actually do produce to be provisional, makeshift. A very interesting analysis of the creative writer's state of mind at this stage of addiction was given by an anonymous American addict, a great admirer of Coleridge, in 1876. In the later stages of addiction, he says, a man's sensibilities are so impervious to all deep feeling that he is in a 'buried-alive condition'. 'No warmth or glow of passion or genial feeling can be aroused. Hence the poetical faculty was annihilated in Coleridge. There is a sort of vitrifying process that chills all sensibility. . . . Whatever is done, is done in pale cold strength of intellect. . . . That exquisite feeling that teaches a writer to know when the best word tips the edges of sensibility, lies buried under the debris of dead tissue'.[31]

But while advanced addiction impoverishes artistic creation in its outward-looking aspect, its commitment to external reality, it may heighten an inward self-consuming proliferation of words and symbols. In an extremely interesting survey of the special vocabulary of narcotic addicts, two American researchers have written: 'As addicts verbalize their reaction to drugs, they also re-enforce the effect which these drugs have on them, and the association of certain terms with specific experiences tends to create an associative pattern which undoubtedly plays a part in the satisfaction which the addict gets from the use of the argot. Many terms in the argot describe vividly and graphically not only the effects which drugs or abstinence from drugs produce, but also, by use of metaphor and suggestion, relate the sensations derived from drugs to other physical and emotional sensations'. Moreover the argot of the opium taker differs 'in character, imagery, connotation and in the life pattern reflected' from that of the marihuana taker, which is comparatively 'thin, obscure and affected'.[32] Opium, in fact, has a language and symbolism of its own, which can invade other areas of the drug-taker's imaginative life.

Memory is the intellectual faculty most affected at the later stage of addiction. For immediate daily concerns, the memory may become nearly useless. It has been habituated by the drug to suppress any anxiety or embarrassment which might disturb the addict's euphoria, and it now does so all too successfully; he cannot call to mind the immediate practical duties of his life, or anything that bores or importunes him or distracts him from his timeless inner world. And so not only do business and family responsibilities vanish in oblivion, but actors forget their lines and singers their notes. Even the bitter memory of the lost mental pleasure they once enjoyed from their drug, though sometimes it is strong enough to cause cured addicts to relapse, may vanish altogether, so that they may be honestly forgetful, not evasive, when they later claim that they never got any pleasure, even at first, from the drug. But certain memories, specially those of childhood, can still be evoked with startling strength and in vivid and precise detail, by an uncontrolled activity of the faculty of association.

Although some recent American researchers have maintained that there is no real evidence that hyperaesthesia is a symptom of addiction at any stage, there is more evidence from earlier case-histories than can be ignored. A laudanum-drinker of many years' habituation reported that sudden shocks and noises were hateful to him; a woman who had taken morphine for four years was tortured by the smallest noises, which she felt as threats or insults; French opium-smokers found the rustling of leaves or of newspapers disagreeably loud and deafening, and footsteps in a room overhead sounded like thunder.[33] Sight, like hearing, becomes intensely acute, so that bright lights and pronounced patterns are painful, and the sophisticated opium-smokers take their drug in bare undecorated rooms with plain hangings, in order not to excruciate their eyes. William Blair recorded that he suffered from a double sense of sight and sound, one real and one visionary, and heard the footsteps of a murderer ascending the stairs, and saw him standing by the bed dagger in hand, while at the same time he heard the real sounds in the house and saw the empty room.[34]

Blair may have been inventing or exaggerating; there is a good deal in his account of his opium experiences that suggests he is not a reliable witness. All addicts, in any case, will lie if they think it will protect their opium habit or their image of themselves, or will make a striking impression; or sometimes merely for the pleasure of teasing and mystifying those who are trying to help them. There is no external proof of anything an addict says about his own mental processes, and it all has to be scrutinized and weighed up against what else is known about him, and what has been gathered from other addicts. All generalizations about the mental processes of addicts are like an Identikit picture of a murderer made up from descriptions by other criminals; the details may be exaggerated for the sake of showing off, or falsified in order to mislead, or inaccurate from sheer irresponsibility, or they may be helpful and true.

An analysis of the visions of the confirmed opium addict is hampered not only by the unreliable reporting of the addicts themselves, but also by the confused terminology used by the medical writers on addiction, many of whom do not really distinguish between ordinary dreams of sleep; the special kind of dream which is known as a nightmare or 'crise nocturne' and which generally wakens the sleeper; day-time rêveries and waking visions; and hallucinations. It is probably safe to say that most advanced addicts no longer experience the partly directed waking rêverie which is the chosen activity of the early stage of addiction; rêverie is now automatic and continuous. Those who were originally non-dreamers still do not have, or do not recall, dreams in sleep, but for those given to dreaming, nightmares may now become a misery and incubus. Opium addicts do not seem often to have actual hallucinations, in the sense that they believe in the objective reality of the visions which they see. Some morphine addicts reach that stage, but these were probably neurotic and unstable personalities originally. Most of the waking visions of opium addicts seem to be recognized as illusions, but they are inescapable tortures all the same. Some of them may be symptoms of withdrawal from the drug rather than of its presence, since most case-histories do not say whether the visions were experienced soon after taking a dose, or during abstinence. In the case of laudanum-drinkers, also, some of the visions may be due to the alcohol in the laudanum rather than to the opium.

After all these provisos, some account can be given of the more usual waking visions and nightmares of advanced addicts. They are often tortured by reptiles and insects—embraced by coiling snakes, trampled on by monsters, crawled on by worms, by ants, by microbes, thrust over precipices by tortoises or fiery dragons.

Setting

Decaying things, still faintly touched with the likeness of beings once loved, stir beside them in rotting debris; their children, as they kiss them, turn to skeletons. Wandering through huge caves, they are forced to step on rotting corpses, and thousands of faces made of blood-red flame flash up and die out in the darkness. There are watching faces everywhere, grinning up through sea-waves, stretching and lengthening and disintegrating, and eyes peer through holes in the wall. There are voices, threatening, insinuating, whispering, imitating each other, telling the addict his own thoughts. He is being spied on, plotted against, shot at, beaten, sawn asunder, drowned. His very identity is in danger— he is falling to pieces, his head is hollow, he is being merged with a character in a book or with the furniture in the room; he has become the opium itself and is being smoked in a pipe by the king of the island of addicts. While he is losing his living individuality, the inanimate creation is coming alive, is vibrating with secret force; the very stitches in his sheets are charged with electricity and give him shocks, and the chairs and the clothes hanging on the door are changing into fantastic animals. All that is safe, loving, stable, is decaying and suffering hideous change, but secret life and revolt are stirring in what were once humble unregarded tools and objects.

These are the miseries at which some addicts may stare day-long, or from which they may wake screaming at midnight. They do not inevitably accompany advanced addiction, there are many well-documented case-histories of addicts who even after many years of drug-taking have never had a vision or a nightmare. But for some addicts, they are the worst wretchedness of all that their slavery inflicts, and it is often in order to escape from them that the effort of withdrawal from the drug is made.

Some addicts seek or are forced to be cured of their habit, either by sudden and complete abstinence from the drug, or by gradual withdrawal—doctors have differed as to which method is most effective, though few now advise an abrupt cutting off of supplies. A few addicts succeed in giving up the drug completely, many relapse during treatment or after the cure has been completed. Some who have no intention of giving up the drug nevertheless undergo cures, simply to be able to start again at the beginning and once more, so they hope, enjoy the pleasurable early stages of addiction. Some, while not undertaking a complete treatment for cure, regulate their doses so as to procure, by a measure of abstinence, the subsequent enjoyments of relief from withdrawal symptoms. In the early stages of the habit, some take opium only once a week, or at longer intervals. There is no invariable pattern of dosage which applies to all addicts at all stages. And even the regular addict, who takes his dose two or three times a day, is not in a uniform state throughout the twenty-four hours; nearing the end of eight hours from the last dose, he begins to experience the first trace of withdrawal symptoms. It is therefore extremely difficult to say of any mental state connected with opium that it is peculiar to the influence of the drug, or to the condition of deprivation of the drug.

But there is no doubt or difference of opinion as to the misery of the process of withdrawal. In its early stages, it is a museum of tortures. The addict is nauseated, suffocated, ice-cold yet sweating; he yawns, sneezes, coughs, weeps, his teeth chatter; he is excruciated by restlessness, by cramps and twitches and burning pains, as though he were being pierced by needles or crawled over by ants. A woman addict subjected to forced abstinence wailed that an insect was rushing about between her skull and her brain. In the first stages of withdrawal the addict cannot sleep, he cannot stay still, he cannot concentrate or think of anything but his misery. Time seems endlessly extended, an hour lasts three months, and the ticking of a clock is unendurable—but when it is stopped, the succeeding silence is still more terrible. 'All created nature seemed annihilated, except my single, suffering self, lying in the midst of a boundless void' wrote one addict who after fifteen years of laudanum-taking finally succeeded in giving it up gradually, while another who was subjected to abrupt withdrawal treatment said that he was being 'torn by an immense void'.[35]

But here we meet the most complete conflict of evidence between nineteenth-century and twentieth-century research.

Setting

An American writing in the 1860s, an emotional but humane man with considerable knowledge of addicts, gave it as his opinion that the tortures of withdrawal were probably greater than being burnt alive.[36] Another American writing in the 1950s, also from a wide experience in the treatment of addicts, said that though withdrawal symptoms 'are undoubtedly uncomfortable, they are seldom more severe than a bad case of gastro-intestinal influenza', and later compared them to 'a moderately severe ten-day illness',[37] while a recent English writer has said that 'there is no need for the addict to feel more than the discomfort of a sharp dose of flu during a modern medically supervised withdrawal'.[38] Much of course depends on the degree of addiction reached before withdrawal is attempted. Addicts vastly exaggerate their sufferings during withdrawal, according to many modern authorities, in order to be allowed some of the drug again as a palliative. Some doctors have gone so far as to say that all withdrawal symptoms are hysterical, not organic, though most experts now agree that opium produces a chemical change in the body which then depends on supplies of the drug and is disorganized by its withdrawal.

No doubt addicts lie about the tortures of withdrawal, as about every other subject; but some of the nineteenth-century accounts of withdrawal were written by cured, or temporarily cured, addicts who had voluntarily given up the drug and were writing with the express purpose of encouraging others to do the same. Such men had no reason to exaggerate the sufferings they had gone through; on the contrary, the purpose of their books required that such sufferings should be minimized. Probably the fear of discouraging addicts from making the attempt has caused some recent medical writers laudably to play down the sufferings of withdrawal. They are, of course, describing gradual withdrawal under medical supervision, helped by tranquillizing drugs, whereas the nineteenth-century accounts mostly, though not all, describe what in the addicts' jargon is called 'cold turkey'— abrupt withdrawal of the drug without palliatives. The choice is grim in any case, a choice between a sharp but probably short agony on the rack, and then freedom, or life imprisonment in a shrinking cell, since the addict who clings to his addiction gets diminishing returns from increasing doses.

I shall not try to describe the gloom, squalor and impotent suspicion of the last stages of opium addiction, since it does not apply to the opium-eating writers to whom this book is devoted, and for comparison with whom this chapter of description has been included. But since it has been suggested by some critics that the withdrawal period is the one most likely to foster literary inspiration and activity, it is worth taking a look at some of the mental symptoms of withdrawal in non-literary addicts.

The immediate effect, as has been said, is to produce a restlessness and irritability so great that concentration, even attention, are impossible. Reading or writing are out of the question; the addict is far too preoccupied with his own sufferings to use his imagination for any other purpose than dwelling on what he is enduring. He is unable to sleep, and sometimes seems to be waiting for someone who never comes. The world and everything in it seems colourless and joyless, and trifling incidents are taken tragically, while no good fortune can win a smile from him. There may be sudden onsets of anxiety and terror, and even violence and hallucinations. These symptoms are at their height between forty-eight and seventy-two hours after the last dose of the drug, and it is unlikely that during this period any work of literature was ever consciously created.

When the first wretchedness is over, a state of mind begins to set in which may well be favourable to literary creation. The mind, so long held in lethargy, starts to work more rapidly, though the ideas flow incessantly through the brain and cannot easily be seized and worked out. One addict, describing the sleepless nights of a withdrawal period during which he lay and heard the clock tick and felt that time had been endlessly extended, says that he composed verses and hymns 'with incredible ease and rapidity', though he had never previously written a line of verse; but they were of no merit, he confessed, and he never wrote them down.[39] Another man, describing his experiences in the later stages of withdrawal, depicts a renewed spring of energy and joy in life, when his power of thought became 'keen, bright and fertile beyond example', his imagination swarmed with ideas of beauty, his sensibility was exquisitely fine, and though he was still too restless, too much unnerved to write down his thoughts, he shone in conversation.[40]

The shadow over this brightening state of mind is that men now again become conscious of what their addiction had concealed from them, and had been welcomed for concealing from them—their own inadequacy. Excessive self-reproach, dwelling on every sin and failure of the past life, and a consciousness of inferiority, dismay the addict who is no longer protected by the drug from these feelings, whose dismal power he had forgotten. One man describes it as 'a sickening death-like sensation about the heart; a self-accusing sense of having committed some wrong —of being guilty before God; a load of fear and trembling'.[41]

The hyperaesthesia experienced when under opium does not disappear during withdrawal. The ticking of a clock or the jar of a heavy footstep can seem unendurably loud. The body feels sensitive all over; the lightest touch, if it is abrupt, gives pain. One man, when a barber began to cut his hair, felt as though each single hair were endowed with intense vitality, and screamed and groaned till the barber stopped.[42] 'The least noise, the feeblest light, the faintest smell, are amplified and become obsessions'.[43] The physical feelings of cold, the shiverings and icy sweats, transform themselves into images of icebergs and stony hands.

The evidence about dreams and visions during withdrawal from opium is most confused. Some authorities report stupendous and fearful dreams during the half-hour spells of sleep snatched during the first forty-eight hours. After that there is little opportunity for dreams in sleep, since insomnia—sometimes lasting for many months—is one of the chief miseries of the withdrawal period. But the waking visions can be terrible, and there are more cases of such visions during withdrawal periods than during addiction. There is no great difference between the visions of addiction and of withdrawal—perhaps because those reporting them have not always made it clear in which state the vision was experienced. But certain visions, specifically dated during withdrawal periods, may be cited. A man whose physical withdrawal symptoms included gnawing stomach pains had a vision of a creature 'like a weasel in shape, but with the neck of a crane and covered with brilliant plumage' which sprang from his breast on to the floor.[44] An actor saw his valise, which lay on the floor beside his bed, grow into the shape and size of an elephant, and strange faces peered at him from dark corners. [45] A preacher felt that boiling water was running in his veins, and tossing against his skull inside the top of his head, and he heard the booming and splashing of breakers on shore, and sharp hissing whispers all round him.[46] Other addicts during withdrawal periods have heard tolling bells and seen shaking lights, and have had dreams in which the dreamer is pursued by disgusting creatures which fling themselves on him; wanders among yawning gulphs and precipices; waters rise and drown him, devouring flames arch over him, he flees from yellow grimacing enemies about to sacrifice him, is shut up in a coffin, is gnawed by worms, and his temples squeezed by hard bony hands. A French soldier in Indo-China, deprived of his habitual drug, saw the earth cracking open in fiery furrows, through which rose up monstrous beings with one blood-red eye in their foreheads.[47]

A mosaic of scraps of case-histories does not catch the light well enough to show a clear outline. These were all real suffering people, but perhaps they have seemed more like dissected limbs and nerves in a laboratory. So I will end with two full-length portraits, of an American and a Frenchman who are not typical addicts—there are no typical addicts, any more than there are typical men—but simply two addicts of whom a good deal is known.

I do not, however, know the American's name. He told his own story, in a little book published in Philadelphia in 1876, *Opium-Eating, an Autobiographical Sketch* by an Habituate. As a young man he had been taken prisoner by the Confederates during the American Civil War, and had suffered terribly from starvation, exposure and scurvy during his prison years. When the war was over he returned home, married, and worked in some subordinate office job which involved keeping strict and regular hours. Crippled by headache and stomach troubles because of the privations he had suffered, he went to a doctor who gave him morphia—without his knowledge, he claimed—and from then on he was caught by the drug.

He maintains that he never got pleasure out of it in any active sense; at first and at best, it stimulated him and left him in 'an extremely sentimental condition of complacency and self-assurance, with a partly-defined feeling that the world had injured me; but that I did not care particularly; that the remainder of my life I could live alone and without it very comfortably'. In the first few minutes after taking the drug, he felt a stimulus and revival of spirits, but this soon passed into a serene untroubled relaxation, tinged with not unpleasurable melancholy but easily upset and confused by any interruption. Still he felt at this stage that his faculties of mind had become more powerful, and after he had come to take the drug daily, he lay awake whole nights with his brain in uncontrollable action. At this stage the addict's intellectual faculties, he says, 'are so adjusted that he needs but call and they obey; discipline and order reign . . . care-soothing peace in rich effulgence shines upon his soul'. But this is only momentary; presently the nerves react under this 'unnatural strain; the harmony of tension has been disturbed and deranged, and now, instead of discipline and equanimity, cruel disorder and distraction rule the hour, and collapse and utter exhaustion follow'. The alternative of 'sickening unnatural excitement' and of gloomy stagnation continued in his case until he became a 'tough, seasoned and dried-out opium eater' and the drug no longer had any power to stimulate him. There was no positive inducement now to make him go on taking opium, but he felt that if he stopped he would 'fall to pieces . . . go into naught', be plunged into a terrifying abyss of darkness and despair. Now if he closed his eyes, by day or night, he saw 'groups of enormous sea-monsters and serpents with frightful heads, coiling and inter-coiling about one another', and was reminded of the slimy things crawling on the slimy sea in *The Ancient Mariner*. His dreams, he firmly maintained, were caused and created solely by 'the subtle and mighty power of opium'.

He continued to take it until he reached a state of numbness, dead to enjoyment or interest, stiff and cold with his fellow men, whom he felt that he no longer understood. He was mild, quiet and submissive to his employers, but shrank from visitors and human contacts. He made an unsuccessful attempt to give up opium, and describes some of his withdrawal symptoms; but when he wrote his book he was back on his regular twelve grains of opium a day, taken at six in the morning and six in the evening; and he described himself as miserable and without hope.

The Habituate was a well-read sensible man, remarkably observant of his own mental processes, and able to describe them objectively. He seems to have had little imagination, or power of imagery; he writes clearly, sensibly and without distinction. He had no particular axe to grind, or none that invalidates what he had to say about opium. His only strong feelings seem to have been resentment at his treatment as a prisoner of war by the Confederates, and veneration for Coleridge, who was his inspiration and his balm; 'numbered with the saints in heaven is the sweet-minded long-suffering Coleridge' he exclaims. Many opium addicts use this ecclesiastical language when writing of their drug and its initiates. De Quincey called himself the Pope of the true church of opium; many French opium-smokers call their drug holy and divine, a god who confers supernatural graces on the faithful and agonies on the renegades who try to withdraw; their opium-smoking is a rite, which it is sacrilege to approach disrespectfully. In this church, Coleridge became a saint for the poor Habituate, whose devotion to him, and defence of him from all criticisms, including De Quincey's, read rather touchingly.

The Habituate's was a self-portrait. The French addict, identified only as D.C., is depicted by his doctor, Roger Dupouy, who warns the reader against the plausible but tainted intelligence with which D.C. describes his own personality and mental states.[48] D.C. was thirty-four and had been an opium-smoker for years. He had a nice taste in the silk hangings, the bed of polished black wood, which should furnish the opium smoker's room and support the perfect rêverie. He was very ready to theorize on the motives of addiction. Men start taking opium, he said, to obtain new sensations and unknown joys, and they continue taking it for fear of losing the physical equilibrium and the new mental experiences which it has conferred on them. The heightening of the imaginative faculty happens only when the addict has taken a moderate well-regulated dose, not when he is abstaining or has taken too much. Those who know how to regulate their doses may never suffer bad effects, and they gain great insight. They see a subtle and hitherto unperceived harmony and relation between the objects on which their eyes rest; they see the relation of colours to each other, the emotion and intensity of beauty which are latent in all visible objects. The slightest sounds have a revealing significance, and the sound of voices can actually be seen as well as heard. The intellectual addict who has once participated in this 'superior existence' is more difficult to cure than the unintelligent addict, who has only to be cured of the craving itself, while the intellectual has also to conquer his memories of 'artificial happiness'.

The mind of the addict, said D.C., works by analogy and association, and by them is able to make an amiable reconciliation of the most antagonistic facts of experience, of Good and Evil themselves. His rêveries take as their themes the thoughts and the experiences of his past life: the conversations of friends, the idea (but not the sensations) of past *amours*, the memory of music heard—but this experience is more like reading a score than attending a concert, the orchestra is seen but the music is not actually heard. He savours poetry, and sees lines and stanzas as statues and bas-reliefs, and he ponders the intentions of the poet, choosing between the dangerous and the orthodox with a will that is still active and deliberate. The addict's mania for combining contraries makes him unable to distinguish clearly between right and wrong; his unimpaired intellect enables him to unravel the most complicated evil doings, but his admiration for the art of the criminal may then make him sympathize with him.

D.C. is less trustworthy than the Habituate. He enjoys a feeling of superiority, he is an intellectual snob who has read Baudelaire and appropriated his ideas about the 'correspondances'. He shows off, and thinks that he is dazzling the unimpressed Dupouy. But he is interesting as a complete contrast with the Habituate; much more sophisticated and philosophic, much less sincere and responsible.

This short ethnological survey of the nation of opium-eaters has mentioned many manners and customs which will be familiar to the readers of Coleridge's letters and notebooks, De Quincey's *Confessions*, and all the biographical material on the literary addicts. But where does all this bear on poetic creation? Not, certainly, by a simple equation. Because the Habituate says that, when he shut his eyes, he saw coiling sea-monsters and was reminded of Coleridge's slimy creatures of the calm, I would not suggest that, even if it could be proved that Coleridge was already an opium addict when he wrote *The Ancient Mariner*, he therefore lifted the creatures of his poem straight and untransmuted from his own drugged visions. Even if Professor Lowes had not identified the books in which Coleridge probably found his sea creatures, and even if dreams of snakes were not among the commonest kind for all dreamers, it still would not be as simple as that. Writers have sometimes transferred their opium rêveries directly into literature, shaping them but not transforming them. The euphoric rêveries of the first stage of the opium habit are directly transcribed in De Quincey's *Pleasures of Opium*, and perhaps in Coleridge's *Kubla Khan*; nightmares of the later stages are related without much transmutation in De Quincey's *Pains of Opium*, Crabbe's *Sir Eustace Grey* and *The World of Dreams*, Coleridge's *The Pains of Sleep*. But there is a more subtle and interesting connection, through the states of feeling, apparatus of images, and manner of presentation which these rêveries display. It is the technique of opium rêveries—their rapid unfolding and linking of associations, the distortion and substitution of sense impressions, the idiosyncrasies of memory—that may influence and train the opium-addicted poets. And the states of mind, the emotions, even the physical sensations produced by the various stages of drug addiction and withdrawal may influence a writer to choose one theme or type of image rather than another. One would look for cosmic flights and vast precarious constructions,

Setting

secret refuges and inescapable eyes, creatures of craving disgust, dead-alive memories, icy footsteps. A man who felt himself isolated, both elect and outcast, in a petrified immunity from human cares, with his thoughts swiftly circling through infinity yet always walled in from communication with external reality—such a man might symbolize his spiritual condition by the figure of a prisoner in a vast cathedral or palace, the Temple of the Pariahs, which is the master image of this book.

III

DREAMS

If De Quincey had never used opium, he might still have written about his dreams. All the Romantic writers thought that there was a strong link between dreams and the processes of literary creation. Dream theory, dreams as sources, dreams as technique, were important to them, and they valued and used their own dreams.[1] A survey of the dream theory and dream experience of the Romantic writers in general may make it possible to isolate those elements in the dreams of the opium-addict writers which were not shared with other contemporary writers, and thus to show the influence of opium on the patterns of their imagination.

I am here concerned only with what the Romantic writers dreamed about, not why they dreamed it; with the plot and scenery of their dreams, the manifest content, not with the latent wishes and fears embodied in these symbols of plot and scenery which make up the manifest content. De Quincey's dream-complex of the deaths of young girls may have been derived from wishes and fears other than the unmixed grief and loss, and consequent death-wish for himself, which he recognized as associated with them, originating in the death of his elder sister when he was a child. But that does not come within the scope of this book. It is the manifest content of dreams with its aura of emotion, the plot and scenery of the dream, that is generally used in poetry; and it is with the use of these dream symbols in these writers' imaginative works, not with the symbols' significance for their personal psychology, that I am concerned.

English literature of all periods has always made use of dreams as a mechanism, a device of plot—to announce or allegorize the theme, to create atmosphere and suspense and dramatic irony; Shakespeare supremely used the device, for all these purposes at once, in Clarence's dream in *Richard III*. Dreams have also long been valued by writers as a clue to man's nature and destiny, explaining the past, perhaps revealing the future, laying bare men's hidden hopes and fears. But till the Romantic period dreams were not generally felt to be in themselves an interesting part of human experience. When Edward Young wrote his *Night Thoughts* (published in 1742), he still felt that his dreams—he was a very active dreamer—were important chiefly as a proof of the immortality of the soul. He did not value them so much because they were intrinsically exciting as because they gave evidence about Man's nature.

' 'Tis past conjecture; all things rise in Proof:
  While o'er my limbs Sleep's soft Dominion spread,
  What though my Soul phantastic Measures trod
  O'er Fairy Fields; or down the craggy Steep
  Hurl'd headlong, swam with Pain the mantled Pool;
  Or scal'd the Cliff; or danc'd on hollow Winds
  With antic Shapes, wild Natives of the Brain?
  Her ceaseless Flight, tho' devious, speaks her Nature
  Of subtler essence than the trodden Clod;
  Active, aerial, tow'ring, unconfin'd,
  Unfetter'd with her gross Companion's fall.
  Ev'n silent Night proclaims my Soul *immortal*:
  Ev'n silent Night proclaims eternal Day.
  For human Weal, Heav'n husbands all Events;
  Dull Sleep instructs, nor sport vain Dreams in vain'.

Later eighteenth-century thinkers like Hartley and Erasmus Darwin were interested more in why and how we dream than in what we dream about. They were concerned with the degree of belief which the mind accords to what it sees in dreams, the extent to which the will is powerless in face of dream events, the connection between bodily sensations and dream feelings. Hartley laid down that 'a Person who has taken Opium, sees either gay scenes, or ghastly ones, according as the Opium excites pleasant or painful Vibrations in the Stomach'. He was

Dreams

not interested in the gay and ghastly scenes except as symptoms,
and in that way resembles mid-twentieth-century psychiatrists.[2]

It was one of the distinctions of the Romantic writers, in
Germany and in England, that they revered dreams not only for
their moral and psychological importance, but also as aesthetic
experiences of intrinsic value. They were uniquely interested—
more than any great writers before or since—in the manifest
content, the actual happenings and appearances of dreams, as well
as in what these stood for. The gift of dreaming vividly in sleep
was cherished and envied among the Romantic writers, as a
necessary endowment of a poet.

Byron produced what might be called the Romantic manifesto
on dreams. Forty years before Gérard de Nerval began *Aurélia*
with the words 'Le Rêve est une seconde vie', Byron wrote

'Our life is two-fold: Sleep hath its own world,
A boundary between the things misnamed
Death and existence: Sleep hath its own world,
And a wide realm of wild reality.
And dreams in their development have breath,
And tears, and tortures, and the touch of joy;
They leave a weight upon our waking thoughts,
They take a weight from off our waking toils,
They do divide our being; they become
A portion of ourselves as of our time,
And look like heralds of eternity . . .
They make us what we were not—what they will,
And shake us with the vision that's gone by,
The dread of vanish'd shadows—Are they so?
Is not the past all shadow?—What are they?
Creations of the mind?—The mind can make
Substance, and people planets of its own
With beings brighter than have been, and give
A breath to forms that can outlive all flesh'.

These lines in *The Dream*, though their starting-point of the
separate world of sleep is as old as Heraclitus, were a gospel for
Byron's contemporaries. They contain the three cardinal
Romantic doctrines on dreams—that they are a revelation of

reality, that they can form and influence waking life, and that the dream process is a parallel and model of the process of poetic creation.

The first of these doctrines owed much to the German Romantics. As Monsieur Albert Béguin showed in his stimulating book *L'Ame Romantique et le Rêve*, for writers like Jean-Paul, Novalis and Hoffmann it was the life of dreams, rather than the world of everyday, that was the realm of enlightenment.[3] There one's eyes, clouded by the mists of ordinary waking life, might be purified by the light from beyond, from the innermost source of essential reality, and thence one might bring back to the waking world the restored perceptions of childhood, and re-establish a right relationship with Nature and with other men. This conception, that

'gleams of a remoter world
Visit the soul in sleep'[4]

was congenial to the English Romantics, who all laid stress on the reality of the dream world, the paradox that it was perhaps the waking life which was illusion and the dream which was essential truth.

The second doctrine, that dreams could be an influence on waking life—that, as Cocteau was to write a century later in his *Opium: Journal d'une Désintoxication*, 'dreams can be a kind of education'—followed from the first. Wordsworth and Shelley both said that dreams could impart strength. They could change the dreamer, 'make us what we were not', as Byron put it. The shock of the strong emotion felt in the dream, and persisting even when the memory of the dream event which had occasioned the emotion was lost, might lastingly re-shape the dreamer's personality. This was what Southey felt when, after recording a horrible dream about a long cold lifeless hand that reached for him through a door, he added 'This was a valuable dream, for an old monk would have believed all to have been verily what it appeared, and I now perfectly understand by experience what their contests with the devil were'. He felt that the boundaries of his experience had been enlarged, he had shared in the consciousness of a mind different from his own.[5]

Dreams

This was valuable to a poet, and equally instructive was the opportunity which dreams gave him of observing, as a spectator without any control over the spectacle, his own imagination at its creative work; he could watch it doing in dreams something like what he made it do in the conscious process of writing poetry. This process could be observed most easily on the borderline of sleep and waking, when he was seeing hypnagogic visions, the moving patterns of light and colour which so many writers have described.[6] De Quincey made them the starting-point of his description of his opium dreams; Coleridge minutely recorded them in his Notebooks; Poe analysed them; Hoffmann launched an aesthetic theory by his study of the phenomenon which he perceived in this 'state of delirium which precedes sleep'. These trains of images were semi-voluntary. 'I can tell them to go, and they go, but sometimes they come when I don't tell them to come' said a child who had hypnagogic visions to De Quincey;[7] and Lamb wrote 'Fiendish faces, with the extinguished taper, will come and look at me; but I know them for mockeries, even while I cannot elude their presence, and I fight and grapple with them'.[8] Wordsworth as a schoolboy at Hawkshead experienced hypnagogic visions as he lay on the verge of sleep. He saw huntsmen and hounds streaming by, files of soldiers mounting upwards, inexplicable grotesque faces melting into one another. Long afterwards he drew a parallel between

'A second-sight procession, such as glides
    Over still mountains, or appears in dreams'

and the process by which the poet's imagination, amid the flux of London crowds, is caught by the spectacle of a single face, and 'as though admonished from another world' receives an insight on which the excited spirit builds poetry.[9]

In their dreams poets could thus watch how imagery was formed. They could also hear scattered sentences and lines of poetry, sometimes harsh and quacking like the voice of a ventriloquist, which were the sound of the mind at play among words as a tuning-up orchestra plays with notes. How odd, and seemingly how unpoetic, are some of the sentences that writers have heard in dreams and hallucinations: Shelley's doppelgänger at Lerici which said to him 'How long do you mean to be content?';[10] Maria Edgeworth's fever-dream which echoed with the continually repeated sentence 'A soldier of the forty-second has lost his portmanteau';[11] Coleridge's opium dream at Malta in which someone said to him 'Varrius thus prophesied Vinegar at his door by damned frigid Tremblings';[12] they all have the meaningless urgency of a Delphic oracle. The verbalizing part of the dreaming mind is indeed something of a clown. When I was writing the chapter on Crabbe in this book, and had gone to sleep as I meditated on his opium habit and on his use of a near-Spenserian stanza for his dream poems, my subsequent dream contained a voice, distinctly heard, proclaiming 'The Spenserian halibut'.

The lines of verse actually remembered from dreams (as opposed to poems based on dreams but written after waking) are generally inadequate and absurd, but one seems to be listening to the very beginning of a process of word-selection, that earliest stage which the conscious mind of the word-choosing poet never hears. Meikle, who was so sure that he composed sublime poetry in his sleep, if only he could remember it, was cruelly disappointed when his wife recalled two lines which she had heard him say in his sleep

'By Heaven, I'll wreak my woes
Upon the cowslip and the pale primrose'

but there is something fascinating about this ungainly lump of un-worked ore.[13] Browning dreamed that at a performance of *Richard III* he heard a line spoken which was not Shakespeare's but his own, and it seemed to him in the dream that it was 'immensely finer than anything else in the play. . . . When I woke I still had hold of the stupendous line, and it was this

"And when I wake my dreams are madness—Damn me" '.

It looks as if Browning in fact had one of those secondary dreams which are devoted to trying to remember a previous dream, and that the 'stupendous line' which finally reached his waking memory was the secondary dream's account of its failure to recall the primary dream's 'stupendous line'.[14]

A world in which words and images are associated with as

much freedom, eccentricity and yet concentration as they are in dreams was bound to be of interest to a generation of poets very conscious of their vocation and very anxious to analyse its techniques and processes. Nearly all the poets of the Romantic period made a point of recording their dreams. Crabbe kept a lamp and writing materials by his bed so that he could set down immediately things that occurred to him in his dreams, and said that he would have 'lost a good many hit' if he had not done so. Southey told his brother that 'two of my old dreams are likely to be introduced, with powerful effect, in this poem' (*The Curse of Kehama*) '—good proof that it was worth while to keep even the imperfect register that I have', and eighteen years later when turning out old papers he found this same register of dreams, and told Caroline Bowles that they had been 'noted down, as you may well suppose, not superstitiously, but for their strange combinations. The use of having kept such a register I felt when writing the *Vindiciae*, and had very often regretted the loss of these few but curious pages'.[15]

Dreams were part of one's professional equipment as a writer. Lamb professed himself mortified by the poverty of his own dreams compared with those of his fellow poets. 'There is Coleridge, at his will can conjure up icy domes, and pleasure-houses for Kubla Khan, and Abyssinian maids, and songs of Abora, and caverns where Alph the sacred river runs, to solace his night solitudes—where I cannot muster a fiddle. Barry Cornwall has his tritons and his nereids gambolling before him in nocturnal visions, and proclaiming sons born to Neptune—when my stretch of imaginative activity can hardly, in the night season, raise up the ghost of a fish-wife' and he ended with the comment 'The degree of the soul's creativeness in sleep might furnish no whimsical criterion of the quantum of poetic faculty resident in the same soul waking' and with a reference to an old friend who used to judge aspiring poets by their answer to the question 'Young man, what sort of dreams have you?'[16]

The whole Gothic Revival in English literature was in fact launched by a dream, on that June night in 1764 when Horace Walpole dreamed that he saw a gigantic hand in armour on the bannister of a great staircase in an ancient castle, and woke to write *The Castle of Otranto*. Many of the Gothick romances, with their unmotivated violence and emotion, their separation from all the hesitations and ambiguities and routine of ordinary waking life, seem to correspond to a human experience of a different order of reality, the experience of dreams, which often have just this disconnected momentousness.

Wordsworth dreamed of a fleeing Arab with a stone and a shell, and wrote the vision into a great passage of *The Prelude*. Keats dreamed of Paolo and Francesca whirling in the icy storm, and wrote a sonnet about it. Southey dreamed of a corpse carried in a sedan chair, and wove the incident into *The Curse of Kehama*. Tennyson dreamed of a hall of maidens and a journey to the sea and a shining ship, and worked the dream into *In Memoriam*. I will carry the topic beyond my period for a moment to include the testimony of Yeats on dream-work and poetry. He dreamed of a jester who sent his soul in a blue robe up to the window of a young queen, and when he made the dream into his poem *The Cap and Bells*, he added a very illuminating note: 'I dreamed this story exactly as I have written it, and dreamed another long dream after it, trying to make out its meaning, and whether I was to write it in prose or verse. The first dream was more a vision than a dream, for it was beautiful and coherent, and gave me the sense of illumination and exaltation that one gets from visions, while the second dream was confused and meaningless. The poem has always meant a great deal to me, though, as is the way with symbolic poems, it has not always meant quite the same thing. Blake would have said "The authors are in eternity", and I am quite sure they can only be questioned in dreams'.[17] Yeats's reference to Blake recalls that Blake was an inspired dreamer, and recorded many of his dreams in visual form. But in his case the borderline between dream and ecstatic vision cannot be traced, and for that reason he is outside the scope of this chapter and this book.

De Quincey, a purist in literary transcriptions of dream-work, felt that he could detect where the dream inspiration had been subsequently falsified. Although he admired Jean-Paul, whose

Dream upon the Universe he translated into English, he considered that in reproducing dreams Jean-Paul 'wanted . . . the severe simplicity, that horror of the *too much*, belonging to Grecian architecture, which is essential to the perfection of the dream considered as a work of art. Too elaborate he was, and too artificial, to realise the grandeur of the shadow'.[18]

Since dreams were considered such a valuable tool in the poet's workshop, it was natural that creative artists should try to procure them artificially if they did not come abundantly by nature. All sorts of physical stimuli were tried. Fuseli, who considered that 'one of the most unexplored regions of art are Dreams', ate raw meat, and Mrs Radcliffe consumed large quantities of indigestible food, to produce dreams of terror. Tennyson, too, thought that a meal of meat, after six weeks of vegetarianism, had produced an unforgettable dream. 'I never felt such joy in my blood. When I went to sleep I dreamt that I saw the vines of the South, with huge Eshcol branches, trailing over the glaciers of the North'.[19] Jean-Paul stimulated his dreams and rêveries by coffee and alcohol. Southey and Humphrey Davy experimented with laughing gas, and had wild cosmic raptures; 'Davy has actually invented a new pleasure, for which language has no name' exclaimed Southey, and Davy tried to get Southey to include in his *Thalaba* one of these nitrous oxide visions, of 'a paradise wholly immaterial—trees of light growing in a soil of ether—palaces of water refracting all rich colours'; a version of this did finally find its way into Southey's *Curse of Kehama*.[20]

Failing a dream of one's own, natural or procured, one borrowed someone else's. One of the starting-points of *The Ancient Mariner* was John Cruikshank's dream of a skeleton ship with figures in it, which was imparted to Coleridge. Mrs Leigh Hunt's dream of a black anchor in the sky, and of tidal waves and burning mountain cities, told to Shelley, reappeared in his poem *Marianne's Dream*.

If all authentic dream sources failed, writers, especially prose writers, let loose their imaginations and invented dreams. There are beautiful or strange and horrible constructed dreams, often inserted purely for their intrinsic interest and not as a device of plot, in Jean-Paul, in Maturin's *Melmoth the Wanderer*, in Mrs Radcliffe and M. G. Lewis, in Hood and Beddoes. Charles Kingsley's *Alton Locke* has a whole long chapter of the hero's fever dreams, partly allegorical but mostly inserted, as far as one can see, for the sheer pleasure of inventing them. Dickens introduces into *Martin Chuzzlewit* a very powerful and vivid dream—of a strange city where to get from one precipitous street to another the dreamer had to descend great depths by ladders that did not reach far enough, and by ropes that rang deep bells; where there were white horses and people strewing flowers and writing on the walls in a strange language—which is quite inappropriate to the mean-souled murderer Jonas Chuzzlewit whose dream it is supposed to be.

Enough has been said to illustrate the general pre-occupation with dreams in early nineteenth-century literature. It was within this climate of the imagination that the special dreams of opium-addict writers unfolded. A survey of the dreams of one of the Romantic poets who did not take opium should provide a standard of comparison for the dreams of the addict writers.

Which poet should be chosen for the comparison? Not Byron or Keats; they took laudanum themselves, though only occasionally, but enough to make the comparison not quite a straight one. Not Lamb, though at first sight he seems a strong candidate. He speculated much about dreams and their value and he was himself a distinct idiosyncratic dreamer, in spite of his mock-humble disparagement of his dreaming powers beside those of Coleridge and Barry Cornwall. He dreamed of architecture and buildings, and in his dreams had 'traversed, for the seeming length of a natural day, Rome, Amsterdam, Paris, Lisbon—their churches, palaces, squares, market-places, shops, suburbs, ruins, with an inexpressible sense of delight—a map-like distinctness of trace, and a day-light vividness of vision, that was all but being awake'. One is reminded at first of De Quincey's statement that in the early stages of his opium habit 'the splendours of my dreams were indeed chiefly architectural'. Do the opium addict and the non-addict dreamer join hands here? But Lamb was not a sufficiently normal man for the comparison to be a fair one. He drank a great deal; but more than that, he had an extra dimension of imaginative experience which disqualified him; he had known what it was to be insane. 'Dream not, Coleridge, of having tasted all the grandeur and wildness of fancy till you have gone mad!' he told his friend.[21]

Shelley might seem an obvious choice for the comparison. He had an absorbed interest in dreams. His peotry is full of references to them. He revered the 'mightier world of sleep' and thought that from his solemn Paradisal dreams man might 'draw new strength to tread the thorns of life'.[22] All his important characters dream constantly; Alastor, Laon, Panthea, Count Cenci, Mahmud, all are dreamers; the Witch of Atlas is a dispenser of dreams. But the dreams that she dispenses are moral allegories, they are not like authentic dreams, and to me almost all the dreams in Shelley's poetry seem constructed. They are often most beautiful, but they are not like real dreams of sleep. None of his poems convincingly conveys a dream of his own. In saying this, I have not forgotten *The Question*; perhaps a faint suggestion for that—the bare incident of gathering flowers with no one to give them to—may have come from a dream, but the lovely though rather self-indulgent poem as a whole does not read in the least like a dream. And *Marianne's Dream*, which clearly is based on authentic dream-work, originated with Marianne Hunt, not with Shelley. Shelley's and Leigh Hunt's letters of November and December 1818 show that Mrs Hunt was proud to have produced a fine apocalyptic dream of her own which Shelley thought worth using in a poem. She perhaps contributed the clanging sounds and the anchor in the sky, the floods and planks and houses on fire and screaming statues; Shelley may have added the radiant mountain landscape, the flaming domes, the winged creatures of quivering marble. This dream poem, alone among Shelley's works, has that incongruity and incoherence in its symbolism which suggests a real untransmuted dream, seized on by Shelley at a moment when he was writing *Laon and Cynthna*, which is full of constructed dreams.[23]

My guess is that Shelley's constant use of dreams as a symbol was not based on much personal experience of distinct dreaming in sleep, or at least of remembering his dreams. It seems now to have been proved that there is no such thing as a non-dreamer. American researchers have recently proved, by an ingenious method of measuring the movements of sleepers' closed eyes, that we all have dreams of some sort every night. But vivid dreams of events and emotions remote from the dreamer's waking experience, which he afterwards spontaneously remembers and which can explain and enrich his waking life, do not seem to be a common endowment; even the most imaginative poet may not possess it, though a number of far lesser mortals do. Shelley very often refers to vanishing memories of dreams, 'wrecks of a dissolving dream', incommunicable dreams, efforts to remember dreams, the secondary dreams in which one tries to recall a previous dream; dreams fading into daylight and leaving only a feeling of lost delight or sometimes of horror, the dreams that shake the dreamer

> 'as the tempest shakes the sea,
> Leaving no figure upon memory's glass'.[24]

The feeling survived, but not the dream image or incident that inspired it, and the attempt that he sometimes made to recall his dreams produced nervous suffering. He both walked and talked in his sleep, and these are alternatives to dreaming, not accompaniments to it. He had many hallucinatory visions—the woman with eyes in her breasts whom he saw after hearing Byron recite *Christabel*, the naked child who rose from the moonlit surf at Lerici, the lacerated and decaying bodies of Jane and Edward Williams coming to warn him of an approaching flood, perhaps the mysterious assailant who fired at him when he was living in Wales—and he was even able to do sketches in his notebooks of these wild faces and watchful eyes; but these were waking hallucinations. Shelley's visionary powers, extraordinary as they were, do not seem to have included the experience of remembered imaginative dreams in normal sleep.

Shelley therefore does not quite fit into the category of the Romantic poet-dreamer needed for comparison with the poet-dreamer-addict. Another possibility is Southey. He certainly qualifies as a dreamer; he had, and recorded, an astonishing collection of dreams. The most vivid, and those which most impressed Southey himself, were ghastly visions of the living dead—of coffins whose occupants struggled out into a vampire life, of rotting bodies that rose up out of the ground, of corpses—naked or horribly decked in gauzes and lace—carried in sedan chairs, of being crushed by the bony arms of skeletons in catacomb niches. He dreamed of giantesses who forced their way in earthquake out of the sides of mountains, and witches who soaked in blood the pages of Bibles, and devils who flew with him on their backs. His sense of smell in his dreams was painfully acute, and brought him horrible stenches of putrefaction, but also pleasant dreams of urbane bodiless heads that sustained themselves by tasting, not smelling, perfumes. He dreamed of saints, of ordeals and talismans and sacrileges and the Last Judgment. Sometimes in his dreams he killed Napoleon with an axe, or poisoned himself to be in the fashion, or going as an ambassador to Haroun al Raschid, beat his interpreters. He was unquestionably a faithful reporter of real dreams of sleep; they have the authentic inconsequence, the lucid illogic, which is always recognizable in true reports of dreams. His experience seems to have been the reverse of Shelley's; he had, and remembered, vivid dreams in sleep but he was seldom able to convey the intense feelings that accompanied them. Reading his dream-register, one gets the same effect that makes his long poems like *Thalaba* and *The Curse of Kehama* so disconcerting. The events and changes of fortune are astonishingly violent, but unmotivated and unfelt, a perpetual seesaw of gigantic but too easy triumphs and disasters. In Southey one can perhaps observe only half the process by which the poet-dreamer makes use of his dreams. The dreams were there, but he was never able to transmute them completely into poetry.

He made many notes on the techniques of dreaming: how 'grief is as intense in dreams as in reality, but we can bear horrors in sleep which would certainly deprive us of our waking senses, if not of life'; how the dreamer partly knows that it is all a dream, and makes efforts to wake; how the power to fly in dreams is dependent on a continuous exercise of the will; how when speaking or reading in dreams we are often discomfited by the disappearance of words from the page, or from articulation; how two incompatible feelings combine in dreams—we see and greet those who are dead, though we are simultaneously mourning their loss, or we decide to stay no longer at school because we are too old for it and must have left it long ago. He felt that here was a whole untapped source of ideas and new combinations which would be useful for poetry. He was a thrifty hoarder of ideas; his bulky Commonplace Books are full of headings such as 'Ground that may be built upon', 'Images for Poetry', 'Subjects for Idylls', 'Would this story mature into a useful volume?'; and perhaps he recognized in his dreaming imagination a wild vivacity beyond the scope of his waking one.[25]

But he could not use what he had got. His Commonplace Book enables one to trace in detail how an idea from a book could combine with his own mental and physical condition at the time, reappear in a dream, and then be noted as a subject for a poem. The whole mechanism is bared, but the result is disappointing. Take the heading 'Subject for Poemlings' in one of his Commonplace Books. He begins the section with a batch of themes ranging from 'The Defeat of Attila' to 'The cold in my head. French blacksmith. Ode', and from a Monodrama on the Death of Cranmer to Meditations on an Empty Purse. Two later consecutive entries read—

'My considering cap. All possible head-coverings. The powdered head—the mitre—the three-tailed wig—the judges'—the helmet.

Laudanum visions. I saw last night one figure whose eyes were in his spectacles; another, whose brains were in his wig. A third devil whose nose was a trumpet'.

One can see just what happened. Southey had been reading about Archbishop Cranmer, and thinking about the essential man and the trappings of office. He had had a cold at the time, and took a dose of laudanum to cure it. This produced a dream or vision, in which the idea of the head-coverings and the heads they cover was embodied in a sort of acted metaphor, as so often in dreams, and he saw someone whose brains were *in* his wig. He never, as far as I know, used this idea for a satirical poem, but if he had it would have been much more poetically effective than his original rather trite scheme for a 'poemling' on 'head-coverings'.[26] But this was Southey's trouble; his conscious mind would not allow him to make real emotive use of the presents which his sub-conscious mind made to him as a poet.

Still he remains one of the most useful parallels, so his dream landscape may be summarily described for comparison with that of the opium-addict poets (among whom he cannot be included, in spite of the recourse to laudanum mentioned in his Commonplace Book; he took it only very occasionally in 1799 and 1800, in small doses). His dream world is a restricted one, there are no wide landscapes or trees or expanses of water, no flowers or animals (although the 'Images for Poetry' sections in his Commonplace Books are full of sensitive observant notes on effects of light and water, colours in birds and leaves). There are few marked faces in his dreams, and not much sense of place, though like Lamb he had a number of architectural dreams, of great churches and staircases, catacombs and low tunnels and vaulted subterranean chambers. His dream world is full of energy and activity and other people who exist in their own right and go about their own concerns; equally far from *Kubla Khan*, from De Quincey's pagodas and crocodiles and haunting faces, and from Crabbe's helpless victim in the freezing marshes under the Northern Lights.

Wordsworth is the only true equivalent for comparison with Coleridge—a great Romantic poet and vivid dreamer who never in his life tasted opium. For Wordsworth the expressions 'dream-like' and 'unreal' were not synonyms, they were antonyms. Dreams to him were more real than most ordinary experiences, they had a glory and freshness which the waking adult eye no longer enjoys, in them one saw things that now one could see no more by day. Describing how he trained his mind to fix and work on images, he said that they thus eventually 'acquired the liveliness of dreams'.[27] Liveliness is an unexpected word in the context, whether it means vivacity or the condition of being alive, or both. But the habitual dreamer knows that it is true; the

intensity of dreams is more urgently real than much of what is
called 'real life'. When Wordsworth says in *Resolution and
Independence* that

> 'the whole body of the Man did seem
> Like one whom I had met with in a dream;
> Or like a man from some far region sent
> To give me human strength, by apt admonishment'

the double comparison makes it clear that for him things seen in
dreams had a power of enlightenment and admonition greater
than anything that came in ordinary waking life.

Wordsworth kept no detailed register of his dreams as Southey
did. He felt no need to make notes and hoard ideas. We know
little of his own dreams except for the ones which he used in his
poetry. There are the nightmares of innocent victims and dungeons and trials before revolutionary courts that he endured
after his stay in France, in which he struggled to plead his cause
before unjust tribunals, feeling treachery everywhere, even in his
own soul.[28] But these seem to have been special to this crisis in
his life, not the usual tenor of his dreams. What that was, we can
only guess. We may think we can trace a true dream origin in the
sonnet *Methought I saw the Footsteps of a Throne*, though Wordsworth
does not expressly say it had one; we may feel convinced that the
jingoistic 1814 *Ode* for which he did claim a dream origin had no
such thing, but was a construction. One famous dream alone,
faithfully told in full with all the unreconciled contradictions of a
true dream, remains to tell us what Wordsworth's dream world
was like—the Arab rider of the *Prelude* with his stone and shell,
pacing across the black sands on his dromedary.

Here I will stop at last in my search for comparisons, and try to
draw to a point the differences between the dream of natural
sleep and the opium dream. To do this I will take an image which
is one of the constants of all dream worlds, those of the ordinary
man and woman as well as those of the poet dreamer and the
addict dreamer. This is the image of the Drowned City, the tidal
wave that submerges a civilization. I have seen it often enough in
my own dreams—a huge shoulder of water, over-topping the
hills, effacing the sky, rolling onwards with irresistible beauty and

Dreams

strength to overwhelm cities. It is found in three nineteenth-
century poems known to be directly drawn from dreams: in
Shelley's *Marianne's Dream*, in Tennyson's *Sea-Dreams* and in the
passage in the *Prelude* about the Arab rider. In Shelley's poem a
raging flood bursts over mountain summits to pour through a city
of flaming domes and palaces. In Tennyson's, a giant wave that is
also a note of music rushes forward from the horizon to break in
cataracts over the façades of ruined cathedrals. In Wordsworth's,
the 'fleet waters of a drowning world' float across the wilderness
in rising floods of glittering light to overwhelm the stone and
shell which are the symbols of civilization. The contexts, the
allegorical meanings, are different, but the image is the same.
Like it, and yet subtly different, is the image of drowned cities in
three visions of writers who took opium—De Quincey's
Savannah-la-Mar, and Poe's City in the Sea (and the related House
of Usher sinking into the black tarn) and Francis Thompson's
Palace of the Occident. No onrushing cataracts, no music, no
glitter, no breath of sea-wind, disturb their dead calm. The great
wave has passed; in silent apathy the cities have sunk into the
depths, and the dream looks down through the lucid water and
sees their towers awash in the sluggish tides, their domes half
turned to bubbles, their bells and horns and organs silenced by
folds of water, the stony faces of their statues faintly flickering as
a passing ripple refracts the light.

IV

CONTEMPORARY IMAGERY

Any writer's stock of imagery is a mixed bag of wild game which he has shot for himself and tame, even tinned, fowls which are obtainable in shops. Many surveys have been made of the fashionable images of the Romantic period: the upas tree, the Aeolian harp, the Sarsar wind, the footless birds of Paradise, the Lapland witches, the battle of the eagle and the snake.[1] The mental iconography of Coleridge, Shelley and Keats has been studied in minute detail; we know much about what they read, and how they picked out what they needed and could use from the works of their predecessors, particularly perhaps from footnotes—how this train of imagery was started off by a note of Erasmus Darwin's, that one by a passage in Hakluyt or Purchas, that other by some echo from Plato or Dante. The commonplace books in which they jotted down their momentary impressions, to be used later in poetic imagery, have been published in faithful detail, and their letters have told us how, for instance, Coleridge went to hear Humphrey Davy's lectures to increase his stock of images, how Keats was afraid of being 'rattlesnaked' into the conventional use of other men's images, while the grand self-confidence of Wordsworth enabled him, as an old man, to dictate in meticulous notes his acknowledgements to his sister and his friends for the images and anecdotes which sank into his retentive memory and rose again in his poems.

A survey of imagery in opium visions has to take into account which images were general property at the time and which were special to the opium landscape, if any of them were. In fact what happened was probably more like an unconscious selection, among standard images, of some which could be made to bear the weight of the special emotions of the opium rêverie. Partly because the process can literally be illustrated, I will concentrate in this chapter on certain visual images which seem specially to have attracted opium addicts because these expressed their unusual experience. The process may be watched by tracing a single image, for instance the image of Memnon, through the literature of the early nineteenth century.

The Greek legend of Memnon, son of Tithonus and the Dawn, who was killed in the Trojan War, and of his bird-haunted tomb which became the eponym for an ancient temple, has always been a standard image in English poetry. The two aspects of it, as they lived in the poetic consciousness of the late eighteenth century, are illustrated by Landor's reference, in *Gebir*, to

'birds that wintering watch in Memnon's tomb'

and by Erasmus Darwin's note in *The Economy of Vegetation*, that 'The gigantic statue of Memnon in his temple at Thebes had a lyre in his hands, which many credible writers assure us, sounded when the rising sun shone upon it. . . . The statue of Memnon was overthrown and sawed in two by Cambyses to discover its internal structure, and is said still to exist. The truncated statue is said for many centuries to have saluted the rising sun with cheerful tones, and the setting sun with melancholy ones'.[2]

Erasmus Darwin's note enshrines all the confusions, dating from Strabo and Diodorus Siculus, by which the colossal statues of Amenhotep III at Thebes, and the neighbouring temple of Rameses II, or User-maat-Re, were all identified with Memnon, the huge statues being known as the Colossi of Memnon and the temple as the Memnonium, or sometimes as the Tomb of Ozymandias, which was the Greek version of User-maat-Re.[3] This complex of legend—the singing statue, child of the dawn, and the ruined temple with its fallen or mutilated statue and its wintering birds—was a stock image, but by the late eighteenth century a more or less inert one. When Coleridge wrote to George Dyer in 1795 that 'The finely-fibred Heart, that like the statue of Memnon, trembles into melody on the sun-beam touch

85

of Benevolence, is most easily jarred into the dissonance of Misanthropy', the simile was frigid, it had no pervasive warmth in Coleridge's imagination.[4]

But twenty-three years later this tired literary image was to spring to life again under the stimulus of visual experience. In 1818 the statue known as the Young Memnon—actually the head and shoulders of a statue of Rameses II—reached the British Museum after the long journey on which Belzoni had launched it from the Ramesseum temple at Thebes. Its arrival was much publicized, particularly in the *Annals of the Fine Arts* to which Leigh Hunt, Haydon and Keats were contributors.

This huge bust of red granite with its regal calm and its faint mysterious smile made a great impression on the writers of the day when it was first exhibited in London. It contributed to the inspiration of Shelley's *Ozymandias*, and also to the sonnet which he wrote in a competition with Keats and Leigh Hunt at Hunt's house on a February evening in 1818 for the best sonnet on the Nile—ancient Egypt had temporarily captured their imaginations. Both Keats and Shelley in their sonnets tentatively explored the mystery of knowledge, which to men can be both a 'soul-sustaining air' and a 'blast of evil', that haunted them from the enigmatic smile of the great granite face from the Nile which they had seen in the British Museum. A variant version of Keats's sonnet speaks of the 'wan smile' on the face of the personified river which he imagines among the desert sands. The image was only beginning to work in his imagination; in the autumn of that year, when he was writing Book II of *Hyperion*, it gave him a simile for the Sun-God's majestic bulk; by September of 1819 in Book I of *The Fall of Hyperion*, the image had grown huge and pervasive, and had become both the vast statue of Moneta's temple and the 'wan face' of the priestess herself.[5]

Memnon, Rameses, Ozymandias—by whichever name the fallen statue was known, it sank deep into the poetic consciousness of the writers who saw it. For Shelley its smile was a 'sneer of cold command' and its overthrow a prophecy of the downfall of tyranny. To Keats it spoke of the devouring strength of knowledge that a poet must bear. To De Quincey it was something

much closer—a presence that lived inside his mind for a lifetime, and beat with his pulses, and multiplied with the ever-
repeated reflections from one opium rêverie to another. In 1845,
when he was writing of the trance which he experienced as a
child in the room where his dead sister lay, he spoke of the
'hollow, solemn, Memnonian, but saintly swell' of the wind
which, then and many times later in his life, he had heard on
summer days. The writing down of the word 'Memnonian'
brought the dream symbol into the daylight of conscious
literary creation, so that a year later, in what started as an article
on *The System of the Heavens as Revealed by Lord Rosse's Telescope*, he
digressed into an extraordinary vision of a hideous gigantic face
seen in a star map, and contrasted it with what he called the
sublimest sight he had ever seen, the Memnon head in the
British Museum. It seemed so much a lifelong part of his imagination that he said he had first seen it thirty-four years earlier—
that is, in 1812, a date at which it was in fact still lying on its face
among the ruined temples of Thebes. For him it was a symbol of
peace, of eternity, and of that love which is 'an emanation from
some mystery of endless dawn'. Its expression was too full of awe
to be called a smile, it had 'the breathlessness which belongs to
a saintly trance; the holy thing seemed to live by silence'.[6] It had
become for him the very face of Rêverie, that timeless experience
which he sought in his opium addiction. [Plate i]

In 1853, when he used in his *Autobiographic Sketches* the passage
about his sister's death which he had printed eight years earlier
as part of *Suspiria de Profundis*, he added a long footnote to his
reference to the 'Memnonian' swell of the wind. He was referring, he said, to the Young Memnon statue in the British
Museum, 'that sublime head which wears upon its lips a smile co-
extensive with all time and all space, an Æonian smile of gracious
love and Pan-like mystery, the most diffusive and pathetically
divine that the hand of man has created'. He evidently thought
that it was this head of Rameses II, not the colossal statues of
Amenhotep III, that sang at dawn, for he goes on to relate the
tradition of its 'solemn and dirge-like series of intonations', and
to compare these with the sounds of the human blood-stream,

Setting

heard through the stethoscope, as an 'elaborate gamut or compass of music, recording the ravages of disease, or the glorious
plenitudes of health, as faithfully as the cavities within this
ancient Memnonian bust reported this mighty event of sunrise to
the rejoicing world of light and life—or again, under the sad
passion of the dying day, uttered the sweet requiem that belonged
to its departure'.[7] His imagination was now lodged inside that
majestic head of stone, and felt the currents of diseased thought
rushing like discordant wind-music through the cavities of his
personality, and informing it with the pathetic mystery of a smile
which he wanted to believe was loving and holy, but which was
in truth withdrawn from life into the inhuman calm of the opium
trance.[8]

That is one example of how the same visual experience can
start different trains of imagery in the minds of differently-con-
ditioned writers. The image itself remains constant, but opium
can add strange shadows to it. One of the most memorable passages in *The Confessions of an English Opium Eater* is the one in
which De Quincey describes the horror which his dreams
imparted to the idea of the East. 'I was stared at, hooted at,
grinned at, chattered at, by monkeys, by paroquets, by cockatoos. I ran into pagodas and was fixed, for centuries, at the sum-
mit, or in secret rooms. . . . The cursed crocodile became to me
an object of more horror than almost all the rest'.[9] It is as though
he had got into a Chinoiserie panel by Huet or Pillement. He
might be that figure, half human and half porcelain, who sits
under an airy pagoda between two dressed-up monkeys in
Christophe Huet's *Singerie* at Chantilly, with birds perched on
hoops, and unsupported terraces leading nowhere, and a crocodile holding a parasol. [Plate ii] But Huet's creatures are light-
hearted and enchanting; De Quincey's were full of horror. He
thought that some of the causes of his own fear must be common
to others and that the Far East was 'in general . . . the seat of
awful images and associations', but in fact he was using a favourite
imagery of the day in an emotional context quite opposite to its
general use. Not only for the Prince Regent and Henry Holland
in the Brighton Pavilion, but for the ordinary English citizen

who had a Chinese Chippendale chair or a japanned commode, a willow-pattern plate on his table or a chinoiserie summer-house in his garden, parrots and pagodas were images of gaiety, not of horror.[10] Perhaps in some opium rêverie De Quincey found himself staring at a looking-glass with a chinoiserie frame, on which spidery figures ascended steps, among icicles and hanging moss, to reach canopied landing-places from which there was no escape; and he became the thing he saw.

At this point, the fashionable image, the pattern of dream-work, and the operation of opium converge. Of all the arts, architecture, the most utilitarian, is the one most seen and enjoyed by the dreamer. There are not many recorded dreams about painting, and though dreamers sometimes hear music, hear or read poetry, they do not bring any precise memory or description of them back to the waking world. They heard divine strains of music, they tell us; but we do not learn whether it was an orchestra or a quartet, a singer or a pianist, or whether they were performing music like Monteverdi's or like Wagner's. As for the wonderful poems heard or composed in sleep, we have seen in the last chapter how little of these, and that little how poor and flat, the dreamer can bring back to waking memory.

But any habitual dreamer has vivid memories of palaces and cathedrals, cities of domes and pyramids, triumphal arches, huge flights of stairs, and can tell you that they were made of black marble or rose-pink stone, that their walls were adorned with swags and trophies and statues in niches, that their spires pierced heaven and their vast terraces darkened the horizon. I myself have seen all these and many more architectural marvels in dreams, and any collection of dreams is full of them. So was the waking imagination of poets, and specially of painters, in Italy and France and England for hundreds of years before De Quincey, though which came first—the dream pattern or the visionary architecture of the painters—no one can say. Many paintings, from the sixteenth century to the eighteenth, portrayed buildings which were certainly in part an embodiment of psychological states, an emanation of a pervasive taste for ruins.[11] The crag cities of Patinir,

Setting

Niccolo del Abbate's tower-studded promontories, the eclipse-shadowed obelisks of Antoine Caron, Claude's golden temples and Poussin's pyramids, the petrified frenzy of Monsu Desiderio's collapsing palaces, Guardi's bridges and Pannini's pompous tombs, the aqueducts of Claude-Joseph Vernet, the fountains and terraces of Hubert Robert, had built a city of the imagination that was neither of this world nor of the next—it was not a vision of the Holy City, but nor was it the likeness of any real town. It had something of the theatrical illusion from which it was often originally derived, of stage décors which had burst through the roofs of the theatre into cloud-high grandeur. It borrowed, too, from the discoveries and surmises of the antiquaries, and a Babylonian hanging garden, a hypogeum from Egypt, a Pompeian terrace, would grow like coral accretions onto the visionary palaces. It was faintly tinged with uneasiness, the remains of the traumatic reaction felt by all Europe when the belfries and façades of Lisbon rocked and crumbled in the terrible earthquake of 1755—a catastrophe which, as Sir Kenneth Clark has suggested in a lecture on *The Sense of Fear in Eighteenth Century Painting*, spread a shade of terror over the imagination of painters and poets, the 'universal Idiom' of fear which Piranesi and Fuseli and Goya were to transfer from dreams into visual experience.

But in the main it was a sophisticated imaginative game, which was occasionally played out in actual stone or brick, as when follies were built to resemble shattered castles, or De Monville put up a huge Corinthian column, broken off in a jagged sky-line and honeycombed with rooms, in his Desert de Retz, or Beckford built that hugest of all follies, Fonthill Abbey. Almost in our own day, Cheval, the postman of Hauterives, built stone by stone with his own hands the grottoes, tunnels, tall doorways, the crypts, galleries, staircases and pinnacles of the Palais Idéal which had been shown to him in a dream. Encrusted, branching, with faces twisting out of concrete surges, it was his paradise, the world in which he wished to live, to sleep.

But mostly this city of the imagination lived on canvas or on paper. It could deviate into wilfulness, as when pictures were painted of the Louvre as it would appear if ruined, or of St

Paul's by a Venetian canal with gondolas floating up to its door. It could hypertrophy, as in the enormous designs of Boullée and Ledoux. Boullée called his creations 'l'architecture ensevelie'— it was meant to suggest to the spectator that it had been partly swallowed by the earth, as though their own gigantic weight had half buried these colossal amphitheatres to hold three hundred thousand people, these huge ziggurats and mausolea and cloud-piercing cones, darkly lit by a stormy moon or a bleak sunrise, towering over barren featureless plains where only a handful of minuscule figures break the vast solitude. These, and Ledoux's houses like hoops, like tops, like upturned footstools, like caves with cascades pouring through them, were supposedly practicable architectural designs, but they were built only in the cities of the mind.

There they multiplied themselves. Recent studies by French scholars have shown how the English painter John Martin was partly inspired by Boullée in his illustration of *Satan Presiding over the Infernal Council* for his *Paradise Lost* series, and that Martin's influence rebounded back on French literature (though not on French painting) and is to be found in Gautier, in Hugo, in Michelet and above all in the fantastic and perhaps opium-inspired cities of Gérard de Nerval's *Voyage en Orient* and *Aurélia*.[12] John Martin's dream world has often been compared with that of the opium writers, with De Quincey and Poe and Baudelaire and even with Coleridge. The Cyclopean architecture of his Nineveh and Babylon and Pandemonium evoked strong echoes among his literary contemporaries. [Plate iii] The working of this influence in its least imaginative form is seen in the stanza by Bernard Barton, friend of Lamb and Southey, on a picture by John Martin

'The awful visions haunt me still!
In thought by day, in dreams by night,
So well has art's creative skill
There shown his fatal might'.

Barton shows the process at its simplest; he saw a melo-dramatic picture, he went home and fell asleep and dreamed about it, he woke up and wrote a poem inspired by his dream about the

Setting

picture. But the spell worked with better poets than Bernard Barton. Shelley perhaps took the Fane in Canto I of *The Revolt of Islam*, with its dome and its ten thousand columns, not only from Coleridge's pleasure-dome in *Kubla Khan* but also from Martin's picture of *Joshua Commanding the Sun to Stand Still*. He certainly referred to Martin when he wrote of a 'hue like that when some great painter dips His pencil in the gloom of earthquake and eclipse'.[13] De Quincey used these lines as the epigraph of his description of the Pains of Opium in *The Confessions of an English Opium Eater*. Baudelaire found them there, and seized on them as 'faithfully rendering the colour of an opium landscape . . . here indeed are the dull sky and veiled horizon which overshadow the brain enslaved by opium'.[14]

In this way the poets, the painters, the architects, built up in each other's imagination new avenues and terraces of the city of the mind. Much has been written, and much remains to be written, about the ricochets between poetry and painting in creating these landscapes of the imagination. Some are conscious borrowings—Constable took his *Leaping Horse* and *Cornfield* from passages in Thomson's *Seasons*, Ward took his *Gordale Scar* from a letter of Gray's; conversely Keats got his 'light blue hills' from Titian. Some of them seem fortuitous parallels, like Shelley's and Constable's cloud shapes, or the almost identical versions of Greta Bridge in Cotman's picture and in Scott's lines in *Rokeby*, or Tennyson's extraordinary feat in reproducing Samuel Palmer's *Cornfield by Moonlight*, Constable's *Salisbury Cathedral from the Meadows* and Crome's *Slate Quarries* in successive stanzas of *The Palace of Art* without referring to, or probably being conscious of, any of the originals.

Two passages in *Hyperion* (II. 5–17, 357–367) are strangely close to John Martin's hauntingly-named and dream-like picture *Sadak in Search of the Waters of Oblivion*, which Keats could have seen —it was painted in 1812, and the artist was a friend of Haydon, who was a friend of Keats.[15] But it could as well be just that the imagination of both Keats and Martin was acclimatized to these visionary landscapes. Aldous Huxley suggested that both Keats and Martin might have been inspired by improvements in the technology of magic lanterns, by 'the intense beamy quality of coloured images on a white sheet in a darkened room'.[16] Even in Martin's own day, Charles Lamb (whose own architectural dreams predisposed him to admire the sublimity of Martin's towered structures, which he felt Martin might have derived from dreams, but who could not forgive the insignificance of Martin's human figures) unkindly compared *Belshazzar's Feast* to a diorama, and in fact it was rapidly reproduced in this form, to Martin's great annoyance.

'Dissolving views' and dioramas, spectacles like Loutherbourg's *Eidophusikon* which showed a 'vast temple of gorgeous architecture bright as molten brass, seemingly composed of unconsuming and unquenchable fire', certainly percolated into poetic imagination. Loutherbourg arranged magical lighting effects for Beckford's twenty-first birthday party at Fonthill; Beckford created in *Vathek* the blazing halls of Eblis, lit by flaming pyramids; and the imaginative transformation which had begun far back with Milton's magnificent City of Hell, and had sunk to a sensational *son et lumière* for a millionaire's party, rose again to the heights, in Keats's burning Palace of Hyperion.[17]

These were some of the visual experiences at work to form the images which streamed through the rêveries of the opium addict writers. But if we want to get inside the landscape of their imaginations, we can get a clearer view of it than any I have yet suggested. We have the testimony of both Coleridge and De Quincey that the closest visual equivalent they had ever seen to their opium visions was one of the *Carceri d'Invenzione* engravings by Piranesi. De Quincey never actually saw it; he described it only from Coleridge's account of it, and he erroneously thought that it was called a 'Dream' of Piranesi, and that it represented vast *Gothic* halls; but so intense was the impression that it made on both of them that before I had ever seen the original, when I knew it only at third-hand, from De Quincey's description of Coleridge's description of it, I visualized its obsessive ramification with horrible distinctness. Here is De Quincey's version. '. . . vast Gothic halls; on the floor of which stood mighty engines and machinery, wheels, cables, catapults, etc., expressive of enormous power put forth, or resistance overcome. Creeping along the sides of the walls, you perceived a staircase; and upon this, groping his way upwards, was Piranesi himself. Follow the stairs a little further, and you perceive them reaching an abrupt termination, without any balustrade, and allowing no step onwards to him who should reach the extremity, except into the depths below. Whatever is to become of poor Piranesi, at least you suppose that his labours must now in some way terminate. But raise your eyes, and behold a second flight of stairs still higher, on which again Piranesi is perceived, by this time standing on the very brink of the abyss. Once again elevate your eyes, and a still more aerial flight of stairs is descried; and there, again, is the delirious Piranesi, busy on his aspiring labours: and so on, until the unfinished stairs and the hopeless Piranesi are lost in the upper gloom of the hall. With the same power of endless growth and self-reproduction did my architecture proceed in dreams'.[18]

Piranesi is said to have conceived the idea of his engravings of Imaginary Prisons when he was delirious with malaria. As a young man of twenty-two he used to wander about the Campagna for whole days, living on cold rice and lighting a camp fire only once a week, while he explored the ruined monuments of Ancient Rome, through the heat of the day and by moonlight among the nocturnal miasmas of that marshy plain. He was bound to get malaria; and the delirious visions when they came to him may have owed something to opium as well as to a high temperature, since opium was then a normal remedy for ague or malaria. But this is conjecture; I do not know of any evidence that Piranesi took opium. The images which were born during his delirious fever were executed and elaborated over many years of fully conscious and controlled labour. I do not believe that a work of art ever actually reaches the point of communication, on paper or canvas or copper, while its creator is in an opium rêverie. The vision comes then, the execution later. Much of the argument about *Kubla Khan* is due to confusion about this. Piranesi seems to have modified his original vision in the course of the twenty years during which he worked and brooded over it. In the second edition of 1761 the strange machines which are scattered among his huge halls—pulleys, cranes, scaffolding, vague suggestions of apparatus for building—were made more definitely into instruments of torture, into spiked wheels and gallows. Madame Marguerite Yourcenar in her essay on the *Carceri* suggests that Piranesi's conscious judgment was operating here to make his prisons more conventionally prison-like;[19] the autonomous logic of dreams was fading, being rationalized away. The visionary halls that he originally saw were not torture-chambers; their anguish was of another kind.

De Quincey said that he recognized in the architecture of the *Carceri* 'the same power of endless growth and self-reproduction' that the buildings in his own opium visions possessed. These huge vaulted spaces, high and wide as they are, have always an opening to some yet higher vault; every staircase has another further staircase running beyond it to a more distant recess; through every arch you see another arch, which opens on to a third; and oubliettes open in the floor, to show that downwards too there is more and ever more space. There is no end to these prisons, but nor is there any way out. Each vast enclosure of space communicates only with another huge sealed crypt. This limitless and yet claustrophobic expansion of space is perceived and conveyed with an agony of hyperaesthesia. The weight of these colossal pillars, the airlessness of these lofty intricate spaces, is felt as one might feel the bony structure, the spongy and capillary matter, of one's own skull and brain. [Plate iv]

The minuscule inhabitants of these vast prisons seem also to be kin to the complacent pariahs of the opium world. Each is alone; a few are chained, but most are free to wander at will over the rickety wooden gangways which swing from one huge pier to another, or to lean over the balustrade of a monumental staircase looking down through the perspective of arches and swinging ropes. They are alone, but not unobserved; there is a sense that they are always under surveillance; invisible enemies and persecutors are somewhere hidden in the shadowy perspectives. Aldous Huxley compared the *Carceri* to Jeremy Bentham's idea of the Panopticon, a circular prison where every convict would be perpetually alone and yet perpetually under the eye of a warder in the centre of the building;[20] and Madame Yourcenar likened them to 'an enormous Eye of Dionysius . . . a formidable silence where the least step, the least sigh of the strange diminutive figures lost among these airy galleries would re-echo from end to end of these vast stone structures. There is no escape here from such noises, and no escape from being watched, in these hollow dungeons, empty so it seems of everything but flights of stairs and shafts leading to other invisible dungeons; and this feeling of being totally unsheltered, totally unsafe, contributes more than anything else to make these fantastic palaces into prisons'.[21]

But their pariah inhabitants, isolated and spied upon, are nevertheless complacent. They take no notice of each other, but pursue their way across dizzy drawbridges in sprightly self-absorption, immune to vertigo, frivolously negligent of the abysses around them, the fetters and gallows. It is pointless for them to go up those stairs, or to stay where they are; there is no way out, no trumpet of deliverance will sound, but they do not now want or hope for that; this is their only home. Théophile Gautier wanted to see *Hamlet* performed in a décor from the *Carceri*. One sees Hamlet himself as one of the chained victims, who knew he was in prison; but Rosencrantz and Guildenstern, incredulous at the suggestion that their familiar world was a place of 'confines, wards and dungeons', would be two of those trim manikins who, poised on fragile cat-walks over the abysses of the *Carceri*, survey their palace prison with a self-satisfaction only faintly tinged with uneasiness.

Whether or not Piranesi had shared the opium experience of Coleridge and De Quincey, he provided the instantly recognizable illustration of their visions. It has been suggested in this chapter that a vast city of visionary architecture, some of it in itself inspired by dreams, was available on canvas and on paper to stimulate the imaginations of the Romantic poets and to form their imagery. But what the opium-addict writers chose from this manual of visionary architecture was rather different from what the others chose. The visionary cities of Wordsworth, of Shelley, of Keats in *Endymion* and the first *Hyperion* were radiant

(i) 'The breathlessness which belongs to a saintly trance'. Granite bust of Rameses II, the 'Young Memnon', in the British Museum, seen by De Quincey as the personification of opium rêverie.

(ii) *The Chinoiserie of De Quincey's opium nightmares—monkeys, paroquets and crocodiles.* Singerie *by Christophe Huet, Musée Condé, Chantilly.*

(iii) 'Des colonnades éblouissantes, des cascades de métal fondu, des paradis de feu' —Baudelaire's description of the 'paysage opiacé', linked with John Martin's illustration of Pandemonium for Paradise Lost.

(iv) '*With the same power of endless growth and self-reproduction did my architecture proceed in dreams*'. Piranesi's Imaginary Prisons, *recognised by Coleridge and De Quincey as the likeness of their opium visions.*

with light and fire, glowing palaces in the clouds or on mountain-peaks; or if they were in caves or deep under the sea, they were yet bright with jewels and springing fountains, peopled with luminous and loving spirits. The cities of the opium writers were sealed underground, like Gérard de Nerval's Hénochia, or sunk deep in stagnant seas, or were themselves enclosed within the shadows of a yet huger building, like the city towards which De Quincey was whirled, a whole night long, across the floor of the gigantic Minster of his Dream-Fugue in *The English Mail-Coach*. And their inhabitants are isolated from each other; in their vast spaces there might be many scattered figures, even sweeping crowds and processions, but they cannot communicate, cannot help or warn each other.

As addiction grows on the opium eater, his visionary palace closes round him. At first, perhaps, he sees it from the outside, glittering across a wide landscape, a 'sunny pleasure-dome with caves of ice' or that 'pomp of cities and palaces' that De Quincey enjoyed in the early stage of his addiction. It was only later that these huge architectural splendours of his turned into the secret rooms and coffin-pinnacles of pagodas, the narrow chambers buried in the heart of pyramids.

When he had described how closely Piranesi's *Carceri* corres-ponded to the architecture of his own opium rêveries, De Quincey went on to quote, as the other closest illustration of these rêveries and dreams, a very different picture, Words-worth's famous passage in the *Excursion* describing a city seen in sunset clouds after a storm. This passage haunted De Quincey all his life; he was for ever quoting it.[22] In the section of *The Confessions of an English Opium Eater* following on the reference to Piranesi, De Quincey quotes Wordsworth's lines in full, and says that the appearance in the clouds was 'in many of its circum-stances' what he saw in his dreams. At first this seemed to me to refute my theory that the opium dreamer's palaces are always dim and enclosed, since Wordsworth's wonderful city of the air blazes with diamond and gold, 'alabaster domes and silver spires'. But De Quincey, after quoting the whole passage, repeats one line, italicizing one of its words

Setting

'Battlements that on their *restless* fronts
Bore stars'

and says that this 'sublime circumstance . . . might have been
copied from my own architectural dreams, so often did it
occur'.[23] It was the idea of buildings restlessly growing and
shape-changing,

'sinking far
And self-withdrawn into a wondrous depth'

in Wordsworth's description that seemed to De Quincey so like
his own dreams. Wordsworth's was a heavenly city,

'the revealed abode
Of spirits in beatitude',

a vision

'beyond all glory ever seen
By waking sense or by the dreaming soul',

with its starry battlements and blazing terraces, high in the open
cerulean sky. De Quincey's purple granite City of Sepulchres,
endlessly extending and withdrawing, remotely deep within the
huge shadowy Minster, and lit by a crimson glare, was a city of
opium.

PART II
THEORY

V

DE QUINCEY (I)

The foregoing chapters have given some idea of the historical context in which these questions could be asked: does opium addiction affect the imagination, and hence the work, of writers who are addicts? If so, in what way does it work on the imaginative process?

Before De Quincey, these questions had never been plainly put. Poems like Charlotte Smith's *Ode to the Poppy*, which De Quincey mentioned with interest in a diary which he kept in 1803, simply describe opium's power to

'agonising pain disarm,
Expel imperious memory from her seat,
And bid the throbbing heart forget to beat'.[1]

Erasmus Darwin's *Loves of the Plants* is slightly less perfunctory on the mental effects of opium. As a doctor with a wide practice in an industrial district where he had opportunities to see cases of opium addiction, then beginning to spread among the workers of the Midlands and North of England, and as a poet (who today is beginning to be reappraised after the scarcely deserved derision of nearly two centuries), he was at the point of intersection between medical theories of opium addiction and beliefs as to its effect on the poetic imagination. Moreover he was a talented collector of ideas which other greater poets would later use. The notes to *The Loves of the Plants* are like a cabinet of curiosities, full of rare shells which Darwin himself merely proffers to the eye in velvet-lined shelves, but which Coleridge and Keats would hold to their ears and in them hear sea voices of everlasting poetry.

Theory

The elegant personifications of Erasmus Darwin's passage on opium in *The Loves of the Plants* are based on his medical knowledge of effects of opium such as its power to stimulate dreams and the feelings of intense cold which accompany withdrawal from it, and on contemporary speculations as to whether opium excited or allayed sexual passion, or first one and then the other. His passage on the opium poppy is a filigree outline of the imagery of opium visions—the pleasure-dome, the airy music, the sorceress, the half-living statue, the embracing lovers in the icy wind—which will be traced later in this book through the works of the addict writers.

> 'Sopha'd on silk, amid her charm-built towers,
> Her meads of asphodel, and amaranth bowers,
> Where Sleep and Silence guard the soft abodes,
> In sullen apathy PAPAVER nods.
> Faint o'er her couch in scintillating streams
> Pass the thin forms of Fancy and of Dreams;
> Froze by inchantment on the velvet ground,
> Fair youths and beauteous ladies glitter round;
> On crystal pedestals they seem to sigh,
> Bend the meek knee, and lift the imploring eye.
> —And now the Sorceress bares her shrivel'd hand,
> And circles thrice in air her ebon wand;
> Flush'd with new life descending statues talk,
> The pliant marble softening as they walk . . .
> To viewless lutes aerial voices sing,
> And hovering loves are heard on rustling wing.
> —She waves her wand again—fresh horrors seize
> Their stiffening limbs, their vital currents freeze;
> By each cold nymph her marble lover lies,
> And iron slumbers seal their glassy eyes'.[2]

In a footnote to this passage Erasmus Darwin explains how opium is extracted from the poppy capsule, cites some of the favourite travellers' tales about Eastern addicts, and gives his verdict on opium: 'in small quantities it exhilarates the mind, raises the passions, and invigorates the body: in large ones it is succeeded by intoxication, languor, stupor, and death'.

De Quincey (I)

Opium exhilarates the mind; it produces scintillating streams of fancy and of dreams. Darwin states the facts as he knew them, but makes no attempt to explain them. In the next fifty years, the theory of how opium affects the literary imagination was to be deeply explored. Theorists and practitioners were not always the same person. Coleridge, the most intellectual writer that ever took opium, gave comparatively little thought to whether, or how, it affected his imagination. Poe and Baudelaire, who contributed greatly to the theory, were not themselves lifelong addicts to opium. Only De Quincey is pre-eminent in theory and in practice, and the study of nineteenth-century theories about opium's action on the literary imagination, which is the theme of this section of my book, must begin with De Quincey. The demonstration of opium's effect on his own writing will be made in a later chapter, in Part III.[3]

De Quincey was the first writer, and he is perhaps still the only one, to study deliberately, from within his personal experience, the way in which dreams and visions are formed, how opium helps to form them and intensifies them, and how they are then re-composed and used in conscious art—in his case in 'impassioned prose', but the process would also apply to poetry. He learned his waking technique as a writer partly from observation of how the mind works in dreams and rêveries under the influence of opium.

It was his belief that opium dreams and rêveries could be in themselves a creative process both analogous to, and leading to, literary creation. He used dreams in his writing not as decoration, not as allegory, not as a device to create atmosphere or to forestall and help on the plot, not even as intimations of a higher reality (though he believed they were that) but as a form of art in themselves. His study of the workings of the imagination in sleep to produce dreams was pursued with as much concentration as some of his contemporaries devoted to the workings of the waking imagination to produce poetry. His waking life and its events came to seem to him interesting chiefly as the raw material of his dreams, but the dreams themselves reached their completion only when he wrote them into literature. He did not fake them, in the sense of making them grander or more interesting than they really were, but he arranged them. Wordsworth did not fake his first impulsive feelings about daffodils or rainbows when he turned them into poems, but he put conscious work into choosing the words to embody his spontaneous feelings. De Quincey did the same with his dream fugues, which were his poems.

His theory of the dream-work of the imagination was the result of a life-time of self-observation when under the influence of opium. He had not yet evolved it when he wrote the first version of his *Confessions of an English Opium Eater* in 1821. His interest was still absorbed by the drug itself, the 'marvellous agency of opium' which was the 'true hero of the tale'.[4] He was like a man who has just explored an almost unknown country, and comes back to astound his own compatriots with his descriptions of it. Such a man does not at first pause to think whether the climate of this new country was healthy, or its political system just and humane; he is too much absorbed by the strangeness and novelty of it all, and comes home to boast about it with uncritical enthusiasm.

De Quincey became the prophet of opium. Addicts often use ecclesiastical terms for their opium slavery, and De Quincey led the way in this disagreeable practice. 'This is the doctrine of the true church on the subject of opium: of which church I acknowledge myself to be the only member' he announced in the original version of the *Confessions*.[5] When he revised the book thirty-five years later, this sentence was significantly changed to 'This is the doctrine of the true church on the subject of opium; of which church I acknowledge myself to be the Pope (consequently infallible)'.[6] This 'true church' now had other worshippers than himself—the martyrs of opium, as he often called them, saluting Coleridge as one such 'poor opium-martyr'.[7] It had produced its own paradises, celestial pleasures, beatific visions, as he dares to name them; he imagined that in a pagan land opium might have had 'altars and priests consecrated to its benign and tutelary powers'.[8] By 1856, now the Pope of his dark church, he was able to write of 'the many (a number that

is sure to be continually growing) who will take an inextinguish-
able interest in the mysterious powers of opium'.[9]

This was miserably true. Anyone who has read many medical
case-histories of opium addicts, in the nineteenth century and
even up to today, constantly meets references to De Quincey as
having first aroused the addicts' curiosity about opium. Francis
Thompson and perhaps Branwell Brontë were inspired to try
opium by De Quincey's work; so were several of the Americans
such as William Blair and Walter Colton whose recorded experiments with opium have been described in Chapter II. The
painter and poisoner Thomas Griffiths Wainewright, who at one
time facetiously claimed to have written *The Confessions of an
English Opium Eater* himself, later became an opium addict when
he was a convict in Australia. De Quincey received letters from
all over the world, written by doctors and by laymen who were
seduced by his doctrine that opium would cure tuberculosis,
remove anxiety, bestow imaginative rapture. Among the addicts
themselves he began to be revered as a high-priest, almost to be
invoked as a saint. The more sensible and cautious ones, such as
the Habituate quoted in Chapter II, saw him as a pernicious influence, though a 'star of literature'. But a novel by Hugues Le
Roux described a circle of opium-takers in Paris, one of whom—
a sculptor who had lost a beloved wife—is depicted as lying
prostrate, after a daily indulgence in two grammes of opium,
gazing at a bust of his wife below which is inscribed De Quincey's
invocation—'Oh just, subtle and mighty opium . . .'.[10] This fatal
prayer, for it is little less, of De Quincey's echoes back and forth
among the accounts of opium addiction. It sounds as musical in
French as in English, and although it was not original—De
Quincey adapted it from Sir Walter Raleigh's 'O eloquent, just
and mighty Death!' passage in his *History of the World*—it has, as a
recent French writer has said, 'an inspiration comparable to that
which breathes through the most ardent prayers of all the
liturgies of the world'.[11]

It is not altogether surprising that some indignant American
doctors of the nineteenth century, who had large practices
among opium addicts, felt that De Quincey's book should be

suppressed and his name buried in oblivion, or that French experts should (once again using an ecclesiastical metaphor) lament the proselytizing power of De Quincey and others, who enlarged on the magical scenery and superb exaltation of the opium trance, without mentioning the degradation that follows.[12] Sometimes, indeed *The Confessions of an English Opium Eater* inspired those who were already addicts to make the effort to give up the drug, as De Quincey described himself doing.[13] There must, too, have often been cases of rash experimenters, who had not really read what De Quincey wrote, and thought they had the capacity to experience all the pleasures and excitements he described, simply by taking one huge dose of opium; the resulting violent illness, unredeemed by any pleasant sensations, deterred them from ever making the experiment again. There is an interesting letter of Southey's to Samuel Cottle, discussing whether it would be advisable for Cottle to publish Coleridge's letter confessing his opium addiction. Southey quotes Thomas Poole as saying that the publication of the letter 'would operate less to deter others from the practice, than it would lead them to flatter themselves in indulging it, by the example of so great a man. That there is some probability in this I happen to know from the effect of Mr De Quincey's book; one who had never taken a drop of opium before, took so large a dose, for the sake of experiencing the sensations that had been described, that a very little addition to the dose might have proved fatal. There, however, the mischief ended, for he never repeated the experiment'.[14]

De Quincey knew that he was blamed for the evil influence of the *Confessions*. When the book was first published, some of the reviewers said that it laid too much emphasis on the pleasures of opium, and not enough on its pains. De Quincey acknowledged that the criticism was just, but said that he would put this right in a further article which he intended to publish; but this never got written.[15] Later he grew more defiant, and rebutted the charge that the *Confessions* had influenced other young men to become opium-eaters. 'Teach opium-eating! Did I teach wine-drinking? Did I reveal the mystery of sleeping? Did I inaugurate the infirmity of laughter?' Opium was already notorious as a drug, long before he wrote about it. There had perhaps been a few cases where 'a man has read a description of the powers lodged in opium; or, which is still more striking, he has found those powers heraldically emblazoned in some magnificent dream due to that agency. This by accident has been his own introduction to opium-eating. But if he never *had* seen the gorgeous description or the gorgeous dream, he would (fifty to one) have tried opium on the recommendation of a friend for toothache, which is as general as the air, or for ear-ache, or (as Coleridge) for rheumatism' and would thus have taken to opium though he had never read about it. 'No man is likely to adopt opium or to lay it aside in consequence of anything he may read in a book'.[16]

It is a weak unconvincing defence. He could have made a much more powerful one, by quoting from the *Confessions* themselves. There, and ever afterwards, he made it clear that opium could only give you interesting dreams if you already had an interesting mind and the power to dream. 'If a man "whose talk is of oxen" should become an opium-eater, the probability is, that (if he is not too dull to dream at all)—he will dream about oxen'. Nothing could be plainer than that, and he repeated it still more emphatically in the Introductory Notice to what was to have been his definitive study of dreams and the imaginative process, his never-completed *Suspiria de Profundis*. Grandeur belongs *potentially* to human dreams, he said; the emphasis by italics is his. The faculty to dream splendidly may be quiescent in a fair number of people, but it is developed in very few. 'A daily experience in-incompatible with much elevation of thought, oftentimes neutralizes the tone of grandeur in the reproductive faculty of dreaming, even for those whose minds are populous with solemn imagery. Habitually to dream magnificently, a man must have a constitutional determination to rêverie'.[17] He himself implied, and it cannot be too often repeated, that the combination of his original endowment of dreaming power with his special use of it is something so rare that it should no more tempt one to imitate him than one is tempted to imitate a lion-tamer or a funambulist. But that is not what most of us want to hear; we do not care to be classed with those whose talk is of oxen; we see ourselves as lion-tamers rather than as ox-herds; so we take what attracts us from De Quincey's books and ignore the rest.

Perhaps De Quincey acquitted himself too easily by that caveat at the beginning of his *Confessions*, and thereafter thought too little of his responsibility when he was describing the extraordinary experiences of the opium addict. He was marvellously observant of the effects of the drug, but he did not at this stage draw many deductions from his observations, or clearly distinguish the pleasures of opium from its pains. He described the serene euphoria, the waking rêveries of the early stage of addiction; the dreams and nightmares, the paralysed will, the mental fragmentation of the later stage; he had begun to suspect how the events of childhood and youth are worked on by the memory and imagination during opium dreams to produce new and interesting patterns of feeling.[18] But though he claimed that 'trances, or profoundest rêveries . . . are the crown and consummation of what opium can do for human nature', he had not yet worked out the full powers or the full dangers of opium in its dealings with human personality.[19] The first version of the *Confessions* is a marvellous heap of thoughts and experiences like unstrung jewels.

For the next twenty-five years, while he turned himself into a full-time working writer, while he fluctuated between deep opium addiction and partial withdrawal, and while he analysed Coleridge's case in the series of articles which he wrote after Coleridge's death, he began to develop his study of the mechanism of opium dreams as a record of the imaginative process. He observed his own mental symptoms during renewed addiction and during withdrawal; he thought back to his mental condition while actually writing the *Confessions*, when he had to take extra opium doses to enable him to write about opium; he watched the material of earlier waking opium rêveries sink down into the sleeping dreams and nightmares which he was now experiencing under more advanced addiction, and surface again in new groupings. He studied the phenomena of sleep: the hypnagogic visions, that faculty of the eye which can paint phantom faces and pro-

De Quincey (I)

cessions on the darkness in the moment before sleep comes; the disturbed rest during which sleep seems to gather and deepen as though it were filling a cup, and then to overflow and so interrupt the slumber; the moment of anguish when the half-awake mind readjusts itself from the world of dream to the world of day, and the woes of the world of day are recovered as though they were then felt with their first pang.[20] He said of himself that he always exercised over the mental symptoms of his own addiction 'a watchful attention which never remitted even under sufferings that were at times absolutely frantic'.[21]

These themes can be traced through his work of the 1830s; through *Klosterheim*, *The Avenger*, *The Household Wreck*, *Recollections of Charles Lamb*, *Murder Considered as one of the Fine Arts*. They are there in passing references, in the choice of symbols, in the climate of feeling. They are more explicit in the articles which he wrote on Coleridge. There is a famous passage in the *Reminiscences of the English Lake Poets* in which De Quincey analyses, with the sympathy of a fellow-sufferer, the anguish of Coleridge's *Dejection* with its terrible recognition of faculties lost for ever, in part through the action of opium, 'blank mementoes of powers extinct' or fugitive revisitings of what once they were, 'phantoms of lost powers, sudden intuitions, and shadowy restorations of forgotten feelings'.[22] For Coleridge, De Quincey realized, all such experiences were torments, positive or negative; but for himself, through the agency of dreams, the shadowy restorations could be re-animated—or so he believed, perhaps lacking Coleridge's more lucid hopelessness.

Through these years he was working out what he called, in his 1839 essay on Wordsworth, the 'germinal principles of the dream'.[23] But it was not till 1843, when he was beginning to emerge from his last deep relapse into opium addiction, that he started to plan a complete book on this theme, which was intended to be his masterpiece, the work by which he wished to be judged by posterity, his *Suspiria de Profundis*. This was to be a sequel to *The Confessions of an English Opium Eater* and 'the *ne plus ultra*, as regards the feeling and the power to express it, that I can ever hope to attain'.[24] If he could have completed the

Suspiria while he was still at the height of his powers, and published it in full in the order in which he planned it, it would certainly have been a great work. But the need to support himself and his family caused him to publish sections piecemeal as they were written, and then to use bits of them for his *Autobiographic Sketches*; some of his notes and drafts were destroyed in an accidental fire, others were irretrievably buried in the chaos of his papers; the fracturing power of his opium addiction prevented him from ever bringing them together, arranging them, and completing the whole pattern; and after his death his editors still further confused the order and keeping of the work. What is left now is only one completed (but disarranged) section out of four, the major part of the second section, a few fragments and titles of what the rest would have been, and scattered hints and rough drafts incorporated in articles on quite other subjects.

Suspiria de Profundis as a record of De Quincey's own dream-work will be considered in Chapter X. Here I am concerned with its contribution to the theory of opium's effect on the literary imagination. In his Introductory Notice to *Suspiria*, De Quincey gave a new turn (at which he had already glanced, in his *Recollections of Charles Lamb*, some years earlier) to what his purpose had been in writing the *Confessions*. They had, he said, been written 'with some slight secondary purpose of exposing this specific power of opium upon the faculty of dreaming, but much more with the purpose of displaying the faculty itself'.[25] In the new work which he was now introducing, the real emphasis was to be still more in this direction. The 'mere medical subject of opium' was to be no more than a dry pole supporting the flowery digressions which it sustained. The digressions—the dreams and rêveries—would not have held together without the pole, would not have grown up unless they had gained strength from it; but he was now interested in the flowers, not in what supported them.[26]

He made this point still more emphatically when in 1856 he issued a revised and much extended version of *The Confessions of an English Opium Eater*. He remodelled the end of the Preface in order to say that what he contemplated in the work was 'to emblazon the power of opium—not over bodily disease and pain, but over the grander and more shadowy world of dreams'.[27] He excused the vast and sometimes tedious expansion of the section on his early life by saying that in it was to be found 'the entire substratum, together with the secret and underlying motive of those pompous dreams and dream-sceneries which were in reality the true Objects—first and last—contemplated in these Confessions'.[28] And he revised the opening passage of the section on the Pains of Opium so as to reiterate that 'the main phenomenon by which opium expressed itself permanently, and the sole phenomenon that was communicable, lay in the dreams (and in the peculiar dream-scenery) which followed the opium excesses. . . . The final object of the whole record lay in the dreams'.[29]

In thus reading back what was now, in 1856, his predominating interest into what he wrote in 1821, De Quincey was being rather disingenuous. In fact the revised *Confessions* of 1856, in spite of some splendid new material, are unhappy to read. They are often sanctimonious, patronizing, self-justifying, in a way that is less attractive than the unashamed revelling in a new experience which the first *Confessions* showed. And they exemplify that mental effect of opium addiction which De Quincey himself described, the 'imbecility in attempting to hold things steadily together'.[30] He knew that he had contradicted himself about the effects of opium, had sometimes said it was a blessing, physical, mental and moral, sometimes that it was a curse, that he had not distinguished its pleasures from its pains. But he was too old and too powerless in concentration to straighten that out. 'Here I pause' he says wearily, after an immense digression on insurance, and helplessly pushes across to the reader the task of sorting out what he has said. 'The reader will infer, from what I have now said, that all passages, written at an earlier period under cloudy and uncorrected views of the evil agencies presumable in opium, stand retracted; although, shrinking from the labour of altering an error diffused so widely under my own early misconceptions of the truth, I have suffered them to remain as they were'.[31] This refers chiefly to the physical effects of opium; he had veered round again, and what he had described ten years earlier as the 'mere medical subject of opium' had become no longer a bare pole, but a favourite hobby-horse.

Like all opium addicts, De Quincey lied, prevaricated and romanced about his addiction. He was a far better observer, and a more honest and responsible man, than most addicts, but everything that even he says about the working of memory and imagination in opium dreams, and the use that can be made of it in literature, has nevertheless to be scrutinized with a reservation because of the witness's infirmity. He is most likely to be reliable when he is not preaching or justifying himself; for this reason I have relied more on the *Suspiria* and on his articles on general subjects than on the *Confessions* for the following analysis of his theories on opium and the imagination.

De Quincey actually gave very little space to describing the first stages of opium addiction and its mental effects,[32] though the ten pages of the first *Confessions* which he devoted to this subject are so attractively written and so famous that they are often read as representing his entire experience as an opium-eater. In fact, they cover only the years before 1813 when he was still taking opium only once in every three weeks, or at most on every Saturday night. None of the dreams and nightmares which he related in the *Confessions* occurred during this period; the pleasures of opium that he described were waking rêveries, enjoyed at the opera or wandering about the streets, and the euphoria which the drug gave to his mind and feelings. From his own experience of this stage of addiction, he deduced that such occasional and properly regulated doses produce effects wholly good. 'The most exquisite order, legislation and harmony' prevail among the mental faculties; self-possession is invigorated, irritation and anxiety are calmed, a warm and serene tranquillity reigns over the impulses of the mind and heart. The intellect, far from being impaired or stupefied into stagnation and torpor, shines in majestic brightness. The spirits are raised rather than depressed, and reactions to visual and aural experiences and to human relationships are intensified.[33] He illustrates this from his own experience of conversations heard and shared with strangers at the opera or in the streets on his nights of opium debauch; but more significant for his later theories of the shaping power of opium over the imagination is his description of how the music affected him at the opera. It is a key passage. 'Opium, by greatly increasing the activity of the mind generally, increases, of necessity, that particular mode of its activity by which we are able to construct out of the raw material of organic sound an elaborate intellectual pleasure. . . . A chorus, etc of elaborate harmony, displayed before me, as in a piece of arras work, the whole of my past life—not as if recalled by an act of memory, but as if present and incarnated in the music: no longer painful to dwell upon: but the detail of its incidents removed, or blended in some hazy abstraction; and its passions exalted, spiritualized, sublimed'.[34] Waking rêveries like these were the first part of the creative process of transformation of past events into 'impassioned prose'; from such rêveries they passed, still under the influence of opium, into dreams of sleep, and rose up again to conscious memory to be turned into literature as 'dream-fugues'. His past experience could be 'incarnated' in the music; by something of the same process, as he sat all night long in an opium trance by an open window overlooking a summer sea, he felt that the ocean typified the mind and mood of the opium-eater who beheld it, and who experienced 'motions of the intellect as unwearied as the heavens, yet for all anxieties a halcyon calm: a tranquillity that seemed no product of inertia, but as if resulting from mighty and equal antagonisms; infinite activities, infinite repose'.[35]

It is a most seducing description, and how seldom does anyone remember that it applied only to the first and inevitably transitory stage of opium addiction. What De Quincey had to say about the later stages is—apart from the stately descriptions of his nightmares in the Pains of Opium section of the *Confessions*—much less musical and much more scattered among his writing. In the *Confessions* he gives a moving but brief description of mental deterioration under advanced addiction. The mind, afflicted with a 'sense of powerless and infantine feebleness', is no longer able to grapple with intellectual problems, but falls prostrate into a kind of imbecility, a torpor of the will, through which the opium-eater still perceives what should be done, but cannot force himself to do it'.[36]

De Quincey's more thorough analysis of the effects of opium in full addiction is scattered among his later articles, especially those on Coleridge and (irrelevantly) on Charles Lamb, and his letters to friends. As early as 1824, in an article called *Madness* from his *Notes from the Pocket Book of a Late Opium Eater*, he acknowledged that both his 'genial spirits' and his intellectual faculties showed signs of decay when he was at the peak of addiction, and that he could understand from the inside how insanity took hold on one. 'As the opium began to take effect, the whole living principle of the intellectual motions began to lose its elasticity, and, as it were, to petrify; I began to comprehend the tendency of madness to eddy about one idea'; and he lost the 'power to abstract—to hold abstractions steadily before me'.

Sixteen years later his ideas about the effects of opium addiction on the intellectual faculties of judgment and memory, and consequently on authorship, were illogically embodied in his *Recollections of Charles Lamb*. The difficulty which he found in clarifying this elusive subject is reflected in the wording of this passage on it, which is much more clotted and opaque than the limpid meanders of his best style. The way in which he wrote about the subject was an instance of what he was writing about—the stranglehold which opium imposes, in the later stages of addiction, on the power to 'hold things steadily together, and to bring them under a comprehensive or unifying act of the judging faculty'. At this late stage, he implies, the addict can no longer formulate, or even follow, a reasoned argument on an abstract subject, so as to form any judgment on its value, and this applies equally to the value of his own recently written works and to the value of philosophical truths. He tautologically laments this 'mere childish helplessness, or senile paralysis of the judgement, which distresses the man in attempting to grasp the upshot and the total effect of the *tout ensemble*'.[37] That sentence itself illustrates painfully what he means; he would not have let such a piece of writing pass when he was in full command of himself. He wrote it in the spring of 1838. Six months earlier his much-loved wife, worn out by anxiety and privation, had died of typhus. De Quincey and his children were living from hand to mouth in Edinburgh on his uncertain revenue from journalism, and he frequently had to take sanctuary in Holyrood from his creditors. Under the pressure of these troubles, he was sinking again into his last deep relapse into opium, which was to last for more than five years. Probably he was not only harking back to his 1821 practice, but also describing his current one, when he said in the article on Charles Lamb that he had managed to write the first half of the *Confessions* by arming himself with a sudden increase of opium doses for a few days running, and thus procuring a glow of spirits and an 'artificial respite' from his usual state of distress, but that he had paid for it by 'a heavy price of subsequent suffering'.[38]

He was to repeat later, in his article on *Coleridge and Opium-Eating* and in the revised *Confessions*, that opium can enable a writer to meet a sudden call for some short effort. 'Opium gives and takes away. It defeats the *steady* habit of exertion; but it creates spasms of irregular exertion. It ruins the natural power of life; but it develops preternatural paroxysms of intermitting power'.[39]

But both he and Coleridge found that if they made such sudden exertions, the work so produced became associated with the disgust of the enforced exertion, and afterwards they could not bring themselves to revise work written in this way, or to write again on the same subject, so impregnated was it with the disgust previously felt.[40] In a wretched letter to Miss Mitford, De Quincey poured out a wild description of his sufferings in this way. 'Whatever I may be writing becomes suddenly overspread with a dark frenzy of horror. . . . No language can give expression to the sudden storm of frightful revelations opening upon me from an eternity not coming, but past and irrevocable. Whatever I may have been writing is suddenly wrapt, as it were, in one sheet of consuming fire—the very paper is poisoned to my eyes. I cannot endure to look at it, and I sweep it away into vast piles of unfinished letters or inchoate essays'.[41] The occasion for this wild lament was merely the need to apologize for not answering a letter of Miss Mitford's, and De Quincey did very often set fire to his papers, and even his own hair, not by any metaphorical blaze of hellish revelations, but by literal clumsiness with his candle; but these facts do not diminish the real misery of his mind in this letter.

The endlessly drawn comparisons between his own addiction and Coleridge's stimulated his unhappy speculations on the effects of opium. His own indiscreet comments on Coleridge in his *Lake Poets* aroused the anger of Coleridge's friends, and Gillman took reprisals, in his *Life of Coleridge*, published in 1838, by quoting Coleridge's comments on De Quincey's addiction. De Quincey in turn retaliated in his *Coleridge and Opium-Eating*, a review of Gillman's book. But in his private meditations, and letters to friends, he was more gloomy about opium's worst powers than in anything he wrote for publication. Brooding over his own mental ruin, he wrote in a letter of 1844 that he comprehended Coleridge's intellectual chaos 'by the darkness of my own, and both were the work of laudanum. It is as if ivory carvings and elaborate fretwork and fair enamelling should be found with worms and ashes amongst coffins and the works of some forgotten life or some abolished nature. In parts and fractions eternal creations are carried on, but the nexus is wanting, and life and the central principle which should bind together all the parts at the centre, with all its radiations to the circumference, are wanting. Infinite incoherence, ropes of sand, gloomy incapacity of vital persuasion by some one plastic principle, that is the hideous incubus upon my mind always'.[42]

When he wrote this letter, he had determined to free himself from his misery by a withdrawal from opium, and after persisting for six months in the struggle to reduce his doses, he 'suddenly found my mind whirled round as if on its true centre. . . . Illimitable seemed the powers restored to me'. Twenty-two years earlier, withdrawing from another peak of addiction, he had written 'I have a greater influx of thoughts in one hour at present than in a whole year under the reign of opium. It seems as though all the thoughts which had been frozen up in a decade of years by opium, had now according to the old fable been thawed at once—such a multitude stream in on me from all quarters'.[43]

But in 1822, and again in 1844, the withdrawal was neither complete nor permanent. If he was to write enough to keep himself and his family alive, he had to give his energy the temporary stimulus of an opium dose,[44] and he was never able to leave it off altogether, though in his last years he took comparatively small amounts. One day in 1854 his friend John Ritchie Findlay called on him and found him in bed with a swollen foot and leg. De Quincey resignedly told him that if he could leave off opium for a few days, his leg would recover, but 'I cannot do that, for without opium I can't get on with my work, which the publishers are urging me to complete. The work must be done; the opium can't be left off; therefore I cannot begin to walk, and the leg must take its chance'.[45]

The question of whether De Quincey really wrote more, or better, during his peak opium periods or his withdrawal periods, will be considered in Chapter X. His theory seems to have been that literature, even great literature—'eternal creations'—might still be conceived and carried on during advanced opium addiction, but it would be in 'parts and fractions', a lyric rather than an epic; a short passage such as his own little masterpieces of 'impassioned prose'. Writing about the effect of opium on Coleridge, he produced a strange theory of poetic inspiration. The drug certainly made Coleridge unhappy, 'but in what way did that operate upon his exertions as a writer? We are of opinion that it killed Coleridge as a poet. "The harp of Quantock" was silenced for ever by the torment of opium . . . poetry can flourish only in the atmosphere of happiness'. Opium might have stimulated Coleridge's metaphysical investigations, but only spasmodically. 'All opium-eaters are tainted with the infirmity of leaving work unfinished, and suffering reactions of disgust'.[46]

In that last bitter sentence De Quincey finally admitted that his hopes, and the hopes of so many opium addicts, of writing a grand philosophical work which would explain the riddle of the universe, were delusions; the great books would never be perfected and published. Coleridge's huge designs which never got further than *Hints towards the Formation of a More Comprehensive Theory of Life*, Poe's *Eureka*, Francis Thompson's resolution to become 'the poet of the return to God', De Quincey's own projected *De emendatione humani intellectus*, all were headless failures. Yet Saintsbury suggests that but for opium De Quincey would have been among the first of British philosophers.[47] De Quincey had once believed in his own destiny to enlighten mankind. When he first wrote to Wordsworth in 1804, he admitted that he had intoxicated himself with the delirious hope of 'elevating my name in authority and kingly splendour above every name that is named upon earth',[48] and in 1818 he could still tell his mother that he hoped to become the benefactor of mankind by accomplishing a great revolution in the intellectual condition of the world.[49] A list which he once drew up of the constituents of human happiness included 'some great intellectual project' in hand,[50] and the hope of completing one great work persisted long, and found its last near-incarnation in *Suspiria de Profundis*. But that was never completed either. He had a contribution to make, a real and important one, to the enlightenment, if not to the amendment, of the human intellect, but opium prevented him from making it—though it also partly provided the evidence on which the contribution would have been made.

So far, I have summarized De Quincey's observations on the effects of opium addiction on the conscious mental processes of writers: will-power and reasoning, the ability to make a synthesis, literary exertion and sustained effort. Similar observations have been made by many other writers on opium (though a good many of these were borrowed, consciously or unconsciously, from De Quincey) and it is not in them that De Quincey's most original discovery lies. That was concerned with the unconscious formation of patterns of feeling, and how these may afterwards be composed into literature.

He never suggested that opium directly stimulated imaginative writing. The process was more complicated than that. The kind of impassioned prose that he wanted to write was the final outcome of a process during which past experience is crystallized into patterns which reflect mysterious and essential truth. This process of crystallization takes place in dreams. Opium precipitates the process by stimulating the faculty of dreaming and rêverie.

That opium had this power, over him at any rate, is proved by the sequence of events in 1803 and 1804. It was during the first months of 1803 that De Quincey, destitute in London, was experiencing those long wanderings with the prostitute Ann through the night streets of London which were to be the central theme of his dreams in later years. In March 1803, after a reconciliation with his mother and his guardians, he went to spend four months in lodgings at Everton, near Liverpool. There he kept a diary, which has survived. It is a detailed record of what was engaging his imagination at the time—the books he was reading and the books he was planning to write, analyses of his own character, fantasies about dying heroines in lake islands and gloomy feudal heroes, lists of his favourite authors in order of priority, apparently the whole furniture of his fancy at the time. There is not one word referring to his recent miseries in London. This can be, and has been, explained in various ways; the miseries never really happened at all, they were pure invention; or they were too recent and painful for him to be able to bear dwelling on them; or, having gained his point with his family by undergoing them, he deliberately put them out of his head and looked forward to the future. However one explains it, the fact is there.

A year later, coming up to London from Oxford and suffering from a bout of excruciating neuralgia, he first took opium; and it was then, during his Oxford days, that his 'visions' began in earnest, 'swept in upon the brain with power, and the grandeur of recovered life, under the separate and the concurring inspirations of opium', which blended memories of his childish grief over his sister's death with his adolescent grief over the loss of Ann.[51] The events of his London destitution were no longer shut off from his idea of himself; they were being integrated into his personality by the agency of dreams induced by opium. He used a perhaps over-dramatic symbol to describe what happened to him at this time. 'My eye had been couched into a secondary power of vision, by misery, by solitude, by sympathy with life in all its modes, by experience too early won, and by the sense of danger critically escaped. Suppose the case of a man suspended by some colossal arm over an unfathomed abyss—suspended, but finally and slowly withdrawn—it is probable that he would not smile for years'.[52] The chatty, touchy, party-going young De Quincey of the Everton diary does not quite fit this tragic unsmiling picture, but it does convey the process of shock, recovery from shock, and final assimilation of the traumatic experience, through which he went, and which opium dreams and rêveries seem to have accelerated.

In the early stages of De Quincey's addiction, he seems to have had more waking rêveries than actual dreams. During these rêveries, the associative faculty worked at full pressure; it has been shown in Chapter II that this is a common symptom of this stage of addiction. At this time the different constituents—memories, impressions, symbols—of what he was later to call an 'involute', a complex of feeling, were drawn together in rêveries under the power of opium over his mental activity. The involutes of the rêveries of his first stage of addiction, the 'Pleasures of Opium' stage, were drawn into the dreams and nightmares of the second, 'Pains of Opium', stage. This explains why some of the dreams, not apparently painful in subject or feeling, are described by him as full of anguish and terror. It was the euphoria and co-ordinating rêverie of the first stage that provided the material for the dreams of the second stage; but since in the second stage the euphoria was past, and feelings of guilt, lethargy and isolation had arrived, the dreams organized by the first stage were coloured by the gloom of the second stage. He revealed this process when, in his *Recollections of Charles Lamb*, he described the struggles of a writer in the advanced stage of addiction, when his imagination is working, not with the failing powers of connected thought which his mind now possesses, but with the memory of the vigorous associative activity of earlier rêveries. Describing how he wrote the dream passages in the *Confessions*, he speaks of 'recoiling from the intricacy and elaborateness which had been made known to me' in the course of considering a subject to which he had given much previous thought.[53] The intricacy and elaborateness of his dreams were *made known* to him, as though they came from outside him; in fact they came from his own earlier rêveries.

Not all his later dreams were formed in this way. He described in the *Confessions* how, as he sank deeper into the trammels of opium, some of his dreams were formed directly by a semi-voluntary process from hypnagogic phenomena. 'As the creative state of the eye increased, a sympathy seemed to arise between the waking and the dreaming states of the brain in one point—that whatsoever I happened to call up and to trace by a voluntary act upon the darkness was very apt to transfer itself to my dreams; so that I feared to exercise this faculty. . . . Whatsoever things capable of being visually presented I did but think of in the darkness, immediately shaped themselves into phantoms of the eye; and, by a process apparently no less inevitable, when thus once traced in faint and visionary colours, like writings in sympathetic ink, they were drawn out by the fierce chemistry of my dreams, into insufferable splendour that fretted my heart'.[54]

It would be a labyrinthine work to trace how De Quincey's dreams formed themselves out of the subtle involutions of his prodigious knowledge and memory. For many years he meditated about his dreams, and then dreamed about his meditations, and then again made a synthesis of his dream experience. He seems to have experienced both dreams and rêveries at all stages of his addiction; in 1856 he referred to 'some twenty or twenty-five dreams and noon-day visions, which had arisen under the latter stages of opium influence' and which he had intended to use as the 'crowning grace' of his revised version of the *Confessions*, but which were lost by accident.[55] Late in his life, when he was trying to couple together in his *Autobiographic Sketches* material originally written for different parts of *Suspiria de Profundis*, he wrote a linking introductory note to the dream which he called *The Apparition of the Brocken*. In this note he explained that 'the echoes, that rendered back the infant experience, might be interpreted by the reader as connected with a *real* ascent of the Brocken; which was not the case. It was an ascent through all its circumstances executed in dreams, which, under advanced stages in the development of opium, repeat with marvellous accuracy the longest succession of phenomena derived either from reading or from actual experience. . . . The playfulness of the scene is the very evoker of the solemn remembrances that lie hidden below. The half-sportive interlusory revealings of the symbolic tend to the same effect. One part of the effect from the symbolic is dependent upon the great catholic principle of the *Idem in alio*. The symbol restores the theme, but under new combinations of form or colouring; gives back, but changes; restores, but idealizes'.[56]

The symbol restores the theme—that was the essence of De Quincey's discovery of this process of the imagination. Only when the original experiences have been drawn into symbolic shape, and that shape has been transmuted by a passage through the mysterious realms where man's nature comes into contact with hidden truth, can it re-emerge into consciousness and be fully communicated as a literary theme.

This was the thesis of *Suspiria de Profundis*. Those profound depths were stirring with life in De Quincey's imagination. His imagery is full of abysses and shafts leading downwards, the ever-expanding palace-prisons of Piranesi's vision. They rise before the eye as one reads the passage in the Introductory Notice to the *Suspiria* in which he announced its theme. 'The machinery for dreaming planted in the human brain was not planted for nothing. That faculty, in alliance with the mystery of darkness, is the one great tube through which man communicates with the shadowy. And the dreaming organ, in connection with the heart, the eye and the ear, compose the magnificent apparatus which forces the infinite into the chambers of a human brain, and throws dark reflections from eternities below all life upon the mirrors of that mysterious *camera obscura*—the sleeping mind'. Of all agencies which assist the faculty of dreaming 'beyond all others is opium, which indeed seems to have a *specific* power in that direction; not merely for exalting the colours of dream-scenery, but for deepening its shadows; and, above all, for strengthening the sense of its fearful realities'.[57]

De Quincey (I)

The realities of dream scenery were *fearful*, in De Quincey's experience. In his dreams many objects not intrinsically horrible—silvery expanses of water, pompous palaces, hedges of white roses, cockatoos, pagodas, anemones, the azure light of tropical seas, the sunshine of summer mornings—were all images of sadness or terror. Grief was specially sacred and revealing to De Quincey. 'Misery is the talisman by which men communicate with the world outside of our fleshly world' he wrote at the end of a letter describing the hell through which he had passed in his last deep relapse into opium addiction.[58] Even from such misery as that—perhaps specially from such misery as that—one could learn. The characteristic power of opium was that it conferred an 'increased power of dealing with the shadowy and the dark', and only by such dealings could one develop the full capacity of the human personality. De Quincey even suggested, half-jestingly, that Milton meant his readers to deduce that the Archangel Michael gave opium to Adam to fortify him against the afflicting visions he was to see, when he

'from the well of life three drops instilled.

So deep the power of these ingredients pierced,

Even to the inmost seat of mental sight.[59]

So it was that what he called the Afflictions of Childhood were at the centre of De Quincey's theory of dream mechanism. His own unhappy experiences in childhood and youth were the nexus round which all his later dream-patterns formed. This is now a commonplace of psychiatry, but in 1845 it was a very original speculation, and De Quincey did not see it as having any wide application. He thought his own childhood sufferings were exceptional. 'The terrific grief which I passed through drove a shaft for me into the worlds of death and darkness which never again closed, and through which it might be said that I ascended and descended at will, according to the temper of my spirits. Some of the phenomena developed in my dream-scenery, undoubtedly, do but repeat the experiences of childhood', which turned into 'those vast clouds of gloomy grandeur which overhung my dreams at all stages of opium, but which grew into the darkest of miseries in the last'.[60]

Theory

There was nothing pleasurable, no rapture, no consolation, in most of these dreams of De Quincey's. Even the faces of his lost sister, wife, children, even the memories of his past happiness, suffered 'poisonous transfigurations'. 'I beheld, forming themselves into solemn groups and processions, and passing over sad phantom stages, all that I have chiefly loved . . . the brilliant, the noble, the wise, the innocent, the brave, the beautiful. With these dreadful masks, and under the persecution of their malicious beauty, wakens up the worm that gnaws at the heart. Under that corrosion arises a hatred, blind and vague, and incomprehensible even to one's self, as of some unknown snake-like enemy, in some unknown hostile world, brooding with secret power over the fountains of one's own vitality'.[61]

That terrible nightmare, which is incongruously buried in an article of 1852 on Sir William Hamilton, gives a different picture of De Quincey's dream world from the uplifting visions of the heavenward-borne sacrificial girl-children, apotheoses of his sister and Ann of Oxford Street, in *The Affliction of Childhood* and *Dream-Fugue*. But De Quincey's religious faith told him that hell could not triumph in the end. All these sufferings, even the worst, must have a meaning. There was a 'root of dark uses . . . in moral convulsions'. He expressed this conviction, in the *Suspiria*, by a personification whom he called the Dark Interpreter. This was a being born of the power of self-projection which exists in 'the dark places of the human spirit — in grief, in fear, in vindictive wrath', one of the 'creative agencies' which are latent in every part of man's nature.[62] The Dark Interpreter stands for the increase in self-knowledge, in understanding of human nature, that comes to everyone, even to children, through suffering, which is necessary to harmonize the whole of experience. This was the power of imagination which enabled him in after years to decipher the meaning of his childish sufferings when they rose up again in dreams under the impetus of opium.[63] It was this Dark Interpreter who, standing beside De Quincey as he watched his own child crying in some infantile pain, showed him that next day the child had made a sudden advance in its powers of attention and observation, it had learned by pain.[64] It was the

De Quincey (I)

Dark Interpreter who dived with the dreaming De Quincey to the drowned streets and churches of Savannah-la-Mar, and told him that the earthquake which had sunk the city and all its inhabitants was a redeeming catastrophe, such as 'raises oftentimes from human intellects glorious vintages that could not else have been'.[65]

I am not here concerned with De Quincey's metaphysical beliefs and their validity. The Dark Interpreter is relevant to the theme of this chapter as an aspect of De Quincey's imagination. De Quincey defined the relationship between his own consciousness and this projection of it with much subtlety. The Dark Interpreter was 'an intruder into my dreams. . . . He is originally a mere reflex of my inner nature, but . . . sometimes swerves out of my orbit, and mixes a little with alien natures. I do not always know him in these cases as my own parhelion'. Generally the Dark Interpreter said in De Quincey's dreams only what he himself had said when waking, but sometimes this being spoke words that De Quincey neither had used, nor could use. His function was not to communicate anything absolutely new, but 'to recall you to your own lurking thoughts—hidden for the moment or imperfectly developed—and to place before you, in immediate connection with groups vanishing too quickly for any effort of meditation on your own part, such commentaries, prophetic or looking back, pointing the moral or deciphering the mystery, justifying Providence, or mitigating the fierceness of anguish, as would or might have occurred to your own meditative heart, had only time been allowed for its motions'.[66]

The Dark Interpreter was the guide who led De Quincey through his dreams. He also had a map, which he himself had made, and which is so enlightening that it is strange it has not been more employed by later travellers in the region. This was his theory of what he called 'involutes'. The word in the sense in which he used it is so rare that the *Oxford English Dictionary*'s only two quotations to illustrate its meaning are both from De Quincey himself, but it is both useful and expressive. His definition of it is that 'far more of our deepest thoughts and feelings pass to us through perplexed combinations of *concrete* objects, pass to us as *involutes* (if I may coin that word) in compound experiences incapable of being disentangled, than ever reach us *directly*, and in their own abstract shapes'.[67] He follows this up with an illustration, to show how the ideas of summer sunshine and of death came to be involved together in his imagination. The constituents of this involute were an illustrated Bible which he and his sisters looked at on dark evenings by the fire when they were children, a favourite nurse who explained to them the story of the Crucifixion and the country in which it took place, the idea of the disciples plucking the corn in brilliant summer sunshine, the names of Palm Sunday and of Jerusalem. But this was only the beginning of the involute; in later years many other feelings were to attach themselves to it: his sister's death in the summer, the words of the Litany and the music of the organ, clouds seen through church windows, the tragedy of Ann of Oxford Street, the death of little Kate Wordsworth; a whole lifetime of experiences which, under the agency of opium dreams, folded inwards round each other and became a single involute of feeling.

Many other such clusters of memories and impressions, fantasticated by opium dreams, can be traced in De Quincey's works. Driving down the Bath Road by mail coach, he often travels with an old coachman whose broad stiff back reminds him of a crocodile; a Malayan beggar who speaks no word of any European language comes to his door in Westmorland; he reads some travel books about the scenery and customs of Egypt and the Asiatic countries, and feels a distaste for anything so alien. Then the power of opium to extend the sense of time and to intensify images by a rampant associative faculty turns this set of disparate impressions into dreams of Eastern terrors, disgusts and imprisonments, endlessly prolonged, through which the crocodile's hideous head looms in a thousand shapes, obsessively incarnating in the very walls and furniture, producing a complex of feelings about a historic civilization such as might, had De Quincey been a poet, have led on to a poem like Yeats's *Byzantium*. Ordinary dreams do not have such intensity and coherence; opium, by strengthening the combining power and heightening the emotion, has already brought these dreams half-way to conscious literary creation.

When De Quincey reprinted in his collected works the essay on *The English Mail Coach* which had first appeared in *Blackwoods* in 1849, and which was meant to be part of *Suspiria de Profundis*, he cut out a very interesting paragraph on the formation and coalescence of symbols in dreams. He had been describing how two very different groups of images—one group composed of a lovely girl, dewy thickets full of deer, and June roses; the other group of a crocodile in a scarlet coachman's uniform, a crowd of monsters, dragons and griffins, a vast armorial shield, and a sculptured clock in the heavens as a warning of mortality—had been united as by a 'confluence of two different keys, though apparently repelling each other, into the music and governing principles of the same dream'. He goes on to speak of 'horrid reconciliation', 'revolting complexities of misery and incomprehensible darkness'. He evidently felt this process to be peculiarly appalling, 'the most terrific that besieges dreams . . . the horrid inoculation upon each other of incompatible natures'. He traces this tendency through the myths of composite creatures such as sphinxes and basilisks, and the heraldic bestiary, but these have none of the horror of the nightmares in which 'the dreamer finds housed within himself—occupying, as it were, some separate chamber in his brain—holding, perhaps, from that station a secret and detestable commerce with his own heart—some horrid alien nature'. He often recurred to the image of the blazon, the heraldic coat of arms which grouped together things incompatible, as a description of dream activity. It was a synonym for the involute. Edwin Muir used it in the same way, to reveal an involute of his own, in the heraldic poem 'Who curbed the lion long ago' in *Variations on a Time Theme*. De Quincey was describing a real dream experience, but he was also describing something very like the process of poetic creation.

He came still nearer to that in his account of the dream involute which I will call the Fatal Choice. He mentions it, almost casually as it seems (but one can never be sure with De Quincey—his design is often buried deep, but still there), in a section of his

Theory

Autobiographic Sketches called *Infant Literature*. He is relating how fond he and his sister were of the *Arabian Nights*, but especially of one passage in the story of Aladdin. This is the incident of the African magician, who knows by his art of the existence of the enchanted lamp in its subterranean chamber, and that it can only be reached by an innocent child with a special horoscope. He lays his ear to the ground and hears the footsteps of every human being all over the globe, and among them, six thousand miles away, the footsteps of the child Aladdin playing in the streets of Baghdad, and in them hears 'an alphabet of new and infinite symbols . . . secret hieroglyphics uttered by the flying footsteps'. That notion, De Quincey said, seized on his mind as a child and became one of the 'involutes of human sensibility, combinations in which the materials of future thought or feeling are carried imperceptibly into the mind'.[68] Round this spindle of childish imagination gathered thread after thread from his later experiences: an excited moment in the Whispering Gallery at Saint Paul's, a lonely evening in an empty ballroom at Shrewsbury during a storm, newspaper accounts of a series of murders; and the filaments twisted together into an involute which patterned his dreams and the imagery of his writings. It was a feeling of being in some unprotected central room of an enormous building, and of hearing footsteps, at first a very long way off but coming nearer and nearer; and linked to that feeling was a conviction that some fatal and irrevocable choice had been made, whose consequences were now at hand.

One has constantly to repeat that De Quincey was describing what happened in his opium dreams, because it reads so much like one of those backward tracings of the constituents of a poem, the kind of analysis to which so many of the works of the Romantic poets have recently been subjected. I will end this survey of De Quincey's dream theory with a suggestion of how he himself worked his dreams into prose-poems, his 'impassioned prose'. The process of selection and shaping began in the dreams themselves. The story of Ann of Oxford Street, he tells us, 'more than any other, coloured—or (more truly I should say) moulded and remoulded, composed and recomposed

—the great body of opium dreams'.[69] Then when he woke from his dreams, he wrote them down. Few of these notes have survived, and those only from the end of his life. In 1855 he related in a letter a recent dream of no great import about his daughters in a room with an expanding floor which melted into a garden rich with flowers. In 1857 during the Indian Mutiny he was haunted by dreams of children standing in the air outside his window, and voices ominously repeating 'Delhi! Delhi!'. His earlier dreams, the ones recorded in the *Confessions* and *Suspiria*, were not always noted down immediately, he owned, but he insisted that they left so strong an impression that even if his notes on them were made some time later, this did not affect their accuracy.[70] Without necessarily accepting this claim, one may note it as showing that De Quincey's dream experiences were not sharply divided from his waking life, but pervaded all his consciousness and were always with him.

De Quincey acknowledged in the *Confessions* that when he came to write the section on dreams 'much has been omitted. I could not, without effort, constrain myself to the task of either recalling, or constructing into a regular narrative, the whole burthen of horrors which lies upon my brain'.[71] Seventeen years later he recalled, in *Recollections of Charles Lamb*, how he had written the dream section of the *Confessions*. The dreams, he said were 'composed slowly, and by separate efforts of thought, at wide intervals of time, according to the actual prevalence, at any particular time, of the separate elements of such dream in my own real dream-experience'.[72] This revealing sentence, and a later one where he refers to the 'principles of *art*' in the sequence of his dreams and visions which governed their presentation,[73] tell us most about the technique that De Quincey learned from his opium dreams and applied in his writing. Had he ever completed *Suspiria de Profundis*, he might have described in full the end of the imaginative process on whose earlier stages he was so wonderfully informative. As it is, we have only the statement that, even when he was consciously composing his dreams into 'fugues', he was still under the control and check of his actual dreams at the time; and that the principle of art behind his *Confessions* and *Suspiria* was an order and a sequence which his imagination had learned in an opium dream.

I will conclude this survey of dreams turning into art by an illustration from personal experience. On the night after I had written this chapter, I had a dream, when I was already emerging from sleep, that I saw (or heard, I am not sure which) the words 'The Embroidered Skeleton'. There was no dream-context, only an impression that this was not a skeleton depicted in embroidery, but that the embroidery was actually stitched into the bones of a skeleton.

I wrote the words down as soon as I was fully awake, because they seemed to me odd and amusing. At that moment I did not recognize them as relating to anything whatever in my experience.

Later the same day I remembered the words again, and now saw that they probably arose from what I had written the day before about De Quincey's dream involutes, and the coalescence of incompatible symbols. But there is nothing about embroidery or skeletons in the passage quoted above about the symbols which suffer a 'horrid inoculation' on one another, though that was certainly the process which produced my embroidered skeleton. Then I made a cast back, and remembered the passage quoted on page 116, De Quincey's letter of 1844 about the ivory carvings among ashes and coffins. There were some of the constituents of my skeleton, but not the embroidery. Harking back further, I remembered the passage in the *Confessions*, which I had quoted earlier in the chapter, about the opera music displaying to De Quincey the whole of his past life like a piece of arras work. My subconscious mind, still milling over the process by which dream patterns are composed, and perhaps over the task of covering with illustrative patterns the bones of my thesis, had selected symbols from two separate passages in which De Quincey described the inhabitants of his mind, married them according to a formula given in a third passage, and produced this peculiar offspring. A poet or a painter could make something of the Embroidered Skeleton; it has got nearly all the way from dream to art; but I have not got the talents that are needed to give it that final development. Nevertheless it does show how the dreaming mind can give a shape to something that the conscious mind wanted to say; and that was the essence of De Quincey's theory of opium dreams.

VI

POE

Many shelves-full of books about Edgar Allan Poe have debated, with passionate conviction or lofty scorn, whether he was or was not an opium addict. It is to some degree a cross-Atlantic battle, the partisans of Poe's opium addiction being mainly French (though with some notable allies in the American camp), the sceptics being mainly American.[1] English studies of Poe have been neither abundant nor very illuminating, and an English writer like myself must land with caution on this heavily-mined beach of scholarship. I will limit myself to summarizing what seem to be the agreed facts about Poe's use of opium.

Poe himself (a very unreliable witness—few writers can have lied so continually about themselves as he did) only once explicitly records that he took laudanum. In November 1848, in the middle of his disastrous courtship of Mrs Whitman, he wrote to Mrs Richmond reminding her of her promise to come to him on his deathbed, and then swallowed an ounce of laudanum. His intention was to post the letter summoning Mrs Richmond, and then take another and final ounce of laudanum when she arrived; but he 'had not calculated on the strength of the laudanum' which took action so quickly that his summoning letter was never posted; 'awful hours' succeeded, hours of drastic nausea, after which he recovered.

It has been argued that this incident proves that Poe was no addict, or he would not have so miscalculated the effect of an ounce of laudanum.[2] It is difficult to accept the story as proving anything either way. It may be pure invention; there is no evidence for it apart from Poe's own. If it really happened, it may or may not have been a genuine attempt at suicide. The tone of his subsequent letter to Mrs Richmond about it suggests that he half intended to kill himself, but afterwards persuaded himself that he had not at any rate deliberately planned suicide.[3] The whole episode reads not unlike Berlioz's description, in a letter of August 1833, of how he took a near-lethal dose of opium in Harriet Smithson's presence when she reproached him for not loving her, but was revived by an emetic. One feels a suspicion that both men took enough opium to produce a dramatic impression but not enough to endanger life. If this gesture of Poe's was consciously contrived, it would argue a fairly experienced knowledge of the effects of opium doses of different sizes.

The only reference to opium-taking which Poe himself made is therefore inconclusive. So are the accounts by his contemporaries on which all subsequent theories have rested. The positive evidence is from his cousin Elizabeth Herring who said, long after his death, that she had had 'the misfortune to see him often in sad conditions from the use of opium' and that he used it freely; and from his slightly imbecile sister Rosalie who claimed, also many years after his death, that when she stayed with the Poes in 1846 she had heard her brother begging for morphine.[4] Against this, English and Carter, two doctors who knew him well and were not disposed to be particularly charitable to him, both said that they had never seen any signs in him of the habitual use of opium, and would certainly have recognized it if it had existed. Others who knew him in his lifetime said the same, when the legend of his addiction began to spread.[5]

Everything else is conjecture. Certain passages in Poe's letters can be read as describing addiction or withdrawal symptoms. 'I am excessively slothful, and wonderfully industrious—by fits. There are epochs when any kind of mental exercise is torture . . . I have thus rambled and dreamed away whole months, and awoke, at last, to a sort of mania for composition. Then I scribble all day, and read all night, so long as the disease endures . . . I live continually in a rêverie of the future'.[6] Then, a year later, 'For the first time during two months I find myself entirely myself—dreadfully sick and depressed, but still myself. I seem to have

just awakened from some horrible dream, in which all was confusion and suffering'.[7]

But Poe's letters were not confessional; they were intended to
impress the recipient and to mask his own real self, they aimed
to attract attention but also to divert it. Moreover anything that
reads like a reference to drug addiction is as likely—more likely,
in fact—to be referring to his recurrent drinking bouts. It is
difficult enough to distinguish the effects of alcohol and of opium
even in the case of otherwise abstemious laudanum-drinkers like
De Quincey, because of the alcoholic content of laudanum. In
the case of someone like Poe who was also a heavy though
occasional brandy drinker, it is impossible. The symptoms of his
occasional dipsomania may have misled his cousin into taking a
hang-over for the effects of opium, or alternatively (since his
dipsomaniac tendencies were well known to his contemporaries)
may have caused his doctor acquaintances to overlook the
parallel symptoms of opium addiction, which might have been
disguised by the effects of drinking bouts. His utterly erratic
behaviour puzzled and confused his contemporaries, as he himself
realized. When his wife was dying of tuberculosis, in an agonizing series of haemorrhages and recoveries, his anxiety, he said,
drove him 'insane, with long intervals of horrible sanity. During
these fits of absolute unconsciousness I drank—God only knows
how often or how much. As a matter of course, my enemies
referred the insanity to the drink, rather than the drink to the
insanity'.[8]

Faced with such slight and conflicting evidence, most
biographers of Poe who believe that he was an opium addict have
based their conviction on two arguments: that his imaginative
works show unmistakable signs of the effects of opium addiction,
and that they constantly refer to opium.

The first argument begs the whole question which I am examining in this book—whether there is such a thing as a recognizable
opium-inspired pattern in imaginative literature. Any conclusions which I have drawn, or am going to draw, about that
are based on the work of known opium-takers—known to be so
by adequate outside testimony as well as their own. To use it in

Poe's case would be to argue in a circle. The opinion most to be respected in his case is that of two other known opium-takers, Baudelaire and Francis Thompson, who both recognized in his works a climate known to them. His world is 'the world of an opium-dream' said Francis Thompson unequivocally.[9] But even their testimony seems to me inconclusive without more direct supporting evidence than seems to be available.

The second point—that Poe frequently wrote about opium and its effects in his *Tales*—is incontestable, but not necessarily conclusive. Since the publication of *The Confessions of an English Opium Eater*, opium had become as much a standard accessory of the Romantic hero as a ruined castle in the Apennines had been a generation earlier, and Poe might have included an opium trance among his heroes' experiences even if he himself had never taken anything stronger than a dose of calomel. Much has been made by some biographers of the fact that Poe deleted descriptions of opium symptoms from later revised versions of some of his tales; it is suggested that the passages were suppressed because they revealed too much.[10] But Poe's reason for deleting some of the references to opium in these stories was probably an artistic, not a personal, one, just as his reason for including them in the first place may have been. He perhaps felt that opium was becoming a sort of signature tune, a too obvious *motif* for the mood which he wished to portray. Opium was for him an image, a piece of machinery for the presentation of certain mental states. His use, or his cancellation, of it in his stories proves nothing either way about whether he was drawing on personal experience. Some of his master images, such as a dying girl or a pool of dark water, were based on things he had seen with his own eyes; others, such as a voyage of exploration or a Gothic castle, he derived from books; but all four are valid images in his work. So was opium, and we cannot tell to which class it belongs.

Perhaps all that can be safely said of Poe in this connection is that he was almost certainly not an opium addict in the sense that Crabbe, Coleridge, De Quincey, Wilkie Collins and Francis Thompson were—laudanum-drinkers over long periods of years, never free from the habit for long throughout their later lives; but that he may have been—like the second James Thomson, like Elizabeth Barrett Browning, perhaps like Keats at the end of his life—an occasional opium-taker, sufficiently addicted to experience rather more than the preliminary stages of its effects. Poe had little resistance to any kind of stimulant—he got dead drunk on an amount of alcohol that would hardly have affected many men—and probably a few doses of laudanum would have carried him far into the depths of the opium landscape.

He may have had personal experiences of opium trance and withdrawal, or he may have simply imagined what such states would be like. As Princess Marie Bonaparte said in her psychiatric study of Poe, whether or not he was an 'opiomane', he was undoubtedly an 'opiophile'. He was deeply interested in all unusual states of consciousness—dreams, hypnagogic visions, swoons, catalepsies, resuscitations, extreme fear and anxiety, loss of identity, obsession, lethargy, melancholia, claustrophobia, vertigo. They were at once symbols and instances of the special insights, not accessible to normal perception, which he most wanted to convey, and he used them as literary tools. What Baudelaire said of Poe's drunkenness may be true also of his opium-taking. It was 'un moyen mnemonique, une méthode de travail, méthode energique et mortelle, mais appropriée à sa nature passionnee. Le poète avait appris à boire, comme un littérateur soigneux s'exerce à faire des cahiers de notes'.[11] It is for Poe's use of opium as a technique, as a 'méthode de travail', that I have included him in this book; not principally as an addict himself—the evidence about that is too uncertain—but as a theorist of the use of opium as an effect in literature.

Four of Poe's heroes—in the original version of *Berenice*, in *Ligeia*, in *The Fall of the House of Usher*, and in *A Tale of the Ragged Mountains*—are opium addicts, and two others (in the original versions of *The Oval Portrait* and *Loss of Breath*) are depicted as feeling, or suffering as though they felt, the effects of opium. Poe identified and described very vividly some of the known effects of opium. His description of hyperaesthesia, as experienced under a régime of daily doses of morphine by Augustus Bedloe in *A Tale of the Ragged Mountains*, is memorable. 'The morphine had its customary effect—that of enduing all the external world with an intensity of interest. In the quivering of a leaf—in the hue of a blade of grass—in the shape of a trefoil—in the humming of a bee—in the gleaming of a dew-drop—in the breathing of the wind—in the faint odours that came from the forest—there came a whole universe of suggestion—a gay and motley train of rhapsodies and immethodical thought'. This intensity of sense perception under opium is depicted more at length in a passage which Poe inserted into the first version of *Loss of Breath*, and then later took out again. Most of this story—both as it first emerged in the *Philadelphia Saturday Courier* as *A Decided Loss*, and as it finally appeared in book form—is grotesque and gruesome fooling. But there is a longish passage in the story as published in 1835 in the *Southern Literary Messenger* which is an intense and serious imaginative experience, quite out of key with the rest. Poe mystifies it, in his self-protective way, with half-mocking references to Schelling, Coleridge, Kant, Disraeli, and even—a genuine mystification as far as I am concerned; I have no idea what he means—to 'synonyms in Crabbe'. But the passage is mainly a serious analysis of a mental state, supposedly the state of a man on the gallows, being hanged, and then coffined and entombed, but also compared with the state of someone 'eating opium, or feasting upon the Hashish of the old Assassins'.

The symptoms of this state include an acute hyperaesthesia, in which the dead-alive narrator's sensations 'assumed, all at once, a degree of intense and unnatural vivacity' so that as he lay in a coffin on a hearse he could hear the rustling of the plumes, the breathing of the horses, could smell 'the sharp acrid smell of the steel screws' in the coffin, could feel the texture of the shroud against his face, and see the variations in light and shadow which the flapping of the black hangings threw across the outside of the coffin.

Roderick Usher, too, who had the hollow weighty voice of the 'irreclaimable eater of opium', suffered from hyperaesthesia, a 'morbid acuteness of the senses' which made strong tastes or smells, bright light and any music except from faint stringed instruments unendurable to him. And the hero of *Berenice*, who in the original version of the tale was given to the immoderate use of opium, was subject to the malady which confers intensity of interest on trivial things—a typographical device in a book, a shadow on tapestry, the flame of a lamp, a commonplace word, on which his attention would be riveted for long unwearied hours. [Plate v] Poe explored many varieties of this riveted unreasoning concentration, 'that terrible state of existence which the nervous experience when the senses are keenly living and awake, and meanwhile the powers of thought lie dormant', when men gaze blankly at flames and reflections in looking-glasses, pore over the rotten deck-timbers of haunted ships, look down from the edge of precipices, cannot drag their eyes away from the eyes or the teeth of some loved enemy.[12]

Poe was not only describing this special stage of consciousness for its own interest. It was a parallel to what he himself was trying to do. Every poet wants to confer intensity of interest on familiar experience. Poe made the parallel yet closer in a passage, later cancelled, in *The Oval Portrait*. The hero of this story, wounded and ill after a battle with banditti, has taken refuge in a lonely castle in the mountains, and doses himself with opium. He is in a room hung with tapestry and gold-framed pictures, in a remote turret of the castle, and as he lies there he feels 'the voluptuous narcotic stealing its way to my brain. I felt that in its magical influence lay much of the gorgeous richness and variety of the frames—and much of the wild interest of the book which I perused. Yet this consciousness rather strengthened than impaired the delight of the illusion, while it weakened the illusion itself'. Poe was watching how the mind of a reader might be affected by an artificial intensity, he was analysing and exposing how illusion operated. It has been plausibly suggested that in this tale, as in *The Domain of Arnheim* and *The Assignation* and even *The House of Usher*, Poe was thinking in terms of the theatre, of painted back-cloths and draped curtains and crimson spot-lights.[13] He was trying all possible short cuts to the creation of illusion, all hooks on which disbelief could be suspended.

Poe's fullest study of an opium addict was the narrator of *Ligeia*. This lugubrious widower was 'habitually fettered in the shackles of the drug' and dwelt perpetually on the memory of his dead wife Ligeia, with 'that sorrow which the living love to cherish for the dead', which, as Poe had said in a note attached to his early poem *Al Aaraaf*, 'in some minds resembles the delirium of opium'. The drug induced in the hero of *Ligeia* a morbid activity of the imagination and the power of sight, so that he saw a perpetual shifting phantasmagoria of shadows and patterns, and even adorned his rooms with gold carpets, ebony beds, lamps of serpentine coloured flames, writhing black patterns and monsters on the perpetually stirring curtains, to conform with his opium visions. 'I had become a bounden slave in the trammels of opium; and my labours and my orders had taken a colouring from my dreams'.

It has often been suggested that the sombre halls and chambers of Poe's tales, with their sumptuous hangings and crimson gloom, are typical of opium dreams.[14] But I know of no other detailed upholstery descriptions of this kind by an addict except the evil chapel of Francis Thompson's *Finis Coronat Opus*, and that is clearly derived from Poe. Poe's *Tales* are full of vast halls deep in remote decaying castles and abbeys, and they are generally cluttered with heavy velvet hangings, pictures, golden ornaments, coloured lamps, marble tables, thick carpets, and censers of smoking perfume, and dimly lit through windows of crimson-stained or leaden-coloured glass, or perhaps only by the flickering flames of braziers. I doubt whether opium provided this furniture of Poe's imagination. Much of it is the conventional stage property of the castles of Gothick romances: the word-pictures of the novelists from Mrs Radcliffe to Walter Scott, the feathery visions of the engravers who illustrated them, the obliquely-lit backcloths of the theatrical designers. Many of Poe's castles and landscapes have actually been traced to individual sources of this kind by researchers.[15] What is peculiar to Poe in these descriptions has a simpler and more pathetic explanation. All his adult life was spent in meanly furnished and sometimes almost bare little rooms in cottages and lodgings, with cheap wooden chairs and tables, cotton curtains, matting on the floors. His starved taste for luxury produced the fantasies of red carpets, gold tassels, rosy lamps, heavy folds of silk and velvet, sweet scents, which culminated in the rather charming absurdity of his crimson and gold perfect room in *The Philosophy of Furniture*. In just the same way Charlotte Brontë, after many years of bleak school-rooms and the austere little parlours of the parsonage at Haworth, indulged herself in Jane Eyre's description of the spacious drawing-room at Thornfield, with its flowery carpets, crimson couches, marble mantelpiece and ruby-red Bohemian glass ornaments.

Poe needed to believe, and to imply, that these luxurious and ancient castles were his habitual surroundings, by heredity and upbringing, that—like Egaeus in *Berenice*—he had emerged at birth into a 'palace of imagination'. He made the most of his memories of the Allens' house at Richmond, the school buildings at Stoke Newington, the university campus at Charlottesville. The narrator of *The Fall of the House of Usher* is carefully made to say that the splendours of that mansion 'were but matters to which, or to such as which, I had been accustomed from my infancy'. This ingenuous and rather endearing snobbery belongs to the simpler more open side of Poe's character, not to the side which the influence of opium could touch.

There is nevertheless one characteristic of Poe's imaginary halls and chambers which links them with the opium world, perhaps by a conscious contrivance of Poe's. They are all strangely lofty and long, and yet they seem claustrophobic. The bridal chamber in *Ligeia* was 'excessively lofty . . . gigantic in height—even unproportionately so'; the communicating halls of Prospero's castle in *The Masque of the Red Death* were many and large, but so disposed that no straight vista through them was possible, and their windows, darkened with coloured glass, opened only onto a corridor. Roderick Usher's study was 'very large and lofty' but the windows were so high up that they were inaccessible, and the roof was lost in shadow. Much of this is cribbed from Beckford's Fonthill, and is a fashionable trimming in which there is nothing peculiar to Poe. But Fonthill stood on a hill-top; Beckford might shut himself up and live in artificial light for three days for a birthday party, but he came out again afterwards. But Roderick Usher's windows were 'altogether inaccessible from within'. One has the sensation of something vast but totally enclosed and even buried, deep underground or under water. The tarn is to close over the House of Usher as the stagnant ocean closes over the City in the Sea. The most horrible of all Poe's imaginary rooms is the one which Roderick Usher created in a painting, and which foreshadowed what was to happen to his sister (and no doubt, like all these visionary halls and chambers, had a physiological equivalent also). This picture 'represented the interior of an immensely long and rectangular vault or tunnel, with low walls, smooth, white, and without interruption or device. Certain accessory points of the design served well to convey the idea that this excavation lay at an exceeding depth below the surface of the earth'.

It is a tunnel in the white bone of a skull. We are seeing the Haunted Palace from inside, as it is seen under opium. Poe makes this clear by the contrasted vision of the House of Usher from the outside, as seen by the narrator, who represents the normal man, seeing as the restored eye sees after withdrawal from opium. He too sees a skull-house, with bleak walls and vacant windows like eye-sockets, but he sees it 'with an utter depression of soul which I can compare to no earthly sensation more properly than to the after-dream of the reveller upon opium—the bitter lapse into everyday life—the hideous dropping off of the veil. There was an iciness, a sinking, a sickening of the heart—an unredeemed dreariness of thought which no goading of the imagination could torture into aught of the sublime'. Here Poe exposes his technique. Opium, whether in its actually experienced effects or in its imagined ones, supplies a goad to the imagination which tortures into the sublime the dreariness of everyday thought.

In *A Chapter of Suggestions* he used the same form of words to explain, implicitly to justify, the use of artificial stimulants to the imagination. Men of genius, he said, use up their mental energy by living too fast; then 'in later years comes the unconquerable desire to goad the imagination up to that point which it would have attained in an ordinary, normal, or well-regulated life. The earnest looking for artificial excitement . . . may thus be regarded as a psychal want, or necessity—an effort to regain the lost—a struggle of the soul to assume the position which, under other circumstances, would have been its due'. De Quincey said much the same thing about Coleridge. 'It is a great misfortune, at least it is a great peril, to have tasted the enchanted cup of youthful rapture incident to the poetical temperament. That fountain of high-wrought sensibility once unlocked experimentally, it is rare to see a submission afterwards to the insipidities of daily life'; when Coleridge's 'youthful blood no longer sustained the riot of his animal spirits, he endeavoured to excite them by artificial stimulants'.[16]

The Haunted Palace of Roderick Usher's song was a house in a skull. We see the head from the outside as we read the poem, but he saw it from within. It may be an allegory for Poe's own mind, or an objective study. It has been interpreted both as an escapist mind happy in its own imaginations but finally destroyed by the hostile realities of the outside world, and conversely as a sane mind finally destroyed by delusions, 'evil things in robes of sorrow'.[17] Poe's explanation that the poem had an 'allegorical conduct' and that by it he 'meant to imply a mind haunted by phantoms—a disordered brain' leaves it open to either interpretation, as he thought all allegories should do; their meanings should run deep underground.[18] He was interested in mental disorder but not in the *causes* of mental disorder. His job was to observe and to express, not to explain.

The peculiar horror of a limitless but yet enclosed space was linked with opium by Poe in the cancelled section of *Loss of Breath*, where the living corpse, whose sensations have been compared with those of an opium-eater, is laid out in 'a chamber sufficiently small, and very much encumbered with furniture—yet to me it appeared of a size to contain the universe. . . . Strange! that the simple conception of abstract magnitude—of infinity—should have been accompanied with pain. Yet so it was'. His fingers, every part of his body, the weights on his eyes, grew to cosmic proportions. Conversely, even when Poe is imagining an angel and a soul after death winging through space, he makes them conscious of the 'continuous gold walls' which shut in the universe.[19]

Books of exploration, romances like *Peter Wilkins*, cosmic fantasies by Jean-Paul Richter, combined to produce the science-fiction element in Poe's works—the colliding and exploding worlds of *The Conversation of Eiros and Charmian* and *The Power of Words*, the mechanical marvels of *Mellonta Tauta* and *Hans Pfaall*, the elusive half-supernatural countries of *The Narrative of Arthur Gordon Pym*. Poe in his turn formulated and handed on a separate category of fiction which Jules Verne and Rider Haggard and so many hundreds of writers since then have exploited. The characteristics of *The Unparalleled Adventures of One Hans Pfaall*— the pawky oddity of the aeronauts' personalities, the loving detail of the mechanical contrivances, the wonders of space described with no sense of wonder—have been repeated again and again in later science fiction. Perhaps they too owe something to a technique derived from opium experience. Near the beginning of *The Narrative of Arthur Gordon Pym*, Poe depicts his hero racking his brains how to procure a light in the dark hold of the ship where he is entombed. 'A multitude of absurd expedients' passed through his brain, 'such expedients precisely as a man in the perturbed sleep occasioned by opium would be apt to fall upon for a similar purpose—each and all of which appear by turns to the dreamer the most reasonable and the most preposterous of conceptions, just as the reasoning or imaginative faculties flicker, one above the other'. The unmotivated violence and eccentricity with which Poe's characters behave has always struck the reader as something specially strange, but they may have been acting according to a dream logic apparent, or intermittently apparent, to Poe, in the moments when absurd expedients seemed perfectly reasonable. The whole movement of *The Narrative of Arthur Gordon Pym* follows a current sunk too deep to be discerned. Most of it is a compilation from sea stories which Poe had read, but planted here and there are clues to a mystery never explained—unrevealed messages are left in bottles

on islands never revisited, chasms of black granite reveal in-
decipherable inscriptions, there is a mounting tension between
the forces of whiteness and blackness, incarnated in various
human and animal forms and in the landscape; there is a veined
purple stream like changeable silk which, according to the
narrator, 'formed the first definite link in that vast chain of
apparent miracles with which I was destined to be at length
encircled'. But though the miracles are apparent, the chain is
not. Poe probably wrote the story in a hurry, aiming at no more
than a pastiche tale of a sea voyage with some fashionable *Ancient
Mariner* horrors and hallucinations, and padded out by a lot of
geography-manual facts. But something else was at work, and
breaking out at intervals in the story, giving it a more imaginative
direction, something that suggested a destination but did not
describe it, so that Poe was left with clues which he could not
work to a conclusion, rather like Coleridge with *Christabel*. Poe
could watch this happening to him, and could even make a virtue
and a technique out of the compulsion he was under; and in doing so, pass on a tradition to all subsequent science fiction, in
which meticulous detail of machinery is combined with dream-
like inconsequence of motive.

Poe did use his dreams for his poems and tales, though it is odd
that in the case of a poet who wrote so many poems about dreams
and dreamland, we should have so few accounts of his actual
dreams, apart from his hallucinations about prisons and white
figures at the end of his life when he was suffering from delirium
tremens. The idea of *Ligeia* came to him in a dream, and so did
the poem beginning 'I saw thee once—once only—years ago';
when he told Mrs Whitman this he added 'Observe the *eyes* in
both tale and poem'. Probably the dream provided only the
shining black eyes which in the story are beautiful and haunting.
He had this dream of eyes again years later, before he wrote the
poem; this progress from dream to writing and back to dream
seems a not unusual experience of writers. When the dream eyes
were given their second incarnation in literature, the effect was
less fortunate than before

'And thou, a ghost, amid the entombing trees

Didst glide away. *Only thine eyes remained.*
They *would not go*—they never yet have gone'.
The italics are Poe's, and reinforce an unlucky association; it is
impossible not to think of the Cheshire Cat's smile which
remained some time after the rest of it had gone.

Nearly everything that Poe said about dreams and how they
work is disappointing; but most of it has reached us through Mrs
Whitman and Mrs Oakes Smith, and it may be supposed that they
sweetened and softened it in the handling, and also that Poe said
what he thought they would like to hear. His magic poems such
as *Dreamland* and *A Dream within a Dream*, and prose-poems like
Silence (which a passage in the original version, later cancelled,
identified as being the landscape of 'those vigorous dreams which
come like the Simoom upon the brain of the sleeper'), depict
realms of dim woods and lakes, melancholy shores and heavy-
headed flowers. But there is no dream of his own, recorded as
such, to confirm that this was his own dream landscape. He has
kept his secret; we do not know whether his own dreams were
of cold still lake-waters, mists and grey woodlands, painted birds
and grains of golden sand, or whether they were of buried
palaces and writhing shadows.

We do, however, know that he saw hypnagogic visions.
Occasionally they were horrible ones, like the grinning evil face
close to his own which he used to see as a young man when he
woke in semi-darkness. But generally the experience was
ecstatically pleasurable, and also awe-inspiring; he felt that the
visions were 'a glimpse of the spirit's outer world'. This strangeness and novelty were so absolute that 'it is as if the five senses
were supplanted by five myriad others alien to mortality'.[20] He
valued them so much that he trained himself to wake, instead of
moving on into sleep, so that he could think over these visions
with full consciousness. Eventually he hoped to embody them in
words, which would startle mankind by the wild originality of
the experiences thus conveyed. Poe seems not to have been
aware, as De Quincey was, how many people, especially children,
see these visions on the borders of sleep. What is interesting is
that he should have made them into what Baudelaire called a

'moyen mnemonique' for future use. He woke himself up in order to transfer the vision 'into the realm of Memory; convey its impressions, or more properly their recollections, to a situation where . . . I can survey them with the eye of analysis'. Here once again, as in his references to mental states produced by opium, one can watch the machinery at work, turning involuntary mental processes into literature.

Everyone who writes about him chooses their own Poe. Some recent American biographers of Poe have been so understandably irritated by the unscholarly fantasies of other biographers that they have reacted almost too far into down-to-earth, matter-of-fact analysis, and have made Poe into such a sober responsible citizen that one feels one is reading about Addison. They are succumbing, just as every reader of Poe succumbs in different ways, to Poe's own propaganda. He liked to believe himself, and to make others believe, that he was an ice-cold logician, perfectly in control of his art, its materials and methods. He wanted to believe this, and he needed to believe it, to fence himself off from the abysses within his own mind. So far in this chapter, I have given way myself to this propaganda of Poe's, and presented him only as a deliberate self-conscious technician. I will end it with a rather different picture, the picture of how Poe's methods and materials sometimes mastered him.

Few, even of the most ardent upholders of Poe as a highly controlled artist, would swallow the whole of his claim in *The Philosophy of Composition*, to have composed *The Raven* by a pure process of logic, beginning with the most suitable length for a poem, and working through the effect it was to produce; the right tone to produce that effect; the right metrical device—a refrain—to give the tone; the right word—'Nevermore'—for the refrain; the right 'non-reasoning creature capable of speech' (it was to have been a parrot at first) to say 'Nevermore'; and so on. Even if it were possible to believe that any poem was ever written like this, enough is known about the sources and early drafts of *The Raven* to show that this particular poem was not. All critics agree that Poe was rationalizing after the event, putting across his favourite picture of himself as a cold mathematical master-mind.

But all the same *The Philosophy of Composition*, taken as a whole, does tell us a good deal about how Poe's imagination worked. At the start of the essay—again as part of his pose as a severely rational logician—he ridicules the idea of the inspired spontaneous poet. The real process of writing poetry, he says, is much less romantic, and much harder work. He lets us in to look at 'the elaborate and vacillating crudities of thought—at the purposes seized only at the last moment—at the innumerable glimpses of idea that arrived not at the maturity of full view—at the fully matured fancies discarded in despair as unmanageable—at the cautious selections and rejections—at the painful erasures and interpolations—in a word, at the wheels and pinions—the tackle for scene-shifting—the step-ladders and demon-traps'.

Any imaginative writer will recognize that as one of the most truthful descriptions ever given of the process of getting ideas onto paper. Poe gave away everything in it, everything that he was to deny later on in the same essay. The wheels and pinions are there, but they are worked by a vacillating hand. Illusion is contrived by stage scenery, but the scene-shifters do not work to a pre-arranged plan. When Poe spoke of the 'true purposes seized only at the last moment' he was revealing that he himself, however he might claim that he always consciously aimed at 'unity of effect', often accepted the 'given' inspiration which he had not planned at all. And in his case the inspiration more often came from below than from above. Again and again in his stories you see a crack opening. *Hans Pfaall* is almost all a cheerful mixture of burlesque and mechanical science fiction, but suddenly in the midst of the mechanical details about ballast and rate of ascent in the account of a balloon voyage to the Moon, there comes this description of a thunder-cloud seen from above as a flash of lightning shoots through it—'I gazed afar down within the yawning abysses, letting imagination descend, and stalk about in the strange vaulted halls, and ruddy gulfs, and red ghastly chasms of the hideous and unfathomable fire'.

This startling vision is quite out of key, in mood and in style, with what comes before and after in the story, until six pages later, we suddenly come to a fantastic and evocative description of the landscape which Hans Pfaall fancies he may find when he reaches the Moon—though the actual landscape, when he does get there, is very perfunctorily and facetiously described. These two passages, both introduced by a reference to freeing or un-shackling the imagination, produce a sudden change of mood, unmotivated and uncalled for in the story, as though Poe's own imagination had suddenly knocked him away from the 'effect' he was consciously aiming at.

Even a story as tedious, facetious and showing-off as *The Duc de l'Omelette* suddenly surprises by a Piranesi vision of a hall in Hell, neither long nor wide but appallingly high, roofed by whirling fiery clouds from which hangs a blood-red chain; and this vision —as surprising in its context as a paragraph from *Vathek* in the middle of a novel by Ouida—is followed by a reference to opium-drugged dreams and beds of poppies. In *Bon-Bon* again, a tale almost entirely on a note of spry facetious gruesomeness which belongs to daylight and full consciousness, a moment of freezing chill comes in the middle of a humorously grotesque description of the Devil—the moment when the Devil takes off his spectacles and 'the space where eyes should naturally have been was . . . simply a dead level of flesh'. This glimpse of horror has no place in the story; Poe has to make his Devil produce a lame laboured explanation for what had obviously come as a thing given, a bottomless crack in the shiny surface of Poe's carefully devised 'effect'.

He believed that he could manipulate horror by logic. It could all be done by formula, and his inner self need not be touched, but could stay aloof and safe. In 1835 he imparted to a friend the complete recipe for producing a successful horror story for the magazines: 'the ludicrous heightened into the grotesque: the fearful coloured into the horrible: the witty exaggerated into the burlesque: the singular wrought out into the strange and mystical'. He cited, among other examples of the genre, *The Confessions of an English Opium Eater* which, he said, was 'uni-versally attributed to Coleridge, although unjustly'.[21] A year later, referring to his own essays in this kind he said, with a half-perception of his own mixed motives, 'most of them were *intended* for half banter, half satire—although I might not have fully acknowledged this to be their aim even to myself'.[22] Two years later still came his public claim to complete mastery over this medium, his *How to Write a Blackwood Article*, in which he imagines the editor of *Blackwood* describing the kind of 'bizarreries' or 'intensities' that go down well. 'There was "The Dead Alive", a capital thing!—the record of a gentleman's sensations when entombed before the breath was out of his body—full of taste, terror, sentiment, metaphysics, and erudition. You would have sworn that the writer had been born and brought up in a coffin. Then we had the "Confession of an Opium-Eater"—fine, very fine!—glorious imagination—deep philosophy—acute speculation—plenty of fire and fury, and a good spicing of the decidedly unintelligible. That was a nice bit of flummery, and went down the throats of the people delightfully'. This witty impudence of Poe's is great fun, and so are the 'Piquant Facts for Similes' which follow, and which are a *bouquet garni* of fashionable images of the time. They are all duly stirred in, slightly wrong, in the spoof *Blackwood* article, *A Predicament* (*The Scythe of Time*) which follows.

There is one extraordinary thing about this jocose and nonsensical piece—it ends with an incident which is a take-off of an utterly serious horror story which Poe himself wrote—five years later. In *A Predicament* the authoress who sets out to write the *Blackwood* article, the Signoria Psyche Zenobia or Miss Sukey Snobbs, climbs up into the tower of a church in Edinburgh, pokes her head out through an aperture in the face of a giant clock, and is decapitated by one of the steel hands of the clock, the 'Scythe of Time'. The gradual decapitation is described with gruesome and jocular detail, though Poe is not always quite able to maintain the detached irony at which he is aiming; the 'huge, glittering, scimitar-like minute hand of the clock', narrowing the mouth of the trap with inconceivable rapidity, is not quite in the tone of its jaunty context. Five years later, in *The Pit and the Pendulum*, Poe used the formula in a tale at which his readers were definitely not meant to laugh—as a torment of a prisoner of the Inquisition, lying bound under a figure of Time whose scythe was a pendulum of glittering steel with a knife edge which swung ever lower and lower, downwards towards the helpless prisoner below.

It is as if, in *A Predicament*, Poe was putting up a frail barrier of ridicule between himself and the edge of the abyss into which he could not help peering. I am reminded of a story which went the rounds when I was at Oxford, a story of two undergraduates, one of whom lived in an old house in Ireland and invited the other to stay during the vacation. The guest thought that his friend and host was rather absurdly superstitious about his house, which was supposed to be haunted; so one night he dressed himself up in a white sheet and went and leaned over his host's bed and woke him up. The host gave such a scream of terror that the guest thought he had gone too far, and said reassuringly 'It's all right, it's only me'.

'I know it's you, you bloody fool. Look behind you.'

VII

BAUDELAIRE AND THE CLUB
DES HASCHISCHINS

Baudelaire's *Paradis Artificiels* is, with *The Confessions of an English Opium Eater*, the twin peak of the literature of drug addiction. Yet this marvellous work of vigilant and sensitive observation has comparatively little to contribute on the subject of opium and the literary imagination. All the first half of *Paradis Artificiels*, with its subtle analyses of mental effects of drug addiction, refers to hashish; and all the second half, which does refer to opium, is a summarized translation of De Quincey's *Confessions* and *Suspiria de Profundis*, with hardly an opinion, let alone an experience, of Baudelaire's own. The method of presentation which Baudelaire chose is misleading, so that although he is always quoting or summarizing De Quincey, it sounds as if he were offering the fruit of his own experience or reflection, and one often sees quotations from this part of *Paradis Artificiels* used to illustrate Baudelaire's thought, when in fact it is De Quincey's. This is not Baudelaire's fault; he stated his intention as plainly as possible. He thought that De Quincey had said all that could be said on the subject of opium addiction, better than anyone else could say it, and that it would be impertinent to do more than abridge De Quincey's work.[1] He added nothing but an occasional sympathetic comment on De Quincey's character or style.

Paradoxically, Baudelaire seems to have had much more personal experience of opium than of hashish. He probably started experimenting with opium when he was a student at the Sorbonne in 1840. During the period when he was living in the Hotel Lauzun he may have indulged more in hashish than in opium, though according to Gautier and others he may have been only a spectator at the Club des Haschischins. If he did take hashish at this period, he later reverted to opium. His letters of the late 1840s often refer to large doses of opium, and there are many later references to it in letters to his mother, to Poulet-Malassis and other friends.[2]

But whereas his descriptions of the mental effects of hashish, collected from his own experiences and those of his friends, are presented with wonderful clarity and detail in *Paradis Artificiels*, his own opinions on the effect of opium on the literary imagination are scattered here and there in poems and articles and notebooks, and seem to be drawn from descriptions by De Quincey and Poe more than from his own experience. As in Poe the mental effect of opium, if he took it, cannot be isolated from the effects of alcohol, so in Baudelaire the effects of opium, which he certainly did take, cannot be isolated from the effects of hashish and other stimulants; it would be rash indeed to say positively of any image or word in Baudelaire's poetry that it was coloured altogether and only by his opium addiction—or only by his hashish taking, since prepared hashish contains a small amount of opium as well as its main constituents of *Cannabis indica* and butter.

It is not suggested that these two drugs have totally distinct actions. Baudelaire himself recorded both similarities and differences in their effects. Both enfeebled the will-power, both riveted the attention inescapably on trivial and minute details, both magnified the sensation of time and space, both inclined the imagination towards visions of moving water—fountains, waterfalls, sea waves. But hashish was much more vehement and disturbing than opium in its immediate effects; hashish was a confusing fury, opium a gentle seducer.[3]

The mental confusion produced by hashish caused one poetic effect much cherished by Baudelaire which opium may not confer —synaesthesia, the confounding of one sense with another, a sensation which, linked to the poetic doctrine of the *correspondances*, became almost a rite of initiation for mid-nineteenth-century poets. Hoffmann had announced in *Kreisleriana* his experience of a synaesthetic cluster of the colour crimson, the scent of carnations and the sound of a tenor clarinet; then Poe proclaimed his simultaneous awareness of the buzzing of a gnat and the orange ray of the spectrum;[4] Gautier both heard and saw pianoforte notes which gushed out in sparks of red and blue;[5] Baudelaire experienced mental transformations between musical notes and arithmetical calculations.[6] Some of these experiences were due to hashish, or possibly to opium, some were a faculty natural to the poet mind, needing no artificial aid.

Another implicit contrast between the effects of hashish and of opium can be found in Baudelaire's work. In *Paradis Artificiels* he insists that the rêveries and hallucinations of the hashish taker, however full of strange monsters and intense colours they may be, all have as their starting point the banal everyday sensations of the particular individual who has taken hashish. They are not like those 'hieroglyphic' dreams which sometimes come in natural sleep, and which are so unexpected, so unrelated to the sleeper's normal character and waking life, that they seem to be a gratuitous grace bestowed from outside.[7]

But towards the end of his life, when he was certainly no longer taking hashish but very probably was taking opium,[8] he had a dream of a terrible landscape which seemed to him such as no mortal had ever seen, a real hieroglyphic dream. His dreaming self, quite distinct from his waking self, could control by its own caprices the architecture of this extraordinary landscape of metal and marble and water, moving but silent and lifeless.[9] This is the imagination that was at work in De Quincey's opium dreams, an imagination that under the influence of opium produced a distinct, recognizable and quite unearthly landscape of vast temples and silvery expanses of water.

The 'paysage opiacé . . . le ciel morne et l'horizon imperméable qui enveloppent le cerveau asservi par l'opium'[10] was a recognizable country to Baudelaire, a country of 'colonnades éblouissantes, des cascades de métal fondu, des paradis de feu, une splendeur triste, la volupté du regret, toutes les magies du rêve, tous les souvenirs de l'opium'.[11] [Plate iii] Its physiognomy suggested to him that the imagination was influenced by the drug towards a certain type of imagery, and might even be despotically ruled by this imagery which imposed itself on the now powerless will of the poet. 'La mémoire poetique, jadis source infinite de jouissances, est devenue an arsénal inépuisable d'instrument de supplices'.[12] There was rapture as well as torture and gloom in these opium landscapes. Baudelaire delighted in the 'sombres et attachantes splendeurs de l'opium'[13] which Poe described in his works, a magic world where the drug had opened out huge vistas of space, and given intensity to all colours, had caused sounds to vibrate with sonorous meaning, and had floated on the far horizon Eastern cities and palaces in a haze of gold.[14]

It is impossible to say how much Baudelaire was drawing on his own experience of opium when he greeted the opium landscapes of De Quincey and Poe with this assurance of recognition. His *Rêve Parisien* may or may not have been an opium dream—he does not tell us. When he names opium in his poetry, it is usually as a symbol or equivalent for some heightening of consciousness, terrifying but enlightening. It can be the insatiable lips of Jeanne Duval or Marie Daubrun's green eyes, or it can be the beacon light which great painters throw upon human experience, or the dauntless love of excess.[15]

> 'L'opium aggrandit ce qui n'a pas de bornes,
> Allonge l'illimité,
> Approfondit le temps, creuse la volupté,
> Et de plaisirs noirs et mornes
> Remplit l'âme au-delà de sa capacité'.[16]

Elegant as the stanza is, its emotion sounds to me faintly second-hand, not deeply or personally felt. There is something ambiguous about Baudelaire's analysis of opium effects, very different from the brilliant certainty of his hashish descriptions, in which, to use his own metaphor, you can see the whole mental mechanism at work as the machinery of a clock in a glass case can be watched. Those of his poems which seem most likely to be descriptions of opium dreams also seem to be possibly the most derivative. *Rêve Parisien* has been thought to derive its inspiration from Poe's *Tale of the Ragged Mountains*.[17] *L'Irrémediable* seems to echo Poe's *Descent into the Maelstrom*, De Quincey's passage on

Piranesi, and *The Ancient Mariner*. Was Baudelaire using other men's experiences, or had all four writers visited the same 'paysage opiacé'?

Baudelaire undoubtedly felt that he could learn from Poe the technique of using opium as a literary device. Among his work notes is one which evidently refers to two favourite passages in Poe's *Ligeia* and *Tale of the Ragged Mountains* about the hyperaesthesia of the opium addict.[18] The note reads 'Appliquer à la joie, au *se sentir vivre*, l'idée d'hyperacuité des sens, appliquée par Poe à la douleur'.[19] Another revealing note, in *Fusées*, reads 'Les milieux, les atmosphères, dont tout un recit doit être trempé (voir *Usher* et en référer aux sensations profondes du haschisch et de l'opium)'.[20] For Baudelaire, Poe's was the supreme authority which must always be cited when the mysterious maladies of the mind are in question[21] because he surveyed exceptional states of mind with scientific minuteness, and deployed them in his work both as content and form.[22] The 'épouvantable mariage de l'homme avec lui-meme' which opium imposed was a constant theme of Poe's which Baudelaire found enthralling.[23] The attraction was professional as well as personal. Baudelaire's comment on Poe's dipsomania as 'une méthode de travail', quoted in the last chapter, led to the main question about drugs and the literary imagination which exercised Baudelaire's mind. Opium could be a symbol for a poetic state of mind; its effects could be used as a technique for presenting states of mind; but could it be something more still? Could it do the mind's thinking for it, could it be a 'machine à penser'?

It was a question, said Baudelaire, which he had often heard put. It must have been passionately discussed in Boissard's salon in the Hotel Lauzun. Perhaps the Club des Haschischins was not such an organized affair as Gautier was to suggest when he described it many years later. But if there was not a great deal of actual indulgence in hashish, there must have been a very great deal of talk about it, the assembled writers and painters comparing their symptoms under hashish or opium, and speculating on how the imagination and the poet's art might be stimulated or betrayed by drugs.

Theory

If anyone were so perverse as to make a pilgrimage to the sites connected with the opium writers, he would find that two very different buildings evoked most clearly for him the life of the writers of this tragic school. One is the little white cottage in Westmorland where De Quincey sat cosily by the fire with his books and his decanter of laudanum, while the winter wind screamed outside. The other is the stately Hotel Lauzun, looking down on the wreathing currents of the Seine, where Baudelaire had an apartment and where the Club des Haschischins used to meet. I myself lived for six years in the Ile Saint Louis, only two streets away from the Hotel Lauzun though on the other side of the island, and I have experienced that feeling of being inside a safe secret privileged retreat which is the magic of the Ile Saint Louis, whose inhabitants proudly call themselves 'les insulaires' and who talk of 'visiting Paris' as though the thirty steps across a bridge were a journey to another world. What place could be more likely to foster the brilliant talk of creative artists exchanging ideas about their art?

The Hotel Lauzun, or Pimodan, presents a reserved face to the outside world, and is not very easy to see; I got inside it only once. It is not of this austere façade with its beautiful iron balcony that one must think, when picturing the Club des Haschischins. One must imagine the guests hurrying through the gateway on an icy winter day, as Gautier described it. The wind on this north side of the island can be piercing indeed on a January evening. They crossed a grass-grown courtyard, whose shadowy corners made its size conjectural, and mounted a staircase with a cast-iron balustrade and an Egyptian sphinx at its foot. They entered by a door hung with velvet, and were welcomed into rooms whose walls were lined with looking-glasses framed in faded gold, whose domed ceilings swarmed with painted allegories, whose tables were covered with Venetian glasses, battered plates of Limoges enamel, and Japanese porcelain saucers filled with the greenish paste of hashish.[24]

Baudelaire, like De Quincey, insists that drugs only produce interesting states of mind in minds that are already interesting. Gross imaginations are stimulated by hashish only to gross visions.

Baudelaire and the Club des Haschischins

It is only in cultivated reflective melancholy minds that hashish can produce its full effect, the excessive development of the poetic spirit.[25] It was from the notes or the talk of such men as these about their long experience of hashish, as well as from his own, that Baudelaire compiled the first part of *Paradis Artificiels*. They compared how, when under the influence of hashish, they reacted to language and to music, to lights, to colours, to the frescoes on walls and ceilings, to clock faces, to the pipes they were smoking; what freezing chills they felt, and how all their senses were acutely sharpened and became interchangeable, how their identities were fused with the objects around them, which became living symbols and allegories; how time and space stretched to infinity; and how, finally, they passed into the 'kief', the sensation of absolute god-like superiority and happiness, a perfect self-satisfaction and complacency which could even admire its own remorse.

Gautier later described experiments with opium as well as with hashish; many kinds of stimulants were tried in the search for new states of consciousness, and these young writers—less scrupulous, or less hypocritical, than Coleridge and De Quincey —did not deceive themselves and others into thinking that the drugs were originally taken only for the relief of pain; they acknowledged that curiosity was their motive. The painter Meissonier hoped for splendid hallucinations when he took hashish, but to his great disappointment he saw nothing but regular symmetrical designs. 'C'était à se croire dans un jardin de Le Nôtre, et je me disais avec désespoir: Dans cette ivresse, je n'aurai donc jamais d'Imagination!'[26]

Meissonier's experience may be compared with Baudelaire's in *Rêve Parisien*. Their starting-point was the same, for to my mind the original inspiration of Baudelaire's dream, if it was a real dream, or at any rate of his poem, was not, as has been suggested, a memory of the very different Oriental City of Poe's *Tale of the Ragged Mountains*, but very plainly the frigid splendours of Le Nôtre's great parks at Vaux-le-Vicomte and Versailles which both he and Meissonier must have seen often enough. These great landscape designs, with their canals and fountains, cascades and statues, stone-edged pools and gravel walks, whose very trees are sculptured and their flower-beds inlaid like marqueterie, always look to an English eye more like architecture than a garden. In them the condition that seemed to Baudelaire so singular in his dream—the banishing of the irregularity of vegetation, the intoxicating monotony of metal, marble and water—seems already achieved.

In Meissonier's hashish hallucination, these landscapes were simply reproduced; but in what may have been Baudelaire's opium dream, they were magically magnified. The difference is of course because Baudelaire was an imaginative genius and Meissonier was not. But something was perhaps also due to the different action of hashish, whose hallucinations keep closely to their visible starting-point, and of opium, which imposes a landscape of its own

> 'Babel d'escaliers et d'arcades,
> C'etait un palais infini,
> Plein de bassins et de cascades
> Tombant dans l'or mat ou bruni . . .'

crystal cataracts, sheets of water stretching millions of leagues to the borders of the universe, rivers pouring from the firmaments into diamond gulfs, oceans channelled through caverns of gems, all lit by a burnished iridescent sheen on the metallic water, watery metal, beneath a sunless sky, and all this slow viscid majesty of movement accomplished in an endless silence— the whole universe becomes one infinite palace, boundless but imprisoning.

Théophile Gautier was more fortunate than Meissonier in his quest for drug visions. The accounts that he wrote thirty years later of his hashish and opium experiences, in *Le Club des Haschischins* and *La Pipe d'Opium*, are obviously part fiction. He has done a good deal of piecing and faking of his memories, making his drug visions neater, more spry, more hilariously grotesque, more consecutive than they probably were at the time, and has fitted in figures from contemporary engravings, from puppet-shows, from the Commedia dell'Arte, from his own ballets, such as *La Péri*, in which Carlotta Grisi incarnated, in her *pas du songe*, the visionary queen of an Oriental paradise of peris revealed in an opium dream.[27] But Gautier's account of his drug visions was not all constructed. In *La Pipe d'Opium*, the vision of the beautiful girl who is to be kept alive by a kiss on the mouth is obviously a chic magazine version of La Belle au Bois Dormant, but some elements of the dream landscape which follows seem to me true untouched-up dreams. Gautier describes himself staring at the ceiling which is turning a deeper and deeper blue, and finally becomes transparent, so that he can see its beams, and then the glittering night sky through them. Sparkling threads and networks twist round him, and white flakes like tufts of wool drift across the vault of the ceiling, and become files of figures spiralling upwards from the cornice —like the processions of white cotton-wool clouds which De Quincey saw in his opium dreams, reconstituting a childish experience. In a later stage of his opium vision, Gautier was being carried past gibbet-like street-lamps and skeleton trees across a barren plain under a lowering sky, to a black city whose houses, small enough for dwarfs, huddled themselves back from the sides of the streets to let Gautier's carriage, with its galloping black horses, force a way through.

Gautier's recorded hashish vision is more famous than his opium one, and to my ear sounds more constructed; the pranks of Daucus Carota, the mandrake man, are too self-consciously whimsical to be very convincing. But Gautier describes himself descending the stairs of the Hotel Lauzun at the end of this vision, which then suddenly assumes an extra dimension of Piranesian grandeur and horror. The stairs had become cyclopean, interminable; when he looked upwards, he saw flight beyond flight, landing above landing; below him stairs wound downwards in whirlpools and giddy spirals as though the staircase pierced right through the centre of the earth—and the steps were soft, and gave way beneath his tread. When he finally reached the courtyard, it seemed to him a vast open space on whose horizon rose huge distant domes and spires and pyramids.

Gautier declared that after about ten experiences with hashish, he gave it up, because 'A real writer needs only his natural dreams, and does not want his thought to be influenced by any external agency whatever it may be'.[28] Balzac, for much the same reason, refused to experiment with hashish at all when It was offered to him at the Hotel Lauzun. He was intensely curious, but he could not bring himself to abdicate any part of his control of his own mind, to violate his will.[29]

It was this question of intellectual and artistic integrity, not any moral guilt about drug addiction, that was the crux of the argument in the Hotel Lauzun about drugs as a 'machine à penser'. Could there be any short cut to true poetic inspiration? Could one get into paradise by the back door? By the time Baudelaire came to write *Paradis Artificiels*, the lesser threat to artistic integrity had been swallowed up in the greater one to moral integrity: the sacrilege, the black magic, of trying to reach through drugs that state of grace, that gratuitous and occasional foretaste of immortality, which should be sought—and afterwards revealed in poetry—only through hard work and contemplation, through the assiduous exercise of the will and unremitting rightness of intention.[30]

That great argument is beyond the scope of this book, which is more narrowly concerned with the effects of opium on the mind of a writer, not on his soul. The considered opinion, on this narrower question, of the most acute intellect—apart from Coleridge—who ever became a drug addict, is decisive. Baudelaire believed that drugs do, to some extent and in some ways, affect the literary imagination; but they give only to those who already have much, they give less than they seem to do, and they take away the power to make use of what they give. To the question 'Whether, at the price of his dignity, his integrity and his free will, a man could extract great intellectual benefit from hashish, could make of it a kind of machine for thinking, a powerful weapon?', Baudelaire replies—'Hashish reveals to a man nothing but himself. It is true that the man is so to speak squared and cubed to infinity, and since it is also true that the memory of his impressions will remain when the debauch is over, those who hope to *make use* of hashish do not seem at first sight to be altogether unreasonable in their hope.

Baudelaire and the Club des Haschischins

But I implore them to realize that the thoughts of which they hope to make so much use are not really as beautiful as they appear in the tinsel magic of their momentary disguise. They are more of earth than of heaven, and owe most of their beauty to the neurotic excitement and desire with which the mind flings itself on them. Also this hope is a vicious circle; even if we admit for a moment that hashish can confer genius, or at least increase it, it must not be forgotten that it is the nature of hashish to weaken the will, and so to give with one hand what it takes away with the other, that is, to bestow imagination without the power to make use of it'. Baudelaire ends with the terrible warning that 'he who makes use of a poison in order to think may soon not be able to think without the poison. Think of the frightful state of a man whose paralysed imagination can no longer work without the help of hashish or opium'.[31]

The last exclamation breaks through the careful judicial objectivity which Baudelaire preserved almost throughout *Paradis Artificiels*. He is no longer austerely presenting impersonal conclusions collected from other men's experience. It is of himself that he is speaking. In the prose poem *La Chambre Double* which he published two years after *Paradis Artificiels* he gives a picture of himself lying in a sordid room full of dirty dilapidated furniture, its cold fireplace filthy with spittle, its grimy windows slime-tracked by rain drops, its air thick with stale tobacco fumes and nameless stenches. This is the world that he has to acknowledge, to live in—and to write in; there is an unfinished manuscript on the table, and the printer's devil is at the door. In this narrow cell, where all is disgust, 'un seul objet connu me sourit: la fiole de laudanum: une vieille et terrible amie'.

PART III

PRACTICE

VIII

CRABBE

In the summer of 1790 passers-by in a street in Ipswich saw a middle-aged clergyman suddenly stagger and fall. He was helped up, one of the helpers muttering to another 'Let the gentleman alone, he will be better by and by', for he was thought to be drunk. They took him back to the inn where he had left his wife, and a doctor was sent for. The clergyman explained that for some time he had been liable to vertigo, and he was afraid it was a symptom of apoplexy. It would be of no use to bleed him, that only increased the symptoms. The doctor pooh-poohed his fears of apoplexy. 'There is nothing the matter with your head, nor any apoplectic tendency; let the digestive organs bear the whole blame; you must take opiates'.

The clergyman, who was the poet George Crabbe, faithfully followed this advice, and took opium regularly for the rest of his life. His son reported this in passing, in his biography of his father, evidently attaching no great importance, and certainly no reproach or concealment, to this habit of his father's. 'From that time' the younger Crabbe reported 'his health began to amend rapidly, and his constitution was renovated; a rare effect of opium, for that drug almost always inflicts some partial injury, even when it is necessary; but to him it was only salutary, and to a constant but slightly increasing dose of it may be attributed his long and generally healthy life'.[1]

Crabbe is the most unexpected of all the opium-addict writers. In his private life he was a respectable reasonably hard-working country parson, living a regular life with an affectionate family on a sufficient income. As a poet he mainly wrote realistic

descriptions, in regular heroic couplets, of the ordinary inhabitants of villages and small country towns, and their ordinary
lives and relationships. Nobody now accepts Hazlitt's con-
demnation of Crabbe as a flat unimaginative writer concerned
only with drab realistic details;[2] but neither his life nor his
poetry suggests at first sight the romantic extravagance usually
associated with opium addiction.

But for this casual reference by his son to his forty years of
opium-taking, it would never have been known. Neither he
himself nor his contemporaries ever mentioned it in his lifetime,
at least in any document that has survived. In the whole of
Crabbe's poetry there are only one or two very passing references
to drugs: to 'cordials' used to stop children crying, with fatal
results; to misleading advertisements for patent medicines,
which are snatched at to deaden pain but give only transient
relief; and, in a very frank account in the unpublished *Hester*,
to the stimulants which prostitutes take to nerve themselves
for their job.[3] Crabbe had been trained as an apothecary before
he became a clergyman, and knew a good deal about the medical
practices and abuses of his day.

Only once, in another poem, *The Flowers*, which was never
published in his lifetime, did he give any hint that he had
personal experience of the dangers of opium.

> 'Deep is the Poppy's blushing red;
> Ah! take it from our joyous bowers.
> With baneful Dew its flower is fed,
> Until, replete with deadly powers,
> Its heavy influence round is shed,
> That ease and cheerfulness o'erpowers.
> No being loves it, all would hate,
> Did it not men intoxicate.
> Ah Lais! thou art like that Herb,
> Its baneful properties are thine,
> So formed the reason to disturb,
> So gaudy, flimsy, flaunting fine,
> And yet thou hast the witchcraft, too,
> That can the sense of men subdue'.[4]

This stanza, as will be shown later, uses one of the themes which suffused Crabbe's opium dreams, and overflowed into his poetry. But the hint is buried in a poem which no one saw in his lifetime.

The chronology of Crabbe's literary output is odd. Between the ages of eighteen and thirty-one he published a number of poems in magazines and several longer poems, *The Library*, *The Village*—which made his name and which in some respects he never afterwards surpassed—and *The Newspaper*. Then for twenty-two years he published nothing at all. In 1807, when he was nearly fifty-three, he published *The Parish Register*, and during the next twelve years he produced three major works, *The Borough*, *Tales in Verse* and *Tales of the Hall*. For the last thirteen years of his life he published nothing more, though he left a considerable amount of poetry which was published post-humously.

The twenty-two-year gap from 1785 to 1807 is not as significant as it looks, and is unlikely to have had any connection with the opium habit which he started in 1790. His continued but moderate use of opium did not stop his substantial literary output from 1807 to 1819, and in fact he continued to write, though not to publish, between 1785 and 1807. He put a great deal of work into a treatise on his favourite subject of botany, and wrote several novels, but his own dissatisfaction or the advice of friends caused him to destroy all these works; his little boys gleefully enjoyed and long remembered these bonfires of manuscripts.[5] No doubt during this long silence—which was partly due to domestic reasons unconnected with his imaginative life; he himself simply ascribed it to 'want of diligence'[6]— Crabbe was re-thinking his poetic vocation. But it cannot be said that the poems which he published after the long interval, during which he had become an opium addict, were altogether different in kind from what he wrote before it. They show more skill and more knowledge of human psychology, but also more detachment from the human predicament; he is attentive rather than helpful to the miseries of mankind. There is perhaps less sense of design and coherence, more absorption in observed details.

Practice

It has been suggested that Crabbe's interest in violence and insanity derived from his opium experiences.[7] But the events of his waking and pre-addiction life already revealed this interest. His father's violent and moody temperament deeply impressed him when he was still a child.[8] As an apothecary and surgeon, and later as a parish priest, he was called on to visit hospitals, lunatic asylums, prisons, workhouses, slums, and to see many varieties of crime, wretchedness, insanity. We know the subject matter of Crabbe's opium dreams, since he wrote three poems which are repertoires of dream experience. They were all concerned with the sufferings of the solitary mind, with alienation from humanity; not with fear of the violence of other men, but with fear of losing contact with them altogether. The influence of his opium habit on his poetry can be traced directly in his three dream poems, *Sir Eustace Grey*, *The World of Dreams*, and *Where Am I Now?* (only the first of these was published in his lifetime, and the last not till 1960), and indirectly in certain themes which spilled over from his opium dreams and rêveries into his narrative poetry.

During the 1790s Crabbe must have been pondering the theme of insanity and its causes, for one of the novels which he then wrote and destroyed, *Reginald Glanshaw, or the Man who Commanded Success*, was, so his son recorded, 'a portrait of an assuming, overbearing, ambitious mind, rendered interesting by some genuine virtues, and gradually wearing down into idiotism'.[9] When in 1807 he at last addressed the public again, he explained his interest in insanity in his preface to this new set of poems. 'It is said of our Shakespeare, respecting madness,—"In that circle none dare walk but he"';—yet be it granted to one, who dares not to pass the boundary fixed for common minds, at least to step near to the tremendous verge, and form some idea of the terrors that are stalking in the interdicted space'. In all his poetry from then on, there are intermittent hoverings on that tremendous verge, and in the 1807 poems there are several studies of incipient madness in *The Parish Register* and *The Hall of Justice*, besides the full-length portrait of a manic-depressive given in *Sir Eustace Grey*. The motto which Crabbe chose for this poem, a tag from Seneca meaning 'Mingling the false with the true', is relevant at two levels. The madman Eustace Grey mingles the true events of his own past with his hallucinations; but it can be shown that Crabbe also invented the framework of Eustace Grey's life to fit round his own remembered—not invented—dreams, and the framework is not a very good fit.

Crabbe's son left two accounts of how his father wrote *Sir Eustace Grey*. He told Fitzgerald that it was 'written or begun' in 1804.[10] In his biography of his father he said 'There was something in the effect of a sudden fall of snow that appeared to stimulate him in a very extraordinary manner. It was during a great snow-storm that, shut up in his room, he wrote almost *currente calamo* his Sir Eustace Grey'.[11] As Canon Ainger pointed out in his life of Crabbe, it is not probable that a poem of fifty-five stanzas with a complicated rhyme-scheme was written at a single sitting. The poem was probably begun in 1804, and elaborated and finished during the following year. But the starting-point, the fall of snow, is there in the poem, and it is part of the dream sequence which is the central and much the most interesting section of this otherwise rather conventional story. These visions are pervaded with a freezing chill, a diamond brilliance of polar wastes and Northern Lights

'They placed me where those streamers play,
Those nimble beams of brilliant light;
It would the stoutest heart dismay,
To see, to feel, that dreadful sight:
So swift, so pure, so cold, so bright,
They pierced my frame with icy wound;
And all that half-year's polar night,
Those dancing streamers wrapp'd me round . . .

And when the morning sun shone bright,
It shone upon a field of snow'.

The great snow-storm recalled to Crabbe a vision of endlessly extended time and of cold, connected perhaps with the chilly sensations which accompany even a short abstinence from opium.

He began to meditate over the many extraordinary visions which he had experienced in the last fourteen years, since he started taking opium, and to shape them into stanzas. When he had written them down, they seemed to him so alien from his ordinary experience that he connected them with the abnormal mental states which had always been one of his special interests. So he incorporated the 'given' passages of *Sir Eustace Grey*, the dream sequence, in a fairly conventional story of a man once happy and prosperous, with a beautiful wife, two lovely children, and a close friend; but the friend seduces the wife, and is killed in a duel by the betrayed husband; the wife dies, the children are swept off by a fever, lands and fortune are lost, and Eustace Grey becomes a homeless and then an insane wanderer, till he finds some comfort, though not cure, in a Methodist 'conversion', and in the firm sympathy of his keepers in the asylum where his wanderings end.

Crabbe's son said that his father confessed to being much moved when he wrote *Sir Eustace Grey*, more so than for all but two others of his poems, and that it was while he was 'describing the terrors of a poor distracted mind' in the poem that he felt this strong emotion.[12] It was not the story but the visions that moved him, in a way in which he was not moved when writing much more terrible, but more external narratives later; this one expressed not what he had observed in others, but what he had felt in himself. These visions are not particularly appropriate to the case-history of Sir Eustace Grey, but they are very much like what other opium addicts have recorded of their own visionary experiences.[13] Crabbe tells of an extreme sensitiveness to light, an endless expansion of space and time, a boundless plain where Time stood still

> 'years were not;—one dreadful *Now*
> Endured no change of night or day'.

Like De Quincey, he was hurried on long inexplicable journeys, through cities of sepulchres; saw vast ruined temples, and was suspended on giddy spires; and walked unharmed and breathing in the depths of the sea over which great tidal waves had rolled. Like Coleridge, he was unjustly blamed

'Harmless I was; yet hunted down
For treasons, to my soul unfit'

just as Coleridge, in his opium poem *The Pains of Sleep*, written a
year earlier than *Sir Eustace Grey* but published nine years later,
had said

'Such punishments, I said, were due
To natures deepliest stained with sin . . .
Such griefs with such men well agree,
But wherefore, wherefore fall on me?'

The original source of some of these visions can be traced in
Crabbe's waking experience, such as the meteor with brilliant
trails of fire which he saw in 1783, an experience of near-
drowning in the River Waveney when he was a young man, and
the giant waves that rolled in upon the crumbling shore and
cottages of his native Aldeburgh; but his opium dreams selected
from his experience those elements that belonged to their own
landscape.[14] Edward Fitzgerald deduced this connection as soon
as he heard of Crabbe's opium habit. 'It probably influenced his
dreams, for better or worse' he scribbled in the margin of the
younger Crabbe's life of his father, against the sentence about
Crabbe's 'constant but slightly increasing dose' of opium, and
added a reference to *Sir Eustace Grey* and *The World of Dreams*.

Crabbe made much use of dreams in his narrative poems. The
dreams of Ellen Orford, Peter Grimes, Allen in *The Parting Hour*,
the Old Bachelor, Lady Barbara, are given in detail, and they
are not merely recounted, but speculated on, in terms sometimes
inappropriate to the characters supposed to be speaking.[15]
Crabbe is working out a dream theory from his own experience
when he makes his old bachelor say, after the sudden death of
his betrothed

'I had a general terror, dread of all
That could a thinking, feeling man befall;
I was desirous from myself to run,
And something, but I knew not what, to shun.
There was a blank from this I cannot fill;
It is a puzzle and a terror still.
Yet did I feel some intervals of bliss,

Ev'n with the horrors of a fate like this;
And dreams of wonderful construction paid
For waking horror'.[16]

There is a revealing footnote to the narrative of the condemned highwayman in *The Borough*, in which Crabbe says that
he has described the distresses and crimes of such men as the
Highwayman and Peter Grimes because most readers are far too
little concerned with the evils and miseries of human nature;
it is a salutary exercise for the mind to contemplate them, and
he hopes that 'more especially the Dream of the Condemned
Highwayman will excite in some minds that mingled pity and
abhorrence which, while it is not unpleasant to the feelings, is
useful in its operation'.[17] Horror, he suggests, can be both
pleasing and useful, and can provide 'dreams of wonderful construction'. Crabbe was determined to fit his abnormal mental
states into a rational framework, and turn them to good uses, but
there is a dislocation in his work between sad and terrible events
and the sadness and terror which would normally accompany
them. This 'indolence', in its original sense of 'non-feeling', was
a symptom which the opium addict writers studied in themselves
with both curiosity and dread. Coleridge's

'I see, not feel, how beautiful they are'[18]

has often been compared with Crabbe's

'It is the soul that sees; the outward eyes
Present the object, but the mind descries'.[19]

Crabbe showed the effect of mood on what is perceived in his
light-hearted tale *The Lover's Journey*, but he himself had probably
gone beyond mere changes of mood into that condition of
hallucination during an opium trance in which real external
objects, plainly perceived, are totally distorted by being linked
with some obsession in the mind.

Crabbe attributes to an inappropriate character—the bullying insensitive George in *Lady Barbara, or the Ghost*—a very
lucid explanation of this form of hallucination. George is
trying to argue away his mistress's belief in a warning dream
that she has had. Some dreams, he says, leave such a strong
impression

> 'that they come again,
> As half familiar thoughts, and half unknown,
> And scarcely recollected as our own'.

They have drawn strong and abiding figures on the brain, and then

> 'in some strong passion's troubled reign,
> Or when the fever'd blood inflames the brain,
> At once the inward and the outward eye
> The real object and the fancied spy.
> The eye is open, and the sense is true,
> And therefore they the outward object view;
> But, while the real sense is fix'd on these,
> The power within its own creation sees;
> And these, when mingled in the mind, create
> Those striking visions which our dreamers state;
> For knowing that is true that met the sight,
> They think the judgment of the fancy right'.[20]

This is not very eminent as poetry, but psychologically it is a remarkable piece of observation.

It was perhaps the world of opium dreams that he was describing in an unnamed fragment which he never published.

> 'This is my Place of pilgrimage: a Vale
> Where piety oft slumbers, while Desire
> Like one new waken'd, snatches up in haste,
> With Grasp insane, Light Joys, fantastic Hopes,
> Remnants of Motley Bliss, confus'dly join'd,
> To woes alternate, sure of something ill,
> When the Good lies beneath'[21]

and there he broke off, aware perhaps that he was losing hold of his theme and that the image of awakening Desire was confusing in a description of sleep and dreams. He was deeply interested in his own dreams, in themselves and as sources for poetry. His habit of keeping a lamp and writing materials by his bed, so that he could record his dreams as soon as he woke, has already been mentioned in Chapter III. He told Lady Scott, who expressed some wonder at this unremitting authorship, by night as well as by day, 'Dear Lady, I should have lost many a good hit, had I not set down, at once, things that occurred to me in my dreams'.[22] None of these immediate records of Crabbe's dreams have survived, as far as I know, but we have a second-hand record of the account that he often gave to his family at breakfast of a recurring dream of his. In a note on *The World of Dreams* Edward Fitzgerald said, on the authority of Crabbe's son, that Crabbe 'was troubled with strange dreams: in one of them he thought he was followed and hooted at by a set of boys, whom he tried to beat off with a stick, but to no purpose because they were made of leather! He would sometimes reply, when he was asked whether he had slept well, "The leather-lads have been at me again" '.

The implications for Crabbe's poetry of this disquieting dream will be discussed later, but it is worth pointing out that it is not a dream inspired by fear of mob violence. If Crabbe was afraid of his fellow men in some way, it was not a fear for his own skin; in face of wars or riots he was unusually brave. During the Gordon riots of 1780 in London, he went out again and again into the streets to watch the mob sacking houses and setting fire to the Old Bailey. When his son woke him one night at Aldeburgh to say that a French invasion had started, he turned over and went to sleep again. During a hotly contested election at Trowbridge, when a mob threatened to destroy his carriage and tear him in pieces if he went to vote, he calmly told them they could kill him if they chose but that they could not otherwise stop him. Even when he was seventy-seven years old, he was with difficulty dissuaded from going out to see the rioting mobs of 1832 in Bristol.[23] He found mob violence interesting, not frightening. The leather lads were disquieting not because they might hurt him, but because he could not hurt them.

Although we cannot see what Crabbe's immediate jottings-down of his dreams were like, we have one entry in his journal which is a same-day record of the disturbance he felt after a vividly wretched dream. Since he not only felt an emotional reaction, but worked it into his second and greatest poem on dreams, it is worth looking in some detail at the circumstances in which this poem, *The World of Dreams*, came to be written, especially since it can be shown fairly certainly that he had taken opium on the night of the dream.

In June 1817 Crabbe came up to London from Trowbridge, where he had been Rector for the past three years. He was now a widower, his wife having died in 1813 after a long period of mental decay. Crabbe was by this time a famous poet. *The Borough*, published in 1810, and *Tales in Verse*, 1812, had both been very successful. When he arrived to stay in London he was sought out and fêted, both by fellow writers such as Rogers and Moore and Campbell, and by the fashionable world, the Hollands, the Spencers, the Lansdownes, the Bessboroughs. His journal is full of duchesses, and it was obviously surprising, droll and interesting to him to find himself welcomed in company so far removed from the world of his youth, specially as memories of his early struggles in London were brought back by revisiting the same scenes.

He found lodgings in Bury Street, where the landlady and the chambermaid mystified him a little; their manner was equivocal —was it merely simple, or was it knowing, indeed inviting? He remained doubtful about this. He observed, without any extravagant admiration, the succession of great houses which he visited, and which included Hampton Court and Holland House, but was much struck by a glorious display of roses in the Spencers' garden at Wimbledon. Talking with Campbell at Holland House, he said that since his wife's death, he had scarcely known positive happiness, but Campbell noted that his manner as he said it was serene. He made some congenial new friends, and it was on the whole a cheerful time for him. 'All this period pleasant, easy, gay, with a tincture of melancholy that makes it delicious. A drawback on mirth, but not on happiness, when our affection has a mixture of regret and pity' he wrote in his journal on July 11th.[24]

On the 18th he was introduced at a party to Lady Caroline Lamb, who asked him to come on to a party of hers. Crabbe was curious, but the year before he had read Lady Caroline's *Glenarvon* and had declared 'the woman absolutely holds for the doctrine of irresistible passion', and he now felt it more prudent to decline 'the woman's' invitation. Next morning he got an extraordinary incoherent letter from her, declaring that his presence soothed her, that she was puzzled and intrigued by the contrast between his benevolent manner and his severe satiric poetry; 'are you false?'. She exclaimed that the thought of having 'mocked at the grey hairs of Samuel Rogers' the previous night was 'like a corkscrew in my heart . . . pray forgive all this do not write an answer I need none and burn this letter' she ended breathlessly. In the course of her letter she also advised Crabbe about his toothache; he should try a leech for it, 'the only cure, for all the opiates inflame the gum'.[25]

Lady Caroline Lamb was by 1817 an excitable, unpredictable, slightly crazy woman, of damaged reputation after her affair with Byron, her near-separation from her husband and her sensational novel *Glenarvon*, but still fascinating in manner and conversation. Like many of Crabbe's contacts during these July days, she was to play a part in his memorable dream. Her reference to toothache makes it clear that Crabbe was in pain at this time, and taking opiates to stifle the pain. He himself noted in his journal that he was 'ill and nervous' on the morning of July 20th, and nearly gave up going to a party at Sir Harry Englefield's, but after walking in the Park he recovered enough to go to the party, and was very glad he had done so, as it turned out to be a delightful evening, in a fine house overlooking Hyde Park, with some of the best conversation he had heard since he came to London, and he did not leave it till one in the morning.

That night he had a dream which painfully disturbed him. His journal entry about it next morning reads 'I would not appear to myself superstitious. I returned late last night, and my reflections were as cheerful as such company could make them, and not, I am afraid, of the most humiliating kind: yet, for the first time these many nights, I was incommoded by dreams such as would cure vanity for a time in any mind where they could gain admission. Some of Baxter's mortifying spirits whispered very singular combinations. None, indeed, that actually did happen in the very worst of times, but still with a formidable resemblance. It is, doubtless, very proper to have the mind thus brought to a sense of its real and possible alliance, and the evils it has encountered, or might have had; but why these images should be given at a time when the thoughts, the waking thoughts, were of so opposite a nature I cannot account. So it was. I had been with the high, the apparently happy: we were very pleasantly engaged, and my last thoughts were cheerful. Asleep, all was misery and degradation, not my own only, but of those who had been. That horrible image of servility and baseness—that mercenary and commercial manner! It is the work of imagination, I suppose; but it is very strange. I must leave it'.[26]

But he did not leave it. He brooded on the experience, and evolved from it a poem which explored the world of dreams as few other poems have done. He never published it in his lifetime, probably because it was too revealing, but in October of that year he referred to its existence; he had among his papers 'some few things in the manner of "Sir Eustace Grey" ' he said.[27] This can only refer to *The World of Dreams*. The two poems, with one other, also about dreams, written a few years later, are in a special eight-line stanza, rhyming ababbcbc, which Crabbe seems to have reserved for his dream poems. The journal entry of 21st July 1817 and the opening stanzas of *The World of Dreams* are linked by one indisputable reference. Crabbe starts the poem by envying, but also pitying, the sound sleeper who knows neither the terrors nor the joys of dreams such as Crabbe himself experiences, dreams which are inspired either by Fancy or by 'Baxter's sprites'. These are 'Baxter's mortifying spirits' of the Journal entry. Andrew Baxter, in his *Enquiry into the Nature of the Human Soul*, had suggested that dreams are caused by the action of spiritual beings. 'Sad emigrants from hell', Crabbe calls them later in the poem, but he knows that the elements of the dream are in his own mind and will-power.

> 'My soul, subdued, admits the foe,
> Perceives, and yet endures the wrong,
> Resists, and yet prepares to go'.

What follows is a phantasmagoric succession of images and events, in which no appearances can be trusted, no identities are stable. The dreamer experiences violent reverses of sorrow and joy, but the joyful moments are masks, there are realities behind which are altogether different. Many of the recent events of Crabbe's life work their way into the dream, coalescing with the permanent images of his dream landscape. He walks through noble mansions, through busy streets, in gardens of perfumed flowers, he sees far-off views of sunny rivers and cities such as he saw from Richmond or Hampton Court. He meets friends whom he has not seen for many years, he is among gay companies of acquaintances—but are they really so welcoming? Has he any right to be among them? And again and again returns the image of a woman, at first recognized as a fiend, a harlot image all too well remembered, with 'tainted bosom bare'; then seen as a lost loved one, his dear affectionate wife, but the smiling mask shifts and there is a stranger's terrifying face beneath it; then again she comes as a brilliant fairy creature hung with gems— and in an instant is a shrivelled old corpse, stinking on a pauper's bed.

Layers of memory were piled beneath this particular vision: at the surface, Lady Caroline Lamb and the ambiguous little chambermaid at his lodgings; below that, his wife in the sad transformation of her madness, perhaps at some moment of crazed immodesty which had deeply wounded his idea of her, and had roused in himself passions of which he was ashamed; below that again, some incident in his early days in London, when he had been inveigled into a brothel, and had seen a bare-breasted prostitute in a filthy room, leering at him. Other memories had grown round it: the sullen stares of madwomen in Bedlams, withered painted faces in workhouses and on booths at fairs, and corpses dissected in hospitals. It was Life-in-Death, the red-lipped nightmare, and it haunted his imagination and coalesced with the drug that coloured his imaginative life, to form what De Quincey would have called an involute.

There are many other powerful images in *The World of Dreams*, and it was evidently not an account of the single dream of 20th July 1817, but an anthology of opium visions. Here is again the overwhelming wave, the vast hall of the dead, the giddy perch on the top of a tower. Crabbe felt himself a 'passive prey' to the powers which inflicted these extremes of bliss and pain in his dreams. But the last stanza of the poem suggests that he may have recognized both the agent that brought on the dreams, and the possibility of escape.

> 'How came I hither? Oh, that Hag!
> 'Tis she the enchanting spell prepares;
> By cruel witchcraft she can drag
> My struggling being in her snares:
> Oh, how triumphantly she glares;
> But yet would leave me, could I make
> Strong effort to subdue my cares!—
> 'TIS MADE!—and I to Freedom wake!'

The personification of opium as the Hag is made more probable by the reference, in the poem earlier quoted, to the Poppy as a harlot with witchcraft to subdue the sense of men.

Crabbe wrote one other dream poem, which was not published till 1960 and cannot be dated more closely than 1819–1822.[28] It is clearly unfinished; it stops in mid-air, and the versification is much less regular and polished than it is in his completed works. It begins with the words 'Where am I now?' which are an echo from Stanza V of *The World of Dreams*. Like that poem, and unlike any other narrative poem of Crabbe's, it is written in the first person in his own character, and it is mainly in the *Sir Eustace Grey* stanza form.

The opening is intentionally chatty and flat; the narrator thinks he is awake, and on a commonplace errand, but gradually his surroundings grow strange, unearthly. He sees giant ruins, he is borne swiftly in a carriage through aisles of trees like De Quincey in the vision of *The English Mail Coach*, he approaches a huge dome radiant with light, he is wafted within to rooms full of music and dancers who suddenly vanish, he gropes through dark passages while distant bells are tolling, and finally finds himself in a room with a mysterious cowled personage. Here the dream effect is dissipated in a dialogue in which Crabbe is evidently trying to put the vision to moral uses; the cowled figure is identified with Satan, and the dreamer struggles against the temptations of this very gentlemanly equivocating fiend, from whom he finally escapes to a further flight across a misty countryside, during which the poem comes to an abrupt stop.

Where Am I Now? has nothing like the power of *Sir Eustace Grey* or *The World of Dreams*, and some of its effects are typical stage properties of the Gothick romance; there are references to Beckford's *Vathek* and Burger's *Lenore*.[29] In the years during which this poem was written, Crabbe was suffering severely from *tic douloureux*, and may have increased his habitual opium dose to deaden the pain, and so brought on a renewal of the dreaming faculty, which normally diminishes with age. He said in a letter of 1822 that he intended to publish some further poems, which would include 'one more essay at the description of a kind of hallucination or insanity'.[30] This may have been *Where Am I Now?* or the then unpublished *World of Dreams*, or the brilliant *Insanity of Ambitious Love*, never published till 1960. Whichever it was, Crabbe did not carry out his intention of publishing it; the 1819 *Tales of the Hall* were the last poems published in his lifetime. He kept his secret. If we are to trace the effects on his poetry of his second life, that night life of the mind which opium bestowed on him, it can only be by hints and inferences.

Crabbe deliberately renounced the poetic use of some of the more striking elements of his dream world. There are no vast ruined castles, no Polar journeys, no floods or volcanoes, no halls full of dead kings, no crying mandrakes or opening graves in any of his poems except the dream ones, or even in his imagery, though he had met all these in his opium dreams and rêveries. In his early poem *The Library* he abjured castles, armoured knights, damsels in distress and churchyard ghosts as poetic subjects,[31] and twenty-nine years later, after twenty years of his opium habit and the dreams it brought, he reiterated and pitilessly exposed why these Gothick subjects are enjoyed by lazy minds—they provide the excitement of danger without any real anxiety, because the happy ending is guaranteed.[32]

He did not practise what he preached; he himself was a great

reader of novels of this kind all his life, his son reported.[33]
Richard, in *Tales of the Hall*, who is one of Crabbe's nearest
approaches to a self-portrait, says of himself

'I lived for many an idle year
In fond pursuit of agitations dear;
For ever seeking, ever pleased to find,
The food I loved, I thought not of its kind;
It gave affliction while it brought delight,
And joy and anguish could at once excite'.[34]

Crabbe knew that agitations were unhealthily dear to him,
and that the insulated excitements of his dreams were not a safe
indulgence, and he tried to exclude them from his poetry.
They had little influence on his imagery which, as Jeffrey suggested, was detachable. 'His similes are almost all elaborate and
ingenious, and rather seem to be furnished from the efforts of a
fanciful mind, than to be exhaled by the spontaneous ferment of
a heated imagination'.[35] Crabbe, when he read this review, said
'Jeffrey is quite right; my usual method has been to think of such
illustrations, and insert them after finishing a tale'. His images
are mainly taken from his favourite pursuit of botany: the rank
growth of weeds, the pliancy of osiers, stifling moss.[36] Others are
scientific—magnets drawing up steel shavings, galvanism animating dead limbs, the cold flames of phosphorescence on a hand
dipped in the sea, beads of mercury sliding about on a floor.[37]
His mandrake dream—the plant growing in the safe shelter of a
tower, which when plucked up gives out a 'sound of anguish
deeply smother'd'—might seem the perfect symbol for his Abel
Keene in *The Borough*, the foolish harmless clerk, happy in his
routine work and his religious convictions, whose beliefs are
mocked and destroyed by his fellow clerks, and who at last goes
mad and hangs himself, leaving behind a piteous dying confession.
But the symbols that Crabbe chooses for Abel Keene are not
from dream mythology, but from everyday—boys sliding on unsafe ice, and a mouse starving in the wainscot.[38]

We know, however, from Crabbe's own statement that he
owed to his dreams 'many a good hit' in his poetry. Some of
these can be traced.

Practice

In a famous portrait in *The Borough*, Crabbe made a sinister use of his dream of the leather lads who could not feel anything however much he beat them. The fisherman Peter Grimes sought out unprotected orphan boys as apprentices because

> 'He wish'd for one to trouble and control;
> He wanted some obedient boy to stand
> And bear the blow of his outrageous hand;
> And hoped to find in some propitious hour
> A feeling creature subject to his power'.

Having found first one, and then another, and having

> 'now the power he ever loved to show,
> A feeling being subject to his blow'

he beat the boys cruelly, and his disapproving but lazy neighbours would say, in the terrible sentence of which Mr Benjamin Britten has made much potent use in his opera on Peter Grimes

> 'Grimes is at his exercise'.[39]

There is no record that Crabbe himself ever committed an act of violence or cruelty against any living creature, but his dream of the leather lads had made him aware of a latent wish to make others suffer, to break through the wall that sometimes seemed to insulate him from his fellow men and place them beyond his reach. In the character of Peter Grimes he explored to the extreme this latent wish. His footnote on the character of Grimes reads in a way as though he were commenting on a character created by some other writer, or at least by some other self. 'This is all the reason I am able to give' he concludes 'why a man of feeling so dull should yet become insane, and why the visions of his distempered brain should be of so horrible a nature'. The visions of Crabbe's own distempered brain had given him a shock, and he was both caricaturing and warning his subconscious self, as it had been revealed to him by his dreams, in the character of Peter Grimes.[40] Grimes had, in fact, a real-life original, a brutal old fisherman of Aldeburgh called Tom Brown who was suspected of murdering his apprentices; but the feelings attributed to Grimes by Crabbe are his own invention—or self-discovery.

The bare-breasted harlot of Crabbe's 1817 opium dream

appeared not only in *The World of Dreams* which he wrote immediately afterwards, but also in *Tales of the Hall*, published two years later, and there too the image was merged with that of a lost wife. 'Asleep, all was misery and degradation, not my own only, but of those who had been. That horrible image of servility and baseness—that mercenary and commercial manner!'—so he described in his journal the prostitute figure of the dream, and her horrible coalescence with the image of his dead wife. He tried to think that it was salutary for the mind to be 'brought to a sense of its real and possible alliances' but the experience was intensely painful. In *The World of Dreams* the coalescence is not made so explicit; but when he used the dream in *Sir Owen Dale*, he gave it in all its plain horror. In that tale, the husband whose wife has left him goes to look for her and finds her at last with her lover, starving in a filthy garret

> 'There she reclined, unmoved, her bosom bare
> To her companion's unimpassion'd stare'

huddled in sordid rags, and gazing provocatively at her former husband.

> 'O! that woman's look! my words are vain
> Her mix'd and troubled feelings to explain;
> True, there was shame and consciousness of fall,
> But yet remembrance of my love withal,
> And knowledge of that power which she would now recall . . .
> So that, for love or pity, terror thrill'd
> My blood, and vile and odious thoughts instill'd'.[41]

When Crabbe had outlived the first horror of his dream, he saw that it gave him an insight into human emotions which never had been fully his own—'none, indeed, that actually did happen in the very worst of times'—but which others might feel, in a situation which combined two separate experiences of his own. Out of this he made the poem of *Sir Owen Dale*.

I will give one more instance of Crabbe's use of dream-material in his poetry, but to do this it is necessary first to look at one *trait* of Crabbe's own character. Crabbe was thoughtful, sincere, merciful and brave, but he was not always able to have easy relationships with other human beings. An air of discomfort breathed round his less intimate contacts with his fellow men. Some of this was mere embarrassment from a change in social class. Crabbe's father was, at the height of his fortune, a very minor local official, and was mostly a warehouse-man and fisherman; and Crabbe's own early days were passed humbly enough, doing menial jobs as an apothecary's apprentice, piling up barrels of cheeses in his father's warehouse, half starving in London while he humbly sued for patronage. His later years, as a famous writer and as the rector of a substantial parish, were passed in a different social milieu. But there was something more than a difficulty in social readjustment behind Crabbe's uneasiness. Thomas Moore, whose origins were quite as humble as Crabbe's, was an instant and resounding success at every social level, up to royalty. If Crabbe could not get his social manner quite right, it was because of something more than a change in social class. An 'infirmity of nerves, or weakness of spirits' made him a looker-on at life, said Jeffrey, or, in Mr E. M. Forster's severer phrase, he had 'an uncomfortable mind', a 'moral gaucherie'.[42] Even his son, who was pardonably proud of his father's gentlemanly appearance and manners, admitted that he did not fit easily into general conversation; and other men who liked and admired him spoke with some amusement of the discomfort which his artificial manners inflicted at the beginning of an acquaintanceship.[43] In his earlier life he had alternated between being too subservient to those whom he considered his social and intellectual superiors, and then too abruptly dogmatic and angular. In later life he worked out for himself a protective manner which was no less disconcerting at first. In conversation with men, unless he knew them really well, he was resolutely non-committal and commonplace, within a narrow range of subjects, avoiding all argument, while they expected him, as a renowned poet, to show a wide-ranging brilliance. With women he was sentimentally polite, soft and affectionate; as one of them said of him 'The cake is no doubt very good, but there is too much sugar to cut through in getting at it'.[44]

He himself was perfectly aware of this. Some of the best descriptions of his social inadequacy are his own. He told his friend Mrs Leadbeater in a letter (he could say on paper all the things he never could convey in conversation) that he preferred the company of women to men because for the latter he was 'not hardy, nor grave, nor knowing enough, nor sufficiently acquainted with the everyday business and concerns of men'.[45] This is an odd confession from a sixty-year-old man celebrated for the grim realism of his poetry; but his profound knowledge of human psychology gave him no confidence in dealing with people; he could diagnose but he could not cure, and he was often made miserable by his own inadequacy. He turned on himself the same searchlight of observation as he did on others, finding in himself a want of 'perseverance and fortitude . . . a mind rather vexed with the present than expecting much from the future, and not sufficiently happy and at ease to draw consolations from variety'.[46] His own 'want of Fortitude or Discernment, or Affection, or Confidence', he said, had caused his wounding blunders towards Charlotte Ridout to whom he was briefly engaged after his wife's death.[47] In his parochial duties he failed, too, because 'I am disgusted where I should pity, and want to run away from the Object who expects from me Consolation and Sympathy'.[48] He felt that he had failed even in his relationship with his wife. There was love between them, but not understanding. On a lively gossipy fond letter of hers he wrote—'Nothing can be more sincere than this, nothing more reasonable and affectionate; and yet happiness was not granted'.[49] It was a life 'almost without incident, invariably cloudy and cheerlessly calm without any storm to cause apprehension or any sunshine to dissipate the gloom'; that was his description, two years after his wife's death, of the last eighteen years of their married life.[50] In the later years of Mrs Crabbe's life when she was intermittently insane, Crabbe's attentive care of her never abated, and when she died, he wrapped up her wedding-ring in a paper on which he had written

> 'The ring so worn, as you behold,
> So thin, so pale, is yet of gold:
> The passion such it was to prove;
> Worn with life's cares, love yet was love'.[51]

Practice

Crabbe's heart was not cold, but his speech had no spontaneous warmth, and his inability to communicate easily when face to face with other human beings cramped his life. His greatest longing was for comfortable companionship, for some being to whom he would really be able to talk freely about all his pleasures, ill-humours, mortifications, or be silent if he felt like it, in un-self-conscious freedom but in an atmosphere of affection; but it would have to be a 'made-on-purpose Creature', he acknowledged —he could not achieve such a relationship with any real person.[52] He could love and be loved, admire and be admired, even have a stable affectionate family life—but he could not be easy.

It is possible to see, in Crabbe's poems which are based on his opium dreams, how opium provided him with the 'made-on-purpose creatures' that he craved for, but how the real faces would break through these sweetly-smiling masks. In *The World of Dreams* Crabbe sees and rapturously greets his lost love, his trusted friends—and then a doubt creeps in; are the beings that he sees really what they appear?

> 'I know not these—
> All strangers, none to me allied—
> Those aspects blood and spirit freeze:
> Dear forms, my wandering judgment spare;
> And thou, most dear, these fiends disarm,
> Resume thy wonted looks and air,
> And break this melancholy charm!
>
> And are they vanish'd? Is she lost?
> Shall never day that form restore?
> Oh! I am all by fears engross'd;
> Sad truth has broken in once more,
> And I the brief delight deplore.
> How durst they such resemblance take?
> Heavens! with what grace the mask they wore!
> Oh, from what visions I awake!'[53]

That is a more intricate state of mind than the simple longing for the dead in Matthew Arnold's

> 'Come to me in my dreams, and then

By day I shall be well again.
For then the night will more than pay
The hopeless longing of the day'.[54]

Crabbe's stanzas reflect more even than the wretched memories
of his wife's altered personality in her madness.

'How durst they such resemblance take?
Heavens! with what grace the mask they wore'.

The dream provides a cherished safety which is then revealed
as a treacherous impersonation. Crabbe was too sane, too
courageous, too clear-sighted, to take refuge altogether in the
world of 'made-on-purpose creatures' who would be all he
wanted, and only that. For a moment the real faces had seemed
frightful, compared with the pleasing masks, but he generally
knew that it was the real beings that he valued, even if he could
not reach them, and that the made-on-purpose masks had a
fiendish life of their own.

But if he would not give way in his waking life to his longing
for made-on-purpose creatures, for the smiling masks of his
dreams, he made use of the longing in his poetry. One of the
most wonderful of Crabbe's studies of madness, a detailed
portrait of schizophrenia, with its vanity, its shiftiness and its
pathos, 'Fine, and yet cunning! Arrogant, yet sly', is his poem
The Insanity of Ambitious Love, never published till more than a
century after his death.[55] In this Crabbe portrays, side by side,
the real situation of the madman—a former servant, of humble
origins, who presumptuously fell in love with his mistress and
then went mad, and now sits in rags among dust and straw and
spiders' webs in a lunatic asylum, ruled by severe warders—and
the madman's picture of himself. He has found the real world
intolerable, and so he has made for himself a personality of a rich
and irresistible Don Juan, who is now waiting, in a luxury of
Persian carpets and flowers, perfumes and purple velvet, for his
mistress, a beautiful Countess, to escape from her cold tyrannical
husband and fly to his arms. His illusion is not total or permanent;
there is a mixture of genuine pathos and anxiety, and of a
cunning wish to impress and soften his visitors, in his cry, as they
brush aside the refuse in his cell

Practice

'Nay Sirs, what mean you to displace
Those lovely flowers? why angry rise
And now again—those Works deface,
That have such Beauty in her eyes?
O! our dear Gifts'
and a mixture of brutality and insight in the warder's rough reply
'Dost thou indeed thy Lye believe?
Or dost thou think that others can? . . .
But dost thou weep? I know the way
Of Crazy Craft—but will be kind'.

The madman had abandoned reality for his made-on-purpose dream-Countess, but he is still sane enough to recognize at times that his delusion is an escape from the unacceptable.

'His lofty Spirit made him half confess
That Madness lightens or conceals distress'.[56]

It is a penetrating psychological study in which—as in the case of Peter Grimes but in a different direction—Crabbe developed a tendency of his own personality, which his opium dreams had pointed out to him, to its extreme, and embodied it in a madman. It has a curious kinship with Baudelaire's *La Chambre Double* whose opium-soaked narrator sees himself in a softly-coloured softly-scented room hung with flowing draperies, where his 'empress of dreams' lies enthroned on the bed—and then wakes to the reality of sordid poverty and filth and brutal intruders.

Crabbe started taking opium purely for medical reasons, but he had two of the predisposing characteristics of the potential addict—curiosity about abnormal states of mind, and a certain inadequacy in human relationships. He never advanced far enough in addiction to show its more extreme effects, but some can be traced. Though he never lost his perception of the wants and miseries of his fellow creatures, he did become insulated from the possibility of helping them. He could, and did, give them money but he could not give them sympathy; he could listen, but he could not respond. Though he never lost the power to concentrate or to finish his works, there was a certain fragmentation and loss of holding-together in his later poetry. He had always had a keen eye for detail, but the hyperaesthesia of opium may have intensified the poring concentration with which, in his later poems, he conveyed some trivial visual experience. The sad splendour of the flowering weeds in *The Village* is seen in a human context; they devour the poor man's wretched crop of rye, and tear and scratch his ragged children.[57] But the weeds described in *The Borough*, that marvellous patch of intricate forms, textures, sickly smells, acrid colours, are intensely seen for themselves alone.[58] They are introduced as part of the real slums that the reformers never visit, the slums of the undeserving poor, but the connection is not felt, as it is in *The Village*. Crabbe has looked at them with something of the opium-eater's intent concentration on any object, whether or not it is pleasing or unpleasing, significant or trivial, which happens to catch his eye and sink into the sluggish stream of association down which his mind is meandering. 'If a settle by the fire-side stands awry, it gives him as much disturbance as a tottering world; and he records the rent in a ragged counterpane as an event in history'; Hazlitt's comment on Crabbe's poetry was made in malice, but it was percipient, it suggested the intensity of absorption which the opium addict turns on the objects within his sight.[59]

In a footnote on yet another passage, in a still later poem, describing a patch of dull weeds in a marsh, Crabbe said that from this vegetation arose 'effluvia strong and peculiar, half saline, half putrid, which would be considered by most people as offensive, and by some as dangerous, but there are others to whom singularity of taste or association of ideas has rendered it agreeable and pleasant'.[60] 'Half saline, half putrid'—it is such a perfect description of one aspect of his own poetry that it is difficult not to see this passage as a conscious allegory of his own mental tendencies—the salt of his principles and commonsense forever counteracting the morbidity of his sub-conscious feelings. Opium, and the dreams and rêveries it brought, opened to him a realm of emotion which fascinated but dismayed him. He found in it, not a *machine à penser*, but a machine for feeling. His bleak clear-sightedness and self-control enabled him to make use as a poet of some of the special experiences which his opium addiction brought him, though he probably did not recognize their

Practice

source. He was aware only of some corruption at work in his personality, which though it might be revealing to him as a poet, poisoned his relationships with other human beings and impaired his taste by its bias towards violence.

IX

COLERIDGE

'O infinite in the depth of darkness, an infinite craving, an infinite capacity of pain and weakness . . . O God save me—save me from myself . . . driven up and down for seven dreadful Days by restless Pain, like a Leopard in a Den, yet the anguish and remorse of Mind was worse than the pain of the whole Body— O I have had a new world opened to me, in the infinity of my own Spirit!'. That is Coleridge's voice, crying from the depths, in letters written on a December day in 1813.[1]

Samuel Taylor Coleridge may have been given opium medicinally as an eight-year-old child, when he had ague after a night spent in a damp field, or when he had rheumatic fever and jaundice as a schoolboy at Christ's Hospital,[2] but the first time he is definitely known to have taken it is during an attack of rheumatism when he was an undergraduate at Cambridge, in 1791.[3] In March 1796, anxious about his wife's illness and the forthcoming publication of his *Poems on Various Subjects*, he took laudanum every night for a time, as a tranquillizer; this was his first recourse to it for mental, not physical, relief.[4] He took it again in November and December 1796 during a violent attack of facial neuralgia,[5] and in March 1798 to relieve the pain from a decayed tooth.[6] At some time during 1797 or the first half of 1798 he also took two grains of it for dysentery, when he was staying by himself in a farmhouse near Porlock on a very memorable occasion.[7] He may have taken it sometimes while he was in Germany in 1798-9.[8]

These were all occasional doses, mostly for the relief of

physical pain. Coleridge had enough experience of opium by 1798 to be able to speak of the delights of rêverie, of those euphoric states of mind which De Quincey, during his initiatory period, called the Pleasures of Opium.[9] But he was not an addict. He could, and did, go without the drug for long periods without experiencing craving or painful abstinence symptoms. He had no notion that opium was a really dangerous or addictive drug, though he used it occasionally as a metaphor for boredom or self-indulgence or fantasy.[10] He could have given it up altogether without difficulty at this stage, and might have done so, if he had not had both emotional stress and a serious illness in the winter of 1800 to 1801 during his first year in Westmorland.[11] His illness—rheumatism, nephritis, gout, whatever it really was —gave him acute pain and swelling in his feet, knees and back, and he started taking both brandy and laudanum to deaden the pain,[12] perhaps on the advice of a writer in a medical treatise.[13] He never again really stopped taking opium for the rest of his life.

During 1801 and early 1802 he was taking slightly over a hundred drops of laudanum a day, with occasional intermissions of a few days.[14] From late 1802 to late 1803 he succeeded in getting his dosage down to twelve or twenty drops, and taking those mainly when his attacks of diarrhoea (caused, though he did not realize this, by withdrawal from opium) became too violent and exhausting, or his nightmares too dreadful to himself and others—the screams with which he woke from them used to arouse the whole house.[15] By the winter of 1803–4 he had realized that he could not do without opium; he still partly believed that it did him no harm.[16] In April 1804 he left by ship for Malta, and during the voyage he made in his private notebook the admission that he was enslaved, and must try to escape. 'O dear God! give me strength of Soul to make one thorough Trial —if I land at Malta, spite of all horrors to go through one month of unstimulated Nature—yielding to nothing but manifest Danger of Life!'[17]

He did not sustain the trial; the danger of his life if he stopped became from henceforth his excuse for continuing to take opium. He took it throughout his two years in Malta and Italy, and although in a letter of August 1806 after his return to England he referred to his 'former detestable habit of poison-taking', he had not given it up, though he still tried to at intervals.[18] He was now experiencing many of the well-known symptoms of advanced addiction, and of attempted withdrawal from it: the infinite expansion of the sense of time, the inability to complete any project, the restlessness and disgust.[19] In 1808 he took medical advice about his addiction, and broke it off abruptly for a time, but he could not keep this up, and convinced himself that he had been told by the doctors that it would be fatal if he stopped it abruptly and altogether.[20]

His opium habit was now known to most of his friends, partly from his confessions in letters,[21] partly from their own observation. The Wordsworths had seen him half stupefied, unable to finish any major work he undertook, and had sadly concluded that he would never again be utterly free from the drug.[22] When he came back from Malta, Southey noticed how opium had dulled his eyes.[23] Cottle was made suspicious by his trembling hand and sallow face.[24]

He made further attempts in 1812 and 1814, under medical direction, to give up the drug, for he had now completely realized its terrible power over him for evil, and wished that after his death the story of his addiction could be told as a warning to others.[25] But he did not always feel guilty; sometimes he would ridicule the solemn protests of his friends, or shrug off his responsibility by attributing the habit to his poor physical constitution and its unavoidable needs, or claim that his obligation to earn a living made it essential for him to keep himself going by opium.[26]

By April 1816 he was in such a miserable state of physical illness and mental despair that he took medical advice once more about his addiction, and it was decided that he should go and live with a doctor in Highgate who would control his supply of the drug and enable him gradually to leave it off.[27] He remained with Dr Gillman for the rest of his life, and his opium dosage was regulated and reduced though he was never able to do without it entirely.[28] At times he used subterfuges to get extra supplies, without the Gillmans' knowledge, as he had done during an earlier attempt at a cure under Josiah Wade's care.[29] He lived on, in poor health but not as a complete invalid, till 1834, and was nearly sixty-two when he died.

How much opium he actually took—at the beginning, the peak, and the later controlled stages of his addiction—is difficult to determine. The proportion of opium in the laudanum which he took varied considerably; he sometimes gives the quantities which he took by weight and sometimes by fluid measures; he mentions 'enormous quantities' but does not specify them; and the accounts given by others vary. He began with about a hundred drops a day in 1801. At his peak in 1814 he was, according to Southey, taking a quart a week, and sometimes as much as two pints a day, which would be nearly 20,000 drops a day.[30] The chemist's assistant who sold him surreptitious supplies of laudanum in the 1820s when he was with the Gillmans said that he took a 12-ounce pint of laudanum every five days, or about 1,000 drops a day.[31]

The story of Coleridge's opium addiction is further confused by his habit of referring to laudanum as a stimulant. Some medical opinion of his day did regard opium as a stimulant,[32] and in any case the alcoholic content of laudanum acted as a stimulant, even if the opium content acted as a sedative. So when Coleridge speaks of his recourse to stimulants—when, for instance, he maintained in his notebook that he took stimulants to quieten mental agitation and ward off nightmares—he may have meant brandy or laudanum or both.[33] Moreover he felt that moral and physical agents which acted as stimulants to other men, had a narcotic effect on him.[34] He never really applied his wonderful powers of self-observation and self-analysis to the task of identifying the effects of his opium habit on himself.

Perhaps the task would have been too painful, and would have told him things that he could not bear to hear; perhaps he deliberately refrained, from conscientious motives, as Humphrey House suggested when he said of Coleridge 'Nor did he ever build up his opium-taking as a virtue of psychological and romantic experimentalism; he never failed to deplore it'.[35] Sometimes in a confessional outburst he could bare the wounds that the 'dirty business of laudanum' had inflicted on his moral nature,[36] but he did not steadily turn his eyes inward to see by what means, and in what directions, the drug was driving his mind and imagination, as De Quincey—braver and more honest, but less sensitive and with less genius—was able to do. The opium habit was the great preoccupation of De Quincey's life, but it was only one of many elements in the huge complex of Coleridge's thought and emotions. A bucket of crimson dye can change the colour of a pond, but will not have much effect on the sea.[37]

Even when Coleridge did turn his mind in this direction, we cannot necessarily believe what he tells us about it. A tendency to lie about the facts of their addiction is one of the most common of all observed symptoms of drug addicts, and everything that Coleridge, or De Quincey, or Baudelaire, or Francis Thompson, tell us about their addiction has to be considered in that light. But everything of value that we know about any process of a poet's mind depends on what he himself tells us; we have to choose what to believe in the light of what else we know about him. One need not take seriously Coleridge's statements about the order of events connected with the start of his addiction, because everything we know about him shows that dates and times were not interesting to him, and he could very easily get them wrong without intention to deceive.[38] We need not believe all that he says about the causes, amount and duration of his addiction, even though this involves finding him guilty of intentional lying. Truth, unlike dates, was important to Coleridge; but he himself, in some terrible moments of truth, admitted that he would lie, had lied, about his opium indulgence.[39] His memory about subjects that did not interest him cannot be trusted, nor can his truthfulness where he felt an overriding need to conceal his secret indulgence or to present a bearable picture of his moral nature. He was less careful to protect his intellectual integrity from dangerous imputations, and this is the doubtful territory. I do not think we can believe what Coleridge says about the causes of his addiction—he gave too many different causes, and protested too much. Can we believe him when he said that opium did not affect his intellectual faculties? Had he observed himself carefully enough to know?

Coleridge's most consistent excuse for his opium habit was that he took the drug as a necessary pain-killer for a long-standing disease. He insisted, over and over again, that it was not, and never had been, the hope of pleasure, but always the fear of pain, that made him take opium. Like all advanced addicts, he disavowed any memory of the euphoria of the early stages, that 'inchantment' of which he had written in a letter of 1798.[40] As early as 1804, he passionately disclaimed having taken stimulants for the sake of any pleasure 'but only as the means of escaping from pains that coiled round my mental powers, as a serpent around the body and wings of an eagle! My sole sensuality was *not* to be in pain'.[41] From then on he constantly repelled the idea that a search for pleasure had made him resort to opium; his conscience, he said, was clear of having yielded to seduction, to any temptation or desire of pleasurable sensations, any craving after gratification or exhilaration.[42] De Quincey's statement, after Coleridge's death, that he had taken opium as 'a source of luxurious sensations'[43] provoked Gillman into publishing a note of Coleridge's accusing De Quincey of just this morbid quest for the pleasures of opium from which he himself, Coleridge, claimed to be free.[44] But Southey, in a hard and chilly but in the circumstances not unjustifiable diagnosis, agreed with De Quincey; he said that Coleridge imputed his habit to bodily causes, 'whereas after every possible allowance is made for these, every person who had witnessed his habits, knows that for the greater—infinitely the greater part—inclination and indulgence are the motives'.[45] Hazlitt, too, who whatever attacks he made on Coleridge did in his heart continue to look up to him, nevertheless classed him with those 'effeminate' characters who want the fortitude to bear pain, and 'have been so used to a studied succession of agreeable sensations, that the shortest pause is a privation which they can by no means endure—it is like tearing them from their very existence. . . . The mind given up to self-indulgence, revolts at suffering; and throws it from it as an unaccountable anomaly, as a piece of injustice when it comes' and therefore lulls itself back to the 'heavy honey-dew' of agreeable sensations by drinking the 'Circean cup'.[46]

Though Coleridge did not admit the guilt of seeking pleasurable sensations by taking opium, he did admit to 'cowardice and defect of fortitude' in taking it to ward off pain.[47] Sometimes he even went further, and admitted that the opium itself magnified his fear of pains which an undistorted imagination would have seen as quite supportable.[48] But this was a late and rare insight. During all the early years of his addiction, he protested that opium was a necessary protection for him against such extreme pain and nightmare horror as darkened his days and nights, and might even kill him in his sleep.[49]

He hardly ever admitted any possibility that opium might alter the nature of his consciousness in any way that could be enjoyable or even interesting. Once, right at the first, he suggested that it brought an increase of 'ease and spirits'.[50] Two or three times he described pleasant rêveries which seem to have been due to opium; one of them he specifically attributed to it.[51] Once in 1803, he conjectured in a passage whose meaning has been much disputed that opium might in some way, by narcotizing new mental growth, release buried memories and associations.[52] But later letters insisted that his intellectual faculties remained unaffected either way by his opium habit. His 'moral feelings, reason, under-standing and senses' remained as sound and well-intentioned as they had ever been, but his volition had become completely dissevered from them, so that he was like a paralysed man, seeing what movements he ought to make but totally unable to make them.[53] In his letter of April 1816 to Byron, one of the most honest letters he ever wrote, he described opium addiction as a 'specific madness which leaving the intellect uninjured and exciting the moral feelings to a cruel sensibility, entirely sus-pended the moral will'.[54] On rare occasions he speculated that opium might, by making the body more under the control of the mind, enable a man to conceive and bring forth thoughts 'hidden in him before, which shall call forth the deepest feelings of his best, greatest and sanest Contemporaries', but he was not sure this was not delusion.[55] And if there was really a new world buried in the depths of his own spirit, which the drug could open up, what sort of a world was it that lay at the bottom of the infinite abyss?[56]

Unlike many of his contemporaries, Coleridge does not seem to have believed that dreams were a doorway into that other world.[57] 'On Coleridge and his dreams a volume might be written', as Professor Coburn said in her note on Coleridge's nightmare of a woman plucking out his eye.[58] It is indeed surprising that no book has yet, as far as I know, been devoted to the single theme of Coleridge's dream-theory, a marvellous framework of acute observation and thoughtful deduction, tending to show how the operations of the mind in dreams and nightmares explained and illustrated waking states of consciousness. Using the speculations of Baxter, Schlegel and Erasmus Darwin as starting-points,[59] and applying them to his own experience of dreams and nightmares, he elaborated a whole science of dream psychology. He defined the difference between dreams and nightmares and analysed the transition from waking to sleep and from sleep to waking, dream transformations of external sensations, the mechanism of hallucination, the phenomenon of paramnesia, the *déjà vu*. From his observations on the absence of surprise in dreams, and the degree of belief accorded by the dreamer to his dream experiences, Coleridge deduced some of his most wonderful ideas about the reader's response to poetic experience; and in the working of the associative faculty in dreams, he found at least a tentative explanation of the existence of moral evil.[60] A poem on dreams, or at least a section on dreams in a longer poem on *Consolations*, was one of Coleridge's many unfulfilled projects. It perhaps came nearest to fulfilment when he was on his way to Malta, on the magical voyage on which his perceptions were so delicate and vibrant that the light and colour of the sea and the clouds, the movements of the sails, even the patterns on the curtains of his bunk, were fused with his thoughts about the mechanism of dreams. During the voyage he actually sketched out the poem on dreams, which was to start with some lines about dream emotion persisting into waking consciousness, and to go on

to analyse the dreamer's partly pleasurable pity for his own past
self, the way in which the dreaming mind can separate events and
the feelings which they usually arouse, and the transformations
and recognitions of identity in dreams. Although this poem was
never written, the ideas sketched out in the summary were
elaborated in scores of later references in Coleridge's Notebooks,
letters, and published essays and poems.[61] Coleridge's dream
theory is too vast a subject for the present chapter, which is
concerned only with whether his opium habit affected his dreams,
and whether these in turn affected his poetry.

Coleridge himself believed for many years that there was no
connection between his opium addiction and his dreams, indeed
that opium was necessary to ward off nightmares. During his
tour with the Wordsworths in Scotland in September 1803, after
two years during which he had become habituated to opium, he
was troubled with terrible nightmares 'with all their mockery of
Guilt, Rage, unworthy Desires, Remorse, Shame and Terror',
from which he awoke with screams of fear and which over-
shadowed and almost stupefied his waking moments.[62] But he had
had, or told the Beaumonts that he had had, a similar spell of
nightmares nine years earlier, that is, long before his opium habit
started. He even said in this same letter to the Beaumonts that the
first version of *The Pains of Sleep*, his poem describing his nightmares, was written during that earlier spell.[63] In notebook
entries of 1805 and 1806 he claimed that it was the fear of nightmares which drove him to take opium in order to ward them
off,[64] and in a letter of 1809 he strengthened this claim, speaking
of 'that accursed Drug, into which the Horrors of Sleep ante-
cedent to my ever taking it seduced me'.[65] It was not till 1814
that he realized, or admitted, that opium was the cause of his
nightmares, and that *The Pains of Sleep*, which he now said had
been written in 1803, was 'an exact and most faithful por-
traiture of the state of my mind under influence of incipient
bodily derangement from the use of Opium, at the time that I
yet remained ignorant of the cause, and still *mighty proud* of my
supposed grand discovery of Laudanum, as the Remedy or
Palliative of Evils, which itself had mainly produced, and at every

dose was reproducing'.[66] Later still, in 1826, he said that *The Pains of Sleep* had been written 'soon after my eyes had been opened to the true nature of the habit into which I had been ignorantly deluded by the seeming magic effect of opium'.[67] In face of so many conflicting accounts by the author, nothing seems certain except that, whether he knew it at the time the poem was written or not, the nightmares described in it were heightened, if not caused, by opium.

He did undoubtedly suffer from nightmares before he became an opium addict. As a child he had seen 'armies of ugly Things' bursting in on him as he lay in bed, fields full of trampling horsemen in blue who had frightened him into screaming tears.[68] He dreamed vividly during his time at Cambridge and in the army, often the frightening but not uncommon dream of falling over precipices.[69] His early poetry is sprinkled with references to wildly-working dreams, distempered sleep, dreamy pangs in feverous dozes, phantoms seen in sleep; it was something more than the contemporary poetic convention of dream reference.[70] If he had not already been a dreamer, opium could not have stimulated in him the more frightful night terrors which he endured after he became an addict.

The peak of terrible nightmares which he reached in the late summer of 1803, which he described in *The Pains of Sleep* (the first known version of which was sent to Southey in a letter of September 1803 as 'a true portrait of my nights'), may possibly have been symptoms of withdrawal, since in 1802–3 he had reduced his dosage, both in amount and in frequency.[71] The comparative share of opium doses, and of withdrawal from them, in producing nightmares, has been discussed in Chapter II, but both of course have their source in the opium habit, since there can be no withdrawal symptoms without previous addiction. This was the description that Coleridge gave of his nightmares in the first draft of *The Pains of Sleep*

> '. . . the fiendish Crowd
> Of Shapes and Thoughts that tortur'd me!
> Desire with Loathing strangely mixt,
> On wild or hateful Objects fixt:

Pangs of Revenge, the powerless Will,
Still baffled, and consuming still,
Sense of intolerable Wrong,
And men whom I despis'd made strong.
Vain-glorious Threats, unmanly Vaunting,
Bad men my boasts and fury taunting.
Rage, sensual Passion, mad'ning Brawl,
And Shame, and Terror over all!
Deeds to be hid that were not hid,
Which, all confus'd I might not know,
Whether I suffer'd or I did:
For all was Horror, Guilt and Woe,
My own or others, still the same,
Life-stifling Fear, Soul-Stifling Shame'.[72]

Coleridge's notebooks for the months when *The Power of Sleep* was written contain no description of the nightmares with which he was plagued, only an occasional reference to 'screamy' nights.[73] A month later he did note down 'I slept again with dreams of sorrow and pain, tho' not of downright Fright and prostration. I was worsted but not conquered—in sorrows and in sadness and in sore and angry Struggles—but not trampled down. But that will all come again, if I do not take care' which suggests that he had detected some preventable cause for his nightmares.[74]

Most of the nightmares recorded in his Notebooks are less horrific than one might expect. He suffers tasks, wrongs and persecutions which generally turn into his being a schoolboy at Christ's Hospital again, so that he was driven to coin a word for the way in which his nightmares 'X-st-Hospitalized the forms and incidents'.[75] There are nightmares of hands and claws that touched him,[76] and a varying but recurrent one of a demon woman, a tall pursuing harlot who tried to mutilate or infect him.[77] But his worst nightmares seem often to have been experiences of almost abstract essential Fear or Pain,[78] not necessarily connected with any dream subject which would naturally arouse horror; or if such causes were present in the dream, they were slight indeed to have produced such storms of terror as those which woke him with screams that startled all the Keswick household out of their sleep, filled him with dread all day and made him fight against the onset of sleep in the ensuing night.[79] He himself felt that the strength of his feelings was disproportionate to the slight physical sensations—disorder of the bodily functions due to illness, or pressure of the bedclothes or of one part of the body on another—which he saw as the cause of most nightmares. 'In a distempered dream things and forms in themselves common and harmless inflict a terror of anguish' he noted,[80] and surmized that this was due to 'an *aggregation* of slight Feelings by the force of a diseasedly retentive Imagination.'[81] He did not speculate on what had diseased his imagination so as to make it retain and assemble past feelings in this way, and create an accumulation of horror.

Coleridge distinguished between his nightmares, which he seems always to have had in very light sleep, when he was partly conscious of external sensations, and his dreams of deep sleep. He often made detailed notes of both dreams and nightmares as soon as he woke from them, in half-finished sentences which seem to vouch for the unembellished fidelity of his dream records. The actual incidents of his dreams are disappointingly dull—dull, that is to say, as events in themselves, and at first sight as material for poetry; they would be far from dull to a psycho-analyst interested in Coleridge's loves and fears of those nearest to him. They consist of slight encounters and dialogues with his wife and children, Sara Hutchinson, Dorothy Wordsworth, his former school friends, all of them often appearing in disguised forms and yet recognizably themselves. The feelings associated with the dreams—anguishes of anxiety for his children, raptures and tortures of love for Sara—are anything but slight, but Coleridge's power of visualizing and story-telling in dreams seems not to have matched his power of feeling in them.[82] None of the dreams recorded in his Notebooks contain any description of landscapes; the nearest he comes to it are, in a single dream, the sight of some magnificent trees overhanging a wall and 'a broad open plain of rubbish with rails and a street beyond'.[83] A few of his dreams were legendary or allegorical narratives—Duns Scotus making love with the daughter of the King of Truth, Adam murdered by the descendants of Cain, Sir Philip Sidney's wife talking to her maid, a shipwrecked mariner on a deserted island making huge stores of goose-quill pens, the dispossessed orphans of a nobleman begging in the streets.[84] But these are rare examples, thinly scattered in the Notebooks, and Coleridge does not record them with the excitement which he bestows on dreams apparently more trivial and unoriginal. I do not think he would have turned to a dream of his own for the characters and incidents of a poem, as Crabbe did. It was emotion, not beings or landscapes, that overflowed from Coleridge's dreams into his poetry. He once said that poetry was 'a rationalized dream dealing to manifold Forms our own Feelings, that never perhaps were attached by us consciously to our own personal Selves.—What is the Lear, the Othello, but a divine Dream, all Shakespeare, and nothing Shakespeare?'[85]

Some of the emotional themes of Coleridge's dreams would have been present in them, and would have flowed on into his poetry, whether or not he had ever taken opium. Others—who can say how many generous energies—may have been petrified by the drug, and never reached their outflow into poetry. Some few may have been concentrated and heightened by opium. It may even be possible occasionally to trace the process.

One tantalizing hint of how the sequence opium/dream/poem worked, or might have worked, in Coleridge's imagination is given in a notebook entry of 1801. 'Laudanum, Friday Septem. 1801. Poem, dream from Dor.—both dead—feelings after death—seeking the children'.[86] That is all. The poem seems never to have been written, and we shall never know whether Dorothy Wordsworth had the dream, or appeared in it, or even if 'Dor.' stands for her.

That is the nearest to a direct clue that Coleridge provided, but the complete process, culminating in a poem, can be traced with some probability in other instances. One example, among several possible ones, may be given of a dream *motif*, linked with a mental state common among opium addicts, which finally built up to one of Coleridge's most moving poems.

Practice

The dream phenomenon of changed or double identity often earned a paragraph of speculation in Coleridge's letters or Notebooks. He dreamed that Humphrey Davy, mutilated by experiments to enlighten humanity, was a wretched dwarf in a hospital bed, and yet still himself.[87] He dreamed that he saw Dorothy Wordsworth as a fat red-haired woman, and yet he knew her instantly.[88] He dreamed of simular transformations of former schoolfellows, and of his own child, utterly changed and yet keeping their own recognizable individuality.[89] Above all, during his years in Malta when he was taking laudanum frequently, he dreamed under many forms and disguises of Sara Hutchinson.[90] Diverse images and recollections combined to suggest, though not to represent, her idea. He found a word—itself coined in a dream—for this process, a word which is his equivalent of De Quincey's 'involute', the word 'polyolbiosis' which, if it has any precise meaning, may mean 'manifold blessedness', Professor Coburn suggests.[91] Many of his dreams led to Sara although no recollection in them actually referred to her, but in some way the whole dream, as he said, 'seems to have been Her—She'. There was a feeling of a person quite distinct from the image of that person, and 'this Feeling forms a most important Link of Associations—and may be combined with the whole Story of a long Dream just as well as with one particular Form no way resembling the true Image'. In another note, written a few days earlier, he says that all his dreams were in some way connected with Sara, 'all their forms in a state of fusion with some Feeling or other, that is the distorted Reflection of my Day-Feelings respecting her'[92] and that he had 'well described' this dream experience in a poem written at this time

> 'All look and likeness caught from earth
> All accident of kin and birth,
> Had pass'd away. There was no trace
> Of aught on that illumined face,
> Uprais'd beneath the rifted stone
> But of one spirit all her own;—
> She, she herself, and only she,
> Shone through her body visibly'.[93]

Coleridge

Identities disguised, doubled or suffused are a fairly common feature of the dreams of opium addicts, but mostly they are associated with suspicion and resentment. It needed a philosophic mind like Coleridge's to observe these dream phenomena objectively, and a poetic faculty like his to turn them into eight lines of such concentrated simplicity—a faculty, moreover, at the height of its powers. He tried a poem on the same theme twenty-five years later, explicitly stating that it was 'a fragment from the life of dreams', but the intensity had evaporated.[94]

All look and likeness caught from earth perhaps expresses an involute of thought and feeling which had not come alive in Coleridge's imagination till he encountered it in his dreams. Perhaps the opposite process may also be traced, of an image originally alive and distinct in his imagination, which opium dreams distorted.

Most Coleridge scholars would now agree with J. L. Lowes and Elisabeth Schneider, against M. H. Abrams and R. C. Bald, that *The Ancient Mariner* does not show the influence of opium. There seems to be no evidence that Coleridge was taking more than a very occasional dose of opium before early 1798 when *The Ancient Mariner* was finished. Its images may have been partly derived from Coleridge's dreams as well as from his reading, but they were not then opium dreams. The image whose later history in Coleridge's imagination I want to trace, the figure of the Nightmare Life-in-Death, seems to me to have been at that stage an unstabilized image, to which Coleridge's imagination had not yet attached any emotional significance important to him, but which was potentially powerful. Professor Lowes showed where Coleridge found the figure of the white-faced yellow-haired spectre woman in the phantom bark. She came from another man's dream, and was dressed in the trappings of Gothick romance.[95] At first she was neither a nightmare nor Life-in-Death; those were later interpolations. She is peripheral to the central theme of sin and redemption in *The Ancient Mariner*. But she has certain attributes which show the part she may play later. She is an icy terror, that 'thicks men's blood with cold', and she is a vampire terror, at whose aspect

Practice

'Fear at my heart, as at a cup
My life-blood seemed to sip'.

This freezing vampire was, I suggest, beginning to grow into a
being far more powerful and subtle, the icy-bosomed Geraldine
of *Christabel*. Nobody now can say—not even Coleridge himself
was later able to say—what the full significance of Geraldine
would have been if he had been able to finish *Christabel*. Was she
to have been an erring mortal expiating a past sin, or a good
spirit sent to inflict vicarious suffering on the martyr Christabel,
or a reluctant vampire, or a demon lover animating a corpse
who ravishes Christabel, or simply a man in disguise? All these
have been suggested by Coleridge scholars.[96] Whatever she was,
she was the central image of the poem, and Coleridge was unable
to finish it. Was it because this image had been defaced in some
creeping landslide of the imagination? He said later that his
quarrel with Charles Lloyd prevented his finishing *Christabel* and
was the first occasion of his having recourse to opium.[97] The
dates of this do not fit, as the quarrel with Lloyd was in 1797–8,
Coleridge's first recorded opium doses of any importance were
in 1796, and his last additions to *Christabel* and the real start of
his opium habit date from 1800. There was certainly a connection between opium and the breakdown of *Christabel*, but
that took place before the effects of real addiction could have
begun to be felt. No doubt the failure to finish *Christabel* was
mainly due to Wordsworth's lack of sympathy, and the petrifaction of Coleridge's poetic power which dried up all his attempts
to finish the poem was due to other things besides opium. But
one specific difficulty with *Christabel* may have been that the
central figure had lost her mythic energy, by becoming identified
in Coleridge's imagination with another kind of agent, one that
sucked vital force and froze impulse—in fact with opium itself.
Life-in-Death with her yellow locks and her phantom ship seems
to have been recognized by other imaginative writers as specially
appropriate to an opium context—by Poe in *Berenice* whose
opium-addict hero is icily haunted by an emaciated and now
yellow-haired wraith of his beloved; by Keats in the cancelled
first stanza of his *Ode to Melancholy*, which combined a skeleton

ship whose cords were a woman's hair with a suggestion of dull
opiates; by De Quincey in his wild-locked woman in a phantom
pinnace in the opium dream of *The English Mail Coach*. Coleridge's
figure of Life-in-Death now haunted his own nightmares. She
was not called Geraldine, but Ebon Ebon Thalud, and she took
her name from a druggist in the *Arabian Nights*. She was pale and
loathsomely affectionate, and her kiss brought disease.[98] She
stood for other things besides opium; she would be the key to
any psycho-analytic interpretation of Coleridge's sexual emotions
at this time. But the image of the icy vampire coalesced with the
idea of opium, loved and loathed, clinging and freezing. In 1816
Coleridge made the alteration to line 193 of *The Ancient Mariner*
which identified the leprosy-white ghost woman who chilled
the very air around her as the Nightmare Life-in-Death; by then
he knew what agency it was that brought his own nightmares.
The image of the icy harlot had made a strange journey through
the labyrinths of his imagination. It began as a vividly seen but
unidentified being; it might have become a great Daemon; it
sank instead through the operation of opium-inspired nightmares
into the likeness of a sordid temptress; and at last was recognized
and named as the bringer of nightmares.

Opium was a symptom, not a cause of Coleridge's tragedy.
When he wrote *The Ancient Mariner* the tragic process, if it had
begun, had not reached the level of his own consciousness. Joy
was still the air he breathed. It was only later that he came to
feel that *The Ancient Mariner* was, in part and among many other
things, an allegory of what had happened to him, and to identify
the Nightmare Life-in-Death with the poison that brought his
nightmares. *The Ancient Mariner* was one of those prophetic
poems (Tennyson's *Tithonus* was another) in which young poets
unconsciously both see and make the shape of things to come to
their own minds and hearts.

Coleridge speculated at intervals on the way in which dreams
might influence the poetic faculty. 'Dreams sometimes useful by
giving the well-grounded *fears and hopes* of the understanding the
feelings of vivid sense' he wrote in 1796.[99] Already, as early as
this, he foresaw the possibility that a time might come when he

would only see, not feel, the beauty of the world, though it is
surely going too far to say, as some critics do, that this poetic
lethargy had already overtaken Coleridge when he wrote *The
Ancient Mariner*, and was its subject.[100] In a poem of 1794 he had
looked forward to a possible living death in a grave of sloth
nodding with poppies, but that was a momentary half-fashionable
fear, not a dreadful ever-present reality.[101]

By April 1802, when he wrote *Dejection: an Ode*, it had become
necessary to deaden his feelings about his unhappy marriage, his
love for Sara Hutchinson, his lack of achievement, and he had
deadened them by hard study of abstract subjects—and by
opium.[102] But when he had thus deliberately narcotized his feelings, he found that he had killed one part of his poetic faculty.
What suited part of his nature had infected the rest, had suspended his imagination and its power to feel and shape into
poetry the beauty of what he saw. Like other poets—Keats, for
instance—he was tortured by the dilemma that either too much
or too little feeling might damage his poetic power. Many poets
need and are attracted by a certain degree of 'indolence', of not-
feeling, which provides the detachment necessary for poetic
creation; but if it goes too far it will kill their poetic faculty
altogether.

Dejection was actually written during a period of comparative
abstinence from opium, but it records a state of mind created
in part by Coleridge's previous opium indulgence, and familiar
to all intellectual addicts: apathy, indifference, chill, a thought
process still in motion but dislocated from all the feelings which
normally accompany it, a preference for abstract metaphysical
speculations. Coleridge's attitude towards his own loss of feeling was ambivalent, he both welcomed and deplored it. 'I suffer
too often sinkings and misgivings, alienations from the Spirit of
Hope, strange withdrawings out of the Life that manifests itself
by existence—morbid yearnings condemned by me, almost
despised, and yet perhaps at times almost cherished, to concenter
my Being into Stoniness'.[103] At times he not only despised but
was terrified by this creeping petrifaction, and felt that anything,
even his nightmares, which gave him violent feelings was to be

welcomed. In 1803 he wrote to his brother George that he sometimes consoled himself by the notion that 'possibly these horrid Dreams with all their mockery of Crimes, and Remorse, and Shame, and Terror, might have been sent upon me to arouse me out of that proud and stoical Apathy, into which I had fallen';[104] and eight years later when he wrote *The Visionary Hope* he still felt that the violent feelings of terrible dreams were better than apathy.[105]

But opium, which had given or promoted the dreams, had taken away the power to profit from them poetically. His night-mares could give him the illusion of strong emotion, but the abstract unrelated Fear and Passion which he felt in dreams were not real enough to be productive of poetry. The poet could use them only as an actor uses emotion, to produce tragic sounds. There are 'dangers of histrionism', as Coleridge was to write much later, in the unreal feelings produced by an 'ever-working Fancy' unreconciled to the reality of experience.[106] It was use-less to turn to one effect of opium to rescue his poetry from the paralysis of feeling which was another effect of it.

Coleridge wrote to Thomas Poole in February 1801, after the four months of rheumatic pains which started his real habituation to opium, 'I shall look back on my long and painful Illness only as a storehouse of wild Dreams for Poems'.[107] A storehouse, not a factory; dreams were to provide materials for poems, not to write them. The only poem which Coleridge recorded at the time as having been actually composed in a dream is not deathless verse.

'Here sleeps at length poor Col., and without screaming,
Who died, as he had always liv'd, a dreaming:
Shot dead, while sleeping, by the Gout within,
Alone, and all unknown, at E'nbro' in an Inn'.[108]

It is evidence that Coleridge's fear of dying in his sleep really haunted him, and was not just a handy excuse for taking opium; but it is not quite at the level of the *Epitaph* which he composed for himself in later years when broad awake. The actual language of Coleridge's dreams, the words and sentences that he heard spoken, have the slightly clownish ambiguity of all the spoken language of dream. 'He who cannot *wait* for his Reward has in reality not earned it'; 'abomination! the full moon came thundering down from Heaven like a Cannon Ball; and seeing that nothing could be done went quietly back again'; 'Varrius thus prophesied Vinegar at the Door by damned frigid Tremblings'; words like 'polyolbiosis', names like the demon woman Ebon Ebon Thalud—those are the voices that quacked and gabbled in Coleridge's dreams.[109] It is hard to believe that he ever expected or allowed a dreaming mind, which spoke in such language as this, actually to write his poetry for him.

Coleridge's opium dreams and nightmares had little influence, and none that was beneficial, on the main body of his poetry. But opium acted on other states of his consciousness besides his sleep. It was, for instance, closely linked with his observations on the mechanism of sight, specially the sight of flames and patterns of light.

Coleridge was fascinated by flames. In the notes which he made of Humphrey Davy's lectures on chemistry at the Royal Institution in 1802, Coleridge paid special attention to the colours and brilliancy with which the various substances burned: blue flames from cochineal, ether burning 'O! how brightly whitely vividly beautiful in Oxygen gas'; iron wire 'most sparklingly'; sulphur blue white and purple; the steady red flame of wood charcoal; tin burning bright violet or crimson blue; copper, blue shading into green, silver 'brighter with a greenish flame'.[110] He was constantly noting down quotations from other writers and observations of his own about candle light—the varying colour of the flames, the strength of their light, their cone-shaped reflections and coral-shaped shadows.[111] More fascinating still were the ocular spectra which luminous objects left on his retina after he had been gazing at them— purple flashes, green lightnings, crystals of orange violet and green that turned into moss, white phosphorescent fringes and lines, angular purple steams streaked with the colours of flesh.[112]

It was not an aimless curiosity. He was studying the nature of

perception, for a book which he intended to write in collabora-
tion with his friend Tom Wedgwood, a book which would
illustrate the connection between perception and the memory
and imagination, and would explain the hallucinations and
apparitions which are the foundation of many ghost stories.[113]
For the purposes of this work he and Tom Wedgwood, who
suffered from mysterious periods of deep depression, and was an
opium-taker, used both to beguile their sleepless nights of pain
and anxiety by taking notes about their visual and aural perceptions and how these were affected by their states of mind, in 'a
multitude of minute experiments with Light and Figure'.[114]
These observations were undoubtedly affected by the opium that
both men took, and the alteration in spatial apprehension, the
hyperaesthesia and perhaps synaesthesia, which it induced.

A very odd notebook entry of Coleridge's in November 1803
makes this clear. He starts by saying that he had taken a considerable quantity of laudanum, and had been reading in bed.
When he put out his candle, he saw a spectrum patterned like a
pheasant's tail; the pattern altered into round concentric wrinkles
which aroused in him a disproportionate attention and anxiety.[115]
Sometimes the appearance of the spectra was associated with
poetic creation. During his winter of illness at the beginning of
his opium addiction, in December 1800 when he was suffering
from inflamed eyes, 'the act of poetic composition, as I lay in
bed, perceptibly affected them, and my voluntary ideas were
every minute passing, more or less transformed into vivid
spectra'.[116] Those spectra were in effect the living illustrations
of his poetry, the kaleidoscopic colours and crystallizations which
were the visual equivalent perhaps of *Christabel* which he then
still hoped to finish. Three years later, though the spectra still
came, he could no longer effectively link them with 'the act of
poetic composition'. In December 1803 'overpowered with the
Phaenomena I arose, lit my candle, and wrote—of figures, even
with open eyes, of squares . . . and of various colours and I know
not what. How in a few minutes I forgot such an Assemblage of
distinct Impressions, ebullitions and piles of golden colours and
thence to think of the Nature of Memory. So intense and yet in

one Minute forgotten! the same is in dreams. *Think of this*, if *perchance*, thou *livest*—ALAS!'[117]

Opium produced in Coleridge a painfully absorbed attention to visible objects, to sounds, to anything touching him.[118] It also had on him its customary effect of disrupting perceptions of relative size and distance, and here he worked closest with Tom Wedgwood, whose posthumously published paper was concerned with 'Our Notion of Distance'.[119] Coleridge found that a pimple or one of his teeth might feel gigantic to the touch; the fire reflected in the window might seem to retreat to a remote distance beyond the garden outside the window; two leaves at the top of a wall, close to the eyes, could be seen as kites soaring high in the air.[120] This last optical illusion, which Coleridge cited seven years later as an example of 'disease of imagination',[121] is reminiscent of Poe's story *The Sphinx* in which a man half crazy with fear of cholera sees, as he thinks, a huge monster advancing down a far-off hill, which was in fact an insect on the window-sash close to his eyes.

It was perhaps Coleridge's first experience of this phenomenon, noted while his eyes were fixed on a smoking fire in the grate of his room, that produced the draft of a poem which was afterwards to be published in a more decorous form

> 'The poet's eye in his tipsy hour
> Hath a magnifying power
> Or rather the soul emancipates his eyes
> Of the accidents of size.
> In unctuous cones of kindling Coal
> Or smoke from his Pipe's bole
> His eye can see
> Phantoms of sublimity'.[122]

Here perhaps he lays bare the mechanism by which an opium rêverie started. The phantoms of sublimity which took possession of his mind floated off from some object close to his eye.[123] I use the word 'rêverie' in the technical sense defined in Chapter II, as that state of mind experienced in the first stage of opium taking, the state of calm enjoyment, free from anxiety, in which long chains of associated images fluently unwind.

Coleridge

Coleridge put some of his rêveries of this kind on record in his letters and Notebooks. One of these records, his 'flighty' letter of 5th November 1796 to Thomas Poole, seems to have been written while the rêverie was still going on. To cure a violent attack of neuralgia he had been taking twenty-five drops of laudanum every five hours, and the letter he wrote under the influence of these doses is a stream of images and associations in which his imagination, launched off from anxiety, floats down liquid convolutions of hope. Bowls, draughts, clouds, lands of milk and honey, conquering armies, hundred-handed fiends, gnawing wolves, burning-glasses, Tartarean suns, wormwood, toe-nails, barley-corns—image after image flits past, unleashed from the normal control of logical sequence.[124]

A letter written nearly a year later, at what may have been the time he took two grains of opium to check dysentery, describes his current mood as mainly one of calm passivity. 'I should much wish, like the Indian Vishna, to float about along an infinite ocean cradled in the flower of the Lotos, and wake once in a million years for a few minutes—just to know that I was going to sleep a million years more'.[125] He used this Hindu rêverie in various forms in successive drafts of plays; one version reads

> 'Deep self-possession, an intense Repose,
> No other than as Eastern Sages feign,
> The God, who floats upon a Lotos leaf,
> Dreams for a thousand ages; then awaking,
> Creates a world, and smiling at the bubble,
> Relapses into bliss. Ah! was that bliss
> Fear'd as an alien, and too vast for man?'[126]

This passage is an anthology of opium symptoms: the feeling of blissful calm, with a shade of uneasiness appearing at the end as the effect of the dose wears off; the sensation of floating; the 'Buddha-like calm' as one addict quoted in Chapter II put it; the endless prolongation of time so that a million years and a few minutes lie side by side; the insouciant god-like power to create a world and then forget about it.

Two years later, when Coleridge was still only taking opium intermittently and therefore still at the stage of experiencing euphoric rêveries, he wrote to Southey that he had been having attacks of rheumatism, 'but when the pain intermits, it leaves my sensitive Frame *so* sensitive! My enjoyments are so deep, of the fire, of the Candle, of the Thought I am thinking, of the old Folio I am reading—and the silence of the silent House is so *most* and very delightful'.[127] The pain presumably intermitted because he had taken laudanum to deaden it, and he then enjoyed a fire-side rêverie with a folio on his knee. Even in 1803, three years after the start of his opium habit, he had a similar rêverie, perhaps because his comparative abstinence for the last few months had diminished his tolerance for the drug and put him back to an earlier stage of addiction.[128] In this rêverie firelight and the sight of his books and the sound of frosty winds outside combined to launch him into the realm of dreams, a rapture of love and softness and sinking through warm seas, and yet he was awake and his reason still in control.[129]

Coleridge's opium rêveries, enjoyed when he first began to experiment with the drug, were states of relaxed mental enjoyment in which the imagination floated freely from image to image in streamy meanders. He was awake, and aware of external sensations like firelight or the sound of wind, and his reason was serenely present, able to direct and organize the pattern of his thoughts and images. But pain, anxiety and fear had vanished, the sense of time had become elastic, new worlds could be decreed without effort or concern. He summed it all up in a famous letter of 1798 to his brother, describing the waking repose and paradisal enchantments that laudanum conferred.[130]

That letter leads at last to the most wonderful of Coleridge's rêveries. It will have been noticed that I have written twenty-three pages about Coleridge, dreams and opium without mentioning *Kubla Khan*. This was done deliberately. Nearly all discussion of the effect of opium on Coleridge's literary powers begins and ends with *Kubla Khan*. I thought therefore that it would be useful to survey first what is known of the workings of opium on the rest of Coleridge's literary output, and to use any lights thrown by that to illuminate the state of mind that produced *Kubla Khan*.

Coleridge

If Coleridge saw Xanadu in a dream of sleep, it was one very
unlike his usual dreams. It has been shown that his dreams were
about his family and friends and his school, and very occasionally
about historical or legendary figures. They contained practically
no landscapes, and very little sense of place at all—some dim
halls, streets and cloisters which tended to turn into Christ's
Hospital. He occasionally dreamed words and sentences, and
once some lines of poetry, but these were aphoristic or grotesque,
not lyrical and evocative. He often wrote down his dreams immediately on waking but, at any rate after his serious opium
addiction began, the vividness of the dream had often already
evaporated even before he was able to write it down.[131]

His nightmares, to which he had always been subject but
which got much worse after he started taking opium, were
mostly crises of fear produced by dream-guilt and dream-
victimization: guilt over lawless desires felt for objects half-
loved half-loathed, or over vague crimes; victimization by
hostile jeering crowds, by vicious women, by monsters, by Fear
itself.

It seems to me, as to many though not all of those who have
written studies of *Kubla Khan*,[132] that it was in a third type of
incomplete consciousness—neither dream nor nightmare, but
the condition of rêverie which generally seems to have been
associated with Coleridge's early experiments with opium, or
with a renewed dose of opium after a period of withdrawal—
that Coleridge conceived the poem. His own two descriptions of
how it came to be written have been endlessly quoted and
analysed,[133] but I cannot avoid quoting them again. At some date
not known, but probably before 1816, Coleridge wrote down a
version of *Kubla Khan* with a note, 'this fragment with a good
deal more, not recoverable, composed in a sort of Rêverie
brought on by two grains of Opium'.[134] In the explanatory note
which he wrote when he finally published *Kubla Khan* in 1816,
he said that he fell asleep, from the effects of an 'anodyne', while
reading a passage in Purchas's *Pilgrimage* about the Khan Kubla
and his palace, and during 'a profound sleep, at least of the
external senses', composed a poem of two or three hundred

lines. When he woke up, he seemed to himself to remember the whole poem distinctly, and started writing it down, but was interrupted and then found that he had forgotten the rest of the poem.[135] He gave to the poem, when published, the sub-title 'A Vision in a Dream', though the word 'dream' does not appear anywhere in the explanatory note attached to it, which describes the landscape of Xanadu simply as 'a vision'.

This is a very circumstantial account, compared with the brief statement that the poem was 'composed in a sort of Rêverie', and whether we reject one or the other, or try to reconcile the two, must depend on what else we know about Coleridge's dreams and rêveries. The decisive testimony, which has always been recognized and quoted as having a very close connection with *Kubla Khan*, is Coleridge's own description of the kind of rêverie that opium induced in him; a description written, not nearly twenty years after the event like the explanatory note of 1816, but within a few months of either of the two generally accepted possible dates for the writing of *Kubla Khan*. We have seen what Coleridge's dreams and nightmares were like; here is his description of what his opium rêveries were like. 'Laudanum gave me repose, not sleep: but you, I believe, know how divine that repose is—what a spot of inchantment, a green spot of fountains, and flowers and trees, in the very heart of a waste of sands'.[136]

Repose, not sleep—that surely is conclusive. It was the euphoric condition which sets in fairly soon after taking a dose of opium in the early stage of addiction, and which is a waking state; sleep may follow later, several hours after the dose. In most addicts, this condition is no more than a freedom from anxiety, a vague sense of happiness; in a mind and imagination such as Coleridge's, it produced a vision of paradisal beauty.

Of course it did not produce it out of nothing. Perhaps no subject in all literature has been more intensely studied than the sources for *Kubla Khan* in Coleridge's reading, old or new, in the landscapes he had seen, in the fashionable images and literary interests of his day.[137] We know from his Notebooks and from many references all through his works that a wilderness-plot, green and fountainous, far away beyond a desert, was an image that always fascinated him, and would at any time have been a likely starting-point for a rêverie of his.[138] And many entries in his Notebooks show how some object actually before his eyes—the crags and caverns in a glowing fire, the meanders of smoke from coal or candle, the sheen on gold-tooled books, the ocular spectra on his retina when he shut his eyes—may have launched him into a stream of rêverie.[139]

It is safer for anyone who has not devoted a life-time of study to the subject to keep away from the problems of Coleridge's sources and intentions in writing *Kubla Khan*. Coleridge experts become extremely impatient with one another, and still more so with any outsider who ventures into their special field. Irony, and a tendency to claim a down-to-earth factual approach compared with the airy fantasies of previous scholars, are very strong in many studies of *Kubla Khan*. Moreover the temptation to cheat in presenting the evidence is very great. You can prove almost anything by italicizing certain words in a poem and ignoring their context; or by picking out scattered images in a long narrative poem and putting them side by side, and then suggesting that they colour the whole of it and must have influenced any later poet who read it; or by deciding that the poet about whom you are writing was obsessed by a particular shape, and then making almost any mountain, group of trees, cloud, light-effect, building, balloon or head that the poet mentions fit that shape. Interpretation exercises are so enjoyable for the interpreter that he sometimes gets carried away. Try as one may, no book like the present one is quite objective. Quotations chosen, as one thinks, to illustrate the tendencies of someone else's intellect may in fact back-project their light on to shallow, odd or unseemly corners of one's own mind. It is necessary constantly to remind oneself that one of the unmistakable signs of genius is the ability to think of several different things, even several different kinds of things, at the same time. Most of us cannot do this, and have to make an effort to remember that what may seem to us incoherent, till we have reduced it to a single formula, may in fact be meant to contain a number of different significances and intentions, whose affinities—though they do exist within the great family of the poet's ideas—will never be apparent to our narrower minds.

I shall therefore skirt round the problem of the dating of *Kubla Khan*; of whether its main sources were early books about voyages or contemporary poems in the Oriental fashion or landscapes in Devonshire and Somerset; of whether it is to be taken literally, as a description of an unsuccessful attempt to write a poem about a Paradise garden, or symbolically—and if so, what it symbolizes—or psycho-analytically, or simply as a pattern of perfect but meaningless sounds and images. These are the most important points to study about *Kubla Khan*, more important than the one with which alone, in this book, I am concerned: whether opium influenced Coleridge in the writing of *Kubla Khan*, and did so by inducing a special state of consciousness, neither sleep nor full waking.

I must use a rather circuitous way of suggesting how Coleridge's imagination may have given birth to *Kubla Khan* when he was in this special state of consciousness. This circuitous route starts with the question of what we actually visualize when we read *Kubla Khan*. Professor Schneider thought that 'the reader could scarcely draw a map of it' but Mr Humphrey House insisted that though 'nobody need keep this mere geographic consistency of the description prominently in mind as he reads . . . once established it remains clear and constant' and Professor Suther gives a precise account of how he sees the topography of *Kubla Khan*.[140]

If we look at some readers' accounts of their impressions of Xanadu, we do not generally find this map-like distinctness. We may take as an example three early accounts by contemporaries of Coleridge's of their memory of one particular feature in the poem, the sunny pleasure-dome. The earliest of all printed references to *Kubla Khan* is contained in the poem to Coleridge by the actress 'Perdita' Robinson, which was written in 1800.[141] This refers to Kubla Khan's 'sunny dome', but by the end of her poem it has become a 'flaming temple studded o'er With all Peruvia's lustrous store'. Her version of Coleridge's dome was therefore clearly covered with gold-leaf. Charles Lamb, writing a few years later about the mortifying dullness of his own dreams, complained 'There is Coleridge, at his will can conjure up icy domes, and pleasure-houses for Kubla Khan'.[142] Lamb's version of the dome is, like the caves of Kubla's palace, made of ice, and is clearly akin to that ice-palace of the Empress Elizabeth of Russia which was such a modish image of the day—first used by Cowper in *The Task*, then by Coleridge to describe Erasmus Darwin's *Botanic Garden*, then by Hazlitt, then by De Quincey to describe Keats's *Endymion*, then by Carlyle in *Past and Present*. Lamb had not listened inattentively to *Kubla Khan*; he adored it, and could never hear Coleridge recite it too often. 'It irradiates and brings heaven and elysian bowers into my parlour' he declared, but the bowers were visualized according to the pattern in Lamb's own mind.[143] Similarly with Shelley; a drawing of his seems to illustrate *Kubla Khan* and certainly has mountains, trees, water and a building with a dome, and Shelley experts have often linked the dome in *Kubla Khan* with the dome in *Adonais*.[144] But that was a dome of many-coloured glass. Gold, ice or glass—which was Kubla's dome meant to be?

Before I began working on this book, I did a small experiment on myself, an attempt simply to visualize certain features of Xanadu. I began with the sunny pleasure-dome. My first picture was of a sun-*lit* dome, the cupola of the Salute church in Venice on a golden October morning. But this did not satisfy me. Ought it perhaps to be a crystal dome? Here Shelley's dome of many-coloured glass rose above the horizon of my mind, to be rather quickly pushed down below it again; there were unpleasing side-associations with the porches of sea-side lodging-houses with panes of magenta and mustard yellow. But next came a more pleasing vision, that opal bloom which one sees through the rounded glass vaults roofing the Grand Palais in Paris as one drives west along the verge of the Seine at sunset. All the same, I did not want Kubla's palace to merge with Victorian exhibition halls in my imagination, so I switched off and thought about its caves of ice. But the first thing that I incongruously visualized was one of those mossy mounds, still be to found in woods near country houses, in which the blocks of ice used to be stored in the summer. An effort for more congruous images only produced a mental reproduction of William Marlow's picture of Saint Paul's with a gondola-studded canal running up Ludgate Hill towards it. Visualization of the pleasure-dome seemed to be getting me further away from it, not nearer; so I turned to the Abyssinian maid and the dulcimer. Most of us, I believe, have a mental picture of the damsel flitting about with something in the nature of a lyre or a lute, and here again it proved a great mistake to visualize her too distinctly, because as I did so, I recalled what a dulcimer really is—a flat box up to three feet wide, standing on a table or on its own legs, most definitely not portable, and played with two hammers. If Coleridge really knew what a dulcimer was, and did not simply choose an instrument with a beautiful name, we must imagine the Abyssinian maid warbling away while wielding a couple of padded hammers, a set concert performance which is not at all what one had imagined or wished for in *Kubla Khan*.

My own attempts at visualization having failed so sadly, I turned to a friend, the daughter of a poet and herself an art historian whose visual sense is very keen. She told me that she had known *Kubla Khan* by heart ever since she was a child, but that it had always been the sound alone that had affected her, and that it was not till, in her late forties, she went to China and flew over a winding river not far from the real Xanadu, that the words 'meandering with a mazy motion' became visual to her at all.

Next I decided that if it was really to prove anything, the experiment ought to be tried out on minds free from all clutter of literary associations, minds that had never heard of anodynes and persons from Porlock, of Bartram or Purchas or the Old Man of the Mountains, and had never read a word of Coleridge biography or criticism; minds to whom *Kubla Khan* was a new poem on a page in a schoolbook, with no background at all.

A friend who teaches English in a secondary school obligingly tried my experiment on one of her junior forms. They were asked simply to read the poem and then describe Kubla's palace and park as though it were a Stately Home which they had just paid half a crown to visit. Although most of them simply wrote a short prose summary of the poem, there were some surprising variations. A quarter of them thought that the dome was reflected in the sea (which one of them firmly identified as the Black Sea) and two of them arranged the fountain and the caves on one side, with the river running out of them past the palace to the sea. Two of them thought that the walls and towers were part of the domed palace. Two thought that the dome was of glass, but looked like ice, while a third said that it was miraculously turned into ice in the course of the poem. The most imaginative of the essays ended with an Atlantis vision— 'Through the noise of the river Kubla seemed to hear a voice telling him that the lovely palace was to be drowned in the dark ocean. It would be a rare achievement, a sunny pleasure dome under the water, with walls of ice'.

It may perhaps be said that in these cases the innocent eye was chiefly the inattentive eye. But if we turn to the scholars, there is still the same confusion. Mr Robert Graves, following Professor Brandl, introduced a fond recumbent couple who are not in the poem at all. These trespassers were rightly banished with contumely by Professor Lowes.[145] But Lowes himself does not seem perfectly clear about the topography of Xanadu; his caves of ice are sometimes beside the fountain in the deep romantic chasm and sometimes attached to the stately pleasure-dome, which is usually supposed to be half-way between the fountain and the opposite caverns measureless to man.[146] But his dome also moves about; on page 286 of *The Road to Xanadu* it is close to the fountain, but on page 406 it is beside the waters where they disappear into the measureless caverns. This would not have worried Lowes, who thought the whole thing was a dream and therefore un-mappable, but it would worry those who regard it as a clear waking description of a landscape. Professor Lowes also gave great pain by referring to the flashing-eyed figure at the end of *Kubla Khan* as 'the Tartar youth'. Miss Maud Bodkin recorded that this gave her a 'shock of surprise' and Professor Schneider rejected it altogether; for both of them the figure is the poet himself.[147]

Practice

The conclusion of this digression is that we are likely to give shocks to ourselves and each other if we try to visualize the details of this poem. This shimmering impression in *Kubla Khan* is often called phantasmagoric and dream-like, but it is not really like a dream—not like Coleridge's dreams, anyway, which were not about landscapes at all, precise or otherwise. Those like myself who do dream about landscapes often see them with detailed distinctness. In my dreams I have seen landscapes of which it would be easy to draw a map, if I could draw at all. The shape of the coast-line, the disposition of hill and valley, forests and grassy uplands, were perfectly clear; the lines of the canals could have been plotted, and the sites of the huge castles related to their surroundings. The magic of *Kubla Khan* does not come from such ordinary dream visions as these. It arises out of a mental state far rarer than the vivid landscape dreams which many of us enjoy; a state in which it is the essence of forest and river, cave and fountain, that is perceived, not individual trees and stretches of water and cave-openings. It has often been pointed out that there are only two colour words in *Kubla Khan*, 'greenery' and 'green'—and yet most people's impression would be that it is full of the play of colour, lights moving across colours and shining through them. The idea of colour is given, without the mention of it.

These are not at all the impressions that we get from much of Coleridge's poetry. When he wanted to, he could make the reader visualize with almost painful distinctness. It is hard to say, for instance, which colour is more instantly and unforgettably vivid—the 'still and awful red' of the charmed water in *The Ancient Mariner* or the 'peculiar tint of yellow green' in the western sky in *Dejection*. But *Kubla Khan* is a different kind of poem, arising out of a different kind of consciousness. Describing how he composed *Kubla Khan*, and speaking of himself in the third person, Coleridge wrote that he spent three hours in a chair, in a 'sleep of the external senses', composing two to three hundred lines of poetry 'if indeed that can be called composition in which all the images rose up before him as *things*, with a parallel production of the correspondent expression, without

any sensation or consciousness of effort'.[148] This sou[n]
much like the phenomenon which he described in D[e]
1800 when, after taking laudanum to dull the pain in
flamed eyes, he found that the act of composing poetry
on his eyes, which perceived ocular spectra correspon[d]
his poetic ideas.[149] Images, with a parallel production
correspondent expressions; ideas, transformed into vivid s[...]
in both cases, the words and some visual equivalent of th[e]
are being produced simultaneously in parallel.

Speaking of the hypnagogic imagery which is often s[...]
children and adults on the borders of sleep, Professor Scl[...]
suggested that though this experience is not peculiar to
addicts, they may enjoy it for longer stretches at a tim[e]
normal people do.[150] Edgar Allan Poe, it will be remem[...]
valued these hypnagogic visions so intensely that he s[...]
trained himself to revert to full wakefulness when h[e]
experienced them, so as to be able to 'transfer them in[...]
realm of Memory'.[151] De Quincey in his opium rêveries
think of anything 'capable of being visually represente[d]
immediately see it so represented in a hypnagogic vision,
which it recurred in his dreams and by them was drawn o[ut]
'insufferable splendour that fretted my heart'.[152] It seem[...]
sible that the special kind of rêverie which Coleridge and
opium addicts enjoyed was a prolonged experience, lasti[ng]
hours, of what in the normal person lasts only for a few sec
Most addicts can produce nothing of value out of this rare
dition, which is neither sleeping nor waking, because they
not got the imagination, the memory, the learning of a Cole[r]
He, with his external senses switched off but his mind still a[...]
and able to observe the linked words and images unwi[...]
simultaneously out of itself, was able to produce at least a
of what was to become Kubla Khan. I do not believe th[...]
emerged complete, word for word as it now stands, fro[m]
rêverie. Its pattern of images and sounds is too polished for
to be possible. He must have worked on it afterwards. Bu[t]
outline emerged from a rare condition produced in hi[m]
opium, and because of that rare condition it has an excepti[...]

effect on its readers. We do not find in it anything that we all recognize as the same, or of which we say to ourselves 'How truly that expresses something that I have often felt'. Examining my own response to *Kubla Khan*, I can find nothing more sophisticated than an impression that it is a vital code message, only partly deciphered, in a language that we are perhaps not allowed to read. But because it is only partly deciphered, we can all find in it whatever we ourselves need and are looking for —a dream, a symbol, a diagram of the creative imagination, a paradise. If you believe in the Paradise of God, you can find that in it; if you believe in nothing but the human body, you can find that too.

Professor I. A. Richards said that it was a 'fraud', when writing about Coleridge, to 'put a ring-fence round a very small part of his thought, and say "We will keep inside this and leave the transcendental and the analytic discussions to someone else" '.[153] I have committed that fraud, because I feel that Coleridge's practice of the imaginative process was more beguiling, if not more important, than his theory about it, and that one can be a gardener without being a soil expert. But I have been concerned with only a small corner of Coleridge's enormous mind, and I have not forgotten that there are vast, and more momentous, tracts beyond this shadowy little valley, about which I have written no more than a footnote to Coleridge's main achievement. But even as a footnote it would not be complete if it ended with *Kubla Khan*. He wrote that poem when he had barely begun to indulge in opium, and had enjoyed only its initial and most transitory pleasures, not yet its pains. After seventeen years of addiction he wrote a poem which to me, far more than *The Pains of Sleep*, suggests the real horrors experienced by the advanced opium addict.[154] It was written during a withdrawal period, in the year after Coleridge had gone to live with Dr Gillman, who had reduced and regulated his opium doses; it was a time of 'misery, sickness, despondence' for Coleridge.[155] The poem was connected with the idea of Purgatory, with an attack on materialism, and with insights gained from dreams,

such as the one which produced *All look and likeness caught from earth*. It is an unfinished fragment, and whatever its ostensible subject, it seems clear what kind of experience it was that he was actually describing. The poem—one draft of which contains some incoherent lines about a creature grotesquely and rather horribly described as a 'skin-pent Druggist'[156] frightening even ghosts as it skims across Acheron—is about a Limbo, a state in which souls shrink, and cower underground away from Light, 'the natural alien of their negative eye', an enemy which they can synaesthetically hear as well as see. There is no normal experience of Time and Space, which are 'Fettered from flight, with nightmare sense of fleeing'. This Limbo is

> 'wall'd round, and made a spirit-jail secure,
> By the mere horror of blank Naught-at-all'.

It is a condition of 'growthless dull Privation', and its only way out is downwards, into absolute and endless Fear. It is the world that Piranesi depicted, and Coleridge and De Quincey both recognized as a world they knew, the underground temple of opium.

X

DE QUINCEY (II)

'Oh, what do you see, dear? What is it that you see?'. The voice this time was the frightened cry of a spectator, De Quincey's wife, as she woke him from the agonized nightmares inflicted on him by opium, which made him shudder and scream in his sleep, and carry back into his waking life a look in his eyes that made Carlyle say that he must have 'been in hell'.

Between the ages of two and four, Thomas De Quincey suffered from ague, or malaria.[1] He later wondered whether he had been given opium at this very early stage, in the form of paregoric elixir, to cure this and other nursery ills, but concluded that this was unlikely.[2] There is no certain record of his ever having recourse to opium until he was an undergraduate at Oxford. His account of the rainy Sunday in the autumn of 1804 on which he first tasted opium is famous. He was in London, and had been suffering from violent neuralgia for three weeks; on the advice of an undergraduate friend he went to a chemist in Oxford Street, and bought less than a shilling's worth of laudanum. Returning to his lodgings he swallowed some of it, and within an hour experienced not only relief from pain but also 'an abyss of divine enjoyment'. Thus early, even at his first taste of the drug, did he associate it with a downward glance into the 'lowest depths of the inner spirit'. He had been admitted, as he put it, to 'the Paradise of Opium-Eaters', to 'celestial pleasures', but this inward paradise was already solemn, shadowy, subterrene.[3]

For nearly ten years he took opium only at intervals, generally once in three weeks, when he indulged himself in what he called an 'opium evening' in London, on a Tuesday or Saturday night. He timed his dose of laudanum so that he would feel its full effect of stimulus and serene glow of pleasure when he was in the midst of the two favourite enjoyments of these opium evenings, listening to the opera or walking about the streets among the crowds of shoppers. This effect lasted eight to ten hours with him, and the final narcotic effects of the dose only came on late at night when he had returned home to bed.[4]

This practice, most unusual for opium takers, of seeking crowds of people among whom to experience the effects of the drug, belonged only to the first few years of De Quincey's opium habit. The later rêveries of that first period of addiction were more often indulged in solitude.[5] But his opium indulgence was not always, even at this period, quite the planned and spaced experiment in pleasure that he described in *The Confessions of an English Opium Eater*. When he was faced with his final examinations at Oxford, he took a large dose of opium, the effect of which was to make him do brilliantly in a translation test that day, and much impress the examiners; but in the reaction of the evening when the drug wore off, he was unable to face the thought of the *viva voce* examination next day, and fled to London, forfeiting his chance of taking a degree.[6]

During these years, when he believed himself to be suffering from incipient tuberculosis, and undoubtedly did suffer from neuralgia, toothache, and various forms of gastric troubles, he also took laudanum medicinally.[7] He later maintained that all through this period when he was taking opium intermittently, he felt no ill-effects; while under its influence he was in an equable glow of pleasure, with his mental faculties stimulated but serene and well-ordered, and his affections benevolent and steady; and when the effects wore off he felt no depression of spirits.[8] He lost all sense of time; everything that he saw, heard or remembered was rejected, selected or re-arranged to fit in with his happy mood.[9] The patterns of feeling thus arranged became the constituents of future dreams and the imagery of future writings.[10]

In 1812, three years after he had moved permanently into the

Wordsworths' former cottage at Grasmere, De Quincey was still taking opium only once a week on Saturday nights.[11] But after a year of mental stress over the death of little Kate Wordsworth, and of physical suffering from a renewal of his gastric disorder, he began in 1813 to take opium daily instead of weekly,[12] and during the next three years his dosage rose to a peak of 320 grains, or 8,000 drops, of laudanum a day.[13] A writer who saw him in Edinburgh in 1815 said that he was then taking opium daily 'as an article of food' but that it had not yet told on his constitution or his wonderful powers of conversation.[14] Lockhart remembered De Quincey helping himself to opium pills from a snuff-box as he sat at dinner.[15] His addiction was now known to all his acquaintances, and was severely criticized by his neighbours and former close friends the Wordsworths, who had already suffered much grief over Coleridge's addiction to the drug.[16] Coleridge himself had suspected De Quincey's addiction much earlier, at the time of their first meeting in 1807, or so he afterwards claimed.[17]

In 1816, under the influence of Margaret Simpson by whom he had a son in that year and whom he married the following spring, De Quincey reduced his opium dosage to a thousand drops a day, and this had the effect of dispelling the 'cloud of profoundest melancholy' which had been resting on his brain, and he was able to resume his philosophical studies and to enjoy a happy year, shut up with his Margaret in the secluded cottage with its views of lake and mountains, until about the middle of 1817.[18] Then he began again to increase his dosage, perhaps eventually to as much as ten or twelve thousand drops a day.[19] The description of the effects of these huge doses—the lethargy, the gloom, the frightful dreams, all the 'Pains of Opium' which he then experienced—is one of the most famous and much-quoted passages of his *Confessions*. Less well known, but equally poignant, is an account of this time which was never published in his lifetime. 'At length I grew afraid to sleep; and I shrank from it as from the most savage tortures. Often I fought with my own drowsiness, and kept it aloof by sitting up the whole night and following day. Sometimes I lay down only in the day-time, and sought to charm away the phantoms by requesting my family to sit round me and to talk, hoping thus to draw an influence from what externally affected me into my internal world of shadows; but, far from that, I infected and stained, as it were, the whole of my waking experience with the feelings derived from sleep'. The beings that he saw in his nightmares were so real and so terrible to him that his wife, unable to bear his groans, would wake him from his sleep by her terrified inquiries what it was that he saw.[20]

In 1819 he was taking varying amounts of laudanum a day, between a thousand and four thousand drops. During 1820 and 1821 he got his dosage down to a much smaller amount, about three hundred drops a day.[21] In 1821 he wrote and published *The Confessions of an English Opium Eater*. To sustain him through the effort of writing it he was forced at times to step up his opium doses;[22] but in the following June he started a determined effort to give them up entirely. He did not succeed in stopping altogether and for good, but he greatly reduced his dosage, sometimes getting it as low as fifty drops a day and once managing to do without it altogether for ninety hours.[23] He suffered all the wretchedness of withdrawal—restlessness, insomnia, sneezing, loss of appetite, breathing difficulties, stomach cramps. Multitudes of thoughts, released from the long mental apathy of his deep addiction, streamed through his brain, but he was too exhausted and restless to write them down. Depression and disgust enveloped everything that he read or wrote.[24] Through all this time he was struggling to write articles and reviews, for his financial situation had become desperate, and he had to earn the money to keep himself and his growing family. He was torn between evils; if he gave way to his craving for opium, it would temporarily give him the stimulus which he had to have to finish the work which he was doing; but he would pay heavily later for any increase in his dosage. One can get a strong and sad impression of De Quincey's struggle during these years from a scrap of paper which is now in the Wordsworth Library at Grasmere—a letter of De Quincey's to the publishers Taylor and Hessey apologizing for his delay in sending a manuscript, which ends 'I must beg you to excuse the stains of laudanum etc which I hope have not made it more difficult to read'. This scrap of paper is marked with brown spots which may also be laudanum stains.

In 1825 De Quincey announced to a friend 'I am quite free of opium'.[25] Reports from his contemporaries make it clear that this was only comparatively true. He had got his daily dose down to a fraction of what it had been at the peaks of 1813–6 and 1817–9, but it was still a daily dose. For the next twelve years he was working hard as a journalist, mainly in Edinburgh with occasional returns to Westmorland, to make a living for his family. Constantly in debt, shifting from one lodging to another, not knowing where the next meal was coming from, the De Quinceys were nevertheless a loving and united family, until two of the sons and then their mother died in the years from 1833 to 1837.

Then De Quincey relapsed again into deep addiction to opium.[26] His daily doses of laudanum were now of ever-increasing size, and anxiety and under-nourishment made him prone to illnesses which were complicated by the effects of laudanum.[27] By 1843 he was again taking enormous doses—eight, ten, even twelve thousand drops of laudanum a day.[28] In the summer of that year he began to feel that the weight of misery and abhorrence of life was insufferable, and at last to acknowledge—as he had never fully done before, and as he was again to deny even later—that even when taken in moderation 'laudanum might be the secret key to all this wretchedness'.[29] That autumn he embarked on a grim struggle to rid himself of his opium habit.[30] He got his dosage down to a hundred drops a day, but had to increase it again, his sufferings were so great.[31] By the summer of 1844 he had stabilized his dosage at about 150 drops a day, and for the rest of his life he never much exceeded that amount.[32] In November 1848 he made one more effort to give up the drug altogether, and abstained completely for sixty-one days.[33] During that time, among all the miseries of withdrawal, he had one or two intermissions of wretchedness which seemed to him to foretell the possibility of complete emancipation and which, as will be seen later, provided the theme for one of the finest of his prose-poems.

But he did not keep it up. The agonies of withdrawal were so insupportable that he decided that total abstinence was impossible for him.[34] He returned to his 150 drops a day, but diluted in water.[35] In 1854, sending an account of his expenses to his daughter, who now managed all his money affairs for him, he totted up washing, laudanum and library subscription as three equally normal items of expenditure, and in these years the laudanum decanter was placed on the dining-room table for him to help himself from, whether or not guests were present.[36] Sometimes he would step up his dose, to enable him to get through a burst of work.[37] His notes in the last three years of his life to his Edinburgh publishers, who were bringing out a collected edition of his works, give a painful impression of anxiety, confusion, loss of memory, as he apologizes for delays and muddles in returning proofs. Working in a room smothered in heaped-up papers, through which he rummaged in weary desperation for missing notes and proofs, he needed more laudanum to enable him to deal with the chaos which laudanum itself had caused.[38]

Late one summer night in 1854 a friend found him on the Dean Bridge at Edinburgh, gazing at the sleeping city, the hills and the sea. He should have been at a dinner-party given by friends, but he had been unable to summon up enough spirits for it. Nothing but a large dose of laudanum, he said, could give him the energy to meet obligations either for work or for social engagements, but he dared not repeat such doses too often, and the intervals were times of misery. 'Oh, my God' he burst out to his appalled friend 'the miseries I have been born to endure; what tortures I have suffered, and what tortures am I yet doomed to suffer!'[39]

The last six pages have recorded the struggle and failure of one side of De Quincey's life, but it was not the only side. The hardworking and much admired writer, the formidable long-winded historian and philosopher, the affectionate and courteous friend, the loved and loving husband and father, the sometimes malicious critic, the joker and punster, the man who walked twenty miles a day, the man who died a Christian death, have not been shown. De Quincey was something more than the Opium Eater, but it is only with the Opium Eater that this book is concerned.

As has been seen, the waxing and waning of De Quincey's opium habit can be fairly precisely dated, and if there were any correlation between them and his literary output, it should be easy to demonstrate. De Quincey himself at times, and some of his contemporaries, seem to have thought that he wrote best when most drugged—'whilst the opium was trickling from his mouth' as Hazlitt brutally put it—and some modern biographers agree with this.[40] But it has also been suggested in recent years that the opium addict writers are productive chiefly in their withdrawal periods.[41] The comparative dates in De Quincey's life do not confirm either conclusion. *The Confessions of an English Opium Eater* was written in the summer of 1821; De Quincey had been gradually reducing his dosage during the previous two years, but in order to get through the writing of the *Confessions* he had to step up his doses again.[42] The years 1823–4, immediately following the sharp reduction of his opium consumption in 1822, were productive, but not of any work of much interest except *On The Knocking on the Gate in Macbeth*. In February 1825 he announced that he was 'free of opium'; but for eighteen months after that his literary output was negligible. Between 1827 and 1840—that is, during a period of low but steady opium consumption and then, in the last three years, of rapidly increasing dosage—he produced some of his best work: *Murder Considered as One of the Fine Arts, Klosterheim, Reminiscences of the Lake Poets*, the first version of his *Autobiographic Sketches, The Revolt of the Tartars*. He began to write what he himself considered potentially his masterpiece—*Suspiria de Profundis*—in July and August 1843, some months before the start of the withdrawal period which brought his dosage down to the mild level of his last years.[43] But probably the main part of it was written in 1844 and early 1845, that is, towards the end of a withdrawal period. *Coleridge and Opium Eating, Joan of Arc, The Spanish Military Nun*, were written in 1845–7, that is, during a period of reduced but steady opium habit. *The English Mail Coach*, a continuation of *Suspiria* which was published in 1849, was almost certainly planned in November 1848 during a two-months' abstinence from opium, but may have been written after he resumed the habit.

There seems, in fact, to be no discernible correlation between the writing of De Quincey's finest works and the state of his opium habit at the time. The most that can be said is that he did not produce any of his longer works—the *Confessions*, the *Autobiographic Sketches*, the *Suspiria*—when he was at the peak of addiction. But partial withdrawal, total abstinence, a low but steady addiction, or intermittent boosts, seem all to have been propitious to his creative powers at one time or another. De Quincey's case reinforces the conclusion that opium neither promotes nor inhibits literary output; it only influences the kind and quality of what is put out.

The theory of the influence of opium on the literary imagination owes more to De Quincey than to any other writer. He gave a quantity of information about what he believed to be its effect on his mental powers. But little material exists from which any objective test of his theory can be made in relation to his own writing.[44] Not many of his letters survive, and the accessible ones are scattered among various memoirs and biographies, in which they are often quoted in mutilated form, and undated. Except for a few months of his life, before he took to opium, he kept no diary; and though he kept whole rooms-full of notes, none of these have survived to be published with the devoted scholarship which has, for instance, been accorded to Coleridge's Notebooks. Moreover he produced no literary works before he became an opium addict, so it is not possible to compare his writing before and after the opium habit started, and then to isolate what might be the effects of opium. The only surviving extended example of De Quincey's writing before he took to opium is the diary which he kept from April to June 1803, when he was living in lodgings at Everton, near Liverpool, after his spell of lonely poverty in London and before he went to Oxford.[45]

Practice

This diary has been interpreted in completely different senses in recent studies of De Quincey.[46] Professor Schneider, in her *Coleridge Opium and 'Kubla Khan'*, contended that the diary shows that all the material for the dream fantasies of the *Confessions of an English Opium Eater* was already present in De Quincey's imagination at this time, before he ever started taking opium. The diary certainly mentions some of De Quincey's main imaginative patterns—the idea that rêveries of suffering are educative, the image of a girl dying in summer-time, the image of a romantic outcast.[47] But these images as presented in the diary were simply part of the romantic paraphernalia of the day, and would probably have been found in the diary of most imaginative youths of seventeen in 1803, and they are combined in De Quincey's diary with a good many other Romantic stage properties which do not re-appear in De Quincey's later work—feudal banquets and carousals, Chatterton on his death-bed, a dark-skinned hero (very unlike his later dream-horrors of the villainous mahogany-dark Malay), a shipwrecked man on a rocky isle, and so on. All that the 1803 diary can show is the repertory of images and ideas from which De Quincey's dreaming mind, under the influence of opium, was later to select those imaginative patterns which conform to the opium addict's mental landscape.

The main effect from opium which De Quincey himself detected in his imaginative process has been analysed in Chapter V. He thought that opium promoted and intensified the dreaming faculty, and that dreams crystallized memories and feelings, particularly feelings of grief, into symbol-patterns, or 'involutes' as he called them.[48] His mind, 'at once systematic and labyrinthine' as Coleridge finely described it,[49] had a special power of 'feeling in a moment the secret analogies or parallelisms that connected things else apparently remote'[50] and thus to produce involutes of feelings and images. These involutes were educative; they interpreted experience, his own and others', to him, and the experience thus crystallized into patterns could then be communicated in literature.

This theme, of the formation of character by sorrow which has been integrated into the imagination, was to be the central idea of his *Suspiria de Profundis*. The key to the whole of this work is the fragment called *Levana and Our Ladies of Sorrow*. De Quincey saw the Roman goddess Levana as the personification of the educative power which 'by passion, by strife, by temptation, by the energies of resistance, works for ever upon children'.[51] De Quincey personified the 'agencies of grief' through whom Levana works on the human personality as three sisters, three Ladies of Sorrow, each of whom was to reign over one section of the experiences, rêveries and dreams which were to make up *Suspiria de Profundis*.[52]

The first of these, Mater Lachrymarum, was to preside over the account of those afflictions of childhood which, in De Quincey's imagination, gathered up into the involute which is made up of a girl child dying in summer as a sacrifice to human cruelty or indifference.[53] Into this involute clustered many poignant memories of his childhood and youth: the death of his sister Jane after ill-treatment by a servant, the death of his sister Elizabeth and the sight of her body in a room flooded by summer sunshine,[54] the deaths of two deaf and dumb girls ill-treated by their parents,[55] the misery of the neglected child-servant in the house in Greek Street where De Quincey slept in his days of destitution in London,[56] the death of Wordsworth's little daughter Kate,[57] and at last, two contrasted girls who drew together all the threads of these emotions of De Quincey's—the prostitute Ann of Oxford Street, and the Westmorland farmer's daughter whom he loved and married and who died, still young, but worn out by suffering and by what De Quincey felt was the heartless ostracism that she had endured from his friends.[58] Linked with these sorrows were images of a grave heaped with gorgeous tropical flowers,[59] of the breathless hush of a midsummer noonday,[60] of stained-glass windows and organ music,[61] of tribunals at which suffering innocence was arraigned, and sometimes vindicated,[62] of Palm Sunday and the name of Jerusalem [63] and the Sacrifice of the Last Supper on which De Quincey's mind dwelt as he lay dying.[64] This involute first reached literary form in the lovely dream in the *Confessions* of the dawn landscape of mountains and hedges of white roses, an

Practice

Easter Sunday and yet a summer one, which turned into a vision of the Holy City with its domes and cupolas, and there under the palm trees was the lost Ann.[65] It came again in *The English Mail Coach*, in the sacrificial sufferings of the girl child and the triumphant organ music of resurrection,[66] and in *The Daughter of Lebanon*, when the outcast Eastern woman, dying with her eyes on a sky of cloudless blue, found redemption.[67] Among fragments unpublished during De Quincey's life are others which embody this theme and which would have been included in the complete *Suspiria*, according to a list which he left.[68] One of these fragments has a haunting title, *Who is this Woman that beckoneth and warneth me from the Place where she is, and in whose Eyes is Woeful remembrance? I guess who she is.* It is a vision of his cottage in Westmorland in summer dawn-light and of the woman who stands at its door, with eyes full of tortured innocence, a vision of his wife and all that she was to bear for his sake, which he claimed to have seen in dreams before ever he saw her or Westmorland.[69]

This group of memories and images, worked into an imaginative pattern by the action of dreams and then written into prose-poems, was to make up the first section of *Suspiria de Profundis*. After a second expository section was to come the third part, over which Mater Suspiriorum reigned and which was to be called *The Pariah Worlds*.[70] De Quincey's sympathy for the outcasts of human society—so influential, through Baudelaire, on the French Symbolists—pervaded his dreams and wound itself up in all his involutes. Many of the suffering daughters of Mater Lachrymarum were also pariahs, subjects of Mater Suspiriorum; they were solitary, neglected, abandoned, abused, like the deaf and dumb twins or the servant in the Greek Street house or, above all, like the prostitute Ann who became, in De Quincey's dreams, the type of 'a lost Pariah woman' pursued by 'some shadowy malice which withdrew her, or attempted to withdraw her, from restoration and from hope'.[71] De Quincey's instinctive sympathy with the rejects and misfits of society was an early and a lifelong feeling. Perhaps it dated from that moment in his childhood when he and his brothers and sisters, playing in their garden, saw beyond the brook which bounded their lawn a mad dog, its eyes glazed with desperation, being hunted along the lane by a shouting mob.[72] This incident, coinciding with the departure of his bullying elder brother, became fixed in his imagination 'heraldically', as he expressed it, that is, in a symbol expressing a complex or involute of feelings.[73] Then and afterwards he identified himself, in a willing humility, with the Pariahs of the world; he had a 'craze for being despised',[74] and felt an anguished sympathy even with the inhabitants of his imaginary kingdom of Gombroon, degraded by his brother's scorn.[75]

But when he first thought of using this theme in literature, he saw it in a rather banal Romantic form. His 1803 diary contained notes for a poem about 'a man darkly wonderful above the beings of this world . . . there is something gloomily great in him; he wraps himself up in the dark recesses of his own soul'; a mysterious stranger, sombrely sublime—in fact, the hero whom Byron was to introduce into popular mythology a few years later.[76] A sympathy for the outcast, the victim of persecution, was a commonplace Romantic symptom, at a time when the French Revolution and the campaign for slave emancipation were elements in everyone's consciousness.[77] Such feelings could be mere self-indulgence, playing at being an exile and outcast, and relying on the presence of spectators who can be impressed when the attitude is struck. But later, perhaps through the influence of opium-heightened dreams, De Quincey's sympathy with pariahs went beyond a mere fashionable attitude. It became an abiding fellow-feeling for those for whom there is no shelter or resting-place in this world—gypsies, Cagots, Jews, and above all the Wandering Jew, the archetype of the pariah;[78] cripples, blind men, lepers; the prisoners, the betrayed, the murdered; the victims of some great catastrophe, like Oedipus, or of some cruel injustice, like Joan of Arc. All of them seemed to him to be denizens of a secret kingdom. In an extraordinary vision of the death of Oedipus, he heard 'from the depth of ancient woods, a voice that drew like gravitation, that sucked in like a vortex, far off yet near—in some distant world yet close at hand' crying out that Oedipus was called to a 'wilderness of pariah eternities', to confront his ancient enemy the Sphinx 'with blazing malice in some pariah world'.[79]

This was the kingdom of Mater Suspiriorum. The visions that were to compose this part of *Suspiria de Profundis* are scattered through De Quincey's work. There are elements of them in his stories *The Avenger* and *The Household Wreck*, in his essays *Joan of Arc* and *The Theban Sphinx*, as well as in the *Confessions*; and at least two of the titles for projected prose-poems in the plan for the completed *Suspiria*—the titles *Cagot and Cressida* and *The Archbishop and the Controller of Fire* (obviously linked with the closing passage of his *Joan of Arc*)—belong to this involute.

The sad realm of Mater Suspiriorum borders on the third region of De Quincey's dreams, that Kingdom of Darkness over which Mater Tenebrarum reigned. Here were assembled the guilts and terrors which thronged De Quincey's nightmares and obsessed the rêveries of his later addiction: murderers, persecutors, processions of death, madmen, monstrous beings, terrors of loathing, of annihilation, of being devoured and transformed. De Quincey first worked these visions of terror into literature in his *Confessions*, in the section on the Pains of Opium; but he used them also in the second part of *Murder Considered as one of the Fine Arts*, in *Klosterheim*, in *The Avenger*, in *The System of the Heavens*.

Suspiria de Profundis, had De Quincey completed it, would have conclusively demonstrated and illustrated what now has to be inferred from scattered references—that his dreams provided both the content and the pattern of much of his finest writing. But how much in those dreams was due to opium? That is the crucial question for the inquiry to which this book is devoted. It cannot be maintained—De Quincey himself never suggested—that opium introduced into his imagination anything that was not already there as a seed. The most that opium could do would be to foster some growths and stunt others.

I do not think that the main theme of *Suspiria de Profundis*—the theme that grief educates us through our rêveries and dreams—owes anything to opium. De Quincy was already meditating

this theme when, in his 1803 diary written before he started
taking opium, he spoke of 'fits of visionary and romantic luxuriat-
ing or of tender pensive melancholy—the necessary and grand
accompaniments of that state of mind to which this system of
education professes to lead'.[80] Two years later, when he was an
undergraduate at Oxford and had already begun to take opium,
he began to dream of Levana, the goddess who educates by grief;
but he expressly said that 'There is no great wonder that a vision,
which occupied my waking thoughts in those years, should re-
appear in my dreams'.[81] Opium, when he began to take it,
worked on the dreaming faculty which he already possessed, and
that faculty made use of the thoughts and images which already
preoccupied his imagination. He was a dreamer from childhood.
One of his earliest memories, which he cites as a proof that his
power to dream was 'constitutional, and not dependent upon
laudanum', was a dream of 'terrific grandeur' about a favourite
nursery-maid, whom he and his sisters loved and who used to
read to them and tell them stories out of the Bible.[82] He has not
recorded much about the subjects of his dreams before he started
taking opium, though a dream of being chased by a lion and
'spellbound from ever attempting to escape' seems to have
recurred with him.[83] He undoubtedly had nightmares in his boyhood, especially in his months of poverty in London when he was
ill with cold and hunger. He does not describe the content of
these nightmares, but says that they were tumultuous, though
'not so awful as those which I shall have to describe hereafter as
produced by opium'.[84] He partly contradicted this by saying that
the nightmares accompanying his descent into serious addiction
in 1813 were 'a revival of all the old dreams' of his London
days.[85]

Judging from case-histories of the dreams and rêveries of other
opium addicts, it appears that some of the main themes of De
Quincey's dreams were not caused by any special selection or
heightening due to opium. The whole group of memories, feelings and images which made up the involute of the child's
sacrificial death in summer—pervaded as it was by an atmosphere
of sunlight and open windows and flowers, compassionate

human love and redeeming divine love—is quite unlike the normal pattern of the opium dream, though its distant domes gilded by sunshine may momentarily recall another writer's opium rêverie. These symbols were selected by De Quincey, at first by a fully conscious choice, for the verities of life which interested him most. These verities concerned the way in which we learn and grow by suffering, and how this explains the otherwise inexplicable mystery of why the innocent should suffer. He would have thought and written about this theme even if he had never taken opium.

What, then, did opium contribute to De Quincey's imaginative powers as a writer? Two shaping forces in De Quincey's work seem to me to be traceable to opium. The first is the tendency of the mind during opium rêveries and dreams to transmute thoughts into patterns. It will be remembered that Coleridge noted, during an illness for which he had been taking laudanum, that his attempts to compose poetry transformed themselves into ocular spectra, and that Poe had similar hypnagogic visions which he valued as the very stuff of poetry, if it could only be pinned down. De Quincey was peculiarly subject to these hypnagogic visions. He refers to them in a famous passage of the *Confessions*, describing how by a voluntary act he traced on the darkness processions of mournful pomp, and how these afterwards transferred themselves to his dreams.[86] 'Heraldries painted on darkness' he calls them elsewhere,[87] and again 'beautiful apparitions starting out of darkness upon the morbid eye, only to be reclaimed by darkness in the instant of their birth'.[88] It is evident that he carefully watched the operation of these ocular illusions, which he regarded as a clue to the mental process by which symbolic literature is created. He expanded this idea in a draft, never published in his lifetime, for the section on the Dark Interpreter in *Suspiria de Profundis*. He began by referring, as he had done in the *Confessions*, to the phenomenon of hypnagogic visions, that semi-voluntary power in the eye which in darkness can project 'a vast theatre of phantasmagorical figures moving forwards or backwards between their bed-curtains and the chamber walls'. He himself had seen myriads of such processions in the darkness, and he recognized all such seeming apparations as self-projections which man's nature, under some excitement whether of violent passion or of a stimulant like opium, could throw off into visible shapes. 'There are creative agencies in every part of human nature' he concluded.[89]

But more important to De Quincey than any visual projection or equivalent of his thoughts was the transmutation, which he sometimes experienced under the influence of opium, of his thoughts and feelings into musical patterns. He had remarkable musical endowments, not as a performer but in appreciation and discrimination.[90] The euphoric rêveries which he enjoyed during the early stages of his opium addiction were closely linked in his imagination with musical patterns. Opium, he said, could 'over-rule all feelings into a compliance with the master key'.[91] Anything that made a discord in the sweetness of his chosen harmony could be resolved by the selective power of opium so that it lost its power to disturb. In the well-known passage quoted in Chapter V he described how when he was listening to the opera, the memories of his past life became incarnated in the music.[92] The pattern of the music then sank into his dreams, and at a later stage, when the dreams had become nightmares under the influence of his deeper opium addiction, the music resounded fatefully as the incarnation of a moment of dreadful decision for all mankind.[93] When De Quincey created his prose-poems out of his dreams, it was often in musical terms that he described their technique. In his essay on *Style* he spoke of 'breaking up massy chords into running variations';[94] the incidents of his childhood were introduced as the *motifs* of his dreams in the revised *Confessions*;[95] he was afraid that in *Suspiria* he might have ruined the whole music by a single false note, a single word in the wrong key.[96] He consciously employed a musical framework of sonata form for some of his longer essays, notably *The English Mail Coach*, which has a symphonic four-part structure, and within its four movements exhibits the musical forms of first and second subject, development, return to the first subject, and coda, with changes of key. He used resounding words—Palm Sunday, Victory, *Non est inventus*, everlasting farewells—as though they were chords struck again and again. His experience under opium of the coalescence of memories and musical forms gave him a technique which underlay much of his subsequent writing.

The second way in which opium shaped De Quincey's imagination, and thence his writing, was by the mythology which it supplied to him. Every imaginative writer needs a mythology, a fixed apparatus of images, for the expression of his thoughts and feelings. Some of De Quincey's contemporaries, like Keats, used and renewed the classical Greek mythology. Some, like Blake, invented their own hierarchies of mythical beings. De Quincey used a mythology derived from his dreams, and some of its gods and demons, its heavens and hells, were animated by opium. His genii were sometimes thoughts or feelings which dreams had personified, like Levana, and sometimes real people casually encountered—a coachman on the Bath Road, a prostitute, a young couple in a gig, a wandering Malayan beggar—whom dreams had elevated into tutelary spirits. The real human beings who meant most to him in his waking life—his mother, his tyrannical elder brother, his guardians, and later Coleridge, the Wordsworths, John Wilson, his own son William—seem hardly ever to have appeared in his dreams in their own shape. Only his little sister and his wife were close to him always, in both his waking and sleeping worlds. His dreaming mind was also curiously selective about the childhood incidents which it revived and enhanced. Some of the most striking incidents which he describes in his *Autobiographic Sketches*, and even in the revised *Confessions* where they were included expressly to give the background of his dreams, seem in fact never to have re-appeared in his dream world. The imaginative games that he unwillingly played with his elder brother had a whole mythology of their own, of island kingdoms, invading armies of ghosts, and men walking head downwards on the ceiling, but none of these recurred in De Quincey's later dreams.[97] The gradual slow approach of the carriage that brought his dying father home by night was elaborated by De Quincey's dreaming mind into innumerable mournful processions;[98] but though he was present at his father's actual death-bed, and heard his delirious complaints that he was deserted by his wife and crushed by unbearable weights, this harrowing scene had no resurrection in De Quincey's dreams.[99] When he ran away from school, the moments of early morning silence just before he stole away from his room remained in his dreaming memory for ever, as a constituent of his involute of the Fatal Choice;[100] but the moment, seemingly far more dramatic, when two mornings later he stood beside the River Dee at Chester and saw the huge onrushing wave of the Bore come tearing towards him, formed no part of the landscape of his dreams.[101] Perhaps this was because it never really happened; one of De Quincey's recent biographers has suggested that he faked his account of that morning in Chester because it was connected with a misdemeanour which he wished to forget.[102] The onrushing tidal wave may have been taken from De Quincey's favourite passage in the *Prelude*, Wordsworth's dream of the Arab on a dromedary pursued by flood waters;[103] De Quincey's description of the Bore as advancing so rapidly that the fleetest dromedary could hardly escape it indicates his source fairly positively.[104] An image, however brilliant and admired, from another man's dream could not enter the landscape of his own dreams. That territory and its inhabitants were shaped by a special influence.

The best way to show how this special influence worked will be to recall those three types of mental characteristics which were mentioned in Chapter II as predisposing a man to opium addiction: first, a curiosity about exceptional states of mind; second, a longing for calm and freedom from anxiety, inadequacy in personal relationships, inability to bear pain and tension; third, a delight in secret societies. The second group of characteristics barely applies to De Quincey, whose personal relationships in adult life were mostly happy and well-adjusted, and who had no craving for solitude and calm. He accused himself of infirmity in bearing misery and pain, his own and others';[105] but his life was on the whole courageous and unfretful. But the first and the third group of predisposing characteristics were pre-eminently De Quincey's.

He had an absorbed curiosity about the extremes of mental

experience, and when the effects, even the physical effects, of his opium habit brought him towards these extremes, his curiosity overpowered every other feeling. One of the well-known symptoms of withdrawal from opium is an intense sensibility to cold, and De Quincey suffered this in full rigour. He had forgotten what it was ever to be thoroughly warm; even in midsummer, even by a blazing fire, even when heaped with cloaks and blankets, still he felt freezing cold.[106] But his interest overpowered his discomfort. Cold was a torment, a frenzy of misery, but 'secretly I was struck with awe at the revelation of powers so unsearchably new lurking within old affections so familiarly known as cold. . . . If cold could give out mysteries of suffering so novel, all things in the world might yet be unvisited by the truth of human sensations'.[107] So frost and the icy Sarsar wind became for him symbols of the revelation of fatal truths.[108] The Sarsar wind was one of the modish images of De Quincey's day, often encountered in Southey's poetry, that reliable repertory of fashionable imagery. As early as 1803, long before he had experienced withdrawal symptoms, De Quincey planned a poem about two young children dying of cold on a frosty moonlight night. But the cold that he felt as a result of his opium habit reappears in his works as something more than a *chic* contemporary device. It gave him, although he never left Britain, the power to create with shuddering vividness the bivouac in the snowy Swabian forest in *Klosterheim*, the rigid frozen corpse poised on the top of the Andean pass in *The Spanish Military Nun*, the icy Central Asian steppes where the fleeing Tartars died of cold round their dwindling camp fires.[109]

This disconnection of experiences from the feelings that usually accompany them, so that painful or horrible events can become simply interesting, is a characteristic of opium addiction which De Quincey showed in other ways. His daughter Florence, who was devoted to him, said of him that he demanded the excitement of fear. 'He was quite incapable of fear in the real sense of the word, so much so that he would not understand it in us as children or young people; and when he was chilling our marrow with awesome stories of ghosts, murders, and mysteries, he only thought he was producing a luxurious excitement'.[110] Like Crabbe, he was fascinated by the idea of the strong passions of madmen and murderers, and above all by the idea of murders in secret. Here in his dreams the kingdom of Mater Suspiriorum, the Pariah Worlds, came too close to the Kingdom of Darkness over which Mater Tenebrarum reigned. His natural impulse of pity for the innocent and persecuted outcast became tainted by too much sympathy for the guilty outcast; the feeling which he laid at the feet of Joan of Arc was also in some measure available to the Thugs. The French addict D.C., mentioned in Chapter II, said that he and his fellow addicts sometimes felt such admiration for the art of criminals that they sympathized with them simply because of the exquisite complexity of their crimes. This movement of mind sometimes appeared in De Quincey. *Murder Considered as one of the Fine Arts* is only half a joke, and the breathless terror of the multiple murders by John Williams described in the second half of De Quincey's essay is no joke at all. De Quincey was enthralled by the idea of a secret murderer, unknown, ubiquitous, not to be kept out; he used it in his novel *Klosterheim*, and again in the uneven but occasionally terrifying tale *The Avenger*. Like Poe, he was keenly interested in the famous murder trials of his day, and often talked about the evidence given by witnesses at the trials, and speculated on the murderer's identity.[111] He could write, of Nero's murder of his mother, 'it would really be pleasant, were it not for the revolting consideration of the persons concerned and their relation to each other, to watch the tortuous pursuit of the hunter, and the doubles of the game'.[112] Or, in a less distasteful vein, he could cogitate the meaning of the knocking on the gate in *Macbeth*, and see it as a re-establishment of the world of day after the 'awful parenthesis' in which Macbeth and his wife by their murder had annihilated time and withdrawn into the kingdom of darkness.[113]

One need not be an opium addict to be interested in murders, but De Quincey's interest, like that of other addicts, had a special tinge. It was murder as the act of a secret society of pariahs, outcast but elect, that interested him. 'Of all the subjects which exercised a permanent fascination over De Quincey, I would place first in order Thuggism in India and the Cagots of Spain and France' wrote James Hogg, who knew him well in his later years. De Quincey was endlessly interested in 'the far-reaching power of this mysterious brotherhood, the swiftness and certainty of its operations, the strange gradations of official rank, and the curious disguises adopted—all these exercised an influence on his mind which never seemed to wane'.[114] The Thugs, the Cagots, the Old Man of the Mountains and his drugged Assassins, haunted De Quincey's imagination.[115] It was the secrecy as much as, or perhaps more than, the crime that enthralled him; he wrote about many kinds of secret societies—Rosicrucians, Freemasons, Essenes,[116] all those hidden fraternities whose principle is to pass down occult wisdom from one generation to another, defying the injuries of time.[117] The secret loyalties of the opium addict peopled his imagination with dark confederacies, and gave a direction to his historical studies.

Among the dreams and hallucinations of opium addicts recorded in Chapters II and III were two myths of human suffering, the image of the drowned city and the terror of watching encircling faces. De Quincey's dream mythology included both these patterns, sometimes in combination. He was haunted by what he called the 'tyranny of the human face'.[118] Crowds of faces that he had seen during his night wanderings in London after a dose of laudanum, in the early stage of his opium habit, rose up close around him in the nightmares which came with deeper addiction, and 'towered into a curse'.[119] When they first appeared in his dreams, they had no 'special power of tormenting'. But now they became a terror to him, terrible above all because they rose into his sight from the ocean depths. 'The sea appeared paved with innumerable faces, upturned to the heavens: faces, imploring, wrathful, despairing, surged upwards by thousands, by myriads, by generations, by centuries'.[120] Then again, the sacrificial girl child who flitted through all De Quincey's dreams would be seen sinking in quicksands, to the sound of funeral bells;[121] or De Quincey himself would sink to the ocean depths, with the weight of twenty Atlantics on him, and would visit the sunken city of Savannah-la-Mar, and float past the bells in drowned belfries.[122] Faces would stare at him, too, from rock forms and veined marbles, haunting him with the idea that they had once been human existences.[123] Identities became unstable; hillocks or waves of the sea would shape themselves into the likeness of a cottage, with a woman waiting at the door.[124] Long before he started taking opium, De Quincey had a tendency to visual hallucinations in moments of grief,[125] and with the increase in his opium habit, this tendency increased too, so that in any time of tension or sickness his eyes played tricks with his surroundings, and people and things lost their identities —a clump of ferns or foxgloves became a lost child with a basket on her head;[126] a coachman became a crocodile, and then, crawling into nightmare, leered from the feet of tables and chairs.[127] This 'horrid inoculation upon each other of incompatible natures' seemed to De Quincey the most terrific of all the miseries that infest dreams. Opium addicts are specially prone to it. Horrible as it is, it bares the imagination at its work of constructing symbols.

The most complete demonstration of how De Quincey's dreaming mind, under the influence of opium, turned a previous waking experience into a powerful symbol in the impassioned prose which he subsequently wrote is the image of the buried temple. The moment when this image first took root in De Quincey's imagination is known. It was the day in July 1800 when, sightseeing in London, he stood in the Whispering Gallery of Saint Paul's Cathedral and fell into a rêverie about those fatal decisions, seeming at the time so trivial, which grow to a huge clamour of irrevocable consequences.[128] From that moment the great domed building and its reverberating gallery, joined with an incident of far-heard footsteps which he had read as a child in the *Arabian Nights*, became for him the symbol of decisions from which there might be no way back.[129] Two years later, in the high echoing emptiness of an inn ball-room at Shrewsbury, on a night of storm, the terror of an irrevocable decision came on him again, and fixed the symbolic link between a huge building and a fatal choice.[130] But this might never have become vivid to his imagination without the aid of his opium dreams, which incarnated this symbol in Cyclopean temples and palaces.[131] In the first stage of his opium habit, his architectural dreams were of magnificent high-piled cities, their domes and terraces towering above the horizon. But in the nightmares of his deeper addiction, the great temple darkened and sank underground and he was imprisoned in chambers buried in its depths.[132]

From then on the symbol of this huge dark building pervaded all his writing. He could not visualize any great house without investing it with a special echoing gloom, a sensation which he believed was inevitably felt by 'any small party assembling in a single room of a vast desolate mansion: how the timid among them fancy continually that they hear some remote door opening, or trace the sound of suppressed footsteps from some distant staircase'.[133] He made terrifying use of this sound of suppressed footsteps in his description of the crimes committed by the multiple murderer Williams,[134] and of Henri IV's prophetic awareness of the still distant oncoming of his assassin.[135]

The dark temple now seemed to enclose De Quincey with its shadows and reverberations wherever he went, even in the open air. Writing about the valleys of Westmorland, he saw them as halls and prison-like chambers,[136] and even the sky hurtling with storms reverberated like a vast enclosed space.[137] Hedge-encircled lawns became studies, corridors and bed-chambers;[138] entangled forest branches on the Andes slopes, and the sunset sky above them, formed into a dome within a dome;[139] the sands of deserts rose up in pillars, eddied into arches and portals;[140] the ocean depths enclosed watery halls within halls,[141] and the sound of a rushing river became the music pouring out from the doors of an illimitable cathedral.[142]

The whole movement of this imagery was inwards and downwards. His symbol for the exploration of human personality was always that of a shaft leading down to a huge dark space.[143] In terms of psycho-analysis such dream images are explicable as equivalents of infantile and sexual experiences, and these must have contributed to De Quincey's imagery. But this has a special architectural form which is not quite a normal dream pattern. 'Yet in the lowest deep there still yawns a lower deep; and in the

De Quincey (II)

vast halls of man's frailty there are separate and more gloomy chambers of a frailty more exquisite and consummate'.[144] His imagery, scattered through his many essays and studies, reflects this downward journey to a buried building, reached through vast avenues of gloom and colossal vestibules, and entered through towering gates, hung with black, which close for ever behind him as he realizes that he can never escape from opium.[145]

Now he is inside the Piranesi prison which he himself recognized as the perfect symbol of his mental processes under opium. His images for these mental operations seem all to be taken from the *Carceri*, which he had never actually seen. His tendency to digression was a landing-place in a flight of stairs[146] (a metaphor borrowed from Coleridge, who also knew the inside of that prison architecture of opium, with its endless staircases and platforms). The unusual analogies which his mind so easily perceived were 'aerial pontoons' over which he passed from one topic to another.[147] His addiction to opium was a mighty ladder, stretching up into shadow 'by which I had imperceptibly attained my giddy altitude—that point from which it had seemed equally impossible to go forward or backward'.[148] It is altogether the world of the *Carceri*, that visionary architecture which, when you first look at it, seems so complete, far stretching, even beautiful, so nobly constructed, of a transcendental dignity. But those magnificent stairs do not lead to anywhere, they stop in mid-air. The aerial bridges that connect everything do not lead *out*, but only round upon themselves. The space is huge, but it is buried and totally enclosed. There is no one else to be seen, but far away, at the furthest end of one of those branching corridors, there is a faint sound that might be a footstep. Down leagues of stone tunnels, a whispering reverberation runs stealthily towards the minute figure at the centre. Some act, some choice, made infinitely long ago, is sending its multiplying echoes towards him from remote recesses.[149] He still has the power to avert the oncoming menace, if he could rouse himself to will it, but he cannot rouse himself.[150] He can only wait there, in the heart of the buried temple, 'alone, utterly divided from all call or hearing of friends, doors open that should be shut, or unlocked that should be triply secured, the very walls gone, barriers swallowed up by unknown abysses . . . whisperings at a distance, correspondence going on between darkness and darkness'.[151]

In the mythology of such opium nightmares as these, De Quincey found the imagery of his prose poems. The most typical example of these, perhaps the only one that he ever fully completed according to his plan, is the extraordinary work which was published under the cheerful Dickensian name of *The English Mail Coach*.[152] The materials of this were present in De Quincey's imagination for many years, and parts of it may actually have been written long before it was published, but it is possible to put an exact date to the moment when its coordinating idea dawned on De Quincey.

In the winter of 1848 he was mainly living in a cottage at Lasswade, near Edinburgh, with his three daughters.[153] His days were spent in writing, much of his nights in long walks, but there were pleasant intervals when he listened to his daughters' music and laughter, and there was no longer any real anxiety over money. At the beginning of November 1848 De Quincey determined to make one more effort to give up opium altogether. He abstained from it completely for over three weeks. On 24th November 1848 he made a memorandum of the stages of his withdrawal symptoms, with all their wretchedness, and with the intermissions which gave him hope. 'The advance will perhaps not be continuous, but intermitting and *per saltum*, but it will burst out more and more at intervals like a fugue until the restoration shall be perfect'.[154]

In the following autumn he published *The English Mail Coach*, a prose-poem patterned like music and incorporating all the main themes and images of his dreams, and among them the theme of opium itself, and his slavery to it and hope of restoration at the last. He called the last section of this study *Dream-Fugue*. It was meant to be included in the *Suspiria de Profundis*, as an example of how incidents of waking life are transformed and idealized in dreams, under the law of association, and an explanatory note on it which he afterwards wrote provided the clues in his waking experience to some of the dream incidents.[155] His mind, forever harking backward and detecting affinities, revelled in this excavation of strata of memory, and a section of *Suspiria*, to be called *Count the Leaves in Vallombrosa*, was to have been devoted to this process, symbolized by the uncovering of palimpsests and the upturnings 'by the searchings of opium' of layer upon layer of dead leaves in aboriginal forests.[156]

The action of opium in fixing events in the memory so that they become dream images is illustrated throughout *The English Mail Coach*. No summary of this prose-poem can make it seem anything but a fantastic string of incongruous incidents and images. It is the rhythm and keeping of De Quincey's style that makes it a coherent structure.

The first two movements of this symphonic work are grouped together under the title *The Glory of Motion*. In the first movement, De Quincey describes the network of mail coaches that used to reticulate all England, the news of victories in the Peninsular War which the coaches sometimes carried hurtling across the country, the thrill of what was then the conquering speed of the fastest vehicle on the roads, and his own undergraduate memories of coach rides on the Bath Road. This movement is the least effective of the four, but De Quincey has woven into it some of his notions about pariahs, and some splendid passages evoking the whirling speed of the heavy coaches and the horses' fiery eyeballs and dilated nostrils and thundering hoofs. He recalls, too, those effects of moving light and shadow cast by carriage lamps on lonely roads at night which were one of the most vivid memories which he retained from childhood journeys, and which were specially distinct to him in the memory of his dying father's night return.[157] This movement ends with a kind of coda in which the theme of his Bath Road journeys, and an old coachman with a pretty daughter remembered from those days, are elaborated by dreams into a wild pattern of roses and crocodiles, heraldries and monsters, and a great clock face in the heavens.

The second movement, *Going down with Victory*, describes a night journey from London in a coach, garlanded with laurels and ribbons and trailing echoes of jubilant horns, which carried the news of the victory of Talavera. It is a journey of triumph, but also of death, for some of those who greet its arrival with shouts and flaring torches will hear soon that their own soldier sons have fallen in the battle.

The third movement, *The Vision of Sudden Death*, is based on an adventure of De Quincey's on a night journey by coach north-wards from Manchester in 1816 or 1817. The theme of this movement especially is that of the fatal choice, the moment in a man's life at which all can be saved or lost, a moment which he had met a thousand times in dreams. De Quincey himself was both actor and spectator in the moment of fatal decision described in this vision. He had taken a dose of laudanum, and was on the box of a mail coach which was thundering through the night along a lonely road between trees which met overhead like a cathedral aisle. He became aware that the coachman and the guard were both asleep. The hurtling coach was under no control, and though the horses would keep the coach on the road, they would run down any less weighty vehicle which they met. The coach whirled round a corner into a long straight stretch of road, and there in the distance was a fragile open cart carrying two young lovers, absorbed in each other and unaware of danger. There was no one but De Quincey—'frail, opium-shattered' as he felt himself to be—to warn them; he thought of trying to blow the guard's horn, but could not reach it in time; he could do nothing but shout, and hope that his feeble cry would carry in time to rouse the threatened couple.

The events that De Quincey is describing can only have lasted a few minutes; but his description of them, stretched out by opium into timeless suspense, convey the everlasting moment in which the fatal choice is made. Would the man in the gig-cart act in time to save himself and his companion? As the coach bore hurtling down on them, and the last-second escape was achieved, and De Quincey looked back at the girl's wild gestures of terror, his opium-influenced eyes recognized a pattern that would sweep into his dreams for ever.

The last movement was called *Dream-Fugue*. It was meant to be heard like music; De Quincey gave it the indication *tumultuosis-*

simamente. He wove into its pattern almost all the themes and images which have been identified in this chapter. Some of them —the images of the threatened girl child, an innocent sacrifice, of sunshine and tropical flowers, of festivals and garlands of white roses, rushing carriages and victories inscribed in gold on midnight skies—have nothing to do with opium, though they echo the themes of the earlier movements. But much of the mythology of opium dreams is in this fugal vision: the phantom ship of Life-in-Death with its demon woman, the funeral bells of the city of drowned children, the vast expansion of space and time, the whisper approaching through darkness. In the climax of the vision, a coach rushes at midnight through the opening gates of a vast cathedral, and all night long at full gallop runs along its floor. Far off like a purple stain on the horizon, but still within the colossal cathedral, is a city of sepulchres, which gradually rises up into huge terraces and sculptured towers as the hurtling carriage draws near it and wheels round its piled sarcophagi. The peril of the girl in the cart, under the cathedral arch of trees, is re-enacted in the vision, in which a girl child in a frail carriage approaches down the illimitable aisle of the dream temple; and a trumpeter sculptured on a tomb wakes from stone to blow a blast which warns and saves her, carrying her up to an altar high in the eastern end of the cathedral through which streams a crimson light from without, a light of dawn at last piercing into the buried temple.

I do not suggest that the whole of *The English Mail Coach* is an autobiographic allegory celebrating De Quincey's hope of escape from opium, but I think that this was one of its themes, one which was certainly in De Quincey's mind when he was writing it. The city of sepulchres, the necropolis enclosed within a huge cathedral, is not prefigured in the waking experiences which De Quincey mentioned in the earlier movements among the constituents of the dream, though in a footnote to *Dream-Fugue* he linked the cathedral with his boyhood visit to Saint Paul's and thus to the involute of the Fatal Choice. The sculptured trumpeter is a denizen of this petrified city of the pariahs. He is also— as De Quincey made clear in his explanatory note to *The English*

Practice

Mail Coach[158]—De Quincey's own 'frail, opium-shattered' self trying and failing to sound the guard's horn to warn the lovers in the cart. Might he at last escape from the petrified city, and by a fierce act of will save his better self?

That hope was not realized in De Quincey's lifetime. He never escaped from the buried temple. He abandoned the attempt to give up opium, and went on taking it for the rest of his life. In his last days, when he was delirious, his rambling words to his daughter showed that he was dwelling on another journey to the altar, in the company of white-clad children. He had been invited, he said, to the 'great supper of Jesus Christ'; but shame and mocking cruelty blocked the way, and his mumbled words did not reveal to the listeners whether he was ever conscious of having reached the altar.[159]

XI

WILKIE COLLINS

In the later years of his life, Coleridge used sometimes to visit the house of the painter William Collins, who had done a portrait of his daughter Sara.[1] Coleridge found Collins and his wife sympathetic, and to Mrs Collins he once confided his grief at his vain struggles against his opium habit, shedding tears as he spoke. Mrs Collins's breezy answer was 'Mr Coleridge, do not cry; if the opium really does you any good, and you *must* have it, why do you not go and get it?'

This at once dried Coleridge's tears, and turning to William Collins he said—'Collins, your wife is an exceedingly sensible woman!'

This conversation was heard by the Collins's small son Wilkie. He cannot have been more than nine years old at the time but, as he told a friend many years later, 'the incident made a strong impression on my mind, and I could not forget it'.[2]

When the boy of nine was a young man of twenty-three, he had to watch his father dying of an acutely painful cardiac disease, and he noted, and recorded in the life of his father which he afterwards wrote, that 'Batley's Drops' (a preparation of opium) was the only medicine that relieved his father's pain and enabled him to sleep.[3] It was therefore not surprising that when in the early 1860s Wilkie Collins himself fell ill—with an agonizing rheumatic complaint which affected his eyes and his feet and legs, and eventually settled into gout—he took laudanum to deaden the pain.[4] He went on taking it for the rest of his life, without concealment and without shame, regarding it as an essential medicine,[5] his 'only friend' as he once said in a moment of bitterness.[6] His dosage gradually crept up, as his tolerance increased, but though at the end of his life he was taking quantities large enough to have been fatal to anyone not habituated,[7] he seems to have been fairly well in control of his habit and never to have indulged in enormous doses such as Coleridge and De Quincey took. He always had a wineglass of laudanum at night to ensure sleep, and at times he also had morphine injections for his neuralgic pains.[8]

All his friends knew about his habit. They had seen the small silver flask of laudanum which he carried with him wherever he went, and some of them had seen him helping himself from a decanter of laudanum at home.[9] Some of his friends, like William Winter, believed that he took laudanum only occasionally,[10] but others knew better. Frederick Lehmann, holidaying with him in Switzerland, was made to go daily to four different chemists to buy supplies of laudanum for his friend; the combined amount was enough to last Wilkie Collins over the night.[11] Others of his friends noticed his extraordinary restlessness and fidgeting at times—most unlike his normal relaxed cheerfulness —in what were obviously periods of temporary abstinence from opium during which he began to experience withdrawal symptoms.[12]

So long as he got his regular supplies of laudanum, he was calm and even complacent about his habit. The actor Squire Bancroft recorded an odd conversation at a dinner-party in his own house. The guests included, besides Wilkie Collins, the eminent surgeon Sir William Fergusson and an oculist called Critchett. During dinner Critchett said to Fergusson 'I have Mr Collins' permission to ask you a question. He has told me the amount of laudanum which he swallows every night on going to bed', and here Critchett named the amount but Bancroft could not recall this. 'I have told him that it would be more than sufficient to prevent any ordinary person from ever awaking. Is not that well within the truth?' Fergusson replied that this dose of opium, to which Wilkie Collins had habituated himself through long usage, was enough to kill every man seated at the dinner-table.[13]

Wilkie Collins would not have allowed such a question to be

put in his presence if he had not felt a certain pride, even boast-fulness, about his opium habit. Hall Caine recorded a very interesting dialogue with Wilkie Collins about his addiction, almost a classic demonstration of such typical opium-addict *traits* as self-justification by the example of others, belief in the beneficent powers of the drug, a mixture of bravado and mis-giving, and fantasies about incidents connected with it.

The two men had been discussing legal matters for some hours when Collins, complaining that his brain was not very clear, opened a cupboard in the corner of the room and took out a wineglass and a bottle, from which he poured out a full glass of what looked like port.

'I am going to show you the secrets of my prison-house' he said. 'Do you see that? It's laudanum', and he drank the whole glass-full.

'Good heavens, Wilkie Collins! how long have you taken that drug?' asked Hall Caine.

'Twenty years'.

'More than once a day?'

'Oh yes, much more. Don't be alarmed. Remember that De Quincey used to drink laudanum out of a jug'. Wilkie Collins then related a long story of how a servant of his had killed himself by taking less than half of one of Collins's opium doses. There is no corroboration of this story, which seems to have been an opium fantasy, perhaps originating with Fergusson's dinner-table remark about Collins's doses being enough to kill a whole party of normal men.

'Why do you take it?' Hall Caine asked him.

'To stimulate the brain and steady the nerves'.

'And you think it does that?'

'Undoubtedly' replied Wilkie Collins, and turned back to the legal matter they had been discussing, saying that he would see it more clearly now, after his laudanum dose. But Hall Caine persisted. Did laudanum have the same stimulating effect on other people as on Collins?

'It had on Bulwer Lytton. He told me so himself'.

Hall Caine, claiming that he himself suffered severely from

nervous exhaustion, asked whether Collins advised him to use the drug. Collins, he records, 'paused, changed colour slightly, and then said quietly "No" '.[14]

As Wilkie Collins began to habituate himself to opium, characters in his novels began to follow suit. In 1862, when his health first gave way seriously and he probably first took laudanum to relieve his bouts of pain, he was writing his novel *No Name*. One of the crucial scenes of this story of a desperate girl plotting to recover her inheritance is the one in which she sits all night long by a window overlooking the sea, with a bottle of laudanum in her hand, wondering whether to kill herself. This is a good example of Wilkie Collins's economical mastery of plot, for the laudanum-bottle is there both to heighten the atmosphere of desperation and as a clue which will be needed later in the story for quite another purpose.

Four years later, in *Armadale*, Wilkie Collins depicted another beautiful woman contemplating a bottle of laudanum, but this time it is the red-haired villainess Miss Gwilt, a much more professional criminal than the daring but ineffective Magdalen Vanstone of *No Name*, and her attitude to opium is gruesomely affectionate. 'Who was the man who invented laudanum? I thank him from the bottom of my heart, whoever he was. If all the miserable wretches in pain of body and mind, whose comforter he has been, could meet together to sing his praises, what a chorus it would be!'. Miss Gwilt took her 'darling' laudanum as a tranquillizer for her nerves, already sufficiently brazen, not for any bodily pain.

In 1868, when Wilkie Collins was suffering such excruciating pain in his eyes that he could not use them for writing, and when he was taking laudanum continually as an anodyne, he dictated his novel *The Moonstone*, the whole plot of which is operated by opium, since the missing diamond turns out to have been actually taken by the hero when sleep-walking under the influence of an opium dose administered to him without his knowledge. And moreover the mystery is discovered by the doctor's assistant Ezra Jennings, himself an opium addict, and the journal in which he describes the experiment in the reconstruction of the somnambulist's movements under the influence of opium also describes the effects on himself of the increased opium doses which he has to take to summon up the energy needed for the experiment. *The Moonstone* has a Chinese box intricacy; the actions of an opium-dosed man are described by an opium addict who is the invention of a writer heavily dosed with opium.

The very odd story of the composition of *The Moonstone* is one of the plainest statements made by any writer of how he produced a major piece of work under the influence of opium. *The Moonstone* was dictated, and its dénouement invented, while Wilkie Collins was in great distress over his mother's approaching death and was under the sway of the laudanum he had to take at that time because of acute pain in his eyes. This was so agonizing that he could not help groaning and crying out even when he was dictating. His male secretary was so much upset by this that he would break off to try and help Wilkie Collins, and finally left because he could not endure the spectacle of so much pain. A second male amanuensis followed suit. Finally a woman secretary was engaged; she was warned of what would happen, and was asked if she could endure it unmoved and carry on with the work. She assured Wilkie Collins that she could manage this, and she did; although while she was working for him he had a worse and more painful attack than any previous one, and lay on a couch writhing and groaning, she stolidly went on writing from his dictation, between his cries and moans—and he stoically went on dictating. But when he had finished, and then read through the last part of the book, he was not only 'pleased and astonished' at the *finale* of the story, but did not recognize it as his own.[15] That this tightly plotted and controlled novel could have been written in such conditions finally disposes of the theory that opium necessarily prevents a writer from doing his work, if further proof were needed in face of the shelves-full of works produced by Coleridge and De Quincey. The fact that Collins afterwards did not recognize it as his own work has parallels in the experience of other writers under the influence of opium, especially Walter Scott's experiences after writing *The Bride of Lammermoor*, as will be related in Chapter XIII. Wilkie Collins knew of this story about Scott;[16] perhaps indeed he slightly worked up his own experience to match it; certainly he rated *The Bride of Lammermoor* extraordinarily high, classing it with *Hamlet* as 'two of the greatest of tragic stories',[17] and perhaps this was because of an affinity with the way in which it was composed.

The fact that Scott and Collins did not recognize as their own work what they had written under the influence of opium does not imply that opium conferred on them something which had never before been present to their imagination. Wilkie Collins's sources for *The Moonstone* have been identified; he had done some fairly thorough research on India, on precious stones, and on somnambulism. The failure in recognition was perhaps connected with that mental symptom recorded by De Quincey as being common to him and Coleridge—the disgust which they felt for anything which they had written under pressure during their opium habit, which made their minds shy away from reconsideration of the subject. The oblivion experienced by Collins and Scott may have been a sub-conscious protective device against this symptom. Every writer, opium addict or not, has had these moments when his work suddenly becomes distanced, no longer his own, and can surprise him by its strangeness. Opium no doubt greatly increases this effect. Deliberately unhitched from painful associations with the effort made to write it, the work appears external and 'given' to the opium-addict writer when he re-reads it.

What Wilkie Collins thought about the mental effects of opium has mainly to be inferred from his novels. He told Hall Caine that it stimulated the brain and steadied the nerves,[18] and said to William Winter that 'Opium sometimes hurts, but also, *sometimes*, it helps. In general, people know nothing about it'.[19] He appears to have felt that it gave him an indispensable stimulus to get through his work, but he does not seem to have speculated on how it affected his imagination, though he was convinced that it was a powerful agent in producing frightful dreams. Ezra Jennings in *The Moonstone* is shown as hesitating between the agonizing pain of his disease and the ghastly dreams which opium will bring if he uses it to deaden the pain, and is made to say 'If I had only myself to think of, I should prefer the sharp pain to the frightful dreams'. Later, pain drives him to opium again—'my full dose—five hundred drops'—and he gains one night of oblivion, 'the night of a man who is stunned', but the following night 'the vengeance of the opium' overtakes him in further appalling nightmares. If this is based on Collins's own experience, he has left no record of that; no nightmares of his seem to have been noted, though in the later stage of his opium habit he seems to have suffered from waking hallucinations—that someone was standing behind him, that when he went up to his room at night the staircase was crowded with ghosts trying to push him down, that a green woman with teeth like tusks was waiting to say goodnight to him by biting his shoulder.[20] This green demon seems to have been conjured up whenever the book which he was writing took a macabre turn; then, as he left his study and made a rush up to his bedroom, the grisly shapeless creature with its green fangs would be waiting for him on the stairs.[21] His account of these hallucinations is half jocular, he used to describe them 'in his fluent dramatic way' said Percy Fitzgerald. He rather enjoyed his terrors, perhaps, and certainly was capable of tracing the origin of some of them to ocular spectra. He spoke of 'certain vagaries of the optic nerves, which persist in seeing a pattern of their own making', which he described as being like black lace, or 'a reptile of the pre-Adamite period'; he even tried to draw a sketch of it.[22] This sounds like the patterned visions seen by both Coleridge and De Quincey under opium influence.

Wilkie Collins does not seem to have used his hallucinations directly in his novels. He constantly made use of dreams in his books, but they were used as a device of plot, not as an atmospheric effect or for their own interest. In his first successful novel *Basil*, the hero has a dream about a woman of the hills and a woman of the woods, which is a rather laboured allegory prophetic of the good and evil geniuses of his life, between whom he has just made a choice. The device is not very well managed in *Basil*, but it is the first example of a technique which he was to use much more powerfully later, specially in *Armadale*—the device of a dream which summarizes the plot of the rest of the book and is shown as reacting on the characters so that, in effect, they will the fulfilment of the dream prophecy. The hero of *Basil* admits that 'I could not dismiss from my heart the love-images which that dream had set up there for the worship of the senses. Those results of the night still remained within me, growing and strengthening with every minute'.

This dream, and one of 1856 in *The Dead Secret*—dreamed by its blind hero and cited by him as showing that he is still sighted in his dreams—are not yet quite structural in Wilkie Collins's novels. But *Armadale*, published in 1866, has a dream and its consequences as the main theme. The hero Armadale has a circumstantial and very matter-of-fact dream, so detailed that Collins actually numbers its constituents to make quite sure that we shall take them in. No attempt is made to invest the dream itself with any terror or menace, and the man who dreams it is not much impressed by it; but he relates it to a friend for whom it at once takes on a haunting threatening significance which is worked out all through the rest of the book. Collins carefully provides a trivial as well as a momentous origin and significance for every feature of the dream. He introduces a doctor who voices the anti-superstitious view that all such dreams are merely jumbled reproductions of recent events. He explains in an Appendix that he has left the reader free to accept whichever view of the dream, natural or supernatural, he prefers. His own view seems to have been that dreams may be a true portent, but not of an inevitable fate; they are a warning of tendencies in man's nature, which man can develop for good or evil.

Dorothy Sayers ridiculed the dream in *Armadale* and its seventeen headings, and thought that Wilkie Collins's mind was too inelastic, too legal, for him to succeed in portraying unusual states of mind. But T. S. Eliot thought that the dream operated the machinery of *Armadale* with a well-managed skill. The doctor's incredulity about the dream makes the reader react in its favour; it creates a tension which pervades the whole book and predisposes the reader to accept situations in themselves implausible. It seems possible that Wilkie Collins's own dreams, like

Coleridge's, were not very portentous or terrifying in their subject-matter, but opium attached intensity and significance to their trivial events so that, like the dream in *Armadale*, they seemed to tower above the future.

The degree to which a dreamer under opium influence actually visualizes scenes, especially landscapes, whose visual impact he can then convey in words, has been considered in Chapter IX when the visual effects of *The Ancient Mariner* and of *Kubla Khan* were compared. The effect of opium in transforming this power of visualizing can be seen in the work of Wilkie Collins.

As a boy he was trained by his painter father to look at landscape in terms of the pictures which could be painted of it. He accompanied his father on journeys to Italy and to Scotland, watched him making sketches and listened to him pointing out the highlights of the landscape.[23] When William Collins died, his son wrote a memoir of him, the greater part of which consists of descriptions of his father's landscape pictures. This was Wilkie Collins's first book, and he had not yet mastered his style or learned to find the precise word; many of the descriptions of pictures are laborious rather than vivid. But they are an attempt to reproduce paint in words. 'The wild, transitory, morning clouds; the bursting sunlight, flashing upon them from the horizon of the fresh, cold, green sea, warmed by one vivid streak of golden light; the shadowy beach, covered in places with the thin transparent flow of water, left by the retiring tide' —that is Wilkie Collins's description of one of his father's last pictures, *Early Morning*, and the reader's eye can translate it back into paint without difficulty.

Three years later Wilkie Collins went on a walking tour in Devonshire and Cornwall, and wrote it up afterwards into a pleasant book, *Rambles Beyond Railways*.[24] All the landscapes that he saw there composed themselves into pictures as he looked at them; one was a Michelangelo, another was a Rembrandt, a third an Italian Primitive. His own word-painting had increased in skill since he wrote the memoir of his father, as is shown by his description of Plymouth Sound. 'The wooded hills rose dark and grand against their transparent background of light. Where the topmost trees grew thinnest, long strips of rosy sky appeared through their interstices; the water beyond us was tinged in one place with all the colours of the prism, in another with the palest and coldest blue—even the wet mud-banks, left by the retiring tide, still glittered with silvery brightness in the waning light'. It is just such a careful landscape note as his father had taught him to make, and one can visualize it at once as the picture his father would have painted of it. But when he goes on to describe the anchored hulks which were used as prisons, and to compare them to water-monsters just emerged from their lairs, the simile falls flat; he can describe with finish, but he cannot evoke images of mystery.

When he started writing novels, he used his trained power of landscape description with telling effect. His weather and landscapes match and underline the feelings of his characters, as in *Basil* where the disastrousness of the hero's marriage is enhanced by downpours of cold rain on the wedding day, and the climacteric meeting between hero and villain is accompanied by a violent thunderstorm. These are fairly conventional effects. Later, at the height of his powers, when he wrote *The Woman in White*, he used landscape descriptions more subtly as an emanation of character. The vague uneasiness and suspicion which Marian Halcombe feels about her brother-in-law is paralleled by her first sight of his house and park, with its dark stifling woods. Collins seems to have suffered from dendrophobia; he hated tree-choked landscapes, such as the one which he powerfully described in *Mad Monckton*, a story otherwise cribbed from Poe's *The Oblong Box*, but impressive for its description of the threatening forests encircling a decaying Campanian monastery. In *The Woman in White* Wilkie Collins was still visualizing landscapes as pictures. His description of Blackwater Park with its shrinking lake, its reedy pools and stretches of mud, and 'lying half in and out of the water, the rotten wreck of an old overturned boat, with a sickly spot of sunlight glimmering through a gap in the trees on its dry surface, and a snake basking in the midst of the spot, fantastically coiled and treacherously still', is both an allegory of Marion Halcombe's prospects and a verbal equivalent of a composition in paint. It is no longer a painting by William Collins, however; it is not at all in his deliberately wholesome cheerful style. It is perhaps a Danby, in the manner of his *Disappointed Love*.

The best known and most often quoted of Wilkie Collins's landscape descriptions is his evocation of Aldeburgh in *No Name*, which almost equals Crabbe's pictures of the same landscape. Wilkie Collins admired Crabbe's poetry, though he almost had to apologize for this taste at a period when no one but Edward Fitzgerald shared it. 'More extraordinary still . . . I am a frequent reader even of Crabbe' he owned deprecatingly.[25] His Aldeburgh seascape, with its calm misty sea and idle ships, is composed like a seascape by Brooking, or perhaps even by Bonington; and as his eye travelled inland, over the desolate marsh with the dull red sunset reflected in muddy pools, over the decaying wharfs and oozing river-banks and the black trees low on the horizon, he arranged what he saw into a word picture reminiscent of a Crome landscape. The foreground, the middle distance and the sky-line are carefully defined, and the colour notation is precise.

Up to this date all Wilkie Collins's landscape descriptions were perfectly translatable into pictorial terms. *No Name* was written in 1862, the year in which Wilkie Collins probably started taking opium regularly. In his next novel, *Armadale*, published in 1866, there is a change. Much the most haunting landscape in this book—the other descriptions, of the Isle of Man and of the Norfolk Broads, do not convey any strong impression—is the one which the murderous Miss Gwilt describes in a letter, a stretch of country on the edge of a little wood. 'There was a dip in the ground, with some felled timber lying in it, and a little pool beyond, still and white and shining in the twilight. The long grazing-grounds rose over its farther shore, with the mist thickening on them, and a dim black line far away of cattle in slow procession going home. . . . The place made an unaccountably vivid impression on me, and I can't help writing about it. If I end badly—suppose we say on the scaffold?—I believe the last thing I shall see, before the hangman pulls the drop, will be the little shining pool, and the long misty grazing-grounds, and the cattle winding dimly home in the thickening night. . . . My fancy plays me strange tricks sometimes—and there is a little of last night's laudanum, I dare say, in this part of my letter'.

That landscape is not paintable, or not in any terms known to painters like William Collins. It is a landscape of the mind; Wilkie Collins's eye was turning inwards to a hidden country of symbols. This change was still more apparent when he came to write *The Moonstone*, under heavy laudanum dosage. Most of the action of the novel takes place in a house near the Yorkshire coast, in a melancholy countryside of sandhills and fir plantations which is only perfunctorily described—except for one feature of the landscape, the little bay filled with a shivering quicksand, into which the pathetic servant Rosanna Spearman throws herself. This horrible place is described with the utmost care, but no longer like a painting. One does not instantly visualize it as a picture in a heavy gold frame, as one does with Collins's descriptions of Blackwater and Aldeburgh. It is a symbolic landscape, not a figurative one; it suggests feelings of menacing calm, of decay, of the dead-alive, of being sucked down. 'I saw the preliminary heaving of the Sand, and then the awful shiver that crept over its surface—as if some spirit of terror lived and moved and shuddered in the fathomless depths beneath'. The objective landscape seen with a painter's eye has been replaced by a subjective landscape of the imagination, as unpaintable as Xanadu or Poe's Dreamland. Rosanna Spearman's swallowing up by the quicksand is paralleled by two earlier opium visions: De Quincey's dream, in *The English Mail Coach*, of the girl engulfed in a quicksand, and Walter Scott's story of Edgar Ravenswood's death in the sinking sands, in *The Bride of Lammermoor*, written when Scott was taking laudanum.

Wilkie Collins wrote many more novels after *The Moonstone*, but none of them contained distinctly-visualized landscapes like the ones in *The Woman in White* and *No Name*. He travelled in France, Italy, Germany, America, but their scenery did not find a way into his later books, which convey almost no sense of place or of external nature. His murder story *The Haunted Hotel* has an ingenious plot, which again makes use of the premonitory dream; but though it is supposed to take place in a Venetian palace, and though Wilkie Collins had been in Venice shortly before he wrote it, there is no Venetian atmosphere; most of the story might as well be taking place in a station hotel in Wigan. The Wilkie Collins who, as a boy in Venice with his father, had noticed every weather-stain on the bridges, every slither of dark water, every drowsy stir of heavy barges in back canals,[26] now could convey nothing of this to his readers. All his skill was turned on portraying the terrors of dreams and the gruesome decay of the severed head which the searchers uncover at last.

This is perhaps one of the most distinct before-and-after signs of opium's effect on the imagination—that it alters a writer's power to convey the visual impact of landscape. The landscapes described by the opium addict writers do not rise up before the reader's eye, they convey to him the emotions connected with landscape, not the landscape itself. Quicksands are despair, weeds on a muddy bank are obsession, sunlit lawns among ancient trees are secret raptures of repose. You feel them, you cannot see them or reproduce them in paint.

Wilkie Collins's father believed, and taught his son, that it was the business of art to reproduce 'all in Nature that was pure, tranquil, tender, harmonious' and to exclude 'all that was coarse, violent, revolting, fearful'. His pictures contained no hurricanes, thunderstorms or shipwrecks, no tragic or vicious human beings.

In his first books, Wilkie Collins tried to practise what his father had inculcated. He was careful to say, in his *Rambles beyond Railways*, that he had dwelt only on the pleasant side of the Cornish character, on the prosperity and hospitality of the people, not on beggars or wreckers or smugglers. But it was not the natural bent of his mind, and even in this sunny little travel-book there are some disquieting shadows: the story of the white boat washed ashore on an icy morning of 1846 with its crew of ten fishermen all frozen to death; the story of the two hermit sisters in a solitary cottage near Tintagel, and how one first died, and then the other, after weeks of silent weeping, was found dead in her chair.

These were the aspects of humanity that fascinated Wilkie Collins most. Like other addicts, he had a sympathy for the pariahs of human society. This was to become a major theme in his novels. When he wrote *Basil*, he had this taste only in the normal Romantic form of the Noble Outcast, the admired being on whom De Quincey had brooded in his youthful diary. Basil is the rejected son of a noble and ancient house, like Crabbe's Sir Eustace Grey, and Francis Thompson's Florentian, and so many of Poe's heroes. This archetypal figure, which owed part of its myth to Byron, lay deep in the sub-conscious minds of the most unlikely personalities in the nineteenth century, just as a cherished James Bond identification probably lurks in the hearts of many respectable civil servants and bank managers today. To be noble but outcast—that seemed the best-fitting *persona* for many nineteenth-century writers: to have the glamour of aristocracy without its conventional restrictions, the freedom of the Bohemian life without its suggestions of squalor. This aspect of *Basil* therefore gave expression to a fantasy which was not peculiar to Wilkie Collins or to drug addicts, though opium, as has been seen, tends to accentuate the pariah theme.

The banal taste for Noble Outcasts was to develop, in the work of Wilkie Collins's best period, into a much more deeply felt sympathy for the real outcasts from normal human destiny—for the deformed, the handicapped, the insane, for recluses and fugitives, for prostitutes, for the illegitimate and the orphaned. The casts of his novels are full of the physically handicapped: a blind hero in *The Dead Secret*, a blind heroine and an epileptic hero in *Poor Miss Finch*, a dumb heroine in *Hide and Seek*, a hunchback girl in *The Moonstone*, and in *The Law and the Lady* the legless and sadistic but not unattractive villain Miserrimus Dexter. Swinburne suggested that Collins 'could not, as a rule, get forward at all without the help of some physical or moral infirmity in some one of the leading agents or patients of the story'. Collins felt that kinship with the pariahs which was so strong in

Wilkie Collins

De Quincey and Poe, in Baudelaire and the second James Thomson. Of characters like the former thief Rosanna Spearman in *The Moonstone* he wrote with a sympathy, almost tenderness, which none of his normal and morally approved characters are accorded by their creator. Magdalen Vanstone, the heroine of *No Name*, the illegitimate girl who plays a lone hand, sometimes by criminal means, to regain her inheritance, is treated with imaginative understanding by her author. In Collins's attitude towards his physically handicapped characters there is at times something of the grace of that affection, without condescending pity or morbid fascination, which De Quincey in his opium dreams felt once again for the deaf and dumb twin girls, repulsive and maltreated, whom he had known in his childhood. But it is Crabbe, rather than De Quincey, whom Wilkie Collins resembles in this mental aspect. Both men were down to earth and unenthusiastic, and yet were interested in abnormal situations and behaviour. Both had a dry compassion for the weak, the handicapped, the unfortunate. Both were affectionate and kind, rather than loving.

Of all the writers discussed in this book, Wilkie Collins is perhaps the least like the conventional idea of a drug addict. To the end of his life he was extremely business-like, a hard and regular worker, friendly and popular; and he organized his emotional life so efficiently that he was able for many years to live with one woman and to keep another, by whom he had several children, only a few streets away, and to maintain this state of affairs without any open scandal or quarrels. He was temperamentally incapable of the extremes of rapture and terror, of the highest aspirations or the deepest feelings of guilt. Opium, which can only work on what is already there, had no spectacular effects on his equable personality or on his ingenious unaspiring work. In his novels he never attempted to illuminate human experience as a whole, or to explore the secret places of the soul. He aimed to write gripping well-constructed stories about striking characters. In this limited aim he succeeded completely when he was at the height of his powers, before the effects of his opium habit began to tell. Then gradually his faculty of observation of external objects began to be deadened; his understanding of normal human beings turned into mechanical characterization; his fascination with abnormal human conditions —deformity, disease, insanity—became more morbid. At its best it was a real humanitarian sympathy, but there was often something less admirable about it, a tinge of excitement, of obsession. The most obvious damage to his literary achievement which the opium habit inflicted was its impairment of the power of sustained concentration needed for the tightly-constructed plots which were his greatest excellence. His later novels do not hold together like the best work of the 1860s. He worked as hard as ever at his novels, but the result was second-rate, and the same cause which made them second-rate weakened his capacity for self-criticism, so that he could not see or remedy what was wrong.[27] He thought that laudanum stimulated his brain and steadied his nerves. It did calm his nervous susceptibilities; in the end it atrophied them.

XII

FRANCIS THOMPSON

In 1880 the wife of a doctor living in Manchester gave her twenty-year-old son a copy of De Quincey's *Confessions of an English Opium Eater*. The son was the future poet Francis Thompson, and there is much conjecture among his biographers whether it was this fatally influential present, or other causes, that bore the chief responsibility for turning him into an opium addict. At that time Francis Thompson, whose devout Roman Catholic parents had intended him for the priesthood but who had been judged unsuited for ordination, was supposed to be studying medicine to qualify him to follow his father's profession. But he was not really attending his medical courses; he was spending his time in libraries and museums and in wandering about the streets of Manchester, though his family did not know this. A year earlier, in 1879, he had had a serious illness, which may have been a first attack of the tuberculosis which eventually killed him; it is possible that he was given laudanum medicinally for this illness, and that his habituation began in that way. Perhaps neither a medical prescription nor De Quincey's influence started him on his opium habit, but rather a sense of failure and a wish to escape from his dreary surroundings and distasteful medical studies into the inner life of the imagination which had always been his chief preoccupation.[1]

Five years later he was still living at home, and had failed several times in his medical examinations. His father began to suspect that there must be some cause for his son's indolence and failure, and may have found that the laudanum supplies in his own surgery were lower than they should have been. There was a sharp quarrel, and Francis Thompson left home for London in November 1885.[2]

For much of the next three years Thompson lived a life of homeless destitution in London, sleeping in common lodging-houses, under archways or on the Embankment, earning a few pence by running errands or selling matches or newspapers.[3] At this time he gave himself over to the deepest indulgence in opium that he ever reached. He afterwards overlaid his life during this period with legends that may be founded on fact, or may have been an unconscious self-identification with earlier protagonists of opium literature. He said that, like De Quincey, he was befriended by a golden-hearted prostitute.[4] He said that, like Poe and Berlioz, he had attempted suicide by laudanum, and actually took half a lethal dose but survived as by a miracle.[5] For some months in 1886 he was actually befriended, housed and given work not by a golden-hearted prostitute but by a philanthropic shoemaker, and he may have given up laudanum during this time, but returned to it in early 1887 after a visit to his family in Manchester.[6] No longer able to perform even the routine work for which the shoemaker paid him, he returned to his homeless life in the London streets.

The story of Francis Thompson's rescue by Wilfrid and Alice Meynell, their launching of him as a poet and their devoted care of him as a man, his achievements in literature, his never-wavering religious faith—these were the most important things in Francis Thompson's life, on which any balanced biography of him ought to concentrate. One recent book on him, Mr J. C. Reid's Francis Thompson, Man and Poet, described his life mainly in terms of his addiction to opium, and is in fact the only full-length study of a poet considered in this particular light which is known to me. But it is inevitably a slanting and distorted light. For the purposes of the present book, I shall concentrate on depicting the stages of Thompson's opium habit, but in this case as in others I have not forgotten that I am ignoring whole segments of his personality and reversing his own scale of values.

When Wilfrid Meynell, editor of the review Merry England, had at last traced and interviewed the ragged pauper who had

sent him an essay and some poems, he arranged for Francis
Thompson to enter a clinic for a cure of his opium addiction.[7]
There he stayed for several weeks, and then went to convalesce
at a monastery at Storrington in Sussex where, for most of 1889,
he endured the miseries of withdrawal from opium and wrote
some of his best-known poetry and prose.

Thompson's letters of 1889 give an unusually detailed picture
of a writer's experiences during a period of withdrawal from
opium. He described the severe physical reactions, which lasted
longer and more obstinately than he had expected, and could
only be endured in the hope that the end was in sight. His nights
were wretched; if he fell into a half-sleep, he experienced
horrible 'attacks' of a nature which he did not specify—they
were perhaps nightmares, the *crises nocturnes* to which many
addicts are subject. To avoid them, he tried like De Quincey to
stay awake all night, and beguiled the time by writing poetry.
At first he had been able to write nothing but letters of the most
banal kind, but presently his poetic powers began to revive, and
during four deliberately waking nights he managed to write
several self-revealing poems.[8] One poem, *Non Pax Expectatio*,
which was written during these months of withdrawal, describes
the breathless pause between crises, the tenuous hope that it
will be just possible to hold out

'I hardly know if I outlast
The minute underneath whose heel I lie,
Yet I endure, have stayed the minute passed,
Perchance may stay the next. Who knows, who knows?'

By the summer of 1889 he was able to write that he had
learned it was possible to bear his fits of depression without
having recourse to opium, and that his mind worked better
without it.[9] At first he had been unable to get on with his writing, but he had pushed at his brain till it began to move—slowly
and unwillingly, but regularly, so that he was able to complete
the essay on Shelley which he had set himself to write.[10] In the
following year, after his return to London, he summed up his
mental condition during this withdrawal period. 'I have been for
months in a condition of acute mental misery, frequently almost

akin to mania, stifling the production of everything except poetry, and rendering me quite incapable of sane letter-writing. It has ended in my return to London, and I am immensely relieved; for the removal of the opium had quite destroyed my power of bearing the almost unbroken solitude in which I found myself'.[11]

Thompson's abstinence did not last long. At some time between 1890 and 1892 he again relapsed into his opium habit, though he never again took such large quantities as during his homeless destitution in London, and may not have taken it as often as daily until his last years.[12] In 1892 Wilfrid Meynell arranged for him to go and stay in the monastery of Pantasaph in North Wales, where it was thought that he would be unable to get supplies of opium.[13] From Pantasaph he was able to write, early in January 1893, '*C'en est fait*, as regards the opium'.[14] He stayed at Pantasaph till the end of 1896, and then returned to London where he spent the last eleven years of his life, working as a journalist. His three volumes of poetry were published in 1893, 1895 and 1897; his output in his last ten years was nearly all prose, principally book reviews. During his four years at Pantasaph, he had almost if not entirely abstained from opium, but at some time after his return to London—perhaps as early as 1897, perhaps not till 1900—he reverted to his opium habit, and continued it till he died.[15]

The Meynell family had now accepted, though not acknowledged, that Francis Thompson's addiction was incurable. They all knew of it—even the children noticed how 'flushed and dozing' his manner sometimes was [16]—but none of them spoke of it. 'We knew that he knew we knew about his drug' wrote Everard Meynell, son of Wilfrid and Alice, who wrote the first biography of Francis Thompson.[17] But the word 'laudanum' was never mentioned between Thompson and his friends and protectors. The Meynells made up their minds that Thompson was partly justified in taking opium because it staved off his tuberculosis and gave him enough strength to go on working,[18] and moreover that it had no effect on any of his important work, neither inspiring nor damaging it.[19] 'The life that opium conserved in him triumphed over the death that opium dealt out to him' concluded Everard Meynell in an affectionate but clear-sighted summing-up which acknowledged the physical degradation, the irresponsibility towards social duties, the haunting guilt of conscience which opium inflicted on Francis Thompson.[20]

'Opium, and its saving of my life' wrote Thompson on a draft of his early poem *Sister Songs*[21]. But at the end of his life he at last spoke out to Wilfred Meynell. 'I am dying from laudanum poisoning' he said.[22] The plain medical truth of the matter probably lies somewhere between these statements. When Thompson started taking opium again at the end of the century, he was able to control his habit.[23] He kept notes of his dosage during the week—a bottle of laudanum on Saturday, three on Sunday, two on Monday, two on Tuesday, one on Thursday; and a chemist's bill found among his papers shows him buying seven 'lots' of laudanum at tenpence, and one at sixpence, between 24th December 1904 and 28th February 1905.[24] The restlessness and discomfort of his abstinence symptoms on any day on which he had not taken his regular dose now became apparent to his friends, and equally apparent was the exaltation of his manner when he had just had his ration of laudanum.[25]

In the last months of his life his dosage was increased to six or even seven ounces a day.[26] So at least his friends reported, but when Thompson himself told a doctor in the hospital where he was dying that he was accustomed to taking seven ounces of laudanum a day, the doctor found this incredible, since the small quantities which he had been given since he entered the hospital had a much more powerful effect on him than would have been possible with anyone habituated to so large a daily dose.[27] Thompson may have been exaggerating, as many addicts do, to get the doctor to allow him a larger dose; or he may really not have known the strength of his doses—the opium content of laudanum often varied; or he may, as Professor Danchin has suggested in his authoritative biography of Francis Thompson, have normally taken small but frequent doses, but have taken much larger ones on rare occasions, especially in the last months of his life. However much or little he took, it was not the cause of his death; he died of tuberculosis, on 13th November 1907, when he was not quite forty-eight.

The connection between withdrawal from an opium habit and the birth or re-birth of poetic impulse can be demonstrated more clearly in the case of Francis Thompson than in that of any of the other writers discussed in this book. Nearly all his poetry was written between the end of 1888 when he started his first 'cure' for addiction, and May 1897 when his *New Poems* were published, at the end of his abstinent period at Pantasaph. There had been a relapse into opium in 1891 and 1892, and in these two years he wrote little of merit. 1889 to 1890 and 1893 to 1896, periods of almost complete freedom from opium, were the years of his finest poetic achievements. After 1897, as he gradually relapsed into opium, he wrote hardly any more poetry. It is arguable that he started taking opium again because he found he could not write any more poetry, rather than that the relapse into opium stopped him writing it; but whichever caused the other, the poetic failure and the renewed addiction coincided.

Alice Meynell was the first to notice the connection. Comparing Thompson and Coleridge, she wrote in 1908 'Let none quote the example of these poets in excuse for that search after a possible inspiration, which is the least pardonable act of ambition . . . Not one of Francis Thompson's poems, except, perhaps, "Dream Tryst"—and this inferior to all others in the first volume —was written with the aid of opium'.[28] She particularly disliked *Dream-Tryst*, which she had first come across one day in 1888, when she was sitting up in bed, reading MSS for her editor husband, and she glanced through the dirty manuscript which Thompson, then a destitute vagrant in the London streets, had sent in, including 'some witch-opium poems' which she found detestable. One of these was *Dream-Tryst*, the celebration of a meeting with a remembered love in the divine air of the house of dreams. Alice Meynell knew nothing of Francis Thompson when she first read the poem; it would be deeply interesting to know whether she really recognized, from the poem itself, that its loved Lucidé was an opium witch, or whether it was only hindsight that caused her to say that she had detected 'evidence of the inspiration of drugs in the poems'.[29]

Her son Everard was equally sure that Francis Thompson's withdrawal periods were the productive ones. 'The renunciation of opium, not its indulgence, opened the doors of the intellect. . . . His images came toppling about his thoughts overflowingly during the pains of abstinence'.[30] Thompson's letters from Storrington in 1889 reveal these mental conditions of withdrawal which are favourable to the composition of poetry: nights of insomnia; a feeling that the brain is being freed from inertia, is beginning to move and to exercise itself; a hyper-sensitivity of the nerves—'I am sometimes like a dispossessed hermit-crab, looking about everywhere for a new shell and quivering at every touch. Figuratively speaking, if I prick my finger I seem to feel it with my whole body'.[31] He was wretchedly uncomfortable and restless, but this state of mind was favourable to poetic creation. He said that he was miserable, almost maniacal sometimes, but this condition, though it disqualified him for most activities, did not stifle the production of poetry.

In late 1893, when he was at Pantasaph, one of his friends there suspected from his 'dull mechanical' manner that he might be 'getting into the old habit'.[32] Perhaps he did give way to a temporary indulgence in opium at this time, for a letter of the following spring suggests that he was again experiencing the poetic impulse connected with withdrawal. 'Am overflowing with a sudden access of literary impulse. I think I could write a book in three months, if thoughts came down in such an endless avalanche as they are doing at present'.[33] Many addicts have reported this tumultuous rush of ideas and images as a symptom of withdrawal, but the origin of the images thus released lies further back, in the action of opium at an earlier stage. Francis Thompson wrote no poems, or none that have survived, when he was in the early euphoric period of his addiction, as Coleridge did in Kubla Khan. But Thompson's Mistress of Vision, written during his later abstinent period at Pantasaph, has often been compared with Kubla Khan, and seems to make use of images from similar opium rêveries of his earlier years. The distinction

which has often been drawn in recent studies between the poetic
creativeness of the addict writers' withdrawal periods and the
literary inertia of their periods of deep addiction is perhaps not a
very revealing one. Withdrawal periods give the writer the
energy to carry on the actual work of composition, but they do
not provide new contents for the writer's imagination.

Thompson himself never discussed the possible effect of either
opium or withdrawal from it on the quality of his imagination.
There are no direct references to opium in his poetry (though
there is a vivid description of the shifting jewelled colours seen
by the smoker of hashish

> 'an eastern Wizard's dreams,
> When, hovering on him through his haschish-swoon,
> All the rained gems of the old Tartarian line
> Shiver in lustrous throbbings of tinged flame').[34]

It has been suggested that in many of Thompson's poems the
sun is a symbol for opium, and its sinking beneath the horizon a
symbol for his deprivation of the drug.[35] But Thompson did not
use the great traditional poetic symbols in this arbitrary way;
they had a fixed equivalence for him, within the framework of
liturgical symbolism.[36] His poetic symbol for opium was the
traditional one of the poppy. This became alive to his imagination on the summer day in 1891 when the child Monica Meynell,
with a symbolic appropriateness amounting to an act of unconscious ritual, picked a poppy in a Suffolk field and gave it to
Thompson saying 'Keep this for ever'. When he used this
incident in his poem The Poppy he hinted at his opium experiences, 'lethargied with fierce bliss', 'drowsed in sleepy
savageries', which cut off his life from normal happiness and
brought him only withered dreams, but dreams from which the
world might benefit. Later, in The Mistress of Vision, he suggested
that poetic inspiration might breathe through opium dreams

> 'And the flowers of dreaming
> Palèd not their fervours,
> For her blood flowed through their nervures'.

The flower of dreaming remained a constant symbol for him.
At the very end of his life, tottering round Wilfrid Blunt's

Sussex garden, he recognized only one among all the flowers. 'Ah, there's a poppy' he said.[37]

Thompson's beliefs about the effect of opium on literary achievement have to be deduced from his studies of other addict writers, not from what he said about his own work. In the many articles and book reviews written in his last years, he discussed almost all the opium-addict writers who have been mentioned in this book, and always with a certain self-conscious curiosity about their opium habit. Reviewing Alfred Ainger's life of Crabbe, he wrote 'It will be news to most that Crabbe was a moderate opium-eater, forced by dyspepsia, and throve on it', and he dwelt on Crabbe's period of poverty in London as the only romantic part of this poet's otherwise drab existence, but added that 'Even that has no picturesque or sordid details'. Crabbe, whose poetry Thompson compared to 'khaki', had obviously not made approved romantic use of this traditional initiatory experience of the opium addicts, as Thompson considered that De Quincey and he himself had.[38]

Coleridge's poems, specially *Kubla Khan* and *Christabel*, were among the earliest that Thompson read, and he revered Coleridge, but did not identify himself with Coleridge as he did with other addict writers. 'Coleridge was always my favourite poet; but I early recognized that to make him a model was like trying to run up a window-pane, or to make clotted cream out of moonlight, or to pack jelly-fish in hampers'. He was severe about Coleridge's addiction and its effect on his literary powers. 'Laudanum by the wine-glassful and half-pint at a time soon reduced him to the journalist-lecturer and philosopher, who projected all things, executed nothing', and he lamented this devastation by opium of 'the mightiest intellect of the day', 'that most piteous and terrible figure of all our literary history'. But Thompson appears to have thought that the splendid poems of Coleridge's youth were inspired by the same agency which afterwards desolated his life and blasted his powers. At any rate he believed that *Kubla Khan* really was composed in a dream, it had a dream character which he recognized from his own experiences.[39] In a later essay he qualified this by adding 'There should be no difficulty, therefore, in admitting the dream-composition of "Kubla Khan"; though how far it was afterwards improved is another matter'.[40]

In Edgar Allan Poe, Francis Thompson recognized a closer affinity with himself, but a dangerous one. Of Poe's tales he said 'One feels the reading of them as it were an unlawful pleasure. . . . The tales are vital with a wrongful vitality. They are told by heroes whose sensitive nerves have the preternatural acuteness of initial insanity; colour, sound, scent—every detail in their rendering becomes morbidly distinct to us, like the ticking of a clock in the dark. . . . The landscapes are preterhuman, painted as with fire, and blinded with a light such as only streams from the fountains of the dreaming brain. . . . Beauty which cannot separate itself from terror, terror tainted by beauty, are the powers which rule this world of an opium-dream. . . . The imagination has seized these things of beauty and terror with more than the closeness of a poet—with the closeness of a dream; and there is no closeness, either to terror or beauty, so appalling as that of a dream'.[41]

There is a distinct note of personal experience in this comment. Thompson recognized a kinship with Poe, and wrote one work in close imitation of him, the prose fantasy *Finis Coronat Opus*. As has often been pointed out, all the trappings of this turgid story are from Poe: the young poet of noble birth in his vast solitary palace, the sinister room with purple velvet curtains and coloured lamps, the horror approaching slowly and secretly, feared and welcomed. But some of its minor constituents seem to come from Thompson's own dream experiences, they are vividly and personally felt, as the symbolic statues and the purple velvet curtains are not. The idol on the altar of the dark chapel, with its copper face soaked in fire and its silver beard that seethed and crept with heat, was perhaps the face of some passer-by which Thompson saw in the light of a street-lamp in his homeless nights in London, but with the crawling fire of his opium vision poured over it. The loud pulse of the throbbing heart, the ticking clock, the great clang of the cathedral bell that announced doom by striking three, seem as if heard by the hyperaesthetic ears of an addict, and the leaf casually seen in the hedge, whose markings suddenly seem to convey a fatal message, suggests the absorbed concentration on trivial objects which overcomes the opium-eater. The effects of light in this story of Francis Thompson's were singled out by M. H. Abrams in *The Milk of Paradise* as specially typical of opium visions; they certainly recall Coleridge's notebook entries about flames and reflections. The greenish writhing tinge of the flame burning on the altar, which presently is streaked and flaked with red; the lamps of amber and peacock blue and green, like the changing lustre on a beetle's back; the flickering spirals of violet, green and flame-coloured glass, undulating in the heat of the lamps; the lights reflected in rainy pools, on the way to the bridge over the dark river—perhaps all these visions in *Finis Coronat Opus* were common bedroom candles and street lamps, seen with opium-blurred eyes on some night when Thompson lay sleepless in rough lodgings or wandered through the wet streets of London and leaned on the parapets of bridges. Thompson in effect signed this story as an opium-inspired one by including in it an incident of a child who gave the poet a flower, recalling the poppy which Monica Meynell had given to him, and which he recognized as the symbol of his addiction and its withered dreams.[42] *Finis Coronat Opus* was written in 1890, that is, during a period of abstinence from opium, but it employed two-year-old memories.

Of Baudelaire, Francis Thompson wrote that he had 'exchanged, as it were, his store of human life blood for strange artistic vibrations, fashioned from these poisoned dreams masterpieces of form, permanent manifestations of what he had purchased from art at the expense of life'. In this comment on Baudelaire, as in some of those on Poe, Thompson seems almost to be identifying the art of poetry with the drug, and blaming those poets who seek from it 'a personal enjoyment, exclusive, exotic, dangerous'.[43] Nearly all his criticisms of other addicted writers tell us more about himself than about them, as when he writes of the Irish poet Mangan that he was a drunkard, not, as his biographers suggested, an opium-eater; a man may be both, but the symptoms of opium with alcohol, or of opium alone, are easily distinguishable. 'A man happens to take a glass of wine, for example, while he is under the influence of opium, and discovers that a powerful and Bacchic exaltation results, very different from the serene and luminous exaltation of opium alone'.[44]

Of all his predecessors, De Quincey was the one with whom Francis Thompson felt the closest kinship.[45] *The Confessions of an English Opium Eater* may actually have influenced Thompson to start experimenting with laudanum, and his flight to London and the life of homeless want that he lived there seems to have been an imitation of De Quincey's. Thompson too had, or imagined that he had, an Ann of Oxford Street who succoured and comforted him. He, too, in later life controlled his opium dosage and struggled against sickness and poverty to make a living by journalism, and the example of De Quincey's 'patient tenacity and purpose' in this struggle was an avowed inspiration to him.[46] He, too, had visions of goddesses of sorrow who brought him revelations of wisdom, or so he claimed in his essay *Moestitiae Encomium* which is an obvious and not very successful pastiche of the style and feeling of De Quincey's *Levana and Our Ladies of Sorrow*. *Moestitiae Encomium* is interesting, all the same, for its opening paragraph which describes a dream landscape of marsh and shadow, grey sky and threatening trees on the horizon, and 'athwart the saturnine marsh, runs long, pitilessly straight, ghastly with an inward pallor (for no gleam dwells on it from the sky), the leprous, pined, infernal watercourse; a water for the Plutonian naiads—exhaling cold perturbation'. This is the rigid canal landscape of Baudelaire's *Rêve Parisien*, but seen as an opium dose is wearing off, not at its climax.

Thompson praised the 'elaborate and thoroughly scientific account of the mysterious workings of opium' given by De Quincey, and marvelled that in spite of it, so many misapprehensions about the effects of opium were still current. 'If only to establish the true effects of the singular drug, to clear it from its fanciful, and confine it to its quite sufficiently real evils', the *Confessions* would be worth reading. But Thompson appears chiefly interested in the moral and physical effects of opium as revealed in the *Confessions*, and has little to say about De Quincey's theories of the operation of opium on dreams and the imagination. He admired De Quincey's writings chiefly for their style, not for their ideas.[47]

Thompson was more concerned with the triumphs and failures of the will than with the workings of the unconscious mind, which did not seem to him the proper stuff of poetry. He was unlikely to use dreams, his own or others', as the substance of any but a slight poem, and he was critical of poetry that explored 'the obscure alleys and lanes of human conduct' as he blamed Browning for doing.[48] Such cogitations were too mortal, in themselves meaningless and useless unless related to faith, so he suggested in *An Anthem of Earth*.

> 'Who the chart shall draw
> Of the strange courts and vaulty labyrinths,
> The spacious tenements and wide pleasances,
> Innumerable corridors far-withdrawn,
> Wherein I wander darkling, of myself?
> Darkling I wander, nor I dare explore
> The long arcane of those dim catacombs,
> Where the rat memory does its burrows make,
> Close-seal them as I may, and my stolen tread
> Starts populace, a *gens lucifuga*'.

He had been in the buried temple, and heard the scurry of light-hating fears, but he was determined not to make poetry out of it. In his essay *Health and Holiness* he acknowledged that most contemporary literature was concerned with the 'contained infirmities' of individual human character; but his own interest was in 'the regality of will'.

There is little evidence that Thompson ever experienced vivid pleasurable dreams in sleep. In his review of a book on *Dreams and Their Meanings*, he mentioned a few characteristics of his own dreams: his senses were heightened in them, new senses were awakened, everything shone with a preternaturally splendid light; as a child he had often had the dream of falling from a height; but he gave little impression that these experiences mattered much to him, or remained vividly in his memory.[49]

Practice

The blissful lethargies of *The Poppy*, the dream experiences recalled in *The Mistress of Vision*, seem to have been the waking
rêveries of the early stage of addiction to opium. Thompson made
this clear in his account of his youthful pleasures in *An Anthem of
Earth*

> 'Dusk grew turbulent with fire before me,
> And like a windy arras waved with dreams.
> Sleep I took not for my bedfellow,
> Who could waken
> To a revel, an inexhaustible
> Wassail of orgiac imageries'.

This passage suggests that Thompson may have experienced
hypnagogic visions, those fiery images seen on the borders of
sleep. Like other opium-addict poets, he may have found that
opium prolonged this borderline experience, and this passage
suggests that the visions directly inspired the formation of poetic
images.

Later he had horrible nightmares, 'a most miserable fortnight
of torpid, despondent days, and affrightful nights, dreams having
been in part the worst realities of my life' he wrote in 1900.[50]
What these nightmares were like may perhaps be deduced from
his description of the *Revelation of Saint John* as being like 'the
pageantry of an appalling dream; insurgent darkness, with wild
lights flashing through it; terrible phantasms, insupportably revealed against profound light, and in a moment no more; on the
earth hurryings to and fro, like insects of the earth at a sudden
candle; unknown voices uttering out of darkness darkened and
disastrous speech; and all this in motion and turmoil, like the
sands of a fretted pool'.[51]

'Like insects of the earth at a sudden candle . . .'; he was
recalling some moment of horror in a filthy lodging, magnified by
opium into an apocalyptic movement of vast crowds, a memory
from

> 'that nightmare-time which still doth haunt
> My dreams'.[52]

His opium habit not only induced nightmares but, once at
least, a waking hallucination during the early part of a with-

drawal period, as he recorded in *Health and Holiness*. He saw a 'minute white-stoled child' sitting in the bell of an arum lily, an apparition which he viewed with delight but no astonishment till, as it vanished, he recognized it as a hallucination. But he was not interested in such mental phenomena for themselves, only for the conclusions which might be drawn from them about the moral justifications and dangers of asceticism. Only two linked poems of his, among the first he ever wrote, are directly drawn from dreams: *Dream-Tryst*, which embodied a dream about a child whom Thompson had met when he was only eleven,[53] and *Not Even in Dream* which described the more enthralling but more terrifying nightmares which displaced the 'divine air' of his early dreams.

Like Coleridge, Francis Thompson seems not to have formulated any theory about the possible effect of his opium habit on his poetic imagination. From his scattered references to the habit in other writers, one may deduce that he thought opium gave a direction and an impetus to a writer's imagination, though an unlawful and dangerous one, paid for by degradation of the moral nature and by a later devastation of the mental powers too. But he was probably incapable of the intense self-scrutiny which De Quincey turned on his own imaginative processes, and, whether capable or not, was unwilling to indulge in it, unless it seemed to confirm the possibility of supernatural intuitions.[54] The influence of opium in Thompson's poetry must be detected by internal evidence, if at all, not with the aid of commentaries supplied by the author.

A poet's choice of imagery has often been used—I have used it myself elsewhere in this book—as an index to the influence of opium on him. But this is a dangerous method at all times, very apt to lead to an argument in a circle. With Francis Thompson it is a nearly impossible method, because his imagery is so profuse and riotous that one can prove nearly anything from it. Suns, stars, seas, flowers, jewels, nymphs, thrones, sepulchres, fortresses, vines, banners, kisses, breasts, veils, sheaves, bees, curls, chaplets, wings, cliffs, trumpets, galleons—they come

Practice

pouring out in what he himself called an 'inexhaustible wassail of orgiac imageries'. The more serious students of his work have been able to analyse and isolate his use of liturgical symbolism, which may perhaps be accepted as the most stable element in his imagery, particularly after he came under the influence of Coventry Patmore.[55] But many of the same symbols were used in a psycho-analytical study of Thompson to prove that he was an example of a 'unique psychical fixation of libido at the oral level. Psychically he was never weaned'.[56] Actually Thompson in his prodigal profusion of imagery uses metaphors of sexual union and parent–child relationships in too much variety—speaking now as the husband, now as the bride, now as the widow, now as the child at the breast or in the womb—for it to be possible to say which, if any, of these images revealed his own needs or lacks or temperament. They reveal no more than that, wishing to describe feelings of obedience, or pursuit, or spiritual dryness, or innocence, he chose symbols from common human experience, some of which may have been his own. In fact, as many critics have pointed out, his imagery owes more to the books he read than to observation of human beings or natural phenomena,[57] and whole areas of his real experience—the squalor and crowded humanity of his nights of poverty in London—are almost excluded from his poetic imagery, though he wrote some memorably vivid prose descriptions of them.[58]

But if it is unsafe to use the imagery of such a profuse image-maker as psycho-analytical evidence against Thompson, it is also unsafe to use it as evidence for the effects of opium addiction. It is therefore with much caution that I will mention his use of certain images which are frequently met in the work of other addict writers, and which do not seem to belong, as plainly as some of his constantly used images do, within the framework of a fixed traditional symbolism, religious or literary.

The speeding up of the sense of time, so that decades and centuries seem to pass in a few moments, is a sensation to which many opium addicts have owned. It seems to have been well known to Francis Thompson, who often used it in his poetry, in a form that suggests an apprehension of Time as a giant building

through which he was being whirled, so that the years flicked
overhead like the arches of a tunnel, or the hours flashed by like
pillars in some endless colonnade, which run together in a blur
as they are passed and left behind by the travelling eye.[59] Space,
like Time, opened huge vistas before his reeling perceptions.
His poems are full of huge circuits among the stars, giddy rides
across 'the long savannahs of the blue'.[60] Music drifts in from
infinite distances, stars shout to each other across the vast
abysses of the universe.[61] Cosmic space expands and contracts, so
that a foot stirring a meadow flower 'flickers the unwithering
stars' or the sunset sky dwindles to a butterfly.[62] This too easy
assumption of giant grandeur, turning planets into toys and
boundless space into a playground and the earth into a trinket
hung from a bracelet, is sometimes very tiresome in Thompson's
poetry. He often, as in *The Hound of Heaven*, used it with a
serious moral significance, but there is something frivolous and
patronizing about his assumption of it all the same, reminiscent
of Baudelaire's description of 'L'Homme-Dieu', the hashish-
smoker in his final development, experiencing 'l'accroissement
monstrueux du temps et de l'espace, deux idées toujours
annexes, mais que l'esprit affronte alors sans tristesse et sans peur.
Il regarde avec un certain délice melancolique à travers les
années profondes, et s'enfonce audacieusement dans d'infinies
perspectives'.[63]

Another notable characteristic of Thompson's imagery is his
use of synaesthesia. This trick of the imagination, as was seen in
Chapter II, is not confined to opium addicts, and some authorities
have thought that it is not among the symptoms of addiction at
all; but there is perhaps sufficient evidence to show that where
this tendency is latent in a writer's imagination, opium greatly
enhances it. Thompson's synaesthetic imagery is one of his most
genuinely brilliant effects, with none of the winsomeness that
spoils much of his poetry, for me at any rate. In his perception
the sun rose in a clash of cymbals and set in 'visible music-blasts'

'I *see* the crimson blaring of thy shawms'.[64]

Tunes rose in twirls of gold, light through the petals of a butter-
cup clanged like a beaten gong, and he could hear

Practice

'The enamelled tone of shallow flute,
     And the furry richness of clarinet'

which last I find a completely accurate transcription of one sense-
perception in terms of another, perhaps influenced by Hoffmann's famous link of clarinet notes with a particular colour and
scent, but more exact.[65]

Thompson thought of himself, with mixed shame and pride,
as a pariah. A schoolboy composition of his shows that this feeling
came to him very early, before his rejection for the priesthood
and well before his addiction to opium,[66] of which it was
one cause, not a result, though as always the opium habit
strengthened this feeling of being an elect outcast. It gave him
some sort of fellow-feeling, though a faint one like most of his
human sympathies, with the drunkards and thieves, and even one
murderer, whom he met in his destitute days in London. In his
poetry he referred to himself as an outlaw, 'a bastard barred from
their inheritance', an 'outcast mark' under the pitiless gaze of the
stars.[67] The touch of complacency about this—the audience,
though hostile, consists of stars and is watching him with great
concentration—robs it of pathos. But I do not suggest that
Thompson's pariah feeling was simply a method of protecting
his idea of himself. He both knew and dreaded the isolation of
spirit which opium inflicts, and he embodied it in an image
known to other addicts.

Two mysterious stanzas in *The Mistress of Vision* link a prospect
of 'tow'rd Cathay' with 'nations underground'. There have been
many interpretations of the main theme of the poem—as a
mystic vision of the Blessed Virgin, as an allegory of poetic
inspiration, as a dream escape from reality. Whatever the main
theme, this further vision of a city buried below the towers of
Cathay, sinking like a dream beyond the horizon of the central
vision, seems to me to stand for opium experience. It is Xanadu,
a palace now sunk underground, that the poet sees eastwards
from the Himalayan peak of his poetic inspiration, that same lost
city that De Quincey imagined his fleeing Tartars reaching at
last, an opium-paradise of rest and relief, but also of melancholy,
of perished memory and lost reason.[68]

Francis Thompson

The image of the sunken city is persistent in Francis Thompson's poetry. It is part of an image-cluster—an involute, De Quincey would have called it—concerned with the processes and failures of poetic inspiration. The imagination, at first winged-heeled like Hermes,

> 'Sure on the verges of precipitous dream,
> Swift in its springing
> From jut to jut of inaccessible fancies'

presently finds itself imprisoned within the rock, enclosed and drawn down through it by the dream, held in icy petrifactions, hardening to marble, crushed like a caryatid with the weight of a monstrous Temple.[69] It is an earthquaked city sinking into the abyss, a hidden world deep under sea.[70] The poet has moments when

> 'like a city under ocean,
> To human things he grows a desolation,
> And is made a habitation
> For the fluctuous universe
> To lave with unimpeded motion.
> He scarcely frets the atmosphere
> With breathing, and his body shares
> The immobility of rocks'.[71]

He saw this petrifaction as potentially a creative process; the poet builds himself into the wall, like the ancient rite of human sacrifice for the protection of a building.[72] The image of poetic creation as a magic palace under the ocean was dear to Thompson. In his essay on Shelley he described the poems of Shelley, Keats and Coleridge as necromantic castles with 'some spirit of pain charm-prisoned at their base', and this is the pattern of his own Palace of the Occident, in *Sister Songs*, with its toppling pinnacles, its mazes and receding labyrinths and stony faces, and at its core,

> 'the unbodied spirit of the sorcerer
> . . . beneath the edifice
> To which itself gave rise;
> Sustaining centre to the bubble of stone
> Which, breathed from it, exists by it alone'.

The necromancer's drowned palace is a beautiful image, but

not as an equivalent for poetic achievement, as Thompson used it. It was perhaps a more vivid image than he knew or intended of the petrifaction of his poetic impulse by his opium addiction. His achievement as a poet was deadened by his experience of that Dream of which he wrote in *Sister Songs*, a power that can seize on a poet and

<blockquote>
'suddenly his limbs entwine,
And draw him down through rock as sea-nymphs
                       might through brine',
</blockquote>

but the rapture of the Dream's embrace died too soon, and the poetry that was conceived in it was a poor unworthy offspring. Neither poetry nor salvation could come from the petrifaction of the drowned palace. The stone had to be turned to start the wing.

XIII

SOME WRITERS WHO TOOK OPIUM OCCASIONALLY

The idea that opium-eating might affect the character of a writer's work was a favourite speculation among literary critics, editors and biographers in the nineteenth century, and many anecdotes about it were recorded. One, which was known to De Quincey and possibly to Coleridge,[1] concerned the actress 'Perdita' Robinson, who was also a poet; the story was related in her *Memoirs*. In 1791, when she was under treatment at Bath for rheumatism, which had brought on crippling lameness, she was ordered by her doctor to take 'near eighty drops of laudanum'. Throughout the ensuing night she dreamt about a miserable madman called Jemmy whom she had seen being pelted with stones and mud in the streets of Bath, and whose wretched condition had seized on her imagination. 'Having slept for some hours, she awoke, and calling her daughter, desired her to take a pen and write what she should dictate. Miss Robinson, supposing that a request so unusual might proceed from the delirium excited by the opium, endeavoured in vain to dissuade her mother from her purpose. The spirit of inspiration was not to be subdued, and she repeated, throughout, the admirable poem of *The Maniac*, much faster than it could be committed to paper. She lay, while dictating, with her eyes closed, apparently in the stupor which opium frequently produces, repeating like a person talking in her sleep. . . . On the ensuing morning, Mrs Robinson had only a confused idea of what had passed, nor could be convinced of the fact till the manuscript was produced. She declared that she had been dreaming of mad Jemmy throughout the night, but was perfectly unconscious of having been awake while she composed the poem, or of the circumstances narrated by her daughter.'[2]

It has been suggested by Professor Schneider[3] that this anecdote put into Coleridge's head the idea of claiming that *Kubla Khan* had been composed in a dream. Mrs Robinson does not seem to have suggested that *The Maniac* was composed while she was asleep; she was awake, but in the euphoric condition produced at first by opium, when the imagination associates freely and actively. The resulting poem was no masterpiece, and its conventional imagery and governess-like moralizing do not sound particularly spontaneous, though there is one interesting stanza

> 'Fix not thy steadfast gaze on me,
> Shrunk atom of mortality!
> Nor freeze my blood with thy distracted groan;
> Ah! quickly turn those eyes away,
> They fill my soul with dire dismay,
> For dead and dark they seem, and almost chill'd to stone!'

which contains the ideas of watching eyes, of cold, of petrifaction, so often found in opium dreams. The anecdote is interesting chiefly for the fact, repeated in later similar cases, that when fully awake Mrs Robinson forgot completely the lines which she had composed in this condition.

The most famous of all stories of this kind is that of Walter Scott when he wrote *The Bride of Lammermoor*. From 1817 to 1819 he suffered a painful illness, whose chief symptom was violent cramps in the stomach, so agonizing that they used sometimes, as he said, to 'send me to bed roaring like a bull-calf'.[4] In the spring of 1819, when he was working on *The Bride of Lammermoor*, he was too ill to write it down himself, and had to dictate it. His amanuenses could hardly bear to carry on when 'his audible suffering filled every pause', but he stoically insisted on continuing; 'though he often turned himself on his pillow with a groan of torment, he usually continued the sentence in the same breath'.[5]

When the pain became unbearably strong—he sometimes had

eight to ten hours of agonizing spasms—he was given large doses of laudanum, but he hated its effects, which in him were only depression and lassitude,[6] and as soon as he was better, he would insist on going for a long ride 'to drive away the accursed vapours of the laudanum I was obliged to swallow last night'.[7] He was convinced that the anodynes which he was obliged to use would be as damaging to his constitution as the pain for which they were prescribed.[8] He had sometimes been given two hundred drops of laudanum and six grains of opium a day, but he was determined to do without opiates as they 'hurt my general health extremely', and he resolutely gave them up.[9]

The Bride of Lammermoor was thus written during bursts of acute pain for which Scott was forced to take considerable doses of laudanum. When the novel was published, and he looked through it again, 'he did not recollect one single incident, character or conversation it contained'. He remembered all the original historical facts on which he had based the novel, but nothing of his own work in moulding these into fiction. His publisher, who recorded Scott's account of this and vouched for its verbal accuracy, remembered that Scott said 'For a long time I felt myself very uneasy in the course of my reading, lest I should be startled by meeting something altogether glaring and fantastic' and that he found it 'monstrous gross and grotesque'.[10] It is significant that Scott not only did not recognize as his own what he had written under the influence of laudanum, but approached this alien creation of his own with some uneasiness, as though it might reveal something fantastic and grotesque, a hidden side of his sunny nature. The difference between the strong-hearted unglamorous Jeanie Deans, heroine of Scott's previous novel, and the lovely but feeble Lucy Ashton, heroine of *The Bride of Lammermoor*, whose neurotic fear and anxiety prepare the way for her outbreak of insanity, is almost an allegory of the difference between Scott's imagination in its natural and in its opium-influenced condition. During this period of intermittent illness, he explained to a friend—who had asked him how he found time, between incessant visitors, to think out his books—how his creative process worked. 'I lie *simmering* over things for an hour

or so before I get up—and there's the time I am dressing to over-
haul my half-sleeping, half-waking *projet de chapitre*—and when I
get the paper before me, it commonly runs off pretty easily'.[11]
The Bride of Lammermoor, product of some of the 'half-sleeping'
'half-waking' moments when Scott was recovering, with the aid
of laudanum, from a crisis of pain, is one of the best-attested
examples of an opium interlude in the work of a non-addicted
writer.

Wilkie Collins adored *The Bride of Lammermoor* which he called
'the greatest of all prose tragedies'.[12] He knew that Walter Scott
took laudanum while he was writing it, and he used this as an
example of the way in which opium could help a writer.[13] Perhaps his knowledge of the anecdote coloured his own account of
the writing of the latter part of *The Moonstone* under the influence
of laudanum. There are many parallels between the two stories—
the amanuensis who could not go on taking dictation because he
was too upset by the groans of the dictating author, the stoicism
of continuing to work in such conditions, the complete forgetting
of the work so produced, so that it seemed entirely alien when
the author later re-read it. One might suppose that Wilkie
Collins had simply appropriated Scott's story for his own, but
for the still earlier story of 'Perdita' Robinson, to which neither
of them refers; the coincidence of the three stories suggests that
this may be a normal experience of writers influenced by
opium.

Wilkie Collins collected reports of writers who had the opium
habit. He told both Hall Caine and William Winter that Bulwer
Lytton had told him that he used opium as a stimulus and a
tranquillizer,[14] and in an article which he wrote on Lytton's *A
Strange Story* he said that Lytton's inspiration for the tale obviously came from laudanum which was the resource that
sustained his work, as he had confessed to Collins.[15] Lytton's
official biographers do not give any details about this habit, and
therefore the possible connection between it and his literary
output cannot be traced; but they do mention the excruciating
fits of earache from which he suffered throughout his life, and
which may well have started him on the opium habit. It is also

possible that he acquired it from his elder brother Henry Lytton Bulwer, who had lived in Constantinople, was subject to violent headaches, and certainly had experience of taking opium, since Monckton Milnes recorded in an unpublished Commonplace Book of 1846–8 that Henry Bulwer had said that 'after taking opium one feels as if one's soul was being rubbed down with silk'.[16]

In the last years of his life Dickens took laudanum occasionally. On his reading tour in America in 1867–8 he had to take it when he went to bed, to calm the nerves which he had wound up for the evening's recital of the death of Tiny Tim, or to subdue the persistent cough which otherwise kept him awake all night.[17] Later, a few weeks before his death, he took it for the pain in his neuralgic foot.[18] He had unpleasant physical reactions, nausea and oppressive feelings, from the opium, but I know of no sign that the small and irregular quantities that he took affected the quality of his writing.[19] But they did help to give him an idea for his last book. John Jasper, the murderer in *Edwin Drood*, is an opium addict. Dickens took trouble to inform himself about the opium habit when he was writing *Edwin Drood*. No doubt he consulted Wilkie Collins, who was not averse to talking about his laudanum habit to his friends, and Dickens may have got the idea of using the effects of opium as an agent in the plot of a novel from *The Moonstone*. John Jasper's addiction was not just put in for atmosphere; it is evident from the last chapter of *Edwin Drood* which Dickens wrote before he died that the old hag whose opium den Jasper frequented was going to contribute to the revelation of his guilt by reporting what she had heard him say during his opium trances. Dickens determined to see for himself what London's opium dens were like. He went with a couple of policemen on their round of slum lodging-houses in Shadwell, and saw just such an old hag, blowing at an opium-pipe made out of an ink-bottle, as he afterwards described in *Edwin Drood*.[20]

The opium scenes in *Edwin Drood* are brilliantly convincing when they describe the dialogue and movements of the drugged man, but sound factitious when they depict his visions of processions, flashing scimitars, and dancing girls. An American

Practice

doctor who had himself experimented with opium-smoking criticized the visions which Dickens bestowed on John Jasper as more like those of a hashish-smoker than an opium-smoker.[21] They are the conventional properties of drug visions in fiction. But Jasper's obsessive brooding, during his opium trances, on his plan of murder is much more convincing. He commits the murder over and over again in his mind. 'I have done it hundreds of thousands of times in this room . . . hundreds of thousands of times. What do I say? I did it millions and billions of times. I did it so often, and through such vast expanses of time, that when it was really done, it seemed not worth the doing, it was done so soon'. When he had actually done the murder in real life, it seemed such a short and trivial thing, compared with the huge sadistic enjoyment of his visions, that he had to return to the opium den to recapture the deeper pleasures of his fantasy murder. [Plate ix]

Dickens is not likely to have indulged in pleasurable fantasies of murdering anybody, as a result of the small doses of laudanum which he occasionally took; but perhaps his account of John Jasper's opium trance reflects some experience of his own when some task before him magnified itself into a vast and fateful operation, endlessly repeated, during the broken laudanum-induced sleep of a night in a strange hotel bed in America, with an evening of tense applauding crowds behind him, and the expectation of exerting himself for another tense applauding audience next day.

Charlotte Brontë claimed that her method of constructing an opium scene in a novel was not, like that of Dickens, by observation and report, combined with a small degree of personal experience, but by a straight exercise of the imagination. Mrs Gaskell asked her whether she had ever taken opium, to account for the vivid scene in *Villette* in which Lucy Snowe, drugged by a 'strong opiate', wanders about the night streets of Brussels. Charlotte Brontë replied that as far as she knew she had never taken opium in any form; to produce this scene, she had used the technique which she always employed when she needed to describe something outside her own experience—she 'thought intently on it for many a night before falling to sleep—wondering what it was like or how it would be—till at length, sometimes after her story had been arrested at this one point for weeks, she wakened up in the morning with all clear before her, as if she had in reality gone through the experience and then could describe it, word for word, as it happened'.[22] Perhaps the luminous colours and fantastic architecture which Lucy Snowe's drugged eye saw in the street lamps and pasteboard decorations of the fête in *Villette* were not entirely evolved by Charlotte Brontë from her unaided imagination. If she herself had never taken opium, her brother Branwell had been addicted to it in the last years of his life, when he was living at home at Haworth. 'In procuring it he showed all the cunning of the opium-eater. He would steal out while the family were at church—to which he had professed himself too ill to go—and manage to cajole the village druggist out of a lump; or, it might be, the carrier had unsuspiciously brought him some in a packet from a distance'.[23] His sister had plenty of opportunities to observe the effects of opium. That she portrayed these convincingly is attested by Mrs Gaskell from her own knowledge. 'The description given in "Villette" was so exactly like what I had experienced—vivid and exaggerated presence of objects, of which the outlines were indistinct, or lost in golden mist'.[24] Mrs Gaskell was probably remembering the aftermath of some isolated medicinal dose; there is no indication that she had the habit.

Some nineteenth-century writers seem to have felt that other writers who took opium as a stimulus to literary exertion were in some way cheating, like trainers who dope horses to win a race. The American poetess Julia Ward Howe, resentful at what she considered the inadequate praise given to her work by the Brownings, published a poem called *One Word More with E.B.B.* in which she accused Mrs Browning of relying on 'pinions other than her own' for her literary flights, because she was inspired by drugs.

Whether or not she was inspired by it, Mrs Browning did indeed take opium. She had probably taken it as a very young woman, in her first serious illness; she was certainly prescribed it during her later years of illness—the result of a broken blood-vessel—from 1837 to 1845. In one of her letters to Browning before their marriage she gave a lively picture of the way in which medical practice of that time used opium. She explained that 'my opium comes in to keep the pulse from fluttering and fainting—to give the right composure and point of balance to the nervous system. I don't take it for "my spirits" in the usual sense; you must not think such a thing. The medical man who came to see me made me take it the other day when he was in the room, before the right hour and when I was talking quite cheerfully, just for the need he observed in the pulse. "It was a necessity for my position" he said. Also I do not suffer from it in any way, as people usually do who take opium. I am not even subject to an opium headache'.[25] Later she tried to convince Browning, who wanted her to give up her morphine draughts, why she had to have them. 'It might strike you as strange that I who have had no pain—no acute suffering to keep down from its angles—should need opium in any shape. But I have had restlessness till it made me almost mad: at one time I lost the power of sleeping quite—and even in the day, the continual aching sense of weakness has been intolerable—besides palpitation—as if one's life, instead of giving movement to the body, were imprisoned undiminished within it, and beating and fluttering impotently to get out, at all the doors and windows. So the medical people gave me opium—a preparation of it, called morphine, and ether—and ever since I have been calling it my amreeta draught, my elixir—because the tranquillizing power has been wonderful'.[26]

Neither Mrs Browning nor her doctors realized that the rest-lessness and insomnia for which she was prescribed opium were caused by previous opium doses, were in fact the classic with-drawal symptoms. She was never enslaved by her opium habit, but was able to reduce it greatly when she married Browning and went to Italy, and to give it up altogether when she was pregnant, and was told it might be bad for the unborn child.[27] She resumed it in later life, but under doctor's orders. She never thought it important, either way; it was a medicine among others, to her, and there is almost no evidence that she connected it in any way with her writing. Once in a letter to her brother she did suggest that her ideal life would be to write all day and all night, all alone in some cedarn grove 'in an hourly succession of poetical paragraphs and morphine draughts'.[28] But she never seems to have speculated on how the morphine draughts might modify the poetical paragraphs. I have analysed in another book the possible influence of her opium habit on her writing, with its effects of hyperaesthesia and synaesthesia, its cosmic infinities, its sudden chills and rotting apparitions, stony faces and cloudy temples, the unexpected juxtapositions of its imagery.[29] The influence is most plainly visible in her 1844 *Poems*, mainly written during the years of ill-health during which she took morphine regularly. The widespread conviction at that time that opium affected a writer's style is shown by the comment of a reviewer in the *Quarterly* who, discussing Mrs Browning's 1844 volume, said that '*A Rhapsody of Life's Progress*, had it not appeared under a lady's name, might have been conjectured to have been written under the influence of opium'. The qualities in this poem which aroused the reviewer's suspicions were probably its giddy effect of expanding and contracting space—at one moment the stars are within reach of a hand, and the tops of the cedar trees brush the feet of angels in heaven, and then there is a sense of 'vast golden spaces like witnessing faces', of huge tides of infinity rolling overhead and cracking the arched vault of human life that shuts them out.

Writers like Walter Scott and Elizabeth Barrett Browning suffered neither character deterioration nor permanent re-orientation of their literary style as a result of their periods of taking opium under medical advice. Their strong wills—and moreover the family love, literary success and sufficient income which they enjoyed—prevented the opium habit from getting a permanent foothold in their personalities. Even with these pro-tective advantages, they may not have found it easy to give up the habit. It was far more difficult for unsuccessful poverty-stricken writers like Edgar Allan Poe and the second James Thomson ('B.V.') to resist. To blot out the very real ills of their lives they sometimes took opium, but in both men one indulgence partly shielded them from another; they were kept out of the full grip of opium by the grasp which alcoholism had on them. There is little evidence that James Thomson took opium regularly or often,[30] and his references to it are mostly to the early euphoric stage of the habit. Some of the despairing inhabitants of the City of Dreadful Night woke to find themselves there after a blissful opium escape

> 'From wandering through many a solemn scene
> Of opium visions, with a heart serene
> And intellect miraculously bright:
> I wake from daydreams to this real night'.[31]

James Thomson was perhaps induced to experiment with opium by his deep admiration for De Quincey, one of his favourite authors from his boyhood on. Several of the titles of his works— *To Our Ladies of Death*, *Mater Tenebrarum*, *A Lady of Sorrow*—are borrowed from De Quincey, and *To Our Ladies of Death*, in which he gives his fullest description of what opium could do for him, follows the pattern of De Quincey's *Levana and Our Ladies of Sorrow*. Thomson's Sisters are not an allegory of death itself, but of the ways of living which lead to different deaths. Our Lady of Beatitudes is the priestess of heroes and saints; Our Lady of Annihilation is the priestess of the sinful, the passionate, the proud, the selfish; but Our Lady of Oblivion corresponds to De Quincey's Mater Suspiriorum, and is the priestess of

> 'The weak, the weary, and the desolate,
> The poor, the mean, the outcast, the opprest'.

She is the Queen of the Pariahs, and carries a poppy-wreath as her 'anodyne of grace', and confers on her followers

> 'An opiate charm to curtain all his days,
> A passive languor of oblivious dream'.

Entwined with 'wreaths of opiate odour' her votaries lie 'passionless, senseless, thoughtless', and when they wake,

> 'arise renewed:
> In soul and body, intellect and will,
> Equal to cope with Life whate'er its mood'.[32]

No such renewal really came to Thomson's impoverished unsuccessful lonely life, only the appalling nights of sleepless restlessness and endlessly extended time which he describes in his poem *Insomnia*, which seems to be an account of a withdrawal experience, perhaps the most vivid and terrible description ever written of this wretched condition. His final collapse and death were due to alcohol, not opium, and the black despair which clouded his life was the cause, not the result, of his indulgence in both alcohol and opium. In them he sought but did not find that blessed condition of indolence celebrated by the first James Thomson, described by his namesake as the state of the 'idlers by grace' who are free from anxiety, live fully in the present, and 'are always all that they are, and seek not to be more or otherwise'.[33] The first James Thomson seems to have given a name and a shape to a condition of equilibrium which many later poets were to recognize as propitious and necessary to poetic creation; some of them were to seek it through the medium of opium. The second James Thomson wrote an essay on *Indolence* and a poem called *The Lord of the Castle of Indolence*, but he never himself achieved the condition of creative detachment which he hymned in these works. He experienced only an 'evil lethargy',

> 'that dull swoon
> Which drugs and with a leaden mantle drapes
> The outworn to worse weariness'.[34]

He, and all the inhabitants of the City of Dreadful Night, were predisposed to despair by natural melancholy of temperament; drink or drugs could only darken what was already black. On a height above the City of Dreadful Night was a huge sombre statue of its Patroness and Queen, the Melancholy portrayed by Dürer.[35] Dürer, himself a vivid dreamer of strange cosmic dreams, seems unwittingly to have created a lifelike image of the peculiar wretchedness of the drug addict when he conceived his *Melencolia*, that moody sultry woman who sits gazing at nothing, the whites of her eyes showing and her shoulders hunched. [Plate vi] This image may be seen evolving towards actual identification with the idea of drug addiction through a series of engravings. Chifflart's frontispiece to Baudelaire's translation of Poe's *Tales* shows a lowering self-absorbed woman, holding a compass and an empty goblet, who is obviously based on Dürer's

Melancholy but is linked with the opium myths of Poe and Baudelaire. [Plate vii] Eugène Grasset's grisly lithograph of a female drug addict takes the identification a stage further; a hypodermic syringe has replaced the compasses, mysterious habiliments have been exchanged for squalid rags, but the derivation from Dürer's image is still unmistakable, and the mood is still the same—a private world of a terror that is almost enjoyed. [Plate viii] Dürer's engraving had a special absorbing significance for other opium-eating writers besides James Thomson. Francis Thompson used the figure of *Melencolia* for his image of the widowed Earth with her brooding gaze in *From the Night of Forebeing*. Gérard de Nerval related in *Aurelia* that the likeness of *Melencolia* once caused him such terror in a dream that his own screams woke him.

Gérard de Nerval in fact may not have been a drug addict at all, though he is often identified as one. The enormous prestige of Baudelaire's *Paradis Artificiels* hangs like a sulphureous cloud over the whole of French mid-nineteenth-century literary mythology, and it would be a work of research far beyond the scope of this book to penetrate through it to the truth about drugs and Gérard de Nerval, or Rimbaud, or Merimée, or Loti. The buried city of Hénochia, subterranean refuge from the waters of the Deluge, in *Voyage en Orient*, and the necromantic dynasties of *Aurélia* in their vast caverns hidden under pyramids, might seem to suggest that Gérard de Nerval's visions owed something to drugs, as well as to his fits of insanity.[36] But recent French studies have shown that he was influenced by the English painter John Martin, and that the source of his fantastic cities and cosmic catastrophes was, partly at least, engravings of *The Fall of Nineveh* and *Belshazzar's Feast*.[37] The fashionable images of the age, as I have suggested in Chapter IV, were available equally to addict and non-addict writers, and none of them can by themselves be used as evidence of drug addiction where there is no supporting biographical evidence.

To produce such evidence for the many French writers of the nineteenth century who were reported to have experimented with drugs, and to analyse their works in the light of it, would have been far beyond my knowledge and would have swelled this book to unwieldy size. I will content myself with tracing one curious arabesque of the opium theme through the arts in nineteenth-century France.

In 1828 Alfred de Musset published what can only be called an impertinent travesty, rather than a translation, of *The Confessions of an English Opium Eater*.[38] He inserted Spanish beauties reclining on blue divans ('couleur inséparable de ces sortes de rêves'), singing boatmen, mountain-top picnics to the tune of mandolines, dissected corpses, decapitated heads, processions of skeletons carrying bluish candles—a whole hotch-potch of visions which are not in the original at all. Moreover he turned De Quincey's sickly pathetic little prostitute Ann into a raven-haired beauty whom De Quincey is made to meet again, hung with diamonds, in a glittering ball-room; and he threw in a wicked lord, a duel, and an elopement. He did, however, translate pretty faithfully De Quincey's passage about the events of his past life becoming incarnated in music under the influence of opium; and he conveyed some idea of De Quincey's visions of the haunting face of a lost girl, and of a sense of doom and guilt and fatal decisions.

Two years later Hector Berlioz composed his *Symphonie Fantastique*, an 'episode in the life of an artist', built round the theme of a young musician haunted by a woman's face which for him is inextricably associated with a musical phrase, the 'idée fixe'. Everywhere, in ball-rooms, in the fields, he sees this ideal woman and at last, despairing of gaining her love, he poisons himself with opium; but the dose, not strong enough to kill him, gives him a horrible vision that he has murdered his beloved, and has been condemned to execution, to which he is carried in solemn procession.

The influence of Alfred de Musset's version of *The Confessions of an English Opium Eater* on the programme of the *Symphonie Fantastique* is obvious not only in the story, but in the idea of human characteristics incarnated in musical phrases; and the connection is underlined by the use of opium for the attempted suicide. Three years later Berlioz, having transformed De Quincey's life (or Alfred de Musset's version of De Quincey's life) into music, carried this process one stage further and attempted to act out his musical theme in his own life. He had a quarrel with the actress Harriet Smithson, with whom he was passionately and impatiently in love, but who was vacillating about marrying him. 'Il y a eu des désespoirs de sa part; il y a eu un reproche de ne pas l'aimer; la-dessus, je lui ai répondu de guerre lasse en m'empoisonnant à ses yeux. Cris affreux d'Henriette!—désespoir sublime!—rires atroces de ma part!—désir de revivre en voyant ses terribles protestations d'amour—émetique!—ipécacuanha!—vomissement de deux heures!—il n'est resté que deux grains d'opium; j'ai été malade trois jours et j'ai survécu'.[39]

Berlioz's biographers seem to assume that this is a dead serious record of an actual event,[40] but it reads almost like a conscious self-parody. He must have been aware of the parallel with the 'Episode de la Vie d'un Artiste'; was he perhaps describing what was actually a fairly banal lovers' quarrel in the heroic symbols of his own symphonic programme, and mocking himself as he did so? The chief objection to this theory is 'ipécacuanha!—vomissement de deux heures!' Narcotics might be employed in an imaginary build-up of the romantic hero, but not emetics. Probably Berlioz did make some attempt to commit suicide with opium, though perhaps, like Poe in his similar attempt, he made sure that the dose was not really a fatal one, just as the hero of the *Symphonie Fantastique* had, according to Berlioz's own programme note, taken a 'dose du narcotique trop faible pour lui donner la mort'.

Berlioz may have experimented with opium when he first read Alfred de Musset's version of the *Confessions*, at the time when he was composing the *Symphonie Fantastique*, but I know of no evidence for this, or for his having taken it before the suicide attempt in 1833, though he was to take it fairly regularly thirty years later, when he was tortured by neuralgia.[41] The *Symphonie Fantastique* is, among many other more important things, an attempt to convey in musical terms the obsessed fixation of the opium addict (in some versions of its 'programme' the opium dose incident is placed in the preamble, which would make the

(v) 'To muse for long unwearied hours . . .'; Egaeus, opium-addict hero
of Berenice. Illustration by Wögel in Baudelaire's translation of Poe's
Tales of Mystery and Imagination.

(vi) 'A lifelike image of the peculiar wretchedness of the drug addict'. Dürer's Melencolia.

(vii) *The* Melencolia *image appropriated for Poe and Baudelaire.*
Chifflart's frontispiece to Baudelaire's translation of Poe's Tales.

(viii) '*A private world of terror that is almost enjoyed*'. *Eugène Grasset's lithograph* Drug Addict, *evolved from Dürer's* Melencolia.

(ix) *John Jasper in the opium den. Illustration by Luke Fildes to Edwin Drood.*

whole symphony, not merely the fourth movement, an opium vision). The love affair of the symphony's opium fantasy is grandiose: exaltations, noble melancholy, tenderness, beauties of nature, delirious passion, guilty violence, heroic expiation. When Berlioz tried to live it out in real life, what he got was frightful shrieks from Harriet and two hours' vomiting. It was the same with Dickens's brilliantly imagined John Jasper in *Edwin Drood*. In his opium dreams the murder he was planning was a thrilling pleasure, endlessly repeated, with his victim terrified and imploring. When he actually committed the murder it was short, easy, almost unimportant, a 'poor mean miserable thing'. Opium may arrange desires into fantastic symphonies, but real events cannot be bent to fit these fantasy lives; they remain intractable, and have to be returned to.

XIV

KEATS

'This morning I am in a sort of temper indolent and supremely careless: I long after a stanza or two of Thomson's Castle of indolence. My passions are all asleep from my having slumbered till nearly eleven and weakened the animal fibres all over me to a delightful sensation about three degrees on this side of faintness. . . . The fibres of the brain are relaxed in common with the rest of the body, and to such a happy degree that pleasure has no show of enticement and pain no unbearable frown. Neither Poetry, nor Ambition, nor Love have any alertness of countenance as they pass by me: they seem rather like three figures on a Greek vase—a man and two women whom no one but myself could distinguish in their disguisement. This is the only happiness; and is a rare instance of advantage in the body overpowering the Mind'.[1]

In this famous letter of 19th March 1819, Keats described one of the states of feeling to which he attached the word 'indolence', and referred it back to the poet who first identified it in terms of the poetic temper. The word comes from the Latin *indolentia*, freedom from pain, and the meaning 'laziness' which is now normally given to it is a secondary one. Its primary meaning in English was either 'insensibility to pain; want of feeling' or 'freedom from pain, a neutral state, in which neither pain nor pleasure is felt', and only thence 'the disposition to avoid trouble; love of ease; laziness; sluggishness'.

Life in James Thomson's delectable Castle of Indolence was easy but not sluggish. As one entered it, one put on slippers and dressing-gown, but though Thomson encouraged one to be comfortable, he did not allow squalor; clean linen was *de rigueur*.

The beds were extremely comfortable and the cooking was superb, but one did more than sleep and eat; one looked at pictures by Claude and Poussin, listened to an Aeolian harp, wrote poetry, strolled about on lawns by beds of poppies, or did a little gardening or fishing. One could even, it almost seems, watch television

> 'One great amusement of our household was
> In a huge crystal magic globe to spy
> Still as you turn'd it, all things that do pass
> Upon this ant-hill earth'.[2]

But one could also get away from it; there was room for everyone to be alone in the landscape if they wanted to. One could do exactly what one pleased, and allow everyone else to do what they pleased. Virtue became 'repose of mind, A pure ethereal calm, that knows no storm', only 'soft gales of passion', just enough to 'gently stir the heart, thereby to form A quicker sense of joy'. It was the Castle of Indolence as Not-Feeling, not of Indolence as Sloth; though Lethargy lay snoring in the dungeon below.

From the moment when it appeared, *The Castle of Indolence* became a favourite poem of other imaginative writers. Young, Collins, Gray, Cowper and Burns are all said to have been influenced by it. Wordsworth carried it about in his pocket and found its allegory a fit framework for a description of his own and Coleridge's poetic temperaments;[3] he once identified 'holy indolence' with the 'wise passiveness' which was the best preparation for creative activity.[4] De Quincey quoted *The Castle of Indolence* to enhance the mood of the most idyllic hour in his *Confessions of an English Opium Eater*.[5] The second James Thomson wistfully imagined a Lord of the Castle of Indolence who could be at once untroubled and intense, indolent and fruitful.[6] Keats found himself longing after a stanza or two of the poem. *The Castle of Indolence* seems to have been recognized by many writers as a close-fitting allegory for a mood which can be auspicious, even indispensable, for the start of poetic creation, though it is dangerous as well as propitious; the not-feeling which took the pang from grief might also at last take the joy from beauty, and everything might be only seen, not felt, as Coleridge dejectedly recognized.

'Indolence' was one of Keats's portmanteau words, like 'identity' and 'ethereal' and 'sensation' and 'intensity'. For him the word enclosed several related and changing meanings. Much has been written about the sense in which he used it at various times, and its value as a necessary pre-condition for poetic creation. Critical comment has concentrated on the point at which Keats's idea of indolence overlapped with his idea of 'abstraction', or detachment, or disinterestedness; on indolence as 'a quiet receptivity of the soul . . . natural and effortless expansion', in Middleton Murry's words,[7] as one extreme of the necessary ebb and flow of poetic power.[8] An analysis of some of the other senses in which he used it will lead to the reason why a chapter on Keats has been included in this book.

Keats sometimes used the word 'indolence' simply as a synonym for laziness or idleness. He was too indolent to fill up his letters from Scotland with details as Charles Brown did, or to write letters at all; as he lolled on two chairs in indolent luxury at the end of a long day's walking, he was affronted by Brown's industry in getting out pen and paper to write up his journal; and when he did write a poem himself, he apologized for being 'so indolent as to write such stuff' instead of something more strenuous.[9] Mental laziness of this kind finds its extreme expression in Keats's reference to the readers whose minds the reviewers have 'enervated and made indolent' so that they no longer bother to think for themselves.[10]

He also used the word 'indolence' for purely physical movements of laziness: Endymion sleepily stretching his indolent arms in the air, the wayward indolence of the foam spreading down the wave's green back, the eagles floating on motionless wings over Loch Awe 'in an indolent fit'[11]—though in this last quotation we cannot be sure that 'indolent' carries no overtones beyond mere laziness; eagles were allegorical creatures for Keats, a type of those 'superior beings' who may look down on the highest human endeavour as though it were an animal's graceful instinctive attitudes.

But he also recognized in himself a kind of indolence which, though not pleasant, might be fruitful, might be a case of *reculer pour mieux sauter*. When his brother George was about to leave for America, he wrote in a state of lethargy, of 'unpleasant numbness which nevertheless does not take away the pain of existence', a state in which he had no interest in anything and would make no effort to save himself from drowning. Nevertheless the results of such an 'indolent' withdrawal from effort and action would be a richer output later on.[12] In another letter a year later, he defined 'easy indolence' as a state in which speculations, even unpleasant and unproductive ones, when indulged in by a poet in solitude, were less of a waste of time than 'uneasy indolence', spent among uncongenial people whose personalities teased him without interesting or rousing him.[13]

Better than this 'easy indolence'—which was withdrawn and perhaps gloomy but not useless—was 'diligent indolence', in Keats's famous and delightful paradox, the mood in which by reflecting on some passage of literature one was led to the starting-post for a voyage of conception;[14] the equivalent of Wordsworth's 'wise passivity', the receptive calm in which the mind was a thoroughfare for all thoughts, and which was a precondition of poetic creation. This was the sense in which Keats was using the word when he spoke of Shakespeare having 'the utmost achievement of human intellect beneath his indolent and kingly gaze';[15] there is the poised eagle high above the world. This sense of indolence, as has often been pointed out, is linked to Keats's great definition of 'negative capability'.

But there was a fourth sense in which Keats used the word 'indolence'—besides the senses of laziness, mental and physical, of withdrawal, and of passivity—and I think it was this fourth and last sense that came to predominate. Its first use in this sense seems to be in the passage in *Endymion* where Keats suggested that the emotions of the past, all except love, tend to turn cool and calm, they become 'indolent'.[16] This is the Latin *indolentia*, freedom from feeling, and it is met again, though not named as indolence, in the Cave of Quietude, reached through the tombs of buried griefs, the dark and silent realm where 'anguish does

not sting; nor pleasure pall'.[17] This characteristic of the Cave of
Quietude has sometimes been equated with the line from the
Ode on Indolence describing that condition in which

'Pain had no sting, and pleasure's wreath no flower'.

But there is a vital difference; in the Cave of Quietude one is
free from pain, but pleasure is not only intense but everlasting;
in the *Indolence* ode neither pain nor pleasure is intensely felt, and
this is the sense in which Keats's conception of 'indolence' developed. In a letter of October 1817 he spoke of an 'indolent
enjoyment of intellect' as opposed to a heart which is always open
to feeling for others. This is the second sense of indolence, 'a
neutral state, in which neither pain nor pleasure is felt'. There
is a link between this use of the word and what Keats sometimes
called 'abstraction', as when in his famous letter to Bailey on
Imagination and Sensation, he asked Bailey 'should you observe
anything cold in me not to put it down to the account of heart-
lessness but abstraction—for I assure you I sometimes feel not the
influence of a Passion or Affection during a whole week';[18] or in
the painful letter of September 1818 when he talked of plunging
into abstract images to free himself from the continual consciousness of his dying brother's face.[19] But this 'abstraction' was produced by a conscious act of the will. The not-feeling indolence
was a mood, not a philosophy; a *feeling* of detachment, not a
theory as to whether a poet should or should not be committed.
I have avoided the difficult question of Keats's idea of the poet's
vocation. Many attempts have been made to reconcile his poet
who must be kept restless by the miseries of this world with his
detached poet who serenely contemplates pain and cruelty as
graceful instinctive attitudes. Keats threw out so many unforgettable phrases in the course of his speculations that by selective
quotation one can prove him to have been an adherent of whatever philosophy one favours oneself; and we should all like to
have Keats on our side. But I do not believe he had made up his
own mind by the time he died—he was against the making up of
minds in any case—and in discussing his notion of 'indolence', I
am not going to attempt an interpretation of the poetic philosophy
to which it was related. It is the mood itself with which I am

concerned—a mood which might be favourable or dangerous to poetic creation. Will and conscience might rationalize it, use it to establish objectivity; but in itself it was not much more than a physical sensation, which came unbidden though, as I shall suggest, latterly not quite unaided.

On 17th March 1819, Keats wrote to his brother and sister-in-law in America about easy and uneasy indolence. In the next two days he had a series of experiences which moved the idea of not-feeling indolence towards the front of his mind as one of the themes that was to pre-occupy him during the following months. He had an accident to his eye which gave him a good deal of pain, he *perhaps* took laudanum to deaden the pain, and he experienced some delightful hours of waking but dreamy euphoria to which he gave the name of indolence and which he described in the words quoted at the beginning of this chapter.

The operative word in my last sentence is 'perhaps'. There is no absolute evidence that Keats ever tasted laudanum before the winter of 1819–20, after he had written all his important poetry. If he really took it then for the first time, he has no place in this book, which is concerned with the effect of opium on the writing of literature. The opium history of Crabbe, Coleridge, De Quincey, Wilkie Collins, Francis Thompson, is documented; there is contemporary evidence that they did take opium before they wrote the works discussed in this book. Keats is the exception, and that is why he appears at the end of this book, out of chronological order, in a chapter of speculation in which the experiences of the other writers previously discussed, and known to have taken opium, are brought to bear for comparison. What I have to say about the possible effects of occasional doses of laudanum on the poetry which Keats wrote in 1819 is not fact but guessing, and is proffered as such.

Many lovers of Keats will be annoyed that it should be proffered at all. The suggestion that Keats may have taken opium fairly often over several months may be resented as a desecration. We are all so fond of Keats that we cannot bear anything that seems like a reflection on him, and to say that a man took opium, even in small quantities for a short time, seems to us now to impugn his courage and will-power. But it must be said once again that this is hindsight when applied to the early nineteenth century. For Keats, himself a qualified doctor, and for other doctors of the period, there was nothing guilty or shameful about taking laudanum regularly yourself, or prescribing it for others. It was a poison if you took too much of it, of course; so were many other medicines in habitual use. To get ourselves into the right frame of mind to consider Keats's possible use of laudanum, a fair parallel to choose would be to imagine what we should feel if it was suddenly discovered that he was addicted to taking Turkish baths, to calm his nerves and keep him in good health. We should be interested, but not at all shocked. If we heard that he had taken to spending all his time in a Turkish bath, neglecting all his duties and never emerging into the light of day, then indeed we might be disappointed and disillusioned. But if we were told merely that he had a Turkish bath once or twice a week; felt occasionally that he was getting rather too dependent on them and enervated by them, and had therefore cut them down to once a fortnight; and, once or twice, when he was feeling particularly rheumaticky, actually slept in the bath-house for a night or two; then we should regard this as one of the experiences, morally indifferent in themselves, which went to make up Keats's character. (We know now that laudanum-taking, even in small quantities, is morally dangerous, not morally indifferent; but few people knew that in 1819.) We should note with interest an increase in Keats's use of images connected with changes of temperature, steam-clouds and expanses of rosy flesh, and of ideas of purgation and ritual ordeals, and we should quote the 'moist anguish' from *La Belle Dame sans Merci* and the 'cold full sponge' to which the arriving guests in *Lamia* were treated. All deductions of this kind are easy to parody, but they are not for that reason all baseless, and my sketch of Keats as an indulger in Turkish baths suggests how we should feel about the possibility that he indulged in laudanum.

Even if it were accepted that Keats was a moderate and intermittent laudanum taker from early in 1819, it would do no more than, at most, cast a little light on some of his imagery and turn of

thought in the 1819 poems. The really important influences on
Keats at this time—his love for Fanny Brawne, the recent death
of one of his brothers and emigration of the other, his deteriorat-
ing health, his feelings about the ill-success of his poetry, his
financial troubles, the books he was reading—are a matter of
fact, not speculation, and have been abundantly studied by
experts. So too have his main poetical themes—man in his
relation to evil and suffering, the consolations of natural and
artistic beauty, the growth of the soul. What follows in this
chapter is not much more than an extended footnote on Keats's
observation of the moods which helped or hindered a poet when
he was embarking on such themes, and on one possible physical
cause of such moods.

Charles Armitage Brown, in the account of Keats's life which
he wrote a few years after his friend's death, said that in the
winter of 1819–20 Keats, having been interrupted by business
while he was writing *The Fall of Hyperion* and *The Cap and Bells*,
found he could not resume them, and became inconsolably
unhappy. 'He was too thoughtful, or too unquiet; and he began
to be reckless of health. Among other proofs of recklessness, he
was secretly taking, at times, a few drops of laudanum to keep
up his spirits. It was discovered by accident, and, without delay,
revealed to me. He needed not to be warned of the danger of
such a habit: but I rejoiced at his promise never to take another
drop without my knowledge'.[20]

If this means, as it has often been interpreted, that as soon as
Keats started taking laudanum it was discovered by accident and
at once reported to Brown, then Keats's laudanum-taking would
have no importance for his work, as by then he had practically
ceased to write. But I think Brown meant that Keats's laudanum-
taking was reported to him as soon as it was discovered, not as
soon as it started; and in that case it may have started at any time.
The two men shared a house at that time, but had separate rooms,
and by no means knew all each other's concerns; Keats, for
instance, did not know for some time that Brown was sleeping
with the servant Abigail Donaghue.

Practice

Brown's account of the incident would probably have been different if he had written it in 1819 instead of in the years between 1829 and 1836. In 1822 De Quincey's *Confessions of an English Opium Eater* had been published; it aroused enormous interest, and what had been regarded as a normal household remedy suddenly acquired notoriety as a dangerous and insidious poison. The friends of addicts like Coleridge already knew and discussed this, before the *Confessions* were published, but to the general public it was a new light. Thereafter no friend or biographer of a poet could reveal, or reader of his poetry could learn, that he had been a laudanum-taker without adding a special tinge to his character. Brown perhaps read his feelings about opium in 1830 back into his discovery in the winter of 1819–20 that Keats had been taking laudanum, and added solemnity to his account of the warning he had given Keats at the time.

Keats himself never mentioned taking laudanum, and the fact that he did mention taking another remedy, mercury, may be seen as evidence against his having experimented with laudanum. There are occasional mentions of opium in his letters and poems, as a synonym for poison or intoxicants,[21] and fairly frequent references to opiates and poppied sleep, to being intoxicated by draughts of poppies, or drowsed with their fume;[22] but these references are mostly symbolic or decorative, or at least without any apparent literal application to himself. The theme of drugs and dreams is one thread in the intricate thought of the beginning of *The Fall of Hyperion*. The image of the fanatical sect of the Assassins, and the paradise into which they were transported, seemingly in a hashish dream, lies behind the opening lines; and Asian poppies, domineering potions and paradise gardens are interwoven with the imagery of the poem, as a parallel for visionary experience. But there seems no evidence that Keats was specially interested in drugs or their mental effects for their own sake. He had, after all, been accustomed to dispensing medicines during his early medical training under Thomas Hammond, the Edmonton surgeon, and had attended lectures on *materia medica* when he was a student at Guy's. He probably thought of laudanum simply as one of several remedies in normal clinical use.

As such, he may have taken it in the spring of 1819 for the complaint which he had by then diagnosed as incipient pulmonary tuberculosis; it was often recommended for this purpose—De Quincey, for instance, believed that it was a sovereign protection against consumption.[23] It seems to be generally agreed now among the experts, though with some dissentients,[24] that Keats contracted pulmonary tuberculosis from his brother Tom, who died of it in December 1818 and whom Keats had been nursing for months in an unventilated room; and that the recurring sore throat from which Keats suffered through the winter of 1818 and spring and summer of 1819 was not laryngeal tuberculosis, already established, but inflammation from teeth or tonsils.[25] For this he at first took mercury in the form of calomel. Whether or not he had previously had syphilis or pellagra—both have been suggested and refuted[26]—is not relevant to the likelihood of his taking laudanum in the spring of 1819. He could have taken it to ease the pain of his sore throat; he could have taken it because he thought he had pulmonary consumption; there is one occasion when he seems to have taken it simply as an anodyne for pain from a sudden injury.

On the afternoon of 18th March 1819 Keats joined in a game of cricket, was hit in the face by a ball, and got a black eye. His friend Brown applied a leech to the eyelid which reduced the swelling. Keats perhaps also took laudanum that evening to deaden the pain of his bruised eye; he certainly had an unusually good night's sleep, and woke very late next morning to a delightful sensation of indolence.[27] In a sonnet, *Why Did I Laugh Tonight?*, written within the previous few days, he had been full of sadness and mortal pain; verse, fame and beauty had seemed intense to him, though death was intenser still. On the morning of the 19th these three personifications reappeared to him in a sort of waking vision as Poetry, Ambition and Love, but now they had no intensity, no alertness of countenance; they were distanced and disguised into three figures on a Greek vase, a man and two women. His physical state was such a happy one that 'pleasure has no show of enticement and pain no unbearable frown'. It was a very different frame of mind from what he had felt a night or two earlier when he wrote *Why Did I Laugh Tonight?*; some potent physical agent may have contributed to the change.[28]

During that day, 19th March, Keats received a note from a friend whose father was dying, and this roused and somewhat changed the current of Keats's thoughts. Continuing with his journal letter to his brother and sister-in-law in America, he wrote the wonderful passages about the Superior Beings who see human sufferings in perspective as humans can see the instinctive actions of stoats and deer. At the end of these passages he copied for his brother the sonnet which he had written twenty-four or forty-eight hours earlier, but with a warning that it should be read in the light of the passages which he had written since, when his passions had subsided.

The effect of laudanum, if Keats did take it on the evening of March 18th, was therefore to switch off not only the physical pain from his black eye, but also the mental misery expressed in *Why Did I Laugh Tonight?*; to produce a condition in which neither pleasure nor pain was strongly felt (a well-known effect of opium—the Habituate quoted in Chapter II reported that the addict feels 'no warmth or glow of passion or genial feeling . . . there is a sort of vitrifying process that chills all sensibility'); and to turn the intensely realized personifications of Verse, Fame and Beauty into un-alert distanced figures on a Greek vase. Keats identified this condition as 'indolence', and it was definitely a physical state. It was not in itself the great creative frame of mind—the 'negative capability', the 'abstraction'—in which poetry should be written, not even the 'wise passivity', the 'diligent indolence' in which poetry is prepared.[29] It was perhaps a still earlier stage in the preliminaries to the creative process—a kind of holiday from emotion, a tranquillity which, in the moment that he was feeling it, he described as 'the only happiness'. In the months that followed he was to see it as both a help and a danger to the creative imagination, and at last perhaps as an unavoidable necessity.

In the middle of April 1819 Keats wrote that he had spent two months without any fruit of literary achievement, a patch of idleness during which he had written nothing.[30] This last seems not to have been literally true; he is thought to have written the last lines of the first *Hyperion* at the end of March;[31] and many scholars have maintained that this was not a 'blank period' at all, but a natural pause, or a condition of 'creative quiescence' or even one of 'intense intellectual activity'.[32] One cannot perhaps quite discount Keats's own view of these weeks as a wasted period, or even altogether rule out Benjamin Robert Haydon's account of him at this time. Haydon's description of Keats's despondency, dissipation and drunkenness at this time—'for six weeks he was scarcely sober'[33]—has given extreme offence to Keats's admirers, and Haydon was certainly an unreliable witness, both in general and specially in this case where he was covering up his own unworthy extortion of a loan from the hard-up Keats.

But the cause of Haydon's unreliability as a witness was generally that he did not understand the real meaning of what he was reporting, not that he was an inaccurate observer. His conclusions about Keats—that he was weak, vacillating, without decision of character or object in life—are utterly worthless; but the sayings of Keats which he quotes in support of his conclusions really sound like Keats's tone of voice, though their real significance is quite different from Haydon's superficial interpretation of them. 'One day he was full of an epic Poem! another, epic poems were splendid impositions on the world! and never for two days did he know his own intentions' says Haydon.[34] That tells us nothing about Keats's real opinion on epics; but we can easily believe that Keats was teasing Haydon's reverence for the epic style, in poetry and in painting, by the sentence about 'splendid impositions' which really does sound like a phrase of Keats's. Keats probably did really tell Haydon his famous tall story about cayenne pepper and claret; it may not even have been a tall story—Keats certainly did enjoy claret, as we know from his own panegyrics on it. Haydon produced the story to show what 'a man of genius does to gratify his appetites when once they get the better of him' and linked it with Keats's despondency over the vicious reviews of *Endymion* and his flight to 'dissipation' as a result, producing alternate elevation and depression of spirits during six weeks. Haydon wished to call attention to his own fortitude in face of hostile criticism, by emphasizing Keats's comparative weakness, and he therefore expanded and distorted what little he knew from actual observation of Keats's manner, in which he may have noticed some absence or oddness, just sufficiently different from Keats's usual manner to fix it in Haydon's memory. That is the sort of point on which Haydon's observation, though not the deductions he made from it, can be trusted; he had a good memory for dialogue, for gestures and expressions.[35]

One possible explanation for the alternation of excited spirits and of despondency which Haydon noticed at this time in Keats's manner is that Keats had begun to take laudanum; this would account for his seesaw of high and low spirits—the euphoria produced by laudanum alternating with the gloom of withdrawal —and also for the weeks of what Keats himself regarded as idleness and poetic sterility. Laudanum may have given him the waking vision of the three vase-figures passing by, on the morning of March 19th; some time early in April it may have given him the dream which he records as having occurred in the middle of many days when he was in a low state of mind. In the dream he was Dante's Paolo, floating in the whirlwind storm of Hell, but 'the dream was one of the most delightful enjoyments I ever had in my life—I floated about the whirling atmosphere . . . with a beautiful figure to whose lips mine were joined as it seemed for an age—and in the midst of all this cold and darkness I was warm—even flowery tree tops sprung up and we rested on them sometimes with the lightness of a cloud till the wind blew us away again. . . . O that I could dream it every night'.[36]

This dream has several of the classic constituents of an opium vision: the feeling of blissful buoyancy, the extension of time ('as it seem'd for an age'), contrasts of temperature, the bliss of the outcast. Professor Schneider, in her *Coleridge, Opium and 'Kubla Khan'*, used this dream as a proof that there is no such thing as a typical opium dream, since these characteristics are found in this dream which was not inspired by opium; but the argument possibly works in reverse.[37]

Keats

We have little information about Keats's ordinary dreams. They seem sometimes to have disappointed him by being mere repetitions of ordinary waking experiences instead of sublime and sunset visions.[38] But if his dreams of full sleep were dull, it seems clear from the opening of the *Epistle to J. H. Reynolds*, and from other passages in his poetry, that on the borders of sleep he saw kaleidoscopic patterns of light against the darkness of his closed eyes. Sleep, he said in *Endymion*, was the key to golden palaces and bespangled caves,[39] and the glittering watery or fiery palaces of *Endymion* and *Hyperion* may owe something to his experiences of hypnagogic visions, such as he described in *Otho the Great*

> 'when I close
>
> These lids, I see far fiercer brilliances,—
> Skies full of splendid moons, and shooting stars,
> And sparkling exhalations, diamond fires,
> And panting fountains quivering with deep glows!'[40]

It has even been suggested that Keats deliberately based the whole of *Endymion* on the technique of dreaming.[41]

His Dante dream in April 1819 is not like the spangled patterns of those earlier visions. It can indeed be shown that the Paolo and Francesca involute, to use De Quincey's word—the idea of lovers floating in icy winds—recurs often in *Endymion*, written long before there is any likelihood of Keats having tasted opium.[42] The sources of Keats's dream of April 1819 are well known; besides Canto V of Dante's *Inferno*, which he himself gives, there is the passage in *Measure for Measure* where the fornicator Claudio shudders out his terror at the icy thrill of Hell, at being 'imprisoned in the viewless winds, And blown with restless violence round about The pendent world', which in its turn was based on Dante, and which Keats marked in his copy of Shakespeare's plays.[43] Then there was Leigh Hunt's *Story of Rimini*, and Keats's own lovers in *The Eve of St Agnes*, warm amid the icy January cold. His dream did not come out of nowhere, even if opium carried it.

But it surprised him for all that, and seemed to him—as his dreams hardly ever did—worthy of being recorded in a letter. And it had a character of its own, not found in the story on which it was based. Dante's lovers were battered and tormented by bellowing tempests in the icy dark; Shakespeare's lover dreaded endless imprisonment in the restless violence of a whirlwind; but Keats and his dream love were warm and rapturous among the cold and darkness, and could rest on flowery tree-tops. Cold, restlessness, endless time, had been disinfected of their terrors. It sounds curiously like the relief of a laudanum-taker who has been suffering from withdrawal symptoms but is now happy again with a new dose.

Some of the rapture had already evaporated when Keats tried to turn this dream into a sonnet, *As Hermes Once Took to his Pinions Light*. In it the lovers are again conscious of the chilly rain, the stinging gusts of hailstones, the melancholy storm in which they float, and their lips are pale with sorrow and cold. The influence of the dream lingered on in other poems which Keats wrote later that year—in the swimming, floating dancers of *Physician Nature!*, in the icy scourging winds, the flights, the frosts and sudden heats of *What Can I Do to Drive Away?* The context and the application are different; it is only the image that persists. A connection has often been noticed between the Paolo and Francesca dream, the sonnet based on it, and *La Belle Dame Sans Merci*, written very soon after the dream.[44] Whatever that magian poem is really about—Death, Temptation, Strangeness, Fanny Brawne, the tragedy of Tom Keats, enslavement to a false ideal of poetry, echoes of Spenser or Burton or Keats's own earlier poetry—it is not a simple transcript of an opium dream, though Keats's recent conversation with Coleridge about dreams no doubt contributed to it. Keats does not mention *Kubla Khan* in his record of that conversation,[45] though the poem, with Coleridge's prologue identifying it as a dream, had been published only three years earlier, and it would be a natural topic for a conversation with Coleridge about dreams. It is possible that the 'honey wild and manna dew' which La Belle Dame gave to the knight at arms owed something to the honey dew on which the poet fed in *Kubla Khan*, and just possible that both had connotations of a forbidden draught of inspiration. If 'honey dew' really had this connotation for Keats, there may be another reference to it in the sonnet *On Sleep* which he wrote late in April 1819, in the lines which originally read

> ' 'ere thy poppy throws
> Around my bed its dewy Charities'.

This lovely sonnet is the perfect expression of that release from anxiety, that enclosed safety, which the opium-eater—though not he alone—hopes to find. But when Keats wrote this sonnet, and during the following weeks when he wrote the great odes, he may have temporarily given up the mild doses of laudanum which he may have previously taken, and his astonishing outburst of creative activity may have been helped by this withdrawal. That sentence is an awkward pile-up of conditional verbs, but intentionally so. There is no external evidence at all for the conjecture, and even if it were undoubted fact, it would only contribute a tiny element to the complex structure of Keats's poetic evolution.

Keats's letters of April and May 1819 express an intention to give a great shake to his mood of idleness; a fear that indolence of mind might make him no longer accept pain for the sake of love; a conviction that pains and troubles were necessary to school the intelligence into a soul; a determination to conquer his indolence and strain his nerves at some grand poem.[46] The first stanza of the *Ode to a Nightingale*, written during these weeks, suggests—among many other themes—that the indolence mood, the drowsy numbness, had again become unpleasant, not welcome, to him; that dull opiates and the Lethean state that they produced, the immunity from weariness, fever and fret enjoyed by the passionless bird, might be dangerous as well as desirable.[47]

In the *Ode to Melancholy*, probably written at the end of May 1819, the danger of the 'indolence' mood to the poet's creative imagination is more definitely stated. The poet is adjured not to go to Lethe, not to drown the wakeful anguish of his soul. I hope it is clear that I do not mean that when Keats wrote 'No, no, go not to Lethe', he was simply warning himself away from the laudanum bottle. Lethe was the not-feeling indolence, the immunity from wakeful anguish, the mood which in this poem he was disposed to regard as inimical to poetry, which demands intensity of feeling, whether joy or sorrow. He probably had not himself detected the connection between the indolence mood and the drug which, I suggest, may have caused it. Or if he had, he may have found it simply a useful symbol for one kind of imaginative relationship with reality, just as he had used wine as the symbol for another kind.[48] When in the *Ode to a Nightingale* he contrasted the dull opiate with the blushful Hippocrene, or in the *Ode to Melancholy* he preferred the taste of grapes against the palate to draughts of Lethe, he was not indulging in a simple moral meditation on the theme that claret is healthier than laudanum. As he prepared himself to write on the great themes of beauty and truth which occupied his mind, he had some introductory thoughts about which of his own moods were most propitious to the writing of poetry, and the cause of such moods. Should the poet be a sharer or a detached observer, and how could participation or detachment be achieved or avoided?

In early June 1819, Keats's feeling about 'indolence' changed again. He had been taking care of his health in late May, not venturing out unless it was a fine day,[49] and perhaps having recourse to laudanum again, and experiencing a repetition of the mood which he had enjoyed when he first took it in March. At any rate, he wrote an ode based on his euphoric vision of the three vase-figures on March 19th, but translated into the summer season in which the poem was written.[50] It was an ode in praise of indolence, which at that moment seemed to him such a desirable state that, just as in March he had described it as 'the only happiness', so he now told a friend that the writing of this poem was 'the thing I have most enjoyed this year'.[51] The works that one has most enjoyed writing are not necessarily one's best; many circumstances—opium among them—may dull a writer's judgment of his own work. The *Ode on Indolence* is not a great poem, but it is an interesting description of a mood of nearly-achieved indifference to any strong desire, and the physical and mental symptoms—heavy eyelids, slow pulse, drowsiness, dreams—that went with this mood. Some of Keats's biographers have equated this final 'indolence' mood with 'apathy';[52] but this, though etymologically exact, is slightly misleading, because the word 'apathy' has come to have a pejorative tinge which is absent from 'indolence'. Indolence is generally felt to be enjoyable and scarcely reprehensible. By the time Keats wrote the *Ode on Indolence*, the word represented for him a state in which he had no strong feelings or reactions about anything; a state which he simply observed in himself, perhaps still without finally making up his mind whether it was favourable or unfavourable to poetic creation, if poetry was still to be created. It might lead to detachment, the faculty of seeing without judging or forming conclusions, the Shakespearian negative capability which he aimed at. On the other hand, it might deaden the imagination, by depriving it of the wakeful anguish which was a needful condition of creative response.

Keats's ambivalent feeling about the indolence mood, and perhaps about the drug that caused it, is reflected in *Lamia*. Indolence was dangerous but also protective to Keats as a poet; it was a parallel to Lycius's situation between the false, escapist but poetical Lamia, and the committed but destructive Apollonius. Finding allegorical interpretations for the characters in *Lamia* has been a favourite sport with critics for many years. If Lycius is generally agreed to be Keats himself, Lamia has been identified as Fanny Brawne, as sensuous beauty, as unreality, as poetry, as the cruelty of sexual passion; Apollonius as Charles Brown, truth, philosophy, reason, and even as the unkind reviewers of *Endymion*.[53] I am tempted to join in this enjoyable game and to interpret the whole of *Lamia* as a neat little medical allegory by Dr J. Keats. Lamia herself would of course stand for opium. That puzzling and superfluous incident about Hermes in pursuit of the nymph at the beginning would now fall into place—Hermes is Mercury, after all, and Keats had previously been taking mercury as a medicine; the pursued nymph would be Syphilis. Apollonius would be a thin disguise for Apollo, and would stand for the healthy bracing walks in the sunshine that Keats ought to have been taking instead of swigging laudanum indoors.

Even this parody interpretation, invented as a reduction to absurdity, begins to seem plausible for a moment as one writes it down. That is the danger with Keats—you can read absolutely anything into his works. The insight and imagination in his poems and letters are so profuse and fluctuating that they can be used to prove almost any thesis about him, quite convincingly. He was changing rapidly all through his short adult life, specially in his ideas about the poet's vocation, and his imagery was not static and fixed in equivalence. He was most truly a chameleon poet. All the different, and often conflicting, descriptions of his intellect and poetic philosophy which I have read have seemed to me true of him at one time or another; it depends on which of the chameleon colours you choose to concentrate on. All I am trying to do is to identify one tinge of colour, not even a colour in itself, but a shadow which blended with one of the colour modifications. If I suggest that vanishing vase-figures, or lovers floating in an icy wind, or huge buildings, are images connected with opium in Keats's poetry, I do not imply that this is their only or main connection.

Huge buildings; there is no lack of them in Keats's poetry at any stage, including the early poems written long before there was any likelihood that he had tasted opium. If I am to apply to Keats the imagery test for opium effects, and to take the central image which I have identified in the imaginative literature analysed in this book—the image of the buried temple—I shall have to show that he used it differently before and after March 1819. There are underground and undersea temples in *Endymion*, and the cavern temple and its approaches in Book II, written in the summer of 1817, have been specifically linked by some critics with Moneta's sanctuary in *The Fall of Hyperion*, written in the late summer of 1819. I was very much surprised when I first came across this identification in Mr E. C. Pettet's illuminating book *On the Poetry of Keats*. He describes Endymion's visit to the cavern temple as 'a descent into the realms of death . . . a hard, bright, sterile world of stone, minerals and jewels, totally bare of vegetation' and compares it with Baudelaire's *Rêve Parisien*.[54]

I first read *Endymion* when I was thirteen, and of all the raptures which it gave me then, Endymion's underground journey provided by far the most thrilling. Perhaps I am only revealing an adolescent death-wish of my own in admitting this, but as far as I can recall my feelings, they were not in the least ambivalent; they were pure unmitigated delight. This, this was what poetry was for—this was what my imagination needed to feed on. I too rushed between sapphire columns, over the fantastic bridge above the crystal flood; I leant over the huge cliff and heard the hundred waterfalls; I went winding down the diamond pathway spiralling in huge loops over the abysses of roaring foam; I teased the fountains with my spear till they rose and interlaced overhead in gauzy lattices. It never occurred to me that this was a picture of the horrors of solitude, it seemed all that was desirable. Now, forty years later, my notion of the highest excellence in poetry is not quite the same as it was then, but even now, re-reading the whole central part of *Endymion* Book II with an attentive eye for signs of horror and the death-wish, I cannot really find them, except when Endymion loses his sense of wonder and pleasure, and gives way to self-pity. ' 'Twas far too strange and wonderful for sadness' Keats tells us at the moment when Endymion enters the underworld; and so it still seems to me—a vision of shifting metamorphosing radiance, of living water, most unlike the austere gloom of Moneta's sanctuary. The likeness at first sight to Baudelaire's dream is stronger. Both are landscapes of metal, water and precious stones; but there is a difference of direction which is, literally, vital. Keats's inorganic landscape is all aspiring to the condition of the organic; the fountains turn into vines and poplars; in Baudelaire's poems the cataracts are hardening into crystal, the rivers are impassive, the oceans are tamed, everything liquid is petrifying into a gem. In Baudelaire's terrifying landscape the 'végétal irrégulier' is banished; in Keats's realm it springs up irresistibly through the marble floor.

I doubt whether the jewelled caverns of *Endymion* Book II had any developed symbolical meaning at all. We are so used to the idea that all dreams have a latent significance, that there must be a symbol under every description, that it does not occur to us that Keats might simply have been describing something that seemed to him intrinsically beautiful. A diamond balustrade miles long—when I read of it at an age a few years younger than

Keats was when he wrote of it, I was quite simply enchanted. No idea of vulgarity or excess entered my mind; diamonds were beautiful, and the more the better. Perhaps if one could re-capture that innocence of eye one might get closer to Keats when he wrote *Endymion* than by the symbolic interpretations— and perhaps also closer to Saint John when he wrote of the City whose every single gate was one pearl.

This digression was not quite irrelevant to my main point, which is to show how Keats's imagination, when affected by opium, may have seized on an image already present in his mind and given it another colouring. This is all that the influence of opium could ever do; there is no objectively real landscape to which opium admits its votaries; it only directs their attention to certain features in the landscape of their own imaginations, and casts a livid shadow over them. There is some warrant for the suggestion that Keats's architectural imagery may have been shaped by the chemical action of drugs which he was taking at the time he wrote. The fiery palace of Hyperion, blazing and glitter-ing with red heat, but also a place of jarring sounds and savours of sick metal, gives an extremely strong impression of an actual physical condition. Sir William Hale-White, in his *Keats as Doctor and Patient*, ingeniously pointed out that doses of mercury cause a metallic taste in the mouth, linked this to the

'Savour of poisonous brass and metal sick'

which corroded Hyperion's palate, and added that Keats had been taking mercury during the month before he wrote this passage[55]—an instance of one of the minor sensations, on the fringe of the poet's consciousness, which may find their way into his poetry.

The 'eternal domed monument' which was Moneta's sanctuary in *The Fall of Hyperion* (the passage was written in September 1819, when Keats may have been taking laudanum inter-mittently for six months) was quite unlike the glittering palaces and temples, astir with moving lights and waters, of Keats's earlier poems. It was vast, misty, silent, light-excluding, filled with sweet fumes, and ice-cold, so bitterly cold that it be-numbed hands and feet and suffocated the heart. Behind the poet as he moved towards the distant altar were black gates that had closed for ever, like the gates 'hung with funeral crape' that De Quincey saw, closed at last and finally barring his retreat.[56] Piranesian perspectives of massive columns leading nowhere, of balustrades and innumerable steps, surrounded him. Far ahead, and only to be reached by an immense effort, was an altar fuming with incense, with a colossal statue enthroned over it. De Quincey too, in his dream, had travelled with desperate effort along the floor of a huge cathedral towards a distant shrine over whose altar, clouded with incense, the shadow of a terrible image was dimly seen; and the outlines of other poetic temples rise up, one behind the other, a phantasmagoria of Poe's City in the Sea, and Thompson's Palace of the Occident, and Baudelaire's 'Babel d'escaliers et d'arcades' and Elizabeth Barrett Browning's temple of the poets with its interlacing aisles and countless columns fading into infinity, its weaving clouds of incense edged with pale flame; even perhaps the crypt of that other 'eternal domed monument' which from without was sunny, but within had caves of ice that communicated with a lifeless ocean. All these architectural visions were huge, stony, silent, freezing and with no way out.

Neither Keats's main sources for Moneta's sanctuary, nor the poetic use for which he devised it, owe anything to opium, if he had indeed taken opium before he wrote this passage. The visionary building was made up of temples and palaces about which he had read—the Parthenon, Egyptian temples, Druid sanctuaries, purgatorial staircases in Dante, infernal palaces in Milton and Beckford; and of things that he himself had seen—the Young Memnon statue in the British Museum, the natural columns of Fingal's Cave, the immensely long nave of the Cathedral at Winchester, where he wrote this passage in September 1819.[57] The profound poetic truths for which he chose this outside shell of symbol, the symbol of the huge sanctuary and the freezing cold, were utterly unlike anything that De Quincey or Poe or Francis Thompson or even Baudelaire was seeking to express. It may seem offensive that Moneta's holy sanctuary should be equated in any way with Poe's corrupted temples of hell, or even with De Quincey's delirious cathedral. But it is the object of worship, not the building where the worship is offered, that makes for holiness or impiety. Opium perhaps provided the vast aisles and branching staircases and freezing pavement of Keats's sanctuary, as mercury may have provided the sickening brassy savours in the earlier poem, as any physical condition may shape a poet's imagery. But Moneta and the deity whose priestess she was and the truths that she revealed —among them the insight that the true poet will not let himself freeze into unfeeling indolence on the pavement of the buried temple—were something more than imagery.

PART IV

VERDICT

XV

THE BURIED TEMPLE

No clear pattern of opium's influence on creative writing—always discernible, recognizable and complete in the work of all writers who took opium—has emerged from this survey. It would not be credible if it had. Opium works on what is already there in a man's mind and memory, and what was already there in the eight writers whose works have been surveyed in this book was extremely varied. They had nothing in common except that they lived in the same century, were imaginative writers, and took opium. In every other way—literary aims and techniques, degree of genius or talent, beliefs, tastes, temperaments—they were as different as possible. Taking only a few straightforward biographical facts which can be easily compared, one can see that there was no common factor in these to account for any similarities in their work.

Their social origins varied widely. Crabbe's father was a warehouseman and fisherman, Keats's father was a groom who rose to keeping a livery stable; Poe's father was an unsuccessful actor, Wilkie Collins's was a painter, De Quincey's a prosperous merchant, Francis Thompson's a doctor, Coleridge's a clergyman, Baudelaire's a tutor in a noble family and later an official.

Coleridge, De Quincey, Baudelaire and Poe had university educations. Crabbe, Keats and Thompson had medical training, and the two former actually practised medicine for short periods. Poe and (very briefly) Coleridge were in the army. Crabbe became a clergyman. Francis Thompson worked briefly for a shoemaker, Wilkie Collins had a spell in a City office. De Quincey and

Verdict

Baudelaire never followed any profession or trade but that of literature, including editing and journalism.

Crabbe, Baudelaire and Thompson for short periods of their lives, and De Quincey and Poe for many years, endured extremes of poverty, including actual hunger. All of them except Collins had to borrow money at some stage; only Crabbe had an assured income for much of his life; but Coleridge and Keats were never hard up and friendless to the point of going hungry, and Collins, though he lived on his literary earnings, was never hard up at all.

Their religious beliefs were as diverse as their social origins or their education. Crabbe was a latitudinarian Anglican parson, Coleridge was at one time a Unitarian and then an undenominational Trinitarian, De Quincey was an Anglican. Baudelaire was a lapsed but, to use his own word, 'incorrigible' Catholic, Francis Thompson an ardently devout Catholic. Poe was a very problematical Deist, Keats and Collins were agnostics.

If we turn to the physical side of their lives, these prove to be equally varied. It is often said that opium produces sexual impotence, but the lives of some of these writers do not support this theory. Crabbe, Coleridge and De Quincey were married and had children; all of De Quincey's children were born after he had been addicted to opium for many years. Poe was married, but his marriage was never consummated and he may have been impotent. Keats, Collins, Baudelaire and Thompson were bachelors, but of very different kinds. We do not know what sexual experience, if any, Keats had, but Wilkie Collins kept two mistresses and had several children by one of them. Baudelaire is generally believed to have had varied sexual experience, and his poetry certainly gives that impression, though some of his contemporaries thought he was impotent. Francis Thompson was probably virgin.

Their state of health was equally unrevealing. Crabbe suffered from dyspepsia, and later from *tic douloureux*, but lived to be seventy-eight. Keats died of tuberculosis at the age of twenty-five, Poe of cardiac disease and intemperance at forty, Baudelaire of a paralytic stroke at forty-six, Francis Thompson of tuberculosis at forty-seven. Wilkie Collins, though suffering much from gout, lived to be sixty-five. Coleridge and De Quincey, the two most advanced addicts, lived to sixty and seventy-four, though Coleridge was prone to some form of rheumatism or gout and De Quincey to neuralgia and gastric troubles.

No common trait emerges from this confused set of biographical facts except that none of these eight writers who took opium was perfectly healthy. Otherwise, all is contrast and contradiction. Early deaths, long lives; prosperity, destitution; happy marriage and devoted fatherhood, or voluntary or involuntary chastity; a stable home, a good education, a great stock of learning, or orphanhood, unhappy adoption, early and enforced application to uncongenial work; secure literary fame or a continual struggle; calm content or anguished misery; devout faith or total unbelief; all these, not in two tidy halves but in every combination, are found among these eight writers.

These were the diverse experiences and temperaments (but with a common factor of creative imagination which is absent from all but a tiny proportion of those who take opium) on which the drug worked. Did it, as Mr M. H. Abrams believed, introduce them all to a world of its own, recognizable but as utterly different from the everyday world as the life of another planet? Or did it, as Professor Schneider maintained, produce no effect at all on the way they wrote?

The strongest evidence for the first hypothesis would seem to be that some who have written under the influence of opium have afterwards not recognized such writing as their own deliberate creation. It was something given, apparently from outside. But although the influence of opium seemed to have shown them something they could not recognize, which they were sure they had never seen before, it was because the action of opium had reorganized their memory, banishing some experiences and recalling others from a great distance. It did not act like a liberating government—it was a reactionary coup d'état; it was Aristides who was banished, Alcibiades or even Hippias who was recalled. These writers had not been taken to a new planet, but were being admitted to caves and prisons and secret hiding-places of their own native Earth, places whose existence they had forgotten or ignored or never observed.

It is the chance of observing these hiding-places more at leisure, and under a stronger light, that seems to be the chief contribution which opium addiction may make to a writer's imaginative equipment. The experiences of the writers described in this book show that the action of opium may unbare some of the semi-conscious processes by which literature begins to be written. These processes are analogous to, and may even be identical with, the mental processes of rêverie, of dreams in full sleep, and of the hypnagogic visions which come on the borders of sleep, and there seems sufficient evidence that opium both intensifies these processes and extends their duration, so that they can be observed while they are happening. The writer can actually witness the process by which words and visual images arise simultaneously and in parallel in his own mind. He can watch, control, and subsequently use the product of the creative imagination at an earlier stage of its production than is normally accessible to the conscious mind.

But he can only do this if he already has a creative imagination and a tendency to rêverie, dreams and hypnagogic visions; and though opium may then present him with unique material for his poetry, it will probably take away from him the will and the power to make use of it. The sophisticated inquiries of Poe and Baudelaire aimed to discover whether opium can provide a *méthode de travail* for the poet, a technique both for collecting material and for presenting it. Poe thought, for instance, that the hyperaesthesia and synaesthesia induced by opium, the intensification and alteration of sense perception, constituted a model and parallel for the intensity of concentrated interest which the writer wishes to evoke from his reader. Opium might provide a short cut, an infallible recipe for producing that immediacy, that heightening of experience, which every poet wants to feel and then to impart. The free flow of association which opium released might wash away the prosaic categories and definitions which canalize the mind, and allow symbols to melt freely into one another. For De Quincey, the way in which feelings and images are presented to the mind during opium dreams and rêveries acted as a model, a lesson in technique, for the writing of prose-poems. Dreams, for De Quincey, for Crabbe, even for Wilkie Collins, gave insight. They crystallized the particles of past experience—sensory impressions, emotions, things read—into a symbolic pattern, an 'involute', which became part of the life of the imagination and could be worked into literature, and this crystallization, in De Quincey's passionately-held opinion, was precipitated by the action of opium.

There is no way of proving whether this is true or not. We know that De Quincey took opium. We know what he afterwards wrote. We do not know what he would have written if he had never taken it. It can be no more than a hypothesis that the action of opium, though it can never be a substitute for innate imagination, can uncover that imagination while it is at work in a way which might enable an exceptionally gifted and self-aware writer to observe and learn from his own mental processes.

But it could only do so at a price which no writer of integrity would ultimately be prepared to pay. I am not referring to moral integrity, but to the poet's responsibility to his own art. One of the most obvious effects of opium addiction on a writer's powers is that it induces indolence, absence of feeling, a state in which the power to observe is detached from the power to sympathize with what is observed. At its very outset, this state of mind can be useful to a poet; there are times when he needs detachment. But in the long run it is deadly. The dislocation of objects and events from the feelings which they normally arouse is in the end destructive of poetic truth. In *Dejection* Coleridge gave, once for all, the classic description of this creeping death of the imaginative impulse, but Crabbe and Keats can also be seen fighting against it, and Poe and Collins yielding to it, and to what comes in its train—the tendency that Coleridge called 'histrionism', the resort to violent attitudes because you no longer have normal feelings. Nearly all the opium-addicted writers indulged in descriptions of violence, gruesomeness, insanity, extremes of fear. The action of opium, by its exaggeration and distortion of normal feelings, may give to one who takes it unusual insights into the mental experience of the wicked, the insane, the terrified, the tortured, the dying, which may be useful and enlightening to a writer; but it only enables him to observe, not to sympathize with, these mental experiences. He feels himself to be a pariah; he recognizes the other pariahs; but he cannot hold out a hand even to them. He is insulated from his fellow-men, and has renounced the obligation of commitment.

Nor is he any longer committed to the physical world in which he lives. Landscapes, which once to him were beautiful in themselves and part of a significant whole, are now only an expression of his mood. No identities are stable and separate, they combine and engraft on each other. There are masks and disguises everywhere, and under the mask there may be only another mask, or nothing at all. Many of these writers felt that they had been endowed with an exceptional insight into the secret of the universe, and could reveal its philosophical framework for the enlightenment of mankind; but the great work could never be finished, because the power to hold things together had gone, everything disintegrated, fell away into fragments. It did not always seem so to them themselves. Among the powers that opium damaged was the power to detect damage; judgment and self-criticism do not make their absence felt by him who has lost them.

It is the great plans that are destroyed. Writers can still write, and in fragments write well, when they have been addicted to opium for many years; and this is not necessarily only during withdrawal periods, though these do in some cases provide the energy to commit to paper the imaginative creations which may otherwise stay uselessly imprisoned in the mind. But the holding-together has gone, the great luminous images which shed light and pattern across all the wide tracts of a writer's imagination do not radiate any more. The images are still there, but some are darkened, some are luridly spot-lit, all are enclosed. The effect of what Baudelaire called the 'paysage opiacé' is produced by blotting out some of the features of a normal landscape of imagery—the groups of people, the flowing streams, the roads,

The Buried Temple

the cottages, the woods, the sun—and high-lighting the solitary figure, the stagnant pools, the cliffs, the castles, the stone faces and slimy claws that show for a moment at the mouths of caves. It is not another planet, it is our own, but in a light of eclipse. The foregoing pages have shown that certain images—pariahs, harlot-ogresses, quicksands, petrified landscapes, freezing cold, drowned or buried temples, watching eyes—do recur in the works of the opium-addicted writers. Some of these images—the fairly obvious poppy, the honey-dew, the temptress, the buried temple—may be conscious or unconscious equivalents for opium itself. Some—the ice-cold, the quicksands, the petrifaction, the floating lovers—may be connected with physical symptoms produced by opium dosage or withdrawal. Some—the idea of the outcast, the images of watching eyes and hybrid shape-changing creatures—may express the addict's isolation and suspicion. None of the images is peculiar to the writing of addicts, and none of the addict-writers use only these images and no others; but they form a recognizable pattern. These eight writers were differently gifted and differently experienced, and opium acted on their diverse natures and powers to produce different modifications of the way they wrote. One can only, as doctors do, deduce that a certain combination of imaginative symptoms, though they may come from separate causes, may add up to a single disease.

A summary like the one which I have just made, an abstract of influences and tendencies, does not do much to convey a frame of mind. I will put the same thing in another way, as a writer's dialogue with himself in Piranesi's prison, the temple of opium.

* * * * *

This place seems very safe. The walls are so thick, and there are miles of solid rock above them. They cannot get at you here. All those demands are shut out. They think that they have triumphed over you, but it is you who have rejected them. You are here, in this great spacious place of your own making, where you can be yourself. There is no hurry any more, and no need to do anything immediately. Already you have been leaning for hours on this railing, looking down through the arches and flights of stairs. Perhaps it has been weeks, not hours; perhaps it has been centuries.

The air is absolutely still. No wind can get in here. The air will always be the same. One could walk about here for ever, it is so spacious and intricate. Across that bridge, and round the pillar, and up the spiral staircase, and along the vaulted tunnel, and over the drawbridge. It ends in mid-air, but that does not matter for you, of course you can overcome that. There is a rope hanging from a pulley, isn't there? Or you can float across. And there you are, back at the pillar. How easy it all is, and how well you do it.

There is a carved mask on the wall, a face ambiguously smiling. Have you seen anything like it before? Look at it again. There, did you see? It has changed. It is she, the one you most want to see—she herself. But why is she leering like that? It is not her at all—it is only a mask. Or was the face you knew a mask, and is this the real one? But we will not think of that anyway—you do not want her here, not now. A stone mask on the wall is better. You came here to be quite safe and alone, didn't you?

This place is so beautiful. It is wonderfully designed. It is a secret Master Plan. You are the only one who understands how the whole place is constructed. You have it all in your mind, the whole immense design. You will explain it all to those others outside, and they will see how wise you are. It explains everything, and you have it all in your head. It doesn't quite all show from here, here where you are standing. You can't see all the way along those openings and passages. But you know—you knew, only just now, you had it all clear, the whole map, all clear in your mind. The staircases lead to—anyway, there is no need to work it out just now, there is time. There is a great deal of time. It was only yesterday that you thought about it last, only a thousand years ago, only a moment ago.

The Buried Temple

There is a great wheel down there, with spikes on it. It is exciting to look at it—one can enjoy that. They were not real people that were broken on it, of course. There are some odd-looking rags and fragments on some of the spikes, but they are not real, there has never been anyone real here except you, so they cannot have felt anything, can they? And it is exciting to imagine it.

You were right to come here. There is everything you need here. You need it more and more. You must have it. They must not take it away. They cannot get at you here.

What an odd pattern of veins and knots there is in the stone of these stairs. You can stand for days looking at them. Are they knots or eyes? Eyes, watching you from the stairs—armies of eyes, advancing one behind the other in thousands, in millions. It is unjust, it is persecution. Why should they watch you? There is nothing there, they have petrified back into patterns in the stone. But suppose they come again? Suppose you put a foot on the stairs, and they turn into eyes, soft and squelching below your foot? Suppose you are sucked down? There is something further down still, waiting for you.

But it is safe here. Outside there are too many people, and the light is too strong, and they worry about everything. It is dangerous out there. There is no protection, there are no walls, nothing to keep things off. Here there are walls. There are openings, but they do not lead to doors. Nothing can get in. There are no doors, are there?

What is that thing on the balustrade beside you, that seems to be coming to pieces? There are scurryings and scuttlings in it. You move, and it moves with you—part of it moves with you, the part that has not quite come to pieces. It is your own hand. Touch yourself with it. It feels like a claw. It feels like a claw that is part of something else close to you, reaching for you. Why do they touch you? Why don't they leave you alone? It is not they, it is your own hand, your hand is perfect, it is not coming to pieces at all, it can do anything. They are jealous of what it can

339

Verdict

do. They say it is not a proper hand any more. It is just their jealousy. You like your hand to be like that, don't you? You are the only one that knows what matters and what doesn't matter. It looks odd, though, that hand. It does not look very nice, does it? It will be better to put it behind your back, what is left of it.

You want to go up those stairs again? Of course you can do it easily. Two flights up already. This landing is a good place to stop for a time. It is much colder up here. One can see all round. One can hear, too. But there is nothing to hear, it is always quite silent in this place. Do you hear anything? A very long way off, like a light footstep? Of course there are no footsteps, there are no doors, no one can get in here. There, did you hear that? But it is too far away, one can't be sure. Only it seems to be not quite so far away as before. They will get in if they can, they will make you do things, they will make you decide. There is nothing there, nothing at all, it is not getting any nearer. But it will be safer lower down.

Perhaps it will be good to have your back against a wall, then no one can get at you. There is a niche out there in that pillar. If you got into that, you would be sheltered from above by the overhang. It is rather narrow, it fits you very well, doesn't it? Almost too well—you won't be able to get out again by the way you came. But there is a way down. Perhaps you had better not look down too much, it is a long way down. You cannot quite see to the bottom, but you can see a very long way down.

But it is easy to get away from the niche after all, isn't it? You need not get out, you can get further in. The stone behind you isn't really stone, you can sink back into it. It is really made of the same stuff as you, or you are made of the same stuff as it. Now you are inside, and it is just the same as outside, all the stairs and pillars and bridges are here too, only not quite so separate as before, and neither are you.

If you stay down here, right down here on the floor, you will be safe. The roof is miles up, all those staircases and gangways are in full view, nothing can get near you without your seeing it coming. You have only to sit quite still. Nothing must be moved, nothing must be touched, nothing must be changed. Just stay quite still, just stay there.

Is this the floor? Is it quite solid beneath you? Are you sure it isn't hollow? There is an opening there, there is a way down. It is not safe unless the floor is solid beneath you. You must have a solid floor, you need it, you must have it. You cannot stay here, you are not safe yet. You need to go down to where the floor will be solid, and keep you up. You need it. You must go on down.

POSTSCRIPT

I was often asked, while I was writing this book, whether I had completed my researches by taking opium myself. It would not have proved anything if I had, since this book is concerned with the effect of opium on the imagination of great creative writers. But in any case, no curiosity or wish for new experience could nerve me to enter such a world of wretchedness. There are voices echoing in my mind, voices that cry 'Oh what do you see, dear? What is it that you see?' . . . 'To know and loathe, yet wish and do' . . . 'Vieille et terrible amie' . . . 'my only friend' . . . 'I see, not feel, how beautiful they are' . . . 'infinite incoherence, ropes of sand' . . . 'Heavens! with what grace the mask they wore' . . . 'the persecution of their malicious beauty' . . . 'O infinite in the depth of darkness, an infinite craving'. Their paradises may have been wholly or partly artificial; their hells were real.

REFERENCES

The sources to which I have referred while writing this book are given in the following notes for each chapter. A few sources which have been quoted frequently throughout the book have been given the following abbreviations:

ABRAMS=*The Milk of Paradise*: *The Effect of Opium Visions on the Works of De Quincey, Crabbe, Francis Thompson and Coleridge*, M. H. Abrams, Harvard University Press, Boston, 1934.

C.E.O.E. 1822=*Confessions of an English Opium Eater*, Thomas De Quincey (Original Version of 1822), ed. Malcolm Elwin, Macdonald, 1956.

C.E.O.E. 1856=*Confessions of an English Opium Eater*, Thomas De Quincey (Revised Version of 1856), ed. Malcolm Elwin, Macdonald, 1956.

DE Q/MASSON=*Collected Writings*, Thomas De Quincey, ed. D. Masson, Black, Edinburgh, 1888–90.

DUPOUY=*Les Opiomanes*, R. Dupouy, Librairie Felix Alcan, Paris, 1912.

LAKE POETS=*Reminiscences of the English Lake Poets*, Thomas De Quincey, ed. J. E. Jordan, Dent, 1961.

LOWES=*The Road to Xanadu*. J. Livingston Lowes, Houghton Mifflin, Boston, 1927.

SCHNEIDER=*Coleridge, Opium and 'Kubla Khan'*, Elisabeth Schneider, University of Chicago Press, 1953.

S.T.C./LETTERS=*Collected Letters of Samuel Taylor Coleridge*, 4 vols., ed. E. L. Griggs, Clarendon Press, 1956 and 1599.

S.T.C./NOTEBOOKS=*The Notebooks of Samuel Taylor Coleridge*, 2 vols., ed. Kathleen Coburn, Routledge and Kegan Paul, 1957 and 1962.

SUSPIRIA=*Suspiria de Profundis* and *The English Mail Coach*, Thomas De Quincey, with *Confessions of an English Opium Eater* ed. Malcolm Elwin, Macdonald, 1956.

All other abbreviated references (e.g. *Letters, Poetical Works, Life,* Gillman, Gittings) in the following notes on individual chapters refer to works of which full titles have been given at the head of the notes on that chapter.

Page references are not given for short articles in periodicals.

All titles mentioned in the notes were published in London unless otherwise stated.

NOTES TO FOREWORD

1 *Drug Addiction*: Report of the Interdepartmental Committee, Ministry of Health, H.M.S.O., 1961.

2 *The Milk of Paradise. The Effect of Opium Visions on the Works of de Quincey, Crabbe, Francis Thompson and Coleridge,* M. H. Abrams, Harvard University Press, Boston, 1934 (hereafter referred to throughout the notes as ABRAMS).

3 *Coleridge, Opium and 'Kubla Khan'*, Elisabeth Schneider, University of Chicago Press, Chicago, 1953 (hereafter referred to throughout the notes as SCHNEIDER).

NOTES ON CHAPTER I. TRADITION

1 Sources for the early history of the use of opium in Egypt and the Near East, Greece and Rome: *Narcotics,* D. W. Cheever, *North American Review CXCVII* October 1862, pp. 374–415; *The Opium Problem,* C. E. Terry and M. Pellens, Bureau of Social Hygiene, New York, 1928; *Phantastica,* Louis Lewin, Kegan Paul, 1931; *Poisons sacrés, Ivresses divines,* Philippe de Félice, Editions Albin Michel, Paris, 1936; *The Trail of Opium,* Margaret Goldsmith, Robert Hale, 1939; *The Pharmacological Basis of Therapeutics,* Louis S. Goodman and Alfred Gilman, Macmillan, 1955; *Drugs and the Mind,* Dr R. S. de Ropp, Gollancz, 1958. See also *Opium: Journal d'une Désintoxication,* Jean Cocteau, Librairie Stock, Paris, 1930; *The Unquiet Grave,* Palinurus (Cyril Connolly), Hamish Hamilton, 1950; *Dreams and Dreaming,* Norman Mackenzie, Aldus Books, London, 1965.

2 *Purchas his Pilgrimes,* 1617; *The Road to Xanadu,* J. L. Lowes, Houghton Mifflin, Boston, 1927, 361–2, 586 n. 11 (hereafter referred to throughout the notes as LOWES); Schneider 139–40.

3 *Purchas his Pilgrimage,* 1613; *Loves of the Plants,* Erasmus Darwin, Canto II; *Narcotics,* D. W. Cheever, *North American Review,* October 1862.

4 Mackenzie 71.

5 Sir Thomas Browne *Works*, Pickering, 1836, III. 491, 492 (Urn-Burial, V), II. 113 (*Religio Medici* II. xii).

6 Thomas Burton, *Anatomy of Melancholy*, Partition II, Section V, Member I, Subsection 6.

7 *Poems*, John Dryden, O.U.P., 1910, 90 l. 20, 91 l. 126, 70 l. 482; *Thomas Shadwell, His Life and Comedies*, A. S. Borgman, New York University Press, N.Y., 1928.

8 *The Mysteries of Opium Reveal'd*, Dr John Jones, London, 1700.

9 *Selected Letters*, Horace Walpole, Dent, 1948, 111.

10 *Life of William Wilberforce* by His Sons, John Murray, 1838, ii. 173–174; *Collected Letters of S. T. Coleridge*, ed. E. L. Griggs, Clarendon Press, 1959, IV. 674–5 (hereafter referred to throughout the notes as S.T.C./LETTERS); *Confessions of an English Opium Eater, in Both the Revised and the Original Texts, With Its Sequels Suspiria de Profundis and the English Mail Coach* by Thomas De Quincey, ed. with introduction and life of De Quincey by Malcolm Elwin, Macdonald, 1956, 94–5 (hereafter referred to throughout the notes as C.E.O.E. 1822, C.E.O.E. 1856 and SUSPIRIA).

11 *Coleridge's Use of Laudanum and Opium*, L. E. Wagner, in *Psycho-analytic Review*, XXV, 3, July 1938, 309–34; *Memoirs of the Life of Sir James Mackintosh*, R. J. Mackintosh, Moxon, 1836; *Dictionary of National Biography* (entries on James Mackintosh and Robert Hall); *Reminiscences of the English Lake Poets*, Thomas De Quincey, ed. J. E. Jordan, Dent, 1961, 277–85 (hereafter referred to throughout the notes as LAKE POETS); *Tom Wedgwood, The First Photographer*, R. B. Litchfield, Duckworth, 1903.

12 *Memoirs of the Turks and the Tartars*, Baron de Tott, Robinson, 1786, l. 160.

13 *C.E.O.E. 1822* 348. cp. Boswell's Life of Johnson, Dent, 1949, II. 436.

14 Terry and Pellens 59.

15 *An Inquiry into the Nature and Properties of Opium*, Samuel Crumpe M.D., Robinson, 1793.

16 *Letters*, Jane Austen, Bodley Head, 1962, 38–9, 41.

17 *Miss Eden's Letters*, Macmillan, 1919, 132.

18 *Wellington and His Friends, Letters of the First Duke of Wellington*, ed. Seventh Duke of Wellington, Macmillan, 1965, 70.

19 *Lake Poets*, 299.

20 *Life and Correspondence of R. Southey*, Longmans, 1849, II. 179.

21 *Byron, a Biography*, L. A. Marchand, John Murray, 1957, II. 559; *Byron, a Self-Portrait. Letters and Diaries 1798–1824*, ed. Peter Quennell, John Murray, 1950, II. 566; *Opium and the Opium Appetite*, A. Calkins, Lippincott, Philadelphia, 1871, 168.

22 *Journal of Thomas Moore*, 1818–41, ed. Peter Quennell, Batsford, 1964, 129; *Letters*, Charles Lamb, 2 vols., Dent, 1917, I. 185; *Letters*, P. B. Shelley, ed. F. L. Jones, Clarendon Press, 1964, I. 232, 246; Schneider 53 and *Fragmentary Remains, Literary and Scientific*, Sir H. Davy, Churchill, 1858, letter of 12th November 1799 from Southey.

23 *Opium and the Opium Appetite*, Calkins, 48.

24 Calkins, 34; *Narcotics*, D. W. Cheever, *North American Review*, October 1862.

25 *The Opium Habit, With Suggestions as to the Remedy*, Horace Day, Harper, N.Y., 1868, 199.

26 *Collected Writings*, Thomas De Quincey, ed. D. Masson, Black, Edinburgh, 1880–90, IV. 216 and XI. 307 n. (hereafter referred to throughout the notes as DE Q/MASSON).

27 *C.E.O.E. 1822* 348.

28 Calkins 33–5.

29 *S.T.C./Letters* III. 125.

30 Calkins 142; *Narcotics*, D. W. Cheever.

31 *C.E.O.E. 1822* 347.

32 *Pharmacological Basic of Therapeutics*, L. S. Goodman and A. Gillman, Macmillan, N.Y., 1955; *Pharmacology of the Opium Alkaloids*, H. M. Krueger, U.S. Public Health Report, 1941, Supplement 165.

33 *C.E.O.E. 1822* 412; *Life of Thomas de Quincey*, H. A. Page (A. H. Japp), Hogg, 1877, II. 89.

NOTES ON CHAPTER II. CASE-HISTORIES

1 *C.E.O.E. 1822* 349.

2 The main sources for this chapter are, in chronological order: *Narcotics*, D. W. Cheever, *North American Review*, Boston, CXCVII. October 1862, 374–415; *The Opium Habit, with Suggestions as to the Remedy*, Horace Day, Harper, N.Y., 1868; *Opium and the Opium Appetite*, A. Calkins, Lippincott, Philadelphia, 1871; *Opium-Eating, an Autobiographical Sketch*, by An Habituate, Claxton, Philadelphia, 1876; *The Drugs That Enslave*, H. H. Kane, Phila-

delphia, 1881; *Opium Smoking in America and China*, H. H. Kane, Putnam, 1882; *Le Morphinisme*, G. Pichon, Doin, Paris, 1889; *Les Morphinomanes*, E. Chambard, Rueff, Paris, 1893; *The Morphia Habit and its Voluntary Renunciation*, Dr Oscar Jennings, Baillière Tindell & Cox, 1909; *Morphinism and Morphinomania*, F. M. Bell, *New York Medical Journal* XCIII, Jan.–June 1911, 680–2; *Les Opiomanes*, R. Dupouy, Librairie Félix Alcan, Paris, 1912 (hereafter referred to throughout the notes as DUPOUY); *The Mental and Nervous Side of Addiction to Narcotic Drugs*, G. C. Wholey, *Journal of the American Medical Association*, Chicago, Vol. 83, No. 5, 2nd August 1924, 324; *Pleasure And Deterioration from Narcotic Addiction*, Dr Laurence Kolb, *Mental Hygiene New York* IX. October 1925. 699–724; *The Opium Problem*, Charles E. Terry and Mildred Pellens, Bureau of Social Hygiene, New York, 1928; *Drug Addiction—a Study of Some Medical Cases*, Dr Laurence Kolb, *Archives of Neurology and Psychiatry*, XX, 1928; *Opium Addiction*, Arthur B. Light and Edward G. Torrance, Philadelphia, 1930; *Poisons Sacrés, Ivresses divines*, Philippe de Félice, Editions Albin Michel, Paris, 1936; *Studies on Drug Addiction*, L. F. Small and others, *U.S.A. Public Health Report*, 1938, Supplement 138; *Pharmacology of the Opium Alkaloids*, H. M. Krueger, *U.S.A. Public Health Report*, 1941, Supplement 165; *Narcotics and Narcotic Addiction*, D. W. Maurer and V. H. Vopel, Thomas, Springfield Ill., 1954; *The Pharmacological Basis of Therapeutics*, L. S. Goodman and Alfred Gilman, Macmillan, New York, 1955; *Treatment and Care of Drug Addicts: Report of the Study Group of the W.H.O.* 1957, *Bulletin on Narcotics* IX, 3, July–Sept. 1957; *Drug Addiction: Physiological, Psychological and Sociological Aspects*, Dr P. D. Ansubel, Random House, New York, 1958; *Problems of Addiction and Habituation*, ed. P. H. Hoch and J. Zubin, Grune and Stratton, New York, 1958; *Drugs and the Mind*, Dr R. S. de Ropp, Gollancz, 1958; *Drug Addiction, Report of the Ministry of Health Interdepartmental Committee*, H.M.S.O., 1961; *Drugs*, Peter Laurie, Penguin, 1967; *Drugs*, Eric Clark, *Observer* 12th, 19th, and 26th February 1967; *Drug Dependence*, Dr David Stafford-Clark, *Times*, 11th and 12th April 1967.

3 Terry and Pellens 516.
4 Terry and Pellens 470.
5 Dupouy 74–7.
6 Ansubel 42, 44.
7 De Félice 46, quoting Louis Laloy, *Le Livre de la Fumée*.

8 Maurer and Vopel 259 et seq.
9 *Drugs*, Eric Clark, *Observer* 26th February 1967.
10 *Narotic Bondage*, Sandor Rado, in *Problems of Addiction and Habituation*, Hoch and Zubin 27.
11 Chambard 60.
12 Day 217.
13 Cheever.
14 Calkins 68.
15 Kane 52.
16 Dupouy 93-4.
17 Krueger 31-2.
18 Dupouy 23-4.
19 Cheever.
20 quoted Dupouy 286.
21 Habituate 93-6.
22 *Turkish Sketches—Effects of Opium*, Rev. Walter Colton, *Knickerbocker Magazine*, VII. 4, April 1836, 421-3.
23 Cheever.
24 Day 185-6.
25 Dupouy 114-15.
26 Dupouy 118.
27 Kolb, *Drug Addiction*.
28 Day 247-9.
29 Dupouy 93.
30 Wholey.
31 Habituate 100-1.
32 Maurer and Vopel 259 et seq.
33 Habituate 96-8; Chambard 31; Dupouy 93-4.
34 Day 189-90.
35 Day 29; Jennings 451.
36 Fitzhugh Ludlow, quoted Day 262.
37 Ansubel 23, 26.
38 Laurie 128.
39 Day 31.
40 Day 223.
41 Habituate 82-4.
42 Day 39.
43 Dupouy 196.
44 Day 30.
45 Kane 67.

46 Day 209.
47 Dupouy 198.
48 Dupouy 123–41.

NOTES ON CHAPTER III. DREAMS

1 Schneider 77–80.
2 *Observations on Man, His Frame, His Duty and His Expectations*, David Hartley, J. Johnson, London, 1791, l. 383–9; *Loves of the Plants*, Erasmus Darwin, Canto III 1. 51 et seq.
3 *L'Ame Romantique et le Rêve*, Albert Béguin, Librairie José Corti, Paris, 1939.
4 Shelley, *Mont Blanc* 11. 49–50.
5 *Correspondence of Southey with Caroline Bowles, to Which Are Added: Correspondence with Shelley, and Southey's Dreams*, ed. Edward Dowden, Longmans, 1881, 366–7.
6 The Marquis d'Hervey reproduced his hypnagogic images in paintings; they were bands, circles, squiggles, shapes like tree-sections, fans, branches, geological strata; mostly yellow but occasionally green, on a black background. Some of them are reproduced in *Dreams and Dreaming*, Norman Mackenzie, Aldus Books, 1965.
7 *C.E.O.E. 1822* 419.
8 *Witches and Other Night Fears, Essays of Elia*, Charles Lamb, Dent, 1913, 80.
9 Wordsworth, *Prelude* VII 11. 600–6; see *William Wordsworth the Early Years*, Mary Moorman, Clarendon Press, 1957, 32.
10 *My Best Mary: Selected Letters of Mary Shelley*, ed. Muriel Spark and Derek Stanford, Allen Wingate, 1953, 121.
11 *Maria Edgeworth: Chosen Letters*, Cape, 1931, 347.
12 *The Notebooks of Samuel Taylor Coleridge*, ed. Kathleen Coburn, Routledge & Kegan Paul, 1956–62, II. 2542 (hereafter referred to throughout the notes as s.t.c./NOTEBOOKS).
13 *Life and Correspondence of Robert Southey*, ed. C. C. Southey, 6 vols., Longmans, 1949, III. 164.
14 *William Allingham: a Diary*, ed. H. Allingham and D. Radford, Macmillan, 1907, 248.
15 *Life and Correspondence of R. Southey* III. 164; *Correspondence with Caroline Bowles* 110.
16 *Witches and Other Night Fears, Essays of Elia*, 81–2.
17 *Collected Poems*, W. B. Yeats, Macmillan, 1963, 71–3.
18 *De Q./Masson* VIII. 33 n.

19 *Alfred Lord Tennyson: a Memoir, by his Son*, Macmillan, 1898, II. 317.

20 *Life and Correspondence of R. Southey* II. 21–2; *Commonplace Book* R. Southey, ed. J. W. Warter, 4 vols., Longmans, 1849, IV. 185; *Curse of Kehama* VII. 10.

21 *Letters of Charles Lamb*, 2 vols., Dent. 1917, I. 16.

22 Shelley, *Mont Blanc*, 1. 55; *Charles I* I. 18–20.

23 *Letters of P. B. Shelley*, ed. F. L. Jones, Clarendon Press, 1964, II. 65 and n.; *Shelley at Work, a Critical Inquiry*, Neville Rogers, Clarendon Press, 1956.

24 Shelley, *Alastor* 1. 39, *Ginevra* 11. 44–5, *Hellas* 11. 130–1, 1065.

25 *Correspondence with Caroline Bowles* and *Commonplace Book*, passim.

26 *Commonplace Book* IV. 20; see Schneider 53–4.

27 Wordsworth *Excursion* I. 183.

28 Wordsworth *Prelude* X. 397–415.

NOTES ON CHAPTER IV. CONTEMPORARY IMAGERY

1 e.g. *The Harp of Aeolus: and other Essays on Art, Literature and Nature*, Geoffrey Grigson, Routledge, 1947.

2 Landor *Gebir* II. 249; Erasmus Darwin *Economy of Vegetation* I. 183.

3 *Egyptian Sculptures in the British Museum*, ed. E. A. Wallis Budge, Department of Egyptian Antiquities, British Museum, 1914; *The Art and Architecture of Ancient Egypt*, W. Stevenson Smith, Pelican History of Art, 1958, 153–4; *The Great Belzoni*, Stanley Mayes, Putnam, 1959, 122–31.

4 *S.T.C./Notebooks* I. 72 n.

5 *Diary of B. R. Haydon*, ed. W. Pope, 5 vols., Harvard University Press, Cambridge, Mass., 1960, II. 492; *Poems*, John Keats, ed. E. de Selincourt, Methuen, 1926, 511 n. 374, 514 n.; *Shelley*, Edmund Blunden, Collins, 1946, 173; *Annals of the Fine Arts*, IX. 323, X. 494, XI. 589–92, June 1818–January 1819.

6 *De Q/Masson* VIII. 17.

7 *De Q/Masson* I. 41.

8 After I had written these paragraphs about the Memnon image, I came across a rather similar analysis on pages 168–70 of *Keats and the Mirror of Art*, Ian Jack, Clarendon Press, 1967.

9 *C.E.O.E. 1822* 426.

10 *Chinoiserie*, Hugh Honour, John Murray, 1961.

11 *Bandits in a Landscape*, William Gaunt, Studio, 1937; *Pleasure of Ruins*, Rose Macaulay, Wiedenfeld and Nicolson, 1953.

12 *John Martin en France*, Jean Seznec, Faber, 1964; *Deux Thèmes Visionnaires de Gérard de Nerval*, Henri Lemaitre, *L'Oeil*, Paris, June 1962.

13 Shelley, *Revolt of Islam*, V. 23; see *John Martin*, Thomas Balston, Duckworth, 1947, 35 n.

14 *Paradis Artificiels*, *Œuvres Completes de C. Baudelaire*, Gallimard, 1961, 422.

15 I find that Professor Ian Jack, in *Keats and the Mirror of Art*, 173, has also noted this parallel.

16 *Heaven and Hell*, Aldous Huxley, Penguin, 1959, 130.

17 *The Mask of Keats*, Robert Gittings, Heinemann, 1956, 103–7; *England's Wealthiest Son: a Study of William Beckford*, Boyd Alexander, Centaur Press, 1962, 83.

18 *C.E.O.E. 1822* 422–3.

19 *Introduction*, Marguerite Yourcenar, to *Carceri d'Invenzione*, *Les Prisons Imaginaires de Gian-Battista Piranesi*, Club International de Bibliophile, Monaco, 1961.

20 *Prisons, with the 'Carceri' Etchings by G. B. Piranesi*, Aldous Huxley and Jean Adhémar, Trianon Press, 1949.

21 Yourcenar.

22 *De Q / Masson* I. 55, VIII. 19 n., X. 389–94.

23 *C.E.O.E. 1856* 318.

NOTES ON CHAPTER V. DE QUINCEY (I)

1 Quoted from *A Diary of Thomas de Quincey*, ed. H. A. Eaton, N. Douglas, London, 177.

2 *Loves of the Plants* Canto II l. 267 et seq.

3 References to De Quincey's main works in this chapter and Chapter X are to the edition *Collected Writings*, 14 vols., ed. David Masson, Adam & Charles Black, Edinburgh, 1889–90 (DE Q/ MASSON) except in the case of the *Confessions of an English Opium Eater*, 1822 and 1856 versions (C.E.O.E. 1822 and C.E.O.E. 1856) and the *Suspiria de Profundis* (SUSPIRIA), which I have quoted from Malcolm Elwin's more accurate edition (Macdonald, London, 1956), and of the *Reminiscences of the English Lake Poets* (LAKE POETS) which I have quoted from another recent and more accurate edition by Professor J. E. Jordan (Dent, London, 1961).

Drafts, letters and a diary of De Quincey unpublished in his lifetime are included in *Posthumous Works of De Quincey*, 2 vols., ed.

A. H. Japp, Heinemann, London, 1891–3; *De Quincey Memorials*, 2 vols., ed. A. H. Japp, Heinemann, 1891; *A Diary of Thomas de Quincey*, ed. H. A. Eaton, N. Douglas, London, 1927; *De Quincey at Work. As Seen in 130 New and Newly Edited Letters*, ed. W. H. Bonner, Buffalo, 1936; *Thomas de Quincey to Wordsworth: a Biography of a Relationship*, ed. J. E. Jordan, University of California Press, 1962.

Biographies and critical studies: *Life of Thomas de Quincey*, H. A. Page (A. H. Japp), Hogg, 1877; *Personal Recollections of Thomas de Quincey*, J. R. Findlay, Black, 1886; *De Quincey and His Friends*, James Hogg, Sampson Low, 1895; *Thomas de Quincey: a Biography*, H. A. Eaton, O.U.P., 1936; *A Flame in Sunlight: the Life and Works of Thomas de Quincey*, Edward Sackville-West, Cassell, 1936; *Thomas de Quincey, La Vie, L'Homme, L'Œuvre*, Francoise Moreux, Presses Universitaires de Paris, 1964 (which contains a particularly thorough analysis of De Quincey's exploration of his opium-dreams); *The Life of Thomas de Quincey*, Malcolm Elwin (in his edition of the *Confessions*, see above), Macdonald, 1956.

4 *C.E.O.E. 1822* 431.
5 *C.E.O.E. 1822* 391.
6 *C.E.O.E. 1856* 265.
7 *Suspiria* 512; *De Q/Masson* III. 203.
8 *C.E.O.E. 1822* 386–7; *De Q/Masson* III. 215.
9 *C.E.O.E. 1856* 293.
10 *Les Morphinomanes*, E. Chambard, 1893, 68–70.
11 *Poisons Sacrés, Ivresses Divines*, P. de Félice, 1936, 40.
12 *Opium and the Opium Appetite*, Dr. A. Calkins, 1871, 95–6; *The Hypodermic Injection of Morphine*, Dr. H. H. Kane, 1880; Dupouy, 74.
13 *The Opium Habit*, Horace Day, 1868, 15.
14 *Reminiscences of S. T. Coleridge and R. Southey*, Joseph Cottle, Houlston & Stoneman, 1847, 409.
15 *C.E.O.E. 1822* 438 n.
16 Page (Japp) II. 271–3.
17 *Suspiria* 447.
18 *C.E.O.E. 1822* 389–91, 414–19, 349, 399, 408, 422, 428.
19 *C.E.O.E. 1822* 398.
20 *C.E.O.E. 1822* 419; *C.E.O.E. 1856* 236; *De Q/Masson* XIII. 191–2.
21 *De Q/Masson* XIV. 265.
22 *Lake Poets* 63–4.
23 *Lake Poets* 129.

24 Page (Japp) I. 338–9, letter of 1844 to Lushington.

25 *Suspiria* 449.

26 *Suspiria* 454–5.

27 *C.E.O.E. 1856*, 99.

28 *C.E.O.E. 1856*, 113–14.

29 *C.E.O.E. 1856* 292.

30 *De Q./Masson* III. 77.

31 *C.E.O.E. 1856* 307–8.

32 This was pointed out by a reviewer in the *Medical Intelligencer*, and De Quincey in his letter of December 1821 in the *London Magazine* acknowledged that the comment was just, and promised to remedy this in the Third Part of the Confessions, which never got written. *De Q./Masson* III. 465 n.

33 *C.E.O.E. 1822* 389–95, 401, 419.

34 *C.E.O.E. 1822* 395.

35 *C.E.O.E. 1822* 399.

36 *C.E.O.E. 1822* 415–19.

37 *De Q./Masson* III. 77.

38 *De Q./Masson* III. 75.

39 *De Q./Masson* V. 206; *C.E.O.E. 1856*, 104, 307.

40 *De Q./Masson* III. 75.

41 Page (Japp) I. 339–40.

42 Page (Japp) I. 325; Eaton, 415.

43 *C.E.O.E. 1822* 438.

44 *De Q./Masson* III. 75.

45 Findlay 39–40; *De Q. at Work*, passim.

46 *De Q./Masson* V. 208.

47 *Essays in English Literature, 1780–1860*, G. Saintsbury, Percival & Co., 1890.

48 *Thomas de Quincey to Wordsworth* 37.

49 *Memorials* II. 111.

50 Page (Japp) I. 107.

51 *Suspiria* 513, 528, 503.

52 *De Q./Masson* II. 55.

53 *De Q./Masson* III. 75.

54 *C.E.O.E. 1822* 419–20.

55 *C.E.O.E. 1856* 102.

56 *De Q./Masson* I. 51.

57 *Suspiria* 448.

58 Page (Japp) I. 329; Eaton 416.

59 De Q / Masson V. 211; Paradise Lost XI. 416-20.
60 Suspiria 453.
61 De Q / Masson V. 305-6.
62 Posthumous Works. I. 7-12.
63 Suspiria 468, 503.
64 De Q / Masson XIII. 135; Posthumous Works I. 11.
65 Suspiria 527.
66 Suspiria 524.
67 Suspiria 466.
68 De Q / Masson I. 128-9.
69 C.E.O.E. 1856 103.
70 C.E.O.E. 1822 413.
71 C.E.O.E. 1822 413.
72 De Q / Masson III. 76, 219.
73 Suspiria 502.

NOTES ON CHAPTER VI. POE

In this chapter I have not given references for Poe's poems and tales as they are short and easily accessible in many editions. I have mainly worked with *Complete Works of Edgar Allan Poe*, ed. J. A. Harrison, 17 vols., New York, 1902. Quotations from Poe's letters are from *Letters of Edgar Allan Poe*, ed. J. W. Ostrom, Harvard University Press, 1948.

Biographies and critical studies: *Edgar Poe, Sa Vie et Ses Œuvres*, introduction to *Histoires Extraordinaires par Edgar Poe*, Charles Baudelaire, Paris, 1856; *Edgar Poe and His Critics*, Sarah Helen Whitman, Rudd & Carleton, New York, 1860; *Edgar Allan Poe, His Life, Letters and Opinions*, J. H. Ingram, Ward Lock, 1891; *The Life of Edgar Allan Poe, Personal and Literary, with his Chief Correspondence with Men of Letters*, 2 vols., G. E. Woodberry, Houghton Miflin, Boston, 1909; *Le Genie d'Edgar Poe*, Camille Mauclair, Albin Michel, Paris, 1925; *Edgar Allan Poe, a Study in Genius*, J. W. Krutch, Knopf, 1926; *Edgar Poe, Etude Psychanalytique*, 2 vols., Marie Bonaparte, Editions Denoel et Steele, Paris, 1933; *The Mind of Poe, and Other Studies*, Killis Campbell, Harvard University Press, 1933; *Edgar Allan Poe*, Una Pope-Hennessy, Macmillan, 1934; *Israfel, The Life and Times of Edgar Allan Poe*, Hervey Allen, Gollancz, 1935; *Le Génie Morbide d'Edgar Poe*, Emile Lauvrière, Desclée de Brouwen, Paris, 1935; *Edgar Allan Poe, a Critical Biography*, A. H. Quinn, Appleton-Century, New York, 1941; *The Histrionic Mr Poe*, N. B. Fagin, Johns Hopkins Press, Baltimore, 1949; *The French*

Face of Edgar Poe, P. F. Quinn, Southern Illinois University Press, 1957; *Edgar Allan Poe, the Man Behind the Legend*, E. Wagenknecht, O.U.P., New York, 1963; *Edgar Allan Poe*, Geoffrey Rans, Oliver and Boyd, 1965.

1 Baudelaire, Roger Dupouy (*Les Opiomanes*), Lauvrière and Marie Bonaparte, among French writers on Poe, and Woodberry, Hervey Allen and Jeannette Marks (*Genius and Disaster. Studies in Drugs and Genius*, Hamilton, 1928) among American writers, have upheld the thesis of Poe as an opium-taker. Woodberry (ii. 428–430) and Allen (298–300, 358 n.) suggested that he resorted to it fairly often, but not habitually. C. Mauclair, A. H. Quinn, E. Wagenknecht, G. Rans, Mary Phillips (*Edgar Allan Poe the Man*, 2 vols., Winston, Chicago, 1926) deny that he took it.

2 A. H. Quinn 592.

3 *Letters*, 16th November 1848 and 21st January 1849 to Mrs Richmond.

4 Woodberry II. 428–30. I have not included the story that Sartain said Poe begged for laudanum when he was in Philadelphia in 1849 (Woodberry II. 428–30; Hervey Allen 474, 461) because it has been shown by A. H. Quinn (618 n.) to be unsound.

5 Woodberry II. 428–30; A. H. Quinn 350, 618 n., 693–4.

6 *Letters* I. 256.

7 *Letters* I. 300.

8 Woodberry I. 302.

9 *A Dream of Things Impossible*, Francis Thompson, *Academy*, 28th September 1901.

10 Marie Bonaparte 278, 347; see also A. H. Quinn 457.

11 Baudelaire, *Edgar Poe, Sa Vie et Ses Œuvres* in *Œuvres en Prose*, E. A. Poe, Gallimard, 1951, 1044–5.

12 *Shadow, MS Found in a Bottle, Imp of the Perverse, Narrative of A. Gordon Pym, Tell-Tale Heart, Ligeia.*

13 N. B. Fagin, *passim*.

14 Hervey Allen 358–60.

15 It has been shown, for instance, that the House of Usher is partly described from Scott's description of the castle in Hoffmann's *Das Majorat* (Woodberry); see also Killis Campbell for the link between *The Masque of the Red Death* and De Quincey's *Klosterheim*, and Hervey Allen (406) for the engravers, Fagin for the stage effects.

16 *Lake Poets* 44–5.

17 G. Rans 58, 69; E. H. Davidson 79–80; Hervey Allen 357.

18 *Letters*, I. 161; essay, *Nathaniel Hawthorne*.
19 *The Power of Words*.
20 *Marginalia: Thoughts and Words*.
21 *Letters* I. 57–8.
22 *Letters* I. 84.

NOTES ON CHAPTER VII. BAUDELAIRE AND THE CLUB DES HASCHISCHINS

1 *Œuvres Complètes*, Charles Baudelaire, Bibliotheque de la Pléiade, Gallimard, Paris, 1961, 349–50. Since in this chapter I am only summarizing Baudelaire's opinions on the effects of opium, not attempting to trace its effects on his own work, there is no occasion to give a source-list of biographical and critical studies of Baudelaire.

2 *Baudelaire*, Enid Starkie, Faber, 1957, 57, 164, 372; *Découverte de l'Ile St Louis*, Paul Guilly, Albin Michel, Paris, 1955, 307–8; *Génies et Realités*, Maurice Nadeau, Hachette, Paris; *Les Opiomanes*, Roger Dupouy.

3 *Œuvres Complètes* 373, 374, 425, 426, 428.
4 Poe, *Marginalia, Works*, vol. XVI, 17–18, November 1844.
5 Gautier, *Club des Haschischins, Romans et Contes*, 1877.
6 *Œuvres Complètes* 364–5.
7 *Œuvres Complètes* 354, 366.
8 Starkie 372–3.
9 *Rêve Parisien*.
10 *Œuvres Complètes* 422.
11 *Œuvres en Prose*, Edgar Allan Poe, traduction par Ch. Baudelaire, Bibliotheque de la Pleiade, Gallimard, Paris, 1951, 1050.
12 *Œuvres Complètes* 428–9.
13 *Œuvres Complètes*, 372.
14 *Œuvres en Prose*, E. A. Poe, 1046.
15 *Sed Non Satiata; Le Poison; Les Phares; Le Voyage*.
16 *Le poison*.
17 *Œuvres en Prose*, E. A. Poe, 1079 n. 4.
18 *Œuvres Complètes* 373, 974.
19 *Œuvres Complètes* 516.
20 *Œuvres Complètes* 1253.
21 *Œuvres Complètes* 372.
22 *Œuvres en Prose*, E. A. Poe, 1046.

23 *Œuvres Complètes* 372.

24 *Le Club des Haschischins*, Theophile Gautier; *Decouverte de l'Ile Saint Louis*, Paul Guilly, 312–13; *Le Quai d'Orleans et l'Ile Saint Louis*, Marius Boisson, Firmin-Didot, Paris, 1931, 75–6.

25 *Œuvres Complètes* 391, 374–5.

26 *Decouverte de l'Ile St Louis*, Paul Guilly, 309.

27 *The Romantic Ballet in Paris*, Ivor Guest, Pitman, 1966.

28 *Decouverte de l'Ile St Louis*, Paul Guilly, 306–7.

29 *Œuvres Complètes* 384.

30 *Œuvres Complètes* 347–9, 386–7; *Œuvres en Prose*, E. A. Poe, 1058.

31 *Œuvres Complètes* 385–6.

NOTES ON CHAPTER VIII. CRABBE

References to Crabbe's poetry in this chapter are to *Poems* by George Crabbe, 3 vols., edited Adolphus Ward, Cambridge University Press, 1905–7 (referred to as *Poems*), to *The Poetical Works of the Rev. George Crabbe, with his Letters and Journals, and his Life by his Son*, 8 vols., John Murray, 1834 (referred to as *Works*), and to *New Poems* by George Crabbe, edited Arthur Pollard, Liverpool University Press, 1960 (referred to as *New Poems*).

Biographies and critical studies: *Memoirs of Eminent Persons* (anonymous autobiographical sketch by Crabbe) in *New Monthly Magazine*, vol. vi. 1st Jan. 1816, pp. 511–17; *Lectures on English Poets*, William Hazlitt, Oxford University Press, 1929; *Life of George Crabbe by his Son*, introduction Edmund Blunden, Cresset Press, 1947 (referred to as *Life*); *Contributions to the Edinburgh Review*, Francis Jeffrey, 3 vols., Longmans, 1846; *The Leadbeater Papers*, Mary Leadbeater, Bell and Daldy, 1862; *Life of George Crabbe*, T. E. Kebbel, W. Scott, 1888; *Crabbe*, Alfred Ainger, Macmillan, 1903; *Un Poète Realiste Anglais: George Crabbe*, R. Huchon, Librairie Hachette, Paris, 1906; *The Romance of an Elderly Poet*, A. M. Broadley and Walter Jerrold, Stanley Paul, 1913; *Introduction*, E. M. Forster, to *Life of George Crabbe, by his Son*, World's Classics, 1932; *Introduction*, Geoffrey Grigson, to *Selected Poems of George Crabbe*, Grey Walls Press, 1950; *Two Cheers for Democracy*, E. M. Forster, Edward Arnold, 1951; *Introduction*, Frank Whitehead, to *George Crabbe: Selections from his Poetry*, Chatto & Windus, 1955; *The Poetry of Crabbe*, Lilian Haddakin, Chatto & Windus, 1955; *George Crabbe*, R. L. Brett, Longmans, 1956.

1 *Life* 138.

2 *Lectures on English Poets* in *Collected Works*, William Hazlitt, ed. A. R. Waller and A. Glover, 13 vols., Dent, 1902, V. 96–8.

3 *Poems* I. 353 (Borough VII ll. 220–9); I. 351–2, 446 ¦(Borough VII. ll. 130–47, XVII l. 231); *New Poems*, 31 (*Hester* ll. 469–76).

4 *New Poems* (*The Flowers* ll. 167–80).

5 *Life* 116, 143–4.

6 *Memoirs of Eminent Persons.*

7 R. L. Brett 30.

8 *Life* 6–7.

9 *Life* 143.

10 Huchon 267 n. 1.

11 *Life* 228.

12 *Life* 169.

13 *Milk of Paradise*, M. H. Abrams.

14 *Life* 108, 33.

15 *Poems* I. 475, 477, 498 II. 38, 39–40, 439, III. 76, 89–97 (*Borough* XX. 192 et seq., 293–5, xxii. 25; *Tales* ii. 418–21, 454 et seq. *Tales of the Hall* x. 334–43, xvi. 39–46, 569 et seq.).

16 *Poems* II. 439 (*The Old Bachelor* ll. 334–43).

17 *Life and Poetical Works of the Rev George Crabbe*, edited by his Son, John Murray, 1847, 251 n.

18 Coleridge, *Dejection, an Ode.*

19 *Poems* II. 135 (*The Lover's Journey* ll. 1–18). See Huchon 339 and Whitehead, *Introduction.*

20 *Poems* III, 96 (*Lady Barbara, or the Ghost*, ll. 820–41).

21 *Poems* III. 496.

22 *Life* 246.

23 *Life* 72, 153, 190, 277.

24 *Life* 207–16.

25 Huchon 509 n.

26 *Life* 220.

27 *Leadbeater Papers* II. 350.

28 *New Poems* 4–5, 52–9.

29 *New Poems* 169–70 n.

30 *Leadbeater Papers* II. 376.

31 *Poems* I. 115–16 (*Library* ll. 535–82).

32 *Poems* I. 471–3 (*Ellen Orford* ll. 29–119).

33 *Life* 136.

34 *Poems* II. 342 (*Adventures of Richard* ll. 343–48). See also *Poems* II. 443–4 (*The Old Bachelor* ll. 490–518).

35 Contributions to the Edinburgh Review, Francis Jeffrey, 4 vols.,
   Longmans, 1844, III. 76.
36 Poems I. 121–2, 456, 220, 315 (Village 63–78; Borough XVIII. ll.
   290–302; Parish Register III. ll. 873–4; Borough IV, ll. 48–55).
37 Poems I. 177, 191, 367, 420, II. 45 (Parish Register I. 747–8, II.
   Borough IX. 105–8, XIV. 802; Tales III. 114–20).
38 Poems I. 482, 487 (Borough XXI. ll. 48, 232, 245–8).
39 Poems I. 493, 494 (Borough XXII. ll. 54–8, 78, 87–8).
40 Life and Poetical Works, 1847, 250 n.; E. M. Forster, George Crabbe
   and Peter Grimes in Two Cheers for Democracy; Geoffrey Grigson,
   Introduction.
41 Poems III. 21–3 (Tales of the Hall, XII. ll. 754–814).
42 Jeffrey, Contributions to Edinburgh Review, III. 79; E. M. Forster,
   Two Cheers for Democracy and Introduction.
43 Life 204–5, 235, 211.
44 Life 234.
45 Leadbeater Papers II. 340–1.
46 Memoirs of Eminent Persons.
47 Romance of an Elderly Poet 82.
48 Romance of an Elderly Poet 110.
49 Life 182. Huchon (247 n.) gives the correct text.
50 Romance of an Elderly Poet 80.
51 Life 185.
52 Romance of an Elderly Poet 89.
53 Poems III. 408–9 (World of Dreams xvii–xx).
54 Longing, Matthew Arnold.
55 New Poems 33–44.
56 New Poems 43–4, 33 (Insanity of Ambitious Love ll. 369–70, 421–2,
   15–16).
57 Poems I. 121–2 (Village I. 63–78).
58 Poems I. 456 (Borough XVIII. ll. 290–302).
59 William Hazlitt, Lectures on English Poets, Complete Works, V. 97.
60 Poems II. 138 (Tales X. 113–28 and note).

NOTES TO CHAPTER IX. COLERIDGE

References to Coleridge's works in this Chapter are to: Complete
Poetical Works of S. T. Coleridge, ed. E. H. Coleridge, 2 vols., Clarendon
Press, 1912; The Notebooks of Samuel Taylor Coleridge, ed. Kathleen
Coburn, 2 vols., Routledge and Kegan Paul, 1957 and 1962 (S.T.C./
NOTEBOOKS); Anima Poetae, ed. E. H. Coleridge, Heinemann, 1895;

Biographia Literaria, Dent, 1956; *Shakespearean Criticism*, ed. T. M. Raysor, 2 vols., Constable, 1930; *Table Talk*, ed. H. N. Coleridge, 2 vols., John Murray, 1835; *Miscellanies, Aesthetic and Literary*, ed. T. Ashe, Bell, 1885; *Inquiring Spirit, A New Presentation of Coleridge from his Published and Unpublished Writings*, ed. Kathleen Coburn, Routledge and Kegan Paul, 1951.

References to Coleridge's letters are to: *Collected Letters of Samuel Taylor Coleridge*, ed. E. L. Griggs, 4 vols., Clarendon Press, 1956 and 1959 (S.T.C./LETTERS); *Letters of S. T. Coleridge*, ed. E. H. Coleridge, 2 vols., Heinemann, 1895; *Unpublished Letters of Samuel Taylor Coleridge*, ed. E. L. Griggs, 2 vols., Constable, 1932; *Memorials of Coleorton*, ed. W. A. Knight, 2 vols., Douglas, Edinburgh, 1887.

Biographies and critical studies: *Early Recollections, Chiefly Relating to the Late S. T. Coleridge*, Joseph Cottle, 2 vols., Longmans, Rees & Co., 1837; *Life of S. T. Coleridge*, James Gillman, William Pickering, 1838; *Reminiscences of Samuel Taylor Coleridge and Robert Southey*, Joseph Cottle, Houlston & Stoneman, 1847; *Letters, Conversations and Recollections of S. T. Coleridge*, T. Allsop, Frederick Farrar, 1864; *Early Years and Late Reflections*, Clement Carlyon, Whittaker & Co., 1856–8; *S. T. Coleridge and the English Romantic School*, Alois Brandl, John Murray, 1887; *Samuel Taylor Coleridge*, J. Dykes Campbell, Macmillan, 1894; *Introduction*, Arthur Symons, to *Poems of Coleridge*, Methuen, 1905; *Coleridge at Highgate*, Lucy Watson, Longmans, 1925; *The Road to Xanadu*, J. L. Lowes, Houghton Mifflin, Boston, 1927 (LOWES); *Archetypal Patterns in Poetry*, Maud Bodkin, O.U.P., 1934; *Minnow Among Tritons*; *Mrs S. T. Coleridge's Letters to Thomas Poole*, ed. Stephen Potter, Nonesuch Press, 1934; *Coleridge on Imagination*, I. A. Richards, Kegan Paul, 1934; *Coleridge's Use of Laudanum and Opium*, Lydia Wagner, in *Psychoanalytic Review*, XXV. 3, pp. 309–34, July 1938; *The Life of S. T. Coleridge: the Early Years*, Lawrence Hanson, Allen & Unwin, 1938; *Samuel Taylor Coleridge, a Biographical Study*, E. K. Chambers, Clarendon Press, 1938; *Coleridge and S.T.C.*, Stephen Potter, Cape, 1938; *The Road to Tryermaine*, A. H. Nethercot, University of Chicago Press, Chicago, 1939; *Coleridge and the Ancient Mariner*, R. C. Bald, in *Nineteenth Century Studies*, Cornell University Press, 1940; *The Starlit Dome*, G. Wilson Knight, O.U.P., 1941; *Coleridge: The Clark Lectures*, Humphrey House, Hart-Davis, 1953; *Coleridge*, Kathleen Raine, Longmans, 1953; *Coleridge Opium and 'Kubla Khan'*, Elisabeth Schneider, University of Chicago Press, Chicago, 1953 (SCHNEIDER); *Samuel Taylor Coleridge and Opium*, E. L. Griggs, in

Huntington Library Quarterly, pp. 357–78. August 1954; *Visions of Xanadu*, Marshall Suther, Columbia University Press, N.Y., 1965.

1 *Letters* III. 463–4.
2 *Letters* I. 353–4; Dupouy 231; Gillman 33; Lowes 415; Hanson 20, 29.
3 *Letters* I. 18, III. xxxi.
4 *Letters* I. 188 and n.; *Edmund Oliver*, Charles Lloyd, I. 210, 245; Lowes 599 n. 13.
5 *Letters* I. 249–50, 252.
6 *Letters* I. 394.
7 *Works* I. 296; Crewe MS, *Letters* I. 348–9. The controversy as to whether *Kubla Khan* was written in the summer or autumn of 1797, in May 1798, or (as suggested by Professor Schneider) in the autumn of 1799 or early summer 1800 does not affect the generally agreed conclusion that Coleridge did not become *addicted* to opium before 1800.
8 Lowes 599–600 n. 14.
9 *Letters* I. 394.
10 *Letters* I. 52, 605. *Notebooks* I. 251.
11 *Letters* III. xxxi–xxxv; Lowes 420; Hanson 29, 133; Potter 62–72; Schneider, *passim*.
12 *Letters* II. 731 and n., 732, III. xxxiv.
13 *Letters* III. 476; Gillman 246; Allsop I. 77–8; *S.T.C. and Opium*, Griggs; *Coleridge's Use of Laudanum and Opium*, Wagner.
14 *Letters* II. 884, 787; *Notebooks* I. 990.
15 *Letters* II. 884, 888–9, 915, 917, 942, 979, 982, 991, 992, 993 III. xxxvi–xxxviii.
16 *Letters* II. 1019. 1027, 1097; but see also 930; *Notebooks* I. 1681, II. 1977.
17 *Notebooks* II. 2091.
18 *Letters* II. 1137, 1178; *Notebooks* II, 2398, 2557, 2602, 2860, 2944, 2990, 3078; Campbell 158.
19 *Letters* III. 22, 28–9, 62–3.
20 *Letters* III. 125–7, 131, 175, 212.
21 *Letters* II. 1178, III. 125, 127, 131, 298 n.; *Early Recollections*, Cottle, II. 149.
22 *Wordsworth, the Early Years*, Mary Moorman, 530; *Dove Cottage*, ed. Kingsley Hart, Folio Society, 1956, 75–6; Campbell 158.
23 *Southey*, Jack Simmons, Collins, 1945, 120.
24 *Early Recollections*, Cottle, II. 149 et seq.

25 *Letters* III. xxxix, 415, 463–4, 476–9, 489–91, 511.
26 *Letters* III. 502, 513, IV. 578, 612.
27 *Letters* IV. 625 n., 626–30.
28 *Letters* III, xl, IV. 638, 644, 660; *Letters* ed. E. H. Coleridge II. 760; *Unpublished Letters* 440–1; *Memorials of Coleorton* II. 246; Allsop I. 81; *Minnow Among Tritons* 48, 165.
29 *Unpublished Letters* I. 328–31; *Coleridge at Highgate* 26–40; *Life of Mary Russell Mitford*, ed. L. Estrange, 3 vols., 1870, I. 271; *S.T.C. and Opium*, Griggs; *Early Recollections*, Cottle, II. 170–1; *Lake Poets*, De Quincey, 69–70.
30 *Reminiscences of S.T.C. and Southey*, Cottle, 373.
31 *S.T.C. and Opium*, Griggs.
32 *Coleridge's Use of Laudanum*, Wagner; *Lake Poets*, De Quincey, 26.
33 *Notebooks* II. 2398.
34 *Letters* I. 125, 367. III. 307; *Biographia Literaria* 128, 166–7.
35 House 39–40; Schneider 54; Raine 13.
36 *Letters* III. 490.
37 Potter 62–72.
38 Lowes 416.
39 *Letters* III. 490, IV. 630; *Notebooks* II. 3078.
40 *Letters* I. 394.
41 *Notebooks* II. 2368.
42 *Notebooks* II. 2398; *Letters* III. xxxii, 127, 331, 477, 489, 491; Gillman 247; Allsop I. 77–8; Bald 25 n. 9.
43 *Lake Poets* 44.
44 Gillman 247–8.
45 *Reminiscences of S. T. Coleridge and Southey*, Cottle, 373.
46 *Table-Talk* William Hazlitt, *Complete Works*, VI. 248–55.
47 *Notebooks* II. 3078; *Letters* III. 477, 489, 491; *Unpublished Letters* 441; *Memorials of Coleorton II.* 246; Allsop I. 76–8.
48 *Letters* IV. 627, 674.
49 *Notebooks* II. 2944; *Letters* II. 984 n., III. 125, 127–8, 212, 477.
50 *Letters* I. 250.
51 *Letters* I. 350, 394, 539; *Notebooks* I. 1718.
52 *Notebooks* I. 576, 1575; Schneider 69–70.
53 *Letters* III. 477, 489. cp. De Quincey *C.E.O.E. 1822* 418–19.
54 *Letters* IV. 626.
55 Bald 36; Schneider 71.
56 *Letters* III, 463–4.
57 *The Friend* I. 246–8, quoted from *Inquiring Spirit*.

58 *Notebooks* I. 848.

59 Schneider 91–105.

60 Only some of S.T.C.'s most important passages on dreams can be given here as references; a complete list would be a book in itself. For the differences between dreams and nightmares, see *Miscellanies, Aesthetic and Literary*, 163–8; *Anima Poetae*, 242–5. For the transition between sleeping and waking, *Notebooks* I. 1726, 1078, II. 2080; Appendix B to *Statesman's Manual, Lay Sermons*. For dream transformations of external sensations, *Notebooks* I. 1620, II. 2064, 2073, 2559. For hallucinations, *Letters* I. 257; *Anima Poetae* 277–8; Carlyon I. 198 et seq. For paramnesia, *Letters* I. 246, 277. For belief and absence of surprise in dreams, *Letters* IV. 641–2; *Shakespearean Criticism* 129; *Miscellanies* 163–8; *Biographia Literaria* 6. For association, *Notebooks* I. 1770; *Letters* II. 974.

61 *Notebooks* II. 2018.

62 *Letters* II. 986, 991, 993.

63 *Letters* II. 993 and n.

64 *Notebooks* II. 2398, 2944.

65 *Letters* III. 212.

66 *Letters* III. 495.

67 Gillman 246.

68 *Letters* I. 348; *Notebooks* II. 2290.

69 *Letters* I. 51, 63, 101, 104, 287.

70 *Works* I. 43, 69, 74, 77, 166; *Osorio* IV. i.

71 Schneider 63–7.

72 *Letters* II. 983.

73 *Notebooks* I. 1492.

74 *Notebooks* I. 1577.

75 *Letters* II. 1028; *Notebooks* I. 432 (ii), 1250, 1176, 1649, II. 2055, 1539; *Biographia Literaria* 5.

76 *Letters* III. 369; *Anima Poetae* 243–5.

77 *Letters* II. 737; *Notebooks* I. 848, 1250, 1726, II. 1998, 2468.

78 *Notebooks* II. 2078, 2838; *Anima Poetae* 243–5; *Remorse* IV. i.

79 *Letters* II. 976, 989–90, 1005, 1028, 1074, 1084; *Notebooks* I. 1619, II. 1863, 1998.

80 *Notebooks* I. 205.

81 *Letters* II. 974.

82 e.g. *Letters* I. 481, II. 776, 832, III. 66; *Notebooks* II. 2061, 2078, 2441, 2600, 2999, 3148.

83 *Notebooks* I. 1726.

84 *Notebooks* I. 1824, 1698, II. 1998, 2489, I. 1649.

85 *Notebooks* II. 2086.

86 *Notebooks* I. 990.

87 *Letters* II. 1028.

88 *Notebooks* I. 1250.

89 *Notebooks* II. 2018, 2441.

90 *Notebooks* II. 2055, 2061.

91 *Notebooks* II. 2061. Cp. Appendix B to *Statesmen's Manual*, *Lay Sermans*, quoted House, Chap. VI.

92 *Notebooks* II. 2055.

93 *Notebooks* II. 2441; *Works* I. 393. Arthur Symons (Notes 218, in *Poems of Coleridge*, 1905) suggests—I do not know on what evidence —that these lines were actually composed in sleep, as *Kubla Khan* was supposed to have been.

94 *Works* I. 484–5.

95 Lowes 274–280.

96 *The Road to Tryermaine*, Nethercot; *A New Reading of Christabel*, *Cambridge Journal* V. No. 2.

97 *Letters* I. 407 n.; Schneider 163, 334 n. 14.

98 *Notebooks* I. 848, 1250.

99 *Notebooks* I. 188.

100 See, e.g., Bodkin 34.

101 *Works* I. 77.

102 Potter 62–72.

103 *Letters* II. 1122.

104 *Letters* II. 1008.

105 *Works* I. 416.

106 Allsop II. 134–7.

107 *Letters* II. 668.

108 *Letters* II. 992; Schneider 82.

109 *Notebooks* I. 848, 1403, II. 2059, 2061, 2542.

110 *Notebooks* I. 1098.

111 e.g. *Notebooks* I. 14, 13, 1024, 841, II. 2409, 2348, 2129.

112 *Notebooks* I. 273, 925, 1039, 1108, 1767; Lowes, 38–9, 452 n. 12 and 474 n. 10.

113 *The Friend* I. 249 quoted from *Tom Wedgwood, the First Photographer*, R. B. Litchfield, Duckworth, 1903.

114 *Letters* II. 707.

115 *Notebooks* I. 1681.

116 *Letters* I. 649.

117 *Notebooks* I. 1750.

118 e.g. *Notebooks* I. 841, 1050, 1307, II. 2359, 2583, 2632; *Letters* I. 539.

119 *Notebooks* I. 1297.

120 *Notebooks* I. 1050, 1297, 894, 1668.

121 Lowes 346.

122 *Notebooks* I. 791.

123 Lowes 484, n. 24.

124 *Letters* I. 249–251; Lowes 602 n. 42.

125 *Letters* I. 349 n., 350. E. L. Griggs definitely associates this Vishnu-on-the-Lotos opium rêverie with *Kubla Khan* which he, for this and other reasons, dates October 1797. See also Lowes 518–19 n. 103, linking the Vishnu-on-the-Lotos passage with the 'dusky light-purple flash' *Notebook* entry (I. 273) in which M. H. Abrams detected the influence of opium. I do not feel quite convinced about that—the entry is too much like S.T.C.'s later notes on ocular spectra, which were not exclusively opium phenomena.

126 *Works* I. 569.

127 *Letters* I. 539.

128 Schneider 68.

129 *Notebooks* I. 1718. Cp. the addict quoted in Chapter II who compared this kind of opium rêverie with floating in a sea of warm milk. All such rêveries, and perhaps especially this one of Coleridge's, no doubt have elements of infantile regression. Otway's line about 'seas of milk' was an oddly favourite quotation of Coleridge's; see Lowes 346–7.

130 *Letters* I. 394.

131 *Notebooks* I. 1750.

132 e.g. M. H. Abrams; but Lowes (343, 401, 403–6) thought it was a real dream of sleep in which all conscious imaginative control was in abeyance, while Professor Schneider thought that there was no distinction between opium rêveries and ordinary rêveries or day-dreams (44, 90, 276–7).

133 See, in particular, Schneider 22–7.

134 Crewe MS., *Letters* I. 348–9.

135 *Works* I. 296.

136 *Letters* I. 394.

137 The classic study is of course Lowes' *Road to Xanadu*, but Professor Schneider, Marshall Suther (*Visions of Xanadu*) and many others have joined in this enthralling sport.

138 *Notebooks* I. 7, 220, 658; *Anima Poetae* 282; *Aids to Reflection,* Conclusion, 383–6.

139 *Notebooks* I. 791, 894, 925, 985, 1718; *Letters* I. 539; Schneider 230–2.

140 Schneider 242, 278; House 114–22; Suther 57–8.

141 *Poetic Works of the late Mrs Mary Robinson,* I. 226–9. See Lowes 354–5, Schneider 86, 216.

142 *Witches and Other Night Fears, Essays of Elia,* 81.

143 *Letters,* Charles Lamb, Dent, 1909, I. 353.

144 *Shelley at Work,* Neville Rogers, Clarendon Press, 1950; *The Starlit Dome,* G. Wilson Knight.

145 Lowes 594–5.

146 Lowes 379–81, 408.

147 Bodkin 94, Schneider 244–5.

148 *Works* I. 296.

149 *Letters* I. 649.

150 Schneider 44.

151 Poe, *Marginalia.*

152 *C.E.O.E. 1822* 420.

153 Richards 5.

154 *Works* I. 429–30 and n. 2.

155 *Letters* IV. 727.

156 Cp. the demon-woman of S.T.C.'s dream of 1800, who took her name of Ebon-Ebon-Thalud from a druggist in the *Arabian Nights* and whom, I have suggested, Coleridge identified with opium. See *Notebooks* I. 848 n.

NOTES ON CHAPTER X. DE QUINCEY (II)

The editions of De Quincey's works and the biographies and critical studies of him which I have consulted are listed with their abbreviations in note 3 of the notes on Chapter V (see pages 353–4).

1 Page (Japp) I. 19.

2 *De Q/Masson* I. 32 n.

3 *C.E.O.E. 1822* 386–8.

4 *C.E.O.E. 1822* 402, 393–4, 389.

5 *C.E.O.E. 1822* 398.

6 *De Quincey and His Friends,* Hogg 107–10; Eaton 128–9.

7 *De Quincey to Wordsworth* 144.

8 *C.E.O.E. 1822* 389–91, 393.

9 *C.E.O.E. 1822* 395, 397.

10 *C.E.O.E. 1822* 397.

11 *C.E.O.E. 1822* 401.

12 *C.E.O.E. 1822* 350–1, 402–4.

13 *C.E.O.E. 1822* 405. Many authorities regard this figure as impossible. Twenty-one grains of heroin a day is a fairly advanced addict's dose now; but the proportion of pure opium in De Quincey's laudanum may have been quite low.

14 *Reminiscences of a Literary Veteran* quoted Page (Japp) I. 189–90.

15 Eaton 200.

16 Elwin 52; Eaton 128.

17 Gillman 248; S.T.C.'s note of 7th January 1830.

18 *C.E.O.E. 1822* 405, 412.

19 Elwin 54.

20 Page (Japp) I. 197.

21 *C.E.O.E. 1822* 431, 435.

22 *De Q/Masson* III. 75.

23 *C.E.O.E. 1822* 435–41.

24 *C.E.O.E. 1822* 414, 431–3, 437–8; *De Q/Masson* III. 71–7.

25 Eaton 304; Elwin 70.

26 Page (Japp) I. 319.

27 Eaton 397–400.

28 *C.E.O.E. 1856* 298.

29 Page (Japp) I. 326; *Suspiria* 450. But see Page (Japp) I. 341 where De Quincey in a letter to Miss Mitford said that any connection between opium and his misery was improbable: see also *C.E.O.E. 1856*, 294–5, 299.

30 Page (Japp) I. 326–31.

31 Page (Japp) I. 328.

32 Page (Japp) I. 330; Elwin 81.

33 Page (Japp) I. 354; Eaton 458 n.

34 Page (Japp) I. 354.

35 Page (Japp) II. 27.

36 Page (Japp) II. 89; *Literary Recollections*, James Payn, 58.

37 Findlay 33.

38 *De Quincey at Work*, W. H. Bonner, *passim.*

39 Findlay 33.

40 *C.E.O.E. 1856* 104, 307; Elwin 61.

41 e.g. by Eaton 425, and by Professor Schneider and Mr J. C. Reid (*Francis Thompson*)

42 *De Q /Masson* III. 73–5.

43 Page (Japp) I. 325–9; Eaton 415–16. The letter of spring 1844 to Lushington which describes this withdrawal period makes it clear that De Quincey tried to cure his misery of summer 1843 by two different methods—walking over ten miles a day, which he started eight months before 23rd February 1844, and reducing his opium dosage, which he started nearly three months before, that is, in December 1843.

44 See Sackville-West vii–x, Eaton vii–ix for main sources.

45 *A Diary of Thomas de Quincey*, ed. H. A. Eaton.

46 Schneider 72–7. See also Sackville-West 63–9, Eaton 88–100.

47 *Diary* 143, 156, 163.

48 *Suspiria* 448, 453, 502–3.

49 *S.T.C./Letters* III. 205.

50 *C.E.O.E. 1856*, 213.

51 *Suspiria* 514.

52 *Suspiria* 520 n.

53 Sackville-West 12–13, 131–2.

54 *Suspiria* 459, 465, 503–4.

55 *De Q /Masson* I. 103–8.

56 *C.E.O.E. 1822* 362–3.

57 *De Q /Masson* II. 443–5.

58 *Posthumous Works* I. 16–21; *Lake Poets* 87 n.

59 *De Q /Masson* I. 58; *Suspiria* 604.

60 *Posthumous Works* I. 14; *Suspiria* 474.

61 *Suspiria* 474–6, 503–4; *De Q /Masson* II. 116.

62 *C.E.O.E. 1822* 399; *De Q /Masson* V. 403–16, XII. 205–7.

63 *Suspiria* 466–7, 523; *De Q /Masson* VI. 152–78.

64 *Suspiria* 466–7; Page (Japp) II. 303.

65 *C.E.O.E. 1822* 428–9.

66 *Suspiria* 610.

67 *C.E.O.E. 1856* 331.

68 *Posthumous Works* I. 5.

69 *Posthumous Works* I. 16–21.

70 *Suspiria* 520 n.

71 *C.E.O.E. 1856* 103.

72 *De Q /Masson* I. 118.

73 *De Q /Masson* I. 120.

74 *De Q /Masson* I. 59; *C.E.O.E. 1856* 123.

75 *De Q /Masson* I. 88–100.

76 *Diary* 156.

77 Eaton 12, 92.

78 *De Q /Masson* I. 100–1.

79 *De Q /Masson* VI. 142.

80 *Diary* 143.

81 *Suspiria* 513, 520 n.

82 *Suspiria* 458, 466; *De Q /Masson* I. 32 and n.

83 *De Quincey to Wordsworth* 86–7; *C.E.O.E. 1856* 196.

84 *C.E.O.E. 1822* 363.

85 *C.E.O.E. 1856* 402.

86 *C.E.O.E. 1822* 419–20.

87 *Suspiria* 516.

88 *De Q /Masson* V. 232.

89 *Posthumous Works* I. 7–12.

90 The best study of De Quincey's musical gifts is in Edward Sack-ville-West's *A Flame in Sunlight*, especially 134–5, 143.

91 *C.E.O.E. 1822* 397.

92 *C.E.O.E. 1822* 395.

93 *C.E.O.E. 1822* 429.

94 *De Q /Masson* X. 140.

95 *C.E.O.E. 1856* 113n.

96 *De Q /Masson* I. 14.

97 *De Q /Masson* I. 62–5, 88–101.

98 *De Q /Masson* I. 57–8.

99 *De Q /Masson* I. 58; *Page (Japp)* I. 168.

100 *C.E.O.E. 1856* 176–7.

101 *C.E.O.E. 1856* 186.

102 Sackville-West 49–52.

103 *Lake Poets* 129–131.

104 *C.E.O.E. 1856* 187.

105 *C.E.O.E. 1822* 403.

106 Eaton 387, 455; *De Q /Masson* XIV. 275–6.

107 *De Q /Masson* XIV, 276.

108 *C.E.O.E. 1856* 176; *Suspiria* 468; *De Q /Masson* II. 108; *Posthumous Works* I. 20.

109 *De Q /Masson* XII. 17, 21, 25, XIII. 194, VII. 397, 400.

110 *Page (Japp)* II. 192.

111 *Page (Japp)* II. 214; Eaton 317.

112 *De Q /Masson* VI. 287.

113 *De Q /Masson* X. 393.

114 *De Quincey and His Friends* 174–5.

115 *De Q /Masson* I. 100–1, XIII. 21–2, 68; *C.E.O.E. 1856* 211.

116 *De Q /Masson* VII. 101–72, 173–246, XIII. 384–448.

117 *De Q /Masson* VII. 184.

118 *C.E.O.E. 1822* 397, 424; *Suspiria* 453.

119 *Suspiria* 453.

120 *C.E.O.E. 1822* 424.

121 *Suspiria* 606.

122 *C.E.O.E. 1822* 430; *Suspiria* 526.

123 *De Q /Masson* VIII. 410.

124 *Posthumous Works* I. 18–19.

125 *Suspiria* 474; *De Q /Masson* XII. 177.

126 *Lake Poets* 323–4.

127 *Suspiria* 570–5; *C.E.O.E. 1822* 420–7.

128 *C.E.O.E. 1856* 176–7.

129 *C.E.O.E. 1856* 181, 194, 195, 197.

130 *C.E.O.E. 1856* 227–8.

131 *C.E.O.E. 1822* 399, 423.

132 *C.E.O.E. 1822* 426.

133 *De Q /Masson* VIII. 438, 414.

134 *De Q /Masson* XIII. 88, 101, 109.

135 *De Q /Masson* VIII. 446.

136 *De Q /Masson* II. 337–8, XIII. 128.

137 *De Q /Masson* XIII. 141, V. 391.

138 *De Q /Masson* XIII. 357.

139 *De Q /Masson* XIII. 204.

140 *De Q /Masson* II. 202, VII. 412.

141 *Suspiria* 529.

142 *Lake Poets* 284.

143 *Suspiria* 448, 453.

144 *De Q /Masson* XII. 158.

145 *Suspiria* 450; *Posthumous Works* I. 25. In the draft of a *Suspiria* vision called *The Princess Who Overlooked One Seed in a Pomegranate* (*Posthumous Works* I. 22–3) De Quincey again linked the involute of the Fatal Choice with his opium addiction.

146 Page (Japp) II. 64.

147 *Suspiria* 480.

148 *De Q /Masson* III. 72–3.

149 *De Q /Masson* I. 128–9; *Posthumous Works* I. 22–3.

150 *C.E.O.E. 1822* 430.

151 De Q/*Masson* XII. 236.

152 Two illuminating analyses of *The English Mail Coach*, particularly of its musical structure, are given in Sackville-West 167–72 and in the *Introduction* (page X) by Professor J. E. Jordan to the Everyman edition of *The English Mail Coach*.

153 Eaton 458 n., 455, 459; Elwin 82.

154 Eaton 458 n.

155 *Suspiria* 612–14.

156 *Suspiria* 512; *Posthumous Works* I. 4.

157 De Q/*Masson* I. 274–5, 57–8. III. 162.

158 *Suspiria* 614.

159 Page (Japp) II. 303–4.

NOTES ON CHAPTER XI. WILKIE COLLINS

In this chapter I have not given references for Wilkie Collins's novels, which are mostly easily accessible in many editions.

Biographies and critical studies: *Some Recollections of Yesterday*, Nat Beard, in *Temple Bar*. July 1894, pp. 320–6; *Studies in Prose and Poetry*, A. C. Swinburne, Chatto & Windus, 1894; *An Artist's Reminiscences*, Rudolf Lehmann, Smith Elder, 1894; *A Few Memories*, Mary Anderson, Osgood McIlvaine, 1896; *Recollections of Wilkie Collins*, Wybert Reeve, in *Chamber's Journal*, June 1906, pp. 458–61; *Memories of Half a Century*, R. C. Lehmann, Smith Elder, 1908; *My Story*, Hall Caine, Heinemann, 1908; *The Bancrofts: Recollections of Sixty Years*, Squire and Marie Bancroft, John Murray, 1909; *Old Friends*, William Winter, Moffat Yard, New York, 1909; *Introduction*, D. L. Sayers, to *Great Short Stories of Detection, Mystery and Horror, First Series*, Gollancz, 1928; *Wilkie Collins, Lefanu and Others*, S. M. Ellis, Constable, 1931; *The Eighteen Sixties*, Walter de la Mare, C.U.P., 1932; *Selected Essays*, T. S. Eliot, Faber, 1932; *Dickens and Daughter*, Gladys Storey, Muller, 1939; *Wilkie Collins*, Kenneth Robinson, Bodley Head, 1951; *Wilkie Collins*, Robert Ashley, Barker, 1952; *The Life of Wilkie Collins*, N. P. Davis, Urbana, Illinois, 1956.

1 Robinson 15, 65; *Memoirs of the Life of William Collins*, Wilkie Collins, 2 vols., Longmans, 1848, I. 148, 250.

2 Winter 213–14.

3 *Memoirs* II. 291, 293, 294.

4 Robinson 93–4, 162–4; Davis 242–3.

5 Robinson 280–3.

6 Davis 299.

7 Bancroft 174; R. Lehmann 233.

8 Robinson 164, 281, 282; Wybert Reeve.

9 Davis 254; Caine 339–40; Wybert Reeve.

10 Winter 211.

11 R. Lehmann 233.

12 Robinson 249, 308, 312; Nat Beard.

13 Bancroft 174.

14 Caine 339–40.

15 Anderson 142–3; Winter 212; Ellis 40.

16 Winter 213.

17 Caine 328, 333.

18 Caine 339–40.

19 Winter 213.

20 Ellis 22–3; Anderson 142–3; Davis 299.

21 Ashley 110.

22 Robinson 308–9.

23 *Memoirs*, *passim*; Davis 26.

24 *Rambles Beyond Railways*, Wilkie Collins, Richard Bentley, 1851.

25 Winter 207.

26 *Memoirs* II. 147.

27 Mr Kenneth Robinson (page 330), after analysing the possible causes of the falling off in quality of Wilkie Collins's later books, dismisses over-production and ill-health, put forward by earlier biographers as causes, and concludes for opium.

NOTES ON CHAPTER XII. FRANCIS THOMPSON

References in this chapter to Thompson's poetry are to *Poetical Works*, Francis Thompson, O.U.P., 1965. *Literary Criticisms of Francis Thompson*, ed. T. L. Connolly, E. P. Dutton, N.Y., 1948, is a valuable anthology of Thompson's critical work.

Biographies and critical studies: *Some Memories of Francis Thompson*, Alice Meynell, in *Dublin Review*, vol. cxlii. January and April 1908; *The Life of Francis Thompson*, Everard Meynell, Burns & Oates, 1913; *Francis Thompson, the Poet of Earth in Heaven*, R. L. Megroz, Faber, 1927; *Francis Thompson and His Poetry*, T. H. Wright, Harrap, 1927; *Alice Meynell, A Memoir*, Viola Meynell, Burns & Oates, 1929; *Francis Thompson and Wilfrid Meynell*, Viola Meynell, Hollis & Carter, 1952; *Francis Thompson: La Vie et L'Œuvre d'un Poète*, Pierre Danchin, Nižet,

Paris, 1959; *Francis Thompson, Man and Poet*, J. C. Reid, Routledge and Kegan Paul, 1959; *Francis Thompson*, P. van K. Thomson, Nelson, N.Y., 1961.

1 E. Meynell 46–54; Danchin 31–2; Reid 21–3; Thomson 32.
2 Danchin 32–3; Reid 23; Thomson 37–8.
3 E. Meynell 64–70; Danchin 39, 41–3; Reid 36–40, 42–3.
4 E. Meynell 81–4; Danchin 50–1; Reid 43–5, 51–2; Thomson 49–50.
5 Danchin 45; Reid 46–7; Thomson 51–2.
6 E. Meynell 70–6; Danchin 39–41; Reid 40–2; Thomson 47–9.
7 E. Meynell 94; Danchin 51; Reid 52–3.
8 E. Meynell 94, 103–4; *F. T. and W. Meynell*, V. Meynell 29–31.
9 E. Meynell 96.
10 E. Meynell 101; *F. T. and W. Meynell*, V. Meynell 31.
11 E. Meynell 123.
12 Danchin 61; Reid 64; Thomson 99.
13 Danchin 65; Reid 65.
14 E. Meynell 180; Danchin 73.
15 Danchin 118, 120 n. 19; Reid 28, 112–13, 138, 160.
16 *F. T. and W. Meynell*, V. Meynell, 177.
17 E. Meynell 52.
18 E. Meynell 49, 231; *Some Memories of F.T.*, A. Meynell; Danchin 134.
19 *Some Memories of F.T.*, A. Meynell.
20 E. Meynell 49.
21 E. Meynell 53; Danchin 144 n. 55.
22 E. Meynell 349.
23 Danchin 134, 144 n. 56 and 57; Reid 34, 170.
24 *F. T. and W. Meynell*, V. Meynell, 177; Danchin 144 n. 57.
25 E. Meynell 342; Danchin 144 n. 60.
26 Danchin 135; Reid 34.
27 Danchin 135.
28 *Some Memories of F.T.*, A. Meynell.
29 Danchin 65 n. 4.
30 E. Meynell 95; see also Danchin 53, Reid 73.
31 E. Meynell 101, 103–4; *F. T. and W. Meynell*, V. Meynell 30–1.
32 Danchin 76–7 and 94 n. 39; Reid 112–13.
33 E. Meynell 184.
34 *Poetical Works* 98.
35 Reid 76, 123, 126, 149.

36 Danchin 261, 288–291; Thomson 138–9.

37 Reid 200.

38 Review of *Crabbe* (Alfred Ainger) in *Academy*, 10th October 1903.

39 Article on Coleridge in *Academy*, 6th February 1897; E. Meynell 10, 96, 344.

40 Review of *Dreams and their Meanings* (H. G. Hutchinson) in *Academy* 30th November 1901.

41 Article on Poe, *A Dream of Things Impossible*, in *Academy* 28th September 1901.

42 Reid (179) sees the whole story as an allegory for Thompson's surrender to opium. See also *Genius and Disaster: Studies in Drugs and Disease*, Jeannette Marks, pp. 158–63. Professor Danchin's comment (p. 533) that this work is known not to have been written under the influence of opium is slightly beside the point; Thompson was not actually under its influence when he was writing, but he was describing experiences of it.

43 Article on Baudelaire, *A Bewildered Poet*, *Academy*, 16th May 1903.

44 Review of J. C. Mangan's Poems, *Academy*, 25th September 1897.

45 E. Meynell 46–54; Danchin 31; Reid 25–6.

46 Review of an edition of *C.E.O.E.*, *A Monument of Personality*, *Academy*, 29th April 1899.

47 Articles on *Seventeenth Century Prose* and *A Monument of Personality*.

48 Article, *Browning Reconsidered*, *Academy*, 25th October 1902.

49 Review of *Dreams and their Meaning*, *Academy*, 30th November 1901.

50 E. Meynell 340.

51 E. Meynell 172–3.

52 *Poetical Works* 29.

53 E. Meynell 14 n.

54 See the very interesting passage from an unpublished MS. quoted by Thomson 74–5.

55 See the very thorough survey of the formation and content of Thompson's imagery in Professor Danchin's study; R. L. Megroz, *passim*; and Thomson 114–22.

56 *Francis Thompson: a Psychoanalytical Study*, Ella Freeman Sharpe, *British Journal of Medical Psychology*, vol. 5, 1925, 329–44.

57 E. Meynell, 30; Danchin 207; Thomson 79–80.

58 Danchin 41–3, and 46–7 n. 10, 11, 15, 16.

59 *Poetical Works* 89, 164–5.

60 *Poetical Works* 259, 197–8, 205–6, 90.

61 *Poetical Works* 193, 190–1.

62 *Poetical Works* 266, 117.

63 *Œuvres Complètes*, C. Baudelaire, 377.

64 *Poetical Works* 184, 264, 96.

65 *Poetical Works* 27, 311, 324,

66 Thomson 28–9.

67 *Poetical Works* 29.

68 *Revolt of the Tartars, De Q / Masson* VII. 368–426.

69 *Poetical Works* 37, 262, 229, 45, 211, 342, 266.

70 *Poetical Works* 195, 34.

71 *Poetical Works* 190.

72 *Poetical Works* 212–13.

NOTES ON CHAPTER XIII. SOME WRITERS WHO TOOK
OPIUM OCCASIONALLY

1 *A Diary of Thomas de Quincey* 163; Schneider 321 n. 102.

2 *Memoirs of the Late Mrs Robinson* II. 96, 129–32.

3 *Coleridge Opium and Kubla Khan* 87–8.

4 *Memoirs of the Life of Sir Walter Scott*, J. G. Lockhart, John Murray,
1827, vol. IV., 58, 59, 82, 105, 137.

5 Lockhart IV. 257–8.

6 Lockhart IV. 83, 107, 233, 239, 242–3.

7 Lockhart IV. 260–1.

8 Lockhart IV. 272.

9 Lockhart IV. 253.

10 Lockhart IV. 274–5.

11 Lockhart IV. 185.

12 *My Story*, Hall Caine, 333.

13 *Old Friends*, W. Winter, 213.

14 Caine 339–40; Winter 213.

15 Article on Lytton by Collins in *The Globe* 4th October 1889.

16 Monckton Milnes's *Commonplace Book* 1846–8, Library of Trinity
College, Cambridge.

17 *Life of Charles Dickens*, John Forster, 2 vols., Dent, 1948, II. 347;
Charles Dickens, Una Pope-Hennessy, Chatto & Windus, 1945, 437.

18 *Letters of Charles Dickens*, 3 vols., Nonesuch Press 1938, III. 776.

19 Forster II. 349.

20 *Letters of Charles Dickens* III. 775; Forster II. 407–8.

21 *Opium-Smoking in America and China*, H. H. Kane, Putman, 1882, 50.

22 *Life of Charlotte Brontë*, Mrs. Gaskell, Dent, 432.

23 Gaskell 227.

24 Gaskell 432.

25 *Letters of Robert Browning and Elizabeth Barrett*, 2 vols., Harper, 1899, I. 277–8.

26 *Letters of R.B. and E.B.B.* I. 451–2.

27 *Elizabeth Barrett Browning*, Dorothy Hewlett, Cassell, 1953, 231.

28 Hewlett 96.

29 *Mrs Browning*, Alethea Hayter, Faber, 1962, 62–8.

30 *Life of James Thomson*, H. S. Salt, Reeves & Turner, 1889, 109.

31 *City of Dreadful Night* XII, Stanza 4.

32 *To Our Ladies of Death*, Stanzas 19–27.

33 Article *Indolence*, 1867.

34 *City of Dreadful Night* XX, Stanza 4.

35 *City of Dreadful Night* XXI.

36 *Voyage en Orient: Histoire de la Reine du Matin et de Soliman des Génies*, VII; *Aurélia, Editions d'Art*, Albert Skira, Geneva, 55–6.

37 *Deux Thèmes Visionnaires de Gérard de Nerval*, Henri Lemaitre, in *L'Oeil*, June 1962; *John Martin en France*, Jean Seznec, Faber, 1964.

38 *L'Anglais Mangeur d'Opium*, Alfred de Musset, 1828.

39 Letter of 30th August 1833. *Les Années Romantiques. Correspondance, 1819–1842*, Hector Berlioz, ed. Julien Tièrsot, Calmann-Levy, Paris, undated.

40 See e.g. *Berlioz and His Century*, Jacques Barzun, Mendian Books, N.Y., 1956, 135.

41 *Life and Letters of Hector Berlioz*, trans. H. M. Dunstan, 2 vols., Remington, 1882, Vol. II, Letters of 8th February 1865, 11th January 1867, 22nd October 1867; Barzun 351, 433 n. 15.

NOTES ON CHAPTER XIV. KEATS

References in this chapter to Keats's poetry are to *The Poetical Works of John Keats*, ed. H. W. Garrod, Clarendon Press, 1958. References to his letters are to *The Letters of John Keats*, ed. M. Buxton Forman, O.U.P., 1960.

Biographies and critical studies: *Life of John Keats*, Charles Armitage Brown, ed. D. Bodurtha and W. B. Pope, O.U.P., 1937; *John Keats*, Amy Lowell, Houghton Miffin, Boston, revised 1929; *John Keats*, Sidney Colvin, Macmillan, 1920; *Keats and Shakespeare*, J. Middleton Murry, O.U.P., 1925; *Introduction*, E. de Selincourt, to *Poems of John Keats*, Methuen, 1926; *The Mind of John Keats*, C. D. Thorpe, O.U.P.,

1926; *Keats's Shakespeare*, Caroline Spurgeon, O.U.P., 1928; *Keats' Craftsmanship*, M. R. Ridley, Clarendon Press, 1933; *The Evolution of Keats's Poetry*, C. L. Finney, 2 vols., Harvard University Press, 1936; *Keats as Doctor and Patient*, W. Hale-White, O.U.P., 1938; *Keats*, H. W. Garrod, O.U.P., 1939; *John Keats's Fancy*, J. R. Caldwell, Cornell University Press, Ithaca, N.Y., 1945; *John Keats, The Living Year*, Robert Gittings, Heinemann, 1954; *Keats*, J. Middleton Murry, Cape, 1955; *The Mask of Keats*, Robert Gittings, Heinemann, 1956; *On the Poetry of Keats*, E. C. Pettet, C.U.P., 1957; *The Consecrated Urn*, Bernard Blackstone, Longmans, 1959; *A Doctor's Life of John Keats*, W. A. Wells, Vantage Press, N.Y., 1959; *John Keats*, Aileen Ward, Secker & Warburg, 1963; *John Keats*, W. J. Bate, O.U.P., 1963.

1 *Letters* 314.
2 *Castle of Indolence* Part I Stanza 49.
3 *Stanzas Written in my Pocket-Copy of Thomson's 'Castle of Indolence'.*
4 'They rest upon their oars . . .' (*Poetical Works* V. 413) and *Expostulation and Reply*; see *Wordsworth: the Early Years*, Mary Moorman, 381 n.
5 *C.E.O.E. 1822* 410.
6 *Lord of the Castle of Indolence*, stanza vi.
7 *Keats and Shakespeare* 61.
8 J. M. Murry *Keats*, 202–9; Blackstone 56–9, 313–14; Ward 91, 165–7, 267, 288; Bate 473–5.
9 *Letters* 201, 194, 200.
10 *Letters* 302.
11 *Poetical Works* 118, 106; *Letters* 188.
12 *Letters* 146–7.
13 *Letters* 312–13.
14 *Letters* 102.
15 Spurgeon 151.
16 *Poetical Works* 95.
17 *Poetical Works* 174.
18 *Letters* 68–9.
19 *Letters* 216–17. On Keats and 'abstraction' see Thorpe, chaps. II and VI; Ridley 217–18; Finney 645–8; Garrod 54; Pettet 255–60; Bate 473–5.
20 *Life of John Keats* C. A. Brown 62–4. Bate (635) dates Brown's discovery 28th January 1820, the day George Keats left to return to America, but does not give his grounds for this particular dating. Amy Lowell (II. 374–5) dated it November/December 1819;

Blackstone (381 n.) late 1819; Joanna Richardson (*Everlasting Spell*, 37) October 1819.

21 *Letters* 325; *Poetical Works* 327.

22 *Poetical Works* 248, 257, 273; *Letters* 352.

23 *C.E.O.E. 1856* 302–3.

24 Lowell I. 513–16, II. 359; Finney 645–6; W. A. Wells.

25 Hale-White 43–51; Gittings 4; Bate 614–15 and 615 n. Miss Ward (257–8) stays on the fence.

26 Lowell I. 512–16; Hale-White 44–5; W. A. Wells; Ward 134.

27 The suggestion that Keats took laudanum on this occasion has been made by Gittings (98–9) and Bate (465–6). Amy Lowell (II. 375) suggested that Keats might have been taking laudanum at the period when Haydon said that Keats was 'scarcely sober', but she dated this period to November/December 1819; it was actually the spring of 1819.

28 *Letters* 314. Miss Ward has shown convincingly (p. 431 n. 30) that this sonnet cannot have been written, as is generally said, on March 19th, since Keats referred to it on that day as having been written at least one night earlier. See also J. M. Murry, *Keats and Shakespeare* (118–123) and Bate (464–6). It has been suggested (Finney 572) that the second half of the section under March 19th in the journal letter must in fact have been written about March 22nd, but his argument rests on the assumption that Keats received only one note from Haslam, but there were evidently two, one saying that his father was dying, and one that he was dead.

29 *Keats and Shakespeare*, J. M. Murry, 203.

30 *Letters* 290, 293.

31 Finney 531; Gittings 101–3; Ward 263–5.

32 Bate 456; *Keats and Shakespeare* 115; Finney 531.

33 *Diary of Benjamin Robert Haydon*, ed. W. B. Pope, 5 vols., Harvard University press, 1960, II. 317.

34 *Diary of B. R. Haydon* II. 317.

35 Gittings (93–8) suggests that Haydon's evidence is not wholly unreliable, but does not link it with laudanum. Amy Lowell (II. 375) did link Haydon's account with laudanum, but dated it wrongly. See also Bate 463–4.

36 *Letters* 325.

37 Schneider 50–1.

38 *Poetical Works* 486.

39 *Poetical Works* 78.

40 *Poetical Works* 376.

41 Caldwell 95–8 et seq.

42 *Poetical Works* 82–6, 101, 169, 173.

43 Spurgeon 114.

44 e.g., Pettet 217–20; Ward 273–4.

45 *Letters* 323.

46 *Letters* 290, 318, 335, 344.

47 Finney 624–33; Pettet 255–60.

48 *Keats* J. M. Murry 312–16; Blackstone 353, 381–4.

49 *Letters* 342–3.

50 Colvin 353. Some authorities, like Professor Blackstone (314 n.) think that the Ode was conceived and possibly written in March, at the time of the vision of the three figures. See also Finney 646, Bate 527–8.

51 *Letters* 346.

52 e.g. Finney 646.

53 *Keats and Shakespeare*, J. M. Murry 157; Pettet 228; Ward 308–10; Ridley 266; Blackstone 299–308; Finney 700.

54 Pettet 161–4.

55 *Letters* 215.

56 *Suspiria* 450.

57 *Moneta's Temple*, J. L. Lowes, in *P.M.L.A.*, L.I. Dec. 1936, 1098–1113; Gittings 178–9; *Keats and the Mirror of Art*, Ian Jack, Clarendon Press, 1967.

INDEX

Index

Index

Index

Index

Index

Index

Index